Reimer Gronemeyer, Michaela Fink,
Marcel Globisch, Felix Schumann

Helping People at the End of their Lives

SOZIOLOGIE

Forschung und Wissenschaft

Band 19

LIT

Reimer Gronemeyer, Michaela Fink,
Marcel Globisch, Felix Schumann

Helping People at the End of their Lives

Hospice and Palliative Care in Europe

Translated by Marcel Globisch

The published study has been funded
by the Robert Bosch Foundation, Stuttgart

LIT

German edition: Reimer Gronemeyer, Michaela Fink, Marcel Globisch, Felix Schumann: Helfen am Ende des Lebens. Hospizarbeit und Palliative Care in Europa. Herausgegeben von der Bundesarbeitsgemeinschaft Hospiz e. V., Wuppertal 2004

Contact:
Project on Hospice and Palliative Care in Europe,
Institute of Sociology,
Department 03: Social and Cultural Sciences
Justus-Liebig-Universität Giessen,
Karl-Glöckner-Str. 21 E,
35394 Giessen, Germany
hospizprojekt@sowi.uni-giessen.de
www.uni-giessen.de/hospizprojekt

The results of this study are also available in
Polish (ISSN 1616-1211, 2nd edition),
Russian (ISSN 1616-1211, 3rd edition),
and French (ISSN 1616-1211, 4th edition)

Translated by Marcel Globisch
Editorial Office by Michaela Fink
Cover by Juliane Conrad

Bibliographic information published by Die Deutsche Bibliothek
Die Deutsche Bibliothek lists this publication in the Deutsche Nationalbibliografie; detailed bibliographic data are available in the Internet at http://dnb.ddb.de.

ISBN 3-8258-8978-5

A catalogue record for this book is available from the British Library

Auslieferung/Verlagskontakt:
Grevener Str./Fresnostr. 2 48159 Münster
Tel. +49 (0)251–62 03 20 Fax +49 (0)251–23 19 72
e-Mail: lit@lit-verlag.de http://www.lit-verlag.de

Distributed in the UK by: Global Book Marketing, 99B Wallis Rd, London, E9 5LN
Phone: +44 (0) 20 8533 5800 – Fax: +44 (0) 1600 775 663
http://www.centralbooks.co.uk/acatalog/search.html

Distributed in North America by:

Transaction Publishers
New Brunswick (U.S.A.) and London (U.K.)

Transaction Publishers
Rutgers University
35 Berrue Circle
Piscataway, NJ 08854

Phone: +1 (732) 445 - 2280
Fax: + 1 (732) 445 - 3138
for orders (U. S. only):
toll free (888) 999 - 6778
e-mail:
orders@transactionspub.com

Content

Foreword by Gerda Graf

With this publication Professor Gronemeyer and his colleagues have provided an international comparison of hospice care that is of great importance in the context of a continent, which is currently expanding and growing together. The results give the opportunity to learn from each other and to modify and integrate concepts from other European countries into its own day-to-day work. Influenced by the guiding hospice idea, this evaluation is an indication of a developing hospice *movement* in Europe. Above all the cultures of the respective countries shape the moving element of hospice work.

Amongst other aspects, this study focuses on volunteers dedicating their time to hospice care. In many Eastern European countries however, the meaning of voluntary support is still that of help between neighbours, with training playing no role. Education in hospice care is a paramount element of voluntary work in other countries (especially in Germany).

Dying patients need to be assured that their destiny lies in the hands of well trained, multi-disciplinary, professional teams because often the dying are no longer capable of caring for themselves and their rights. Still the question remains how much training and education a volunteer needs to be able to offer humane support without getting caught in the maelstrom of professionalisation.

The study also provides a basis for the discussion on how far voluntary work in times of economic recession may be forced to close a gap inevitably. In case of inappropriate assignments or excessive demands, symptoms of fatigue could appear, which would hinder the original aims of the hospice movement.

The "added value of the good" needs comparison and its individual, creative design in order to allow the development of the care for the dying from isolation towards a more general provision in all areas of the society.

The *Bundesarbeitsgemeinschaft Hospiz* would like to thank Professor Gronemeyer and his team for this exceptional scientific study, which is an incentive for us and at the same time signalises an atmosphere of departure for the development and further growth of hospice work.

Gerda Graf,
Chairwoman of the *Bundesarbeitsgemeinschaft Hospiz e.V.*
October 2004

Foreword by Dr Katalin Hegedus

In the summer of 2003 two young German men, Marcel Globisch and Felix Schumann visited me in the hospital where I was leading the hospice team at the time. They told me that they have started a great, comprehensive hospice survey. During the interview with me and fact-finding in Hungary, it was clear how thoroughly they prepared for this work; their questions and competence amazed me.

It was especially interesting for me to know that a comprehensive study is being performed in this field at last. Until now – though various works have summarized and dealt with the development of palliative care in different countries of the world – comparisons were hindered by many factors. Development of hospice/palliative care in the Western and Eastern European countries was compared only within the regions during the execution of Pallium and International Observatory on End of Life Care projects.

Members of the Giessen research group have laid specific emphasis on having the 8 Western and 8 Eastern European countries representing each region (North, South, East, and West) of Europe and to have countries of the most different developmental stage represented. It is of great importance that the authors use the same standardised viewpoints and measuring instruments so differences in quality and quantity can be precisely measured. In this new research demographic and historical synopses, information on national peculiarities, the actual situation, training and the role of volunteers and the detailed introduction of some specific services provide priceless information for researchers who wish to immerse themselves in the topic.

I feel honoured that I had the opportunity to participate in the edition of the summary on my home country, Hungary, and as a result of joint work such a detailed and up-to-date country-review was created that has never been written by Hungarian authors before.

As the only Eastern European board member of European Association for Palliative Care I consider the international level development of palliative care in the Eastern European region as especially important. One of the EAPC's important and actual purpose is – while preserving the European countries' international peculiarities – to build a bridge between developed and developing countries reducing the existing differences on this level as well. ‚Connecting diversity' is the slogan of the 10th EAPC congress that is being organised in Budapest in 2007. The book that you are holding in your hands is the most beautiful example of how to introduce diversity and how to connect developed with the developing.

Dr Katalin Hegedűs,
President of the *Hungarian Hospice-Palliative Association*
Member of the Board of Directors of the *European Association of Palliative Care*

Foreword by Prof Dr Stein Husebø

Since the beginning of mankind, people are born and people die. The time in between is called life. 100 years ago, the average life expectancy was approximately 50 years old and almost half of the population died before reaching 20 years old. Today, the average life expectancy has exceeded 80 years old in nearly all industrialised countries and the Infant Mortality Rate is less than 2 percent.

In earlier times, we were born, lived and died at home. There were few hospitals or care institutions and in those cases where they did exist, they were only for the wealthy. This changed with the development of the industrialised societies.

There is more than sufficient documentation to support the fact that death, in earlier times, was less than comfortable. In the Middle Ages, Doctors often fled when they heard that death was imminent. They did not want their healing powers to fall into disrepute. Often, the only way the pain was eased of those dying, was through death.

In the Twentieth Century a new Religion evolved. Until this time, the source of the origin and development of all known Religions was death and life after death. The new Religion was called *Science*. It was, above all, the belief in natural sciences that instilled new hope in people which was previously the belief in a kind hearted God and life after death.

Microcosm and Macrocosm were researched; Atoms and Quarks described and outer space was visited. For many people, the advances in Medicine were most joyous. With the development of Anaesthetics, many operations could be carried out painlessly. Large break-throughs such as Antibiotics and Insulin saved lives and drastically improved the quality of life for others.

In 2004, European countries saw 7 - 8 times more Doctors than 50 years ago. The number of nurses has increased 20 - 30 times in the same period of time. The Medicine faculties of universities have increased in size and in some places are the same size as all other faculties put together.

The main factors supporting the radical increase in life expectancy in industrial countries are: improved hygiene, nutrition, drinking water, and general living conditions. If the two most important causes of death were to suddenly become curable, it would mean that by treatable Cancer, life expectancy would increase by 1.5 - 2 years and by Heart Disease, 3 - 4 years. In such a case, other illnesses would become the main causes of death. Radically said, it is more than questionable whether the modern health care system is delivering the improvements for the people who believe in it and above all pay for it.

Our birth is, for those people involved unplanned. If we are lucky, it is planned and wanted by our parents. It is dramatic. The pain and agony associated with it for the mother and child is unbearable. It can and is, however, suffered and coped with as the mother has the relevant motivation for the situation: a child is being born. The mother also knows that the agony is abruptly over with as soon as to child is born. Today, families and health care institutions make sure that the birth and health of the child takes centre stage.

Death is different. Today, death is neither planned nor wanted. Through the attitude and practice of modern medicine, the preparation for death and time to say goodbye is taken away from the person dying and their relatives. The physical agony and pain is often more than unbearable. It is often not sufficiently noticed or alleviated.

This development led to a counter movement. In the 1950s pioneers began to publicise the hardships and loneliness of terminally ill and dying tumour patients and to talk about the possibilities of support. These pioneers were: Dame Cicely Saunders, Elisabeth Kübler Ross and Norbert Elias. A new era in Medicine was started in 1967 when Cicely Saunders opened *St Christopher's Hospice* – the first modern Hospice for the terminally ill and dying in London. This was followed by the opening of the first Palliative ward by Balfour Mount in Montreal in 1972. This movement received the name Hospice movement or Palliative Care.

At the beginning, taken serious by only some, in 1980 there were just a dozen Hospices or Palliative wards. After around 1980, the field gained national and international attention. In 1989 the *European Association for Palliative Care* was established in Milan. In 1992 the first edition of the *Oxford Textbook of Palliative Care* was published. During this time the first *Journal of Palliative Care and Palliative Medicine* were also published. Important for the global development has been the engagement of the *World Health Organisation (WHO)* led by Jan Stjärnswerd and the release of *Cancer Pain Relief* in various languages.

Today, hundreds of scientific articles are published every year on Palliative Care. There is a vast variety of books in almost all languages. Hundreds of hospices and Palliative wards are to be found in almost all countries in the world.

Many surveys have asked patients the question: *Should you find yourself suffering from a life threatening illness and death is near, what would you hope to receive from us the most?*

The main answers are: *I do not want to unnecessarily suffer or that my death should be prolonged by artificial ways and means. I would like the Doctor to be open and to discuss the situation with me so I am able to say goodbye to my loved ones. I do not want to be alone when I die. I want my relatives to receive the best support possible after my death.*

And these are the main contents of this movement – to sufficiently ease pain and suffering. To make truthful communication possible when death is near. No unnecessarily prolonging the process of dying. Multidisciplinary care and integration of families and children into the treatment. Support for the people affected after the death of someone close. And above all – acceptance of death as part of life.

There are however many challenges to overcome. With the exception of Anglo-Saxon Countries and Scandinavia, Palliative Care is rarely taught or tested by Universities and Higher Education institutes and when done so, then usually only as an optional subject. The further education in medical occupations has so far been less then poor. This means that a small minority of personnel are competent in giving the appropriate and necessary care to patients in Palliative care.

Despite the positive development and increasing number of Hospices, Palliative wards and services, only a fraction of dying patients are cared for in such institutions. In Europe approximately 1 in 80. Those who are treated and cared for in Palliative wards have specific characteristics: they have Cancer in the advanced stages. They are young – hardly any over 70 years old – the average age in Palliative institutions is approximately 50 - 60 years old.

There is also an obvious difference in concept. In Anglo-Saxon Countries and Scandinavia the hospices and Palliative wards are identical with respect to concept and resources. The only difference is Palliative wards are connected to hospitals and Hospices are usually independent. Both concepts are impossible to imagine without numerous full-time Doctors. This is, however, not the case in many European countries and in the USA where the concept is mainly supported by voluntary work.

Other differences are also obvious. In all European countries, the cost development in the health care system has become a central problem. Money is being saved everywhere. Exceptions are rare. One of these exceptions is Palliative Care where the decision makers are becoming increasingly aware of the deficit in the system for the provisions for terminally ill and dying patients. This message is quickly being realised by people in established divisions of conventional medicine. They now know that in the near future, their resources will be limited but that there is still possibilities to expand with respect to offering Palliative Care.

This development has led to many clinics organising special Palliative Care wards for Cancer patients without taking into consideration the actual concept of Palliative Care. In some of the institutions chemotherapy, radiotherapy and expensive operations are offered to the dying patients as if the ultimate result was non-existent. With only a few exceptions, again in Anglo-Saxon countries and Scandinavia, there is no common concept or standard on how offers of Palliative Care should be organised.

One central challenge is the development of the legalisation and practice of Euthanasia (or Medically Assisted Suicide). Three European countries have legalised Euthanasia in the past few years: the Netherlands, Belgium and Switzerland. We know, from publications made in the Netherlands, that 4000 patients are medically assisted in committing suicide every year, of which around 1000 who do not specifically asked for it. It is more than likely that in the coming years, further European Countries will follow and legalise Euthanasia. If all European Countries were to follow the Netherlands and the results it has produced, it would mean the number of patients practicing Euthanasia could rise to 250 000 annually, of which 60 000 patients who have not specifically asked for it.

Almost no one can doubt the fact that there are situations where people are faced with unbearable and agonising suffering before death and it is more than understandable that some want to have the right to depart from this life. This wish is especially understandable when these terminally ill people, suffering or the elderly are faced with inadequate provisions and treatment. At the same time, there is a risk that Euthanasia is used as an easy means to save money by society and politicians in a time where an ageing population is being taken seriously and resources are limited. In addition to this, many weaker citizens could feel forced into taking up this "final solution" if they feel they are becoming a burden to their relatives and to society.

Another paradox becomes visible. In some European Countries, especially Germany and Austria, strong action is being taken against the legalisation of Euthanasia. One example in Germany is that of Dementia patients who are no longer able to express their will and are often fed through a tube even in situations where they are still able to eat and drink for themselves. It is often the case that many old people are moved into hospital in their final days to receive the maximum amount of treatment even though they could be cared for at home or an actual care home with a higher quality of life.

A number of critical questions remain:

- Can we carry on accepting that modern medicine and society want to hide dying and death from us?
- Should a "nice" death only be restricted to those receiving Palliative Care?
- Which offers of Palliative Care do we want to give to the increasingly ageing population in their final years?
- Can we be sure that all terminally ill and dying patients, irrespective of age, diagnosis and residence, are guaranteed dignity and directness and help to ease pain and other agonising symptoms?
- How can we stop patients being artificially kept alive against their will?

It is more than satisfying to see that the book *Helping people at the end of their lives – Hospice and Palliative Care in Europe* will be the first publication released in various languages critically describing and comparing the differences in Palliative Care.

A movement like that of the Hospice movement and the development of Palliative Care has led to a small revolution in Europe in the treatment and care for the terminally ill and dying. Professor Reimer Gronemeyer and his Team have done well in critically analysing the contents and developments of this revolution.

I hope this book attracts many readers!

Stein Husebø Professor at *IFF – Palliative Care und Organisation Ethics* (*Faculty for Interdisciplinary Research and Further Education* at the University of Klagenfurt, Graz and Vienna) Doctor and Project Director at the *Bergen Røde Kors Care Home,* Norway

Foreword

Important things are always very simple
Dame Cicely Saunders

During the course of our research project, the situation changed dramatically in the care of the dying. The topic "death and dying", often a taboo in the past, has become a widely discussed topic in the media and in European societies in general. On one side the changes have put hospice care, still the most adequate term from the general public's point of view, into the spotlight. On the other hand, it cannot be overlooked that all over Europe the debate on Euthanasia is under way. In 2002, Dianne Pretty, from the United Kingdom, claimed that the English director of public prosecutions was wrong to refuse to grant immunity to her husband if he helped her to commit suicide on the basis that English laws outlawing assisted suicide contravened the European Convention on Human Rights. The European Court for Human Rights (ECHR) unanimously rejected Mrs Pretty's request for Euthanasia.[1] Mrs Pretty suffered from motor nerone disease and died in May 2002.

In 2003, the case of 22-year-old Vincent Humbert who was left mute, blind and paralysed following an accident sparked a nation-wide debate over Euthanasia in France after his mother put an overdose in his drip eventually causing his death.[2] Opinion polls suggest that the majority of French people believe Marie Humbert was right to carry out her son's request for Euthanasia.[3] Hundreds of thousands of viewers attended Spanish cinemas in 2004 as the true story of Roman Sampredo was told. "Mar adentro" ("The sea inside") is the true story of activist Ramon Sampedro, who fought the Spanish government for thirty years for his right to die. Sampedro broke his neck in a horrific diving accident. Bedridden, Sampedro decided to end his life rather than live with paralysis. He did not want his family or friends prosecuted for their assistance, so he unsuccessfully challenged Spain's laws prohibiting Euthanasia.[4]

In Germany members of several parties [Social Democrats (SPD), Green Party and the Liberals (FDP)] got together to introduce a bill that allows Euthanasia.[5] Belgium discussed plans to extend the country's Euthanasia law to allow the procedure for

1 http://www.euro-fam.org/scripts/spop/articleINT.php?&LG=EN&LJ=FR&XMLCODE=2003-03-27-2025
2 Vincent Humbert: Je vous demande le droit de mourir. Paris 2003.
3 http://news.bbc.co.uk/1/hi/world/europe/3142246.stm
4 http://www.blackfilm.com/20041217/reviews/theseainside.shtml
5 Frankfurter Rundschau 08./09.04.2004.

children, starting at the age of 12, as well as dementia patients, who have completed a corresponding declaration of intention.

For the fourth time, the *Council of Europe* discussed a draft which promotes the introduction of a European law on Euthanasia.[6] According to opinion polls the majority of European citizens support a law on Euthanasia and at the same time does not know what hospice and palliative care stand for.[7]

The current situation appears to be confusing for several reasons: the care of the dying has become more and more difficult in the ageing European societies; hospitals seem to be unsuitable places to be acquainted with the delicate issues death and dying; life prolonging measures are contentious. As there are strong interest groups who support the practice of Euthanasia, Europe is at the crossroads: Palliative Care or Euthanasia? Switzerland, the Netherlands and Belgium already have, in different ways, legalised Euthanasia. At the same time everywhere in Europe, hospice and palliative care services offer care for the dying and proclaim themselves as alternatives to the practice of Euthanasia. Medical, economical, legal, humanitarian, ethical and religious arguments are thrown into the mix and intensify the impression that Europe will face extremely delicate and difficult questions concerning the care of the dying.

We hope that this comparative study on hospice and palliative care in Europe will contribute to the ongoing discussion. Presumably the questions involved with the issue will be among the most important for the future of Europe. The answers given may set the tone for the development of the growing European Union. Will Euthanasia disguise a "civil killing culture", which draws its arguments from demographic pressure and economical crisis and gain influence? Or will hospice and palliative care services herald the development of a humane European society?[8]

In the following we use "palliative care" as defined by the *WHO* as the term that describes various forms of in-patient, out-patient and home care services. Whereas in some countries palliative care and hospice care are used more or less synonymously (for example England, Norway, Netherlands), in other countries such as Germany explicit distinctions between services located in hospital settings (palliative wards) and other voluntary hospice services, still exist.

We present our report with some concerns: A small team dealing with a big topic. Palliative care is undergoing rapid change and development so that figures and data are changing constantly. Nevertheless we hope to present a useful study which should interest people working in the field of palliative care who would like to know: What is happening in other countries? How can we learn from each other? What mistakes

---

6 Parliamentary Assembly of the European Council. 10.09.2003. Doc. 9898. Report by Dick Marty, Switzerland. http://assembly.coe.int/Mainf.asp?link=http://assembly.coe.int/documents/workingdocs/doc03/edoc9898.htm

7 cp. Emnid-survey 2003: "Was denken die Deutschen über Palliative-Care?" ("What do Germans think of palliative care?"). On behalf of the Deutsche Hospiz Stiftung (German Hospice Foundation).

8 cp. Bioskop-AutorInnenkollektiv: "Sterbehilfe" Die neue Zivilkultur des Tötens? Frankfurt am Main 2002.

can be avoided? The latter point could be especially interesting for activists in those countries where palliative care is still in its infancy.

Above all this study aims to promote the international discourse.

Although the study is a team product, the responsibilities for the individual country reports have been marked.

We dedicate this book to Heinrich Pera, who has been influential for the hospice movements in Germany and Eastern Europe. He supported our work in his distinctive generous manner. We would have liked to discuss the results with him. Heinrich Pera died suddenly and unexpectedly on March 2, 2004. His calm, thoughtful and experienced voice will be sorely missed.

Reimer Gronemeyer, Michaela Fink, Marcel Globisch, Felix Schumann
Giessen, March 2005

Acknowledgments

We would like to thank the Robert Bosch Foundation, Stuttgart, – in particular Dr. Almut Satrapa-Schill – who enabled this study through their funding and support. Throughout our work we have been grateful for the interest and support of the German Umbrella Organisation for Hospice care (Bundesarbeitsgemeinschaft Hospiz) and their president Gerda Graf. Of course we thank all the people who were interviewed for the study: carers, politicians, volunteers, patients and relatives. We are deeply impressed by the kindness and willingness shown by the interviewees and experts during our research. Without them our book would not have been possible.

This also applies to several individuals who have given extensive and vital help. The list of people we owe our gratitude is long and probably incomplete:

Brian Archibald, Ole Bang, Dr Johann Baumgartner, Martin Böker, Verena Bottenhorn, Denise Brady, Larissa Budde, Wolfgang Buff, Marcela Buhlmann, Natalie Butz, Guiseppe Casale, Miriam Cejkova, Prof Dr David Clark, Leslie Clarke, Juliane Conrad, Dr Tomasz Dangel, Ria de Korte-Verhoef, David Distelmann, Raffaella Dobrina, Dominic Dobson, Mark Dobson, Thorsten Euler, Sebastian Eumann, Kathrin Feick, Christine Ursula Feigs, Ralf P. Frenger, Dr. Michele Gallucci, Rita Garnier, Heidi Globisch, Rüdiger Globisch, Stefan Globisch, Jean-Pierre Greiveldinger, Martin Hassa, Dr Dagny Faksvåg Haugen, Dr Katalin Hegedus, Prof Dr. Andreas Heller, Annegret Horbach, Dr Bettina Sandgathe Husebø, Prof Dr Stein Husebø, Avril Jackson, Miles Jackson, Barbara Kállo, Rafal Kaminski, Helga Keller, Horst Keller, Thile Kerkovius, Dr Bernadette Klapper, Dr Peter Krizan, Marta Kuerschner, Yevgeniya Kononenko, Christel Lauterbach, Dr Christian Metz, Becky Millinger, Rachel Millinger, Claudia Monti, Andrea Newerla, Peter Otto, Mimi Parker, Claudia Paul, Christine Pfeffer, Elzbieta Piotrowska, Wolfgang Polkowski, Dr Georgia A. Rakelmann, Melissa Reddish, Dr Harald Retschitzegger, Dr André Rhebergen, Dr Matthias Rompel, Josef Roß, Sophia Rudzki, Ingeborg Schumann, Prof Dr Michael Schumann, Till Schumann, Carolin Seitz, Prof Dr Arvydas Seskevicius, Dr Ondrej Slama, Alan Sparhawk, Dr Jolanta Stokłasa, Victoria Southworth, Melinda Szöllősi, Peter Tebbit, Paul Timmermanns, Dr Tove Vejlgaard, Heidi von Gruenewaldt, Ilka Weinbrenner, Prof Dr Herbert Willems, Dr Giovanni Zaninetta, Tina Zielesny.

Part One – Palliative Care in Europe

1. Objectives and methods of the study

The 2-year project began in February 2003 and was preceded by two international hospice conferences held at the Faculty of Sociology at Justus-Liebig-University in Giessen, Germany. The aim of the study was to complete a **comparative study on palliative care in sixteen European countries**. The countries covered here are: Austria, Czech Republic, Denmark, England, Estonia, France, Germany, Hungary, Italy, Latvia, Lithuania, Netherlands, Norway, Poland, Slovakia and Ukraine. [1]

However our study also builds on previous research in the field: International research projects carried out by David Clark and Michael Wright, Andreas Heller, Stein Husebø and Eberhard Klaschik. [2] The work of European organisations has also been very important for our study. Above all the *European Association of Palliative Care (EAPC)* [3] and the *European Federation of Older People (EURAG)*.

The project was divided into three components:

---

1 The research and country report on the Ukraine was completed by Yevgeniya Kononenko. Miss Kononenko is Ukrainian and works at the Institute of Sociology at Justus-Liebig-University Giessen. Revision by Michaela Fink.

2 cp. most notably the following studies: Cicely Saunders/Robert Kastenbaum (Eds.): Hospice Care on the International Scene. New York 1997; Friedemann Nauck/Eberhard Klaschik: The role of health policy in the development and organisation of palliative medicine. Nijmegen: Pallium Report 1998; Henk ten Have (Eds.): Palliative Care in Europa: Concepts and Policies. Amsterdam 2001; Henk ten Have/David Clark (Eds.): The Ethics of Palliative Care: European Perspectives. Buckingham 2002; David Clark/Michael Wright: Transitions in End of Life Care: Hospice and related developments in Eastern Europe and Central Asia. Buckingham 2003; Stein Husebø/Eberhard Klaschik: Palliativmedizin. 3rd edition Berlin et al. 2003; European Commission Community research: Promoting the Development and Integration of Palliative Care Mobile Support Teams in the Hospital. The fifth framework programme 1998 - 2002 "Quality of life and management of living resources". Other individual studies supplement the ones mentioned above: for example Claude Fusco-Karmann/Gianna Tinini: A review of the volunteer movement in EAPC countries. In: European Journal of Palliative Care. Vol. 8. No.5/2001, p. 199 - 202; cp. also: European Economic and Social Committee. Plenary Assembly 20 and 21 March 2002. Hospice work – an example of voluntary activities in Europe. On the Internet: http://www.esc.eu.int/documents/summaries_plenaries/2002/synt_03_en.PDF. The brochure "The last hours and days" sets standards for Palliative Care. An edition of 50,000 issues was published in five different languages (English, German, Italian, Spanish and Norwegian) (Bettina Sandgathe Husebø/ Stein Husebø: Die letzten Tage und Stunden. Oslo 2001).

3 Dr. Carlos Centeno leads the EAPC Task Force on Development of Palliative Care in Europe.

Quantitative information and data

Relevant quantitative information and data of the sixteen European countries focusing on: demographics, population structure, health care system, legal status of palliative care, stats of palliative care services (national and regional data). The quantitative data was gathered from governmental, public health and NGO sources (such as National and regional Umbrella organisations), publications as well as conference abstracts and documentations.

Qualitative data

The analysis of palliative care in the respective countries concentrates on: sponsorship, funding, education and training of professional and voluntary staff, management, patient groups, role of relatives and friends, and the history of palliative care. The main sources for the research on the successes, failures and perspectives of palliative care are approximately 150 **qualitatively drafted interviews** with experts in the various countries.

Comparison

The individual country reports, which are presented in a standardised pattern, are the basis for the comparison. With the help of MAXqda2, a software programme for **computer assisted analysis of qualitative data**, a systematic analysis and interpretation of the texts was carried out. The sixteen country reports were categorised in a code system in accordance with the standardised pattern used in each report to ensure the elaboration and verification of theoretical conclusions. The varying degrees and forms in which information and data from the different countries was available **made comparison more difficult.** Similar experiences have been made during other international studies. [4] Perhaps the incomparableness is worth protecting. Efforts are being made to implement standards and definition in this sensitive field. This could eventually lead to "quality controlled dying" the threatens to carry the phenomenon of levelling into the latter stages of life.

At the same time Palliative care structures benefit from the interest in cross-boarder exchange of information. Over the past few years, a number of important international palliative care conferences took place. [5] It is the explicit desire of this study to encourage and support the ongoing international and interdisciplinary discourse.

---

4 cp. et al.: Henk ten Have/David Clark (Ed.): The Ethics of Palliative Care: European Perspectives. Buckingham 2002, p. 35 et seq.

5 Apart from the regular national and international conferences the following are worth special attention: The Antea conference in Rome (The International Meeting of Hospices, 06.-07.11.2003), EURAG conference in Brussels (Making Palliative Care a Priority Topic on the European Health Agenda, 23.01.2004), Four Countries Conference in Cleveland, USA, ("End of Life Care" 16.-18.07. 2004) and Workshop by IFF Vienna and the Austrian Red Cross in Vienna (Palliative Care in Old Age – Dignity for the Weakest Old, 02.-04.04.2004).

The first aim of this comparative study is to document the current situation of palliative care in the sixteen countries: How is palliative care progressing in Europe? By comparing the different developments

- existing and developing *European similarities* are identified and
- *regional and national particularities* are highlighted.

2. Background

Beyond all visible differences, **two common tendencies** can be observed in Europe that consistently influence the development of palliative care: European societies are getting older and as a result of demographic changes, a European wide crisis of health care systems is obvious.

Ageing societies and their consequences

There is a visible process of ageing in the continent's population. The percentage of over-65-year-olds in Europe will increase from 14.7 per cent in 2000 to 21.3 per cent in the year 2025, and is expected to climb to 27.9 per cent by the year 2050. The percentage of over 80-year-olds is predicted to rise from 2.9 per cent in 2000 to 5.2 per cent in 2025 and then to 9.5 per cent by 2050 (see table 1).[6] At the same time it is anticipated that birth rates will decline throughout the continent. These developments will have considerable effects on the health systems and health expenditure in each individual country.

For a long time the issue of obsolescence has been ignored in European societies. Now the consequences of demographic change are discussed widely. Recently, questions have been asked such as: Will the welfare system collapse? How can we (further) save the expenses for health care? Will we be able to cover pensions on a long-term basis? Will the dominance of the elderly change Europe? How is death supposed to take place in modern societies where family ties are eroding, where the comfort brought by religion is disappearing, where – in the direct and metaphysical sense – the act of dying is becoming homeless? Everywhere from Riga to Madrid, from London to Bratislava, the traditional model is disintegrating.[7] Without a doubt, this European crisis will also effect the care of the dying.

[6] Source: Population Division of the Department of Economic and Social Affairs of the United Nations Secretariat, World Population Prospects: The 2002 Revision Population Database: http://esa.un.org/unpp (medium variant).

[7] cp. Reimer Gronemeyer: Kampf der Generationen. München 2004.

Country	Population 65 or older in 2000 (in %)	Population 65 or older in 2050 (in %)	Population 80 or older in 2000 (in %)	Population 80 or older in 2050 (in %)
Austria	15.5	30.6	3.5	12.8
Czech Rep.	13.8	32.2	2.3	9.3
Denmark	15.0	24.9	4.0	9.3
Estonia	15.1	31.2	2.6	9.3
France	16.0	26.4	3.7	10.3
Germany	16.3	28.0	3.5	11.7
Hungary	14.6	28.8	2.5	7.6
Italy	18.1	34.4	3.9	13.5
Latvia	15.1	30.8	2.6	9.6
Lithuania	14.0	24.9	2.4	8.5
Netherlands	13.6	24.7	3.2	9.5
Norway	15.4	26.1	4.5	10.3
Poland	12.1	28.4	2.0	7.6
Slovakia	11.3	27.3	1.8	7.1
UK	15.9	23.0	4.1	8.5
Ukraine	13.8	28.6	2.3	7.8
Europe	14.7	27.9	2.9	9.5

Table 1: Ageing societies in Europe [8]

The crisis of health care systems

Total expenditure on health services increased from 5 per cent of the gross domestic product in 1970 to over 8 per cent by 1998. The overall proportional growth in the number of elderly citizens is leading to increased demand for long-term medical and nursing care. From age-related ailments and illnesses to around-the-clock nursing, those concerned have to be cared for over long periods of time. Health expenditures for the elderly are startlingly higher than for young people. [9]

8 Source: Population Division of the Department of Economic and Social Affairs of the United Nations Secretariat, World Population Prospects: The 2002 Revision Population Database: http://esa.un.org/unpp (medium variant).

9 Commission of the European Communities. Communication from the Commission to the Council, the European Parliament, the Economic and Social Committee and the Committee of the Regions. The future of health care and care for the elderly: guaranteeing accessibility, quality and financial viability. 05 December 2001, p. 4. On the Internet: http://europa.eu.int/eur-lex/en/com/cnc/2001/com2001_0723en01.pdf

Within Europe the individual health systems exhibit very different financial conditions and organisational structures. [10] However, one can see that in almost all parts of the continent, attempts have been made to limit costs. These costs are already having an effect on palliative care – and in the future this will only be intensified – in particular because end-of-life medical and nursing care can be extremely expensive. Questions concerning the costs for care at the end of life are no longer taboo. In the United States E. Emanuel and M. Batin raised the question in how far physician-assisted suicide could save costs at the end of life. [11] Such questions are a commonly debated topics in the European Union as well.

Palliative care can be provided at a cheaper rate than intensive medicine. In respect to the ageing of Europe, there is the threat of palliative care being misused. From an attempt to guarantee better care for the dying, in a worst-case scenario it could become a more cost-effective human disposal structure and reinforce the inequity in the health care system by consolidating current structures.

The swift ability of the new concept of palliative care to assert itself owes much to the fact of fundamental changes. End of life these days is, in stark contrast to the 19th century, characterized by the **institutionalisation** and the **medicalisation** of dying that confront professionals involved with difficult tasks. "All physicians face the problem of balancing technical intervention with a humanistic orientation to their dying patients." [12] Often care of the dying in primary care is considered inadequate and unsatisfying.

3. Palliative care – the development of a new global provision structure

Although most human beings express the wish to die at home, dying in institutions is increasing normality. In Germany approximately 80 percent of all people die in nursing homes, hospitals or other institutions. [13] Even though this is the case in most European countries, there are some exceptions such as the Baltic countries or the Netherlands. In the latter, 65 percent spend their last hours in familiar surroundings. [14] In different contexts, tendencies can be observed but at the same time generalisations are inappropriate as provision structures in the countries vary considerably. The careful

---

10 ibid., p. 9 et seqq.

11 E. Emanuel/B. Batin: What are the Potential Cost Savings from Legalizing Physician-Assisted Suicide? In: New England Journal of Medicine. Volume 339. 1998, p. 167 - 172.

12 David Clark has published a very interesting and notable article on the medicalisation of dying and its effect on palliative care. David Clark: Between hope and acceptance: the medicalisation of dying. In: British Medical Journal. Volume 324. 13. April 2002, p. 905 et seqq.

13 Klaus Dörner: Der gute Arzt. Lehrbuch der ärztlichen Grundhaltung. Stuttgart 2001, p. 97 et seqq.

14 A.L. Francke/ D.L. Willems: Palliatieve zorg vandaag en morgen. Feiten, opvattingen en scenario's. Maarssen: Elsevier gezondheidszorg, 2000. As cited by Ministry of Health, Welfare and Sport in the Netherlands: Palliative care for terminally ill patients in the Netherlands. Dutch Government Policy. The Hague 2003, p. 5.

consideration of the places of death shows that generalisations appear foreshortened and inappropriate.

In the face of staff shortages in institutions and dominating economical issues in hospitals, dying has become a "problem" in European societies. Often patients do not want high-tech medicine. At the same time worries are openly expressed to limit the costs of chronic diseases and geriatric illnesses. Such concerns also regard the care of the dying.

The hospice movement and palliative care forged out of hopelessness: for example, eroding family boundaries, the excessive demands care services face, and the inadequate care of the dying in hospitals. This has led to the development of palliative care that today, is present in all European countries. It is worth mentioning that this widely accepted phenomenon of a model for the handling of dying and death has been able to make a breakthrough in the comparatively short period of 25 years.[15] Palliative care started in England and since then has been widely established in Northern industrial societies. Today palliative care is provided in large parts of the world, or in some cases, is on its way to becoming established today. At present palliative care structures are growing in parts of Africa that are particularly hit by the HIV/AIDS epidemic.

It is not really evident where palliative care belongs. In a sense palliative care cannot be part of the traditional health care system as it "lacks" the primary aim of health care which is to cure people. This is highlighted by the fact that the hospice movement, in the beginning, was mainly carried by a voluntary and civil movement that cared for the dying outside hospitals. Palliative care started as hospice *movement* that was set into motion by Cicely Saunders as a personally and religiously motivated model outside traditional medicine structures. In the meantime there is doubt that palliative care has become a part of the health care system and traditional medicine. Until the 19th century the deathbed was the sanctuary of the family and religious figures, virtually excluding doctors. The moment *facies hippocratica* – the signs of death – became visible on the face of the dying person, the doctor left the room to make way for the priest and the family. It remains to be seen whether the increased involvement of physicians in the process of dying and the integration of palliative care into existing health care structures will be beneficial on the long term.

The ***World Health Organization*** **(*WHO*)** has played an important part in the establishment of palliative care. The WHO's-definitions of palliative care in 1990 and 2002 are respected world-wide.[16] Palliative Care is defined as

> an approach that improves the quality of life of patients and their families facing the problem associated with life-threatening illness, through the prevention and relief of suffering by means

---

[15] The beginnings of modern Hospice Care, founded by Dame Cicely Saunders, date back much longer. However, palliative care, as a European phenomenon, became evident more recently.

[16] cp. above all the publications by WHO/Europe. Elizabeth Davies/ Irene Higginson (Eds.): *Palliative Care – The Solid Facts*. WHO Regional Office for Europe. Copenhagen 2004. On the Internet: http://www.euro.who.int/document/E82931.pdf and Elizabeth Davies/ Irene Higginson (Eds.): Better Palliative Care for Older People. Copenhagen 2004. On the Internet: http://www.euro.who.int/document/E82933.pdf cp. as well: http://www.who.int/cancer/palliative/definition/en/

of early identification and impeccable assessment and treatment of pain and other problems, physical, psychosocial and spiritual. Palliative care:

- provides relief from pain and other distressing symptoms;
- affirms life and regards dying as a normal process;
- intends neither to hasten or postpone death;
- integrates the psychological and spiritual aspects of patient care;
- offers a support system to help patients live as actively as possible until death;
- offers a support system to help the family cope during the patients illness and in their own bereavement;
- uses a team approach to address the needs of patients and their families, including bereavement counselling, if indicated;
- will enhance quality of life, and may also positively influence the course of illness;
- is applicable early in the course of illness, in conjunction with other therapies that are intended to prolong life, such as chemotherapy or radiation therapy, and includes those investigations needed to better understand and manage distressing clinical complications.

On the whole one can say that in Europe today there is a **model of palliative care**, which is receiving general acceptance from medical, nursing, administrative, political and charitable authorities. Predominantly in the past ten years different models of services have been established in Europe: Free-standing hospices, palliative care units in hospital settings, hospital mobile teams, nursing homes, day care and home care services.

It is widely recognised that palliative care should include the following elements:

- Out-patient services are generally preferred to in-patient provision which should, as a matter of principle, come into place when home care is no longer possible or impossible at all.
- Pain relief, as quoted in the *WHO's*-definitions of palliative care, is one of the key priorities.
- A multi-disciplinary team (medical, psychological, care-staff, volunteers) cares for the patient, their family and friends.
- Special training for example special courses for the professional and voluntary team members are necessary.
- Palliative care should – as far as possible – guarantee quality of life right to the end.
- As a result, the necessity to secure palliative care through professionalisation, standardisation and quality control has grown.
- Palliative care is part of the regular health care system and as such, costs are partly or fully covered within regular funding structures.
- National policies providing guidelines should be in place.

The **success of the concept of "palliative care"** is understandably based on the fact that family members are less willing to, and also less capable of taking care of a dying family member alone in their home: They do not have the time, the space, the money, and – in view of the medicalisation of the dying – no longer have the competence to care of a moribund family member. On the other hand the model of radical medicalisation of dying has come under criticism because it has become clear that a dying person's dignity can be harmed even with the best medical care. It is in this gap, between the failures of the family and medicine, that palliative care has flourished. In this respect the success of palliative care is evidence for the ability of European societies to react to social and cultural challenges.

4. Results

4.1 Introduction

What are the results of our study? When one looks at the results of our study of palliative care, what are the similarities, what are the differences in the sixteen countries that have been part of the study? Which trends can be observed? What are the main tasks the European "palliative care community" faces in the future?

In the whole of Europe, the WHO-defined model of palliative care has established itself. Over the course of ten years, new palliative care structures have spread in a rapid and substantial manner. Almost everywhere in Europe in-patient and out-patient services co-exist. The principle "out-patient in favour of in-patient" has become widely accepted among planners from various backgrounds (state, private, non-profit, church) in order to fulfil the wishes often expressed by patients to die in familiar surroundings. Nevertheless it can be observed that public attention often focuses on in-patient units. Normally fundraising for in-patient units is less problematic than for home care services. As the establishment of an inpatient hospice is also a question of prestige (for example for local politicians or cities), at times planners do not elevate the needs for such a service.

In most European regions state-run and voluntary structures exist parallel to each other. National or regional legislation regarding the provision of palliative care have been introduced in many countries, regulated funding systems exist increasingly (either financed by the state or health insurance companies). Palliative Care more and more becomes a public issue, and also a matter for European authorities such as the European Commission. This implicates a push towards professionalisation that ranges from university courses on palliative medicine to the training of volunteers. This changes the economical, social and ethical situation significantly: Palliative care becomes a special discipline. [17]

At the same time palliative care is on its way to establish itself as the third pillar in European health policy: Next to the treatment of diseases (1) and the care of elderly people (2), palliative care takes the place of the care for the terminally ill (3). We explicitly speak of terminally ill patients and not exclusively of the dying as studies show that today, in most countries, palliative care occurs much earlier in the course of the illness as in the beginnings of the hospice movement. Palliative care in countries

[17] In general, palliative care is ascribed to Dame Cicely Saunders and the origins of the modern hospice movement. Whether the current European palliative care structures have much in common with the origins of the hospice movement remains questionable.

such as Great Britain and the Netherlands has increasingly disengaged from the label of being solely responsible for the care of the dying. In other countries like Norway or Denmark, this is sometimes visible in the names of institutions: KamillianerGaarden Hospice in Denmark also carries the name "Center for relieving treatment", while the five Centres of Excellence in Norway are called *Kompetansesenter*.

The **"new features of palliative care"** are ambivalent:

- On one hand, the earlier palliative care takes place in the course of a terminal illness, the better for the patient.[18] The care is no longer restricted to the last few days, a holistic approach in the original sense of hospice care can be accomplished more easily.
- On the other hand, the earlier terminally ill patients receive palliative care, the more the accentuation is on "life quality", one of the primary aims of palliative care. In fact there seems less talk of "dignity of the dying" and more discussion of "securing the quality of life" for the dying. Thus arises the danger that the ideals of quality control and standardisation will suppress the very personal and humanitarian elements of palliative care that are especially represented by the volunteers.

In light of this development, the statement by Dame Cicely Saunders seems to be of particular interest:

> We must not forget that all our patients are eventually going to die and we must not so much concentrate on quality of life up to dying that we forget the actual problem of the dying, the last days and weeks, the families, the bereavement and so on.[19]

4.2 Origins

The history of hospice and palliative movement originated in England under the driving force of Dame Cicely Saunders. Hospice and palliative care services world-wide are still deeply connected with Dame Cicely. In various interviews, experts from all over Europe regard Dame Cicely and *St Christopher's Hospice* as the main inspirations to set up their own hospice services.

Particularly in Eastern Europe palliative care services are still very much modelled on Western concepts with Poland an exception to the rule. In Poland the developments took course much earlier and more independently than in other Eastern European countries.

Of course the history of origins in Europe has been different (see table 2). Nevertheless two traces can be identified:

- **Bottom-up**: A (civil)-movement that was founded mainly outside the regular health care system and without state-aid. Mostly initiated by charismatic personalities who – often despite serious resistance in their countries – served as pioneers of the movement to improve the care of the dying (for example Germany, Slovakia).

---

[18] cp. et al.: Johann Baumgartner et al.: Pilotprojekt "Stationäre Palliativbetreuung" in der Steiermark. Die wissenschaftliche Begleituntersuchung. Graz 1999, p. 160.

[19] Interview with Dame Cicely Saunders, 16 March 2004, in London.

- **Top-down**: The development of palliative care structures was most of all the result of administrative measures taken by either state authorities or from within the regular health care system (for example Netherlands, Norway).

Table 2 gives an overview on the origins of hospice and palliative care services in the sixteen European countries which were part of the study.

Country	Year	Type of service	Name of service
Austria	1989	Home care	Charity Archdiocese, Vienna
Denmark	1992	Inpatient hospice	St. Lukas Hospice, Copenhagen
Germany	1983	Hospital inpatient palliative care unit	University Clinic, Cologne
England	1967	Inpatient hospice	St Christopher's Hospice, London
Estonia	1997	Home care service	Cancer Centre, Talinn
France	1983	Home care service	Association Jalmalv, Grenoble
Italy	1980	Home care programme	Pain Therapy Division of National Cancer Institute of Milan and Floriani Foundation
Latvia	1997	Hospital inpatient palliative care unit	Cancer Centre, Riga
Lithuania	1993	Mobile hospice team	Kaunas Terminal Care Hospital
Netherlands	1991	Inpatient hospice	Johannes Hospice, Vleuten
Norway	1977	Home care service	Fransiskushjelpen, Oslo
Poland	1976	Unit for terminally ill patients	Jeromsky Hospital, Krakow
Slovakia	1995	Hospital inpatient palliative care unit	National Cancer Institute, Bratislava
Czech Rep.	1992	Hospital inpatient palliative care unit	Hospital for pulmonary diseases, Babice
Ukraine	1996	Inpatient hospice	Public hospital No. 2, Kiew
Hungary	1991	Home care service	Hungarian Hospice Foundation, Budapest

Table 2: Founding specialist hospice and palliative care services in sixteen European countries [20]

[20] Sources: Data taken from country reports.

4.3 Inpatient service provision

The total provision of palliative care beds across the sixteen countries proved difficult to determine.[21] For some countries:

- **precise nationwide statistics** are on hand (Austria, England, France, Germany, Hungary, Netherlands),
- **divers statistics existed,** which were contradicting (Italy, Poland),
- **no official national statistics** are available at all, so that the calculation for those countries, where the number of inpatient units are still low and ascertainable, are put together from the data collected in our extensive research (Czech Republic, Denmark, Estonia, Latvia, Lithuania, Slovakia). In countries with extended palliative care structures, the statistics are on estimations based on consultations with experts (Norway, Ukraine).
- In addition, the definition of palliative care beds in the countries differs so the degree to which comparisons could be drawn are restricted as similar studies have asserted in the past.[22] Whereas in some countries palliative care beds in care- and nursing homes are regarded as inpatient beds (for example Norway), they are not covered in official statistics in other countries (for example Germany). Furthermore it is imperative to consider the number of beds in relation to the specific structure of care provision. In countries where home care provision is well-developed, and caring family members are still very much involved, the need for inpatient beds might be lower than in regions with hardly any home care services existing.

For all that, the total provision of inpatient palliative care beds shows the continuing disparity of palliative care provision available to Europeans that has been observed in former studies before.[23] In order to make a comparison possible we present the number of palliative care bes in relation to the total population (table 3).

---

21 Other projects had to cope with similar problems: cp. et al.: Henk ten Have/David Clark (Ed.): The Ethics of Palliative Care: European Perspectives, Buckingham 2002, p. 41.

22 ibid.

23 Henk ten Have/David Clark (Ed.): The Ethics of Palliative Care: European Perspectives, Buckingham 2002, p. 41.

Country	Population in million (2000)[24]	Number of beds	Ratio of beds to population	Beds per 1 million habitants
UK	58.689	3.195	1: 18.369	54.44
Norway	4.473	190	1: 23.542	42.51
Netherlands	15.898	590	1: 26.946	37.11
Italy	57.536	2.133	1: 26.974	37.07
Poland	38.671	1.268	1: 30.498	32.79
Austria	8.102	190	1: 42.742	23.46
Germany	82.282	1.788	1: 46.019	21.73
Latvia	2.373	50	1: 47.460	21.09
Czech Rep.	10.269	185	1: 55.508	18.01
France	59.296	772	1: 76.808	13.02
Denmark	5.322	65	1: 81.877	12.22
Estonia	1.367	16	1: 85.438	11.70
Hungary	10.012	106	1: 94.452	10.59
Ukraine	49.688	500	1: 99.376	10.06
Slovakia	5.391	54	1: 99.833	10.02
Lithuania	3.501	30	1: 116.700	8.57
Total	**412.870**	**11.132**	**1:37.089**	**26.96**

Table 3: Inpatient hospice and palliative care beds in Europe[25]

Based on epidemiological research in the UK population and literature review Irene Higginson provided a palliative and terminal health care needs assessment. According to Higginson there is an estimated need of 50 specialist palliative care beds per million inhabitants.[26] The study is well-respected and has been adopted in many European countries. If one applies this calculation to the sixteen countries – for all given concerns in view of the different conditions in the countries – it would add up to a total need of 20.666 inpatient palliative care beds. Based on the best available figures, there are 11.132 beds in the sixteen countries. This means only 26.96 beds per million citizens are provided at the moment, just a little more than half of the 50 beds required per million inhabitants. As a result, the UK is currently the only country with

24 Source: Population Division of the Department of Economic and Social Affairs of the United Nations Secretariat, World Population Prospects: The 2002 Revision Population Database: http://esa.un.org/unpp (medium variant)

25 Sources: Stats taken from country reports.

26 Irene Higginson: Palliative and Terminal Care. In: A. Stevens/ J. Raftery (Eds.): Palliative and Terminal Care Health Care Needs Assessment. Oxford 1998, p. 1 - 45.

a sufficient number of inpatient palliative care beds (see table 3). In addition a significant steep incline between the provision in Western and Eastern Europe is obvious: Whereas on average there are 31.23 beds per million inhabitants in the eight Western European countries, on average only 16.58 do currently exist in the eight researched countries located in Eastern Europe (see table 4).

4.4 East-West distinctions

With the exception of Poland and the two Baltic countries Estonia and Latvia, the Eastern European states remain bottom of the table. Poland's outstanding position corresponds with the findings of a 2003 study by David Clark and Michael Wright: 69 percent of the palliative care services in fifteen [27] researched countries in Central and Eastern Europe were located in Poland. [28] Amongst the eight Eastern European nations that were part of our research, the 1.268 beds in Poland make up 63 percent of the total number of beds. If the beds in Poland were not considered among the statistics, the provision of palliative care beds would drop significantly from an average 16.69 to 9 beds (see table 4).

The high ranking of Latvia is based on two inpatient units in the capital of Riga with 25 beds each. This deceives the otherwise rather poor provision with palliative care in the rest of Latvia. A similar situation can be stated for Estonia.

Although Hungary, as one example, is placed behind Estonia and Latvia, the provision with palliative care is much further developed than in the two Baltic countries (see table 6).

The development in most parts of Eastern Europe is often characterised by a strong commitment shown by individuals and small groups whereas the establishment of cross regional structures proves to be very difficult.

Region [29]	**Population in million (2000) [30]**	**Beds**	**Ratio of beds to population**	**Beds per 1 million habitants**
Western Europe	291.598	9.108	1:32.016	31.23
Eastern Europe	121.272	2.024	1:59.917	16.69
Total	**412.870**	**11.132**	**1:37.089**	**26.96**

Table 4: Inpatient hospice and palliative care beds in Western- and Eastern Europe

[27] The fifteen countries were: Albania, Bosnia-Herzegovina, Bulgaria, Croatia, Czech Republic, Estonia, Hungary, Latvia, Lithuania, Macedonia, Poland, Romania, Serbia, Slovakia and Slovenia.

[28] David Clark/Michael Wright: Transitions in end of life care: hospice developments in Eastern Europe and Central Asia. Buckingham 2003, p. 21.

The **Prosperity incline** from West to East is unmistakably evident in the financial provisions of palliative care institutions. Whereas in Italy, for example, there are many almost luxurious hospices, palliative institutions in the Czech Republic and the Baltic countries are of a more basic nature.

In contrast to the relatively slow development of palliative care structures in Eastern Europe, an **enormous growth of services in Western Europe** can be observed. This can be exemplified by contrasting the current state of provision with comparable data from a study carried out by Henk ten Have and David Clark in 1999.[31] In this study, the number of hospice and palliative beds in seven Western European countries[32] were investigated. Whereas in 1999, ten Have/ Clark found out there were merely 30 beds in Italy at the time, today the number of beds has risen to 2.133. This signifies an astonishing increase of over 700 percent of palliative care beds.[33] A similar development can be seen in the Netherlands: The quantity of inpatient palliative care beds climbed almost five fold from 119 in 1999 to 590 beds in 2004. In Germany, the number of beds has almost doubled in the same span of time from 899 (1999) to 1.788 (2004). In the UK the number of palliative care beds has been almost the same. Hence, it is not surprising as palliative care provision in the UK had already been well-developed five years ago and it can be assumed that the needs of beds have been fulfilled although regional distinction is also evident in the UK.

There are also **regional differences** within the countries that have to be considered. This applies to the high developed palliative care provision in England as well as in Italy where disparities between North and South are highly visible.

For the majority of the **Eastern European** countries, problems securing **long-term funding** is often the main reason for slow developments. Often palliative care is regarded as a luxury by policy makers that cannot be afforded. Although funding by the National Health Services or insurance companies is established in most countries, the money made available is often not enough to cover occurring costs completely. This is particularly evident in the Baltic countries.

---

29 For this table, the following eight countries are considered as Western European: Austria, Denmark, Germany, France, Italy, Netherlands, Norway, UK. The eight Eastern European countries include: Czech Republic, Estonia, Hungary, Latvia, Lithuania, Poland, Slovakia, Ukraine.

30 Source: Population Division of the Department of Economic and Social Affairs of the United Nations Secretariat, World Population Prospects: The 2002 Revision Population Database: http://esa.un.org/unpp (medium variant).

31 Henk ten Have/David Clark (Ed.): The Ethics of Palliative Care: European Perspectives, Buckingham 2002.

32 The seven countries were:, Belgium, Germany, Great Britain, Netherlands, Italy, Spain, and Sweden.

33 It is important to note that the information of different sources in Italy differ to a great extent. The used stats here have been gathered from a official statistic by the National Ministry of Health (see country report Italy). The immense rise in palliative care beds over the past five years poses the question whether this rapid increase is the result of "rededications" of "common" beds into "palliative care beds" sometimes at the expense of qualified palliative care staff educated and trained in the care of the dying.

4.5 The role of states for palliative care

What are the consequences for palliative care when public funding is provided for networks, national curricula, research and practice? What are the advantages and disadvantages when state authorities are actively involved in palliative care?

- **No involvement of state authorities or public funding (bottom-up situation):**
  - Advantages: Self-determination, no obligations towards funders.
  - Disadvantages: Makeshift equipment and facilities, high degree of reliance on volunteers, lack of professional staff, no reliable funding. Threat of stagnation (for example Slovakia).
- **Strong state commitment (top-down situation):**
  - Advantages: Stable structures (for example the Centres for Palliative Care in Norway and the Netherlands), secure funding through integration in health care system.
  - Disadvantages: Narrow guidelines by the implementation of standards (Obligatory membership in regional networks as precondition for national health care funding in the Netherlands), under certain conditions institutions do not fit into the structured patterns (due to the funding system in Norway, hospices there are forced to release patients early to be able to gain essential money from new admissions).

Table 5 shows a summary of the state's role in palliative care. The list shows main activities in the field of palliative care by the countries state authorities and is not exhaustive. More extensive information can be found in the respective country reports. The summarised findings once again provides information on the strong variations that exist in terms of state planning and funding that go along with the reflections on the advantages and disadvantages of state commitment.

Country	**National policy**	**State funding**	**Purpose and aim**
Austria	2002	yes	The *Familienhospizkarenz* (family rest period) is a legal claim that allows employees a reduction, change or release of their usual working time in order to care for a dying relative. In case of hardships applications for special support can be filed to the Federal Ministry for Social Security and Generations.
Czech Republic	No	yes	The Ministry of Health subsidises inpatient hospices.

Denmark	1999	yes	Since 2003: 55 Mill. DKK (approx. 7,4 Mill. €) have been provided by the state to build and run inpatient hospices. Aim: The establishment of 16 inpatient hospices on a medium-term.
England	1987	yes	The *NHS Cancer Plan* provided *specialist palliative care* services with £50 Million British pounds for 2003. Aim: To improve care for cancer patients; to tackle inequalities; to build for the future through investments in workforce and research.
Estonia	No	yes	Palliative care is funded like regular care.
France	1999	yes	1999: Three-year plan for the promotion of palliative care. 2002 - 2005: *Programme National de Dévelopment des Soins Palliatifs*, under the direction of the Ministry of Health. Aim: To improve home care; the further integration of palliative care into the regular health care system; to improve the awareness of involved professions for palliative care.
Germany	1998	yes	Support of regional initiatives and funding of research projects and conferences.
Hungary	1997	yes	In September 2004, a 2-year model program started in the course of which the National Health Insurance will pay altogether 300 million Hungarian Forint to 21 home care services and 9 inpatient hospital departments which offer hospice care for patients and their families. Aim: By taking this measure it is hoped to increase the number of people who have access to hospice care.
Italy	1999	yes	1998 - 2002: approx. 200 Mill. €have been provided for the different regions. Aim: To raise the number of hospices to 184.
Latvia	No	yes	Palliative care is funded like regular care.
Lithuania	No	yes	A daily rate is provided to services that provide palliative care in the so called *Nursing Hospitals*. The state covers the costs for four month of treatment for every patient per year.

Netherlands	1997	yes	Since 1998 the Dutch Ministry of Health has spend 15 Mill. €on the development of palliative care services and their integration into public health care. Meanwhile palliative care is a integral part of the public health system.
Norway	N/a.	yes	Palliative care in Norway is part of the public health care system and to a great extent is covered by the public social insurances that fund palliative care in hospitals and services in the primary health care sector.
Poland	1991	yes	In 1993 for the first time, the government supported palliative care with approx. 16 Mill. €. A further approx. 250 Mill. €was provided for palliative care between 1999-2004. The money was distributed to all provinces.
Slovakia	N/a.	yes	In order to support hospice services the Slovakian government provided 490.000 €from lottery incomes at the end of 2001. 25% of the money was allocated to the expansion of hospice services, 75% were provided for running costs of those institutions.
Ukraine	No	yes	Normally services that have been founded by the state are also run by the state although the provided funding does not cover all costs.

Table 5: The role of the State in the field of palliative care [34]

With the subject of state intervention we once again encounter the question of who should be allowed to run hospices and hospice services (in regard to palliative medicine, the question is of less relevance). Until now there has been a spectrum of different formats in Europe from voluntary hospice groups through charity associations to state-run organisations. The further palliative care is formalised, the more emphatic the confronting questions of **quality control and standardisation** become. Thus, it becomes unavoidable that when discussing the ultra-sensitive area of cost-calculation the question of economising death creeps in. Palliative care representatives from different countries have expressed their concerns that in the course of a "economisation

[34] Sources: Data taken from country reports. The abbreviation N.a. (not available) stands for insufficient state of data at present.

of death", hospice services could be forced to operate on merely economical rather than humanistic reasons. [35]

4.6 Professional education and training

With the exception of Poland and Hungary there is a **lack of education and training** prospects in **Eastern Europe**. Instead interested individuals are often forced to gain their expert education abroad. Primarily, doctors and nurses are trained abroad, most notably in Poland, England and the USA. The **scarcity of trained professionals** has sustainable consequences: the establishment and maintenance of palliative care provision is difficult. Sometimes the lack of palliative care specialists is compensated by the employment of "professionals" who have only minimum or no education or training in palliative care. This "false labelling" can cause counterproductive consequences as those services are often run by professionals with neither special expertise in palliative care nor a multi-professional approach. The development of new specialist palliative care services can be obstructed by those "low-standard" services. It is worth adding that this is by far a solely Eastern European phenomenon. This can also be observed or assumed for some Western European countries (for example Denmark, Italy).

The introduction of a **consultant in palliative medicine** has extensive consequences for the establishment of palliative medicine as a separate medical discipline. So far Great Britain is the only European country with the possibility to become a consultant in palliative medicine. Owing to circumstances a consultant in palliative medicine must not necessarily be a target (for example Netherlands). In keeping with a generalistic approach, it is expected that health professionals acquire basic knowledge in palliative care within their education.

4.7 Volunteers

Whereas in Western Europe the **co-operation and help of volunteers** plays an extremely important role, Eastern European countries are finding problems attracting them. This can be, first and foremost, regarded as a result of former socialist planned economies. Again, the situation in Poland is different. Their voluntary commitment has a long tradition as it was one way to express an independence under the rule of socialism.

It should not be forgotten that in some parts of Europe, volunteers founded the hospice movement and with it initiated the development of palliative care. In a world where disorientation and senselessness are a common experience for many people, the commitment for the care of the dying seems to offer a possibility to do something meaningful and sensible. This, above all, applies to women whose children have left

---

[35] cp. concerns expressed by Klaus Dörner: Whereas outpatient and home care services often have to overcome financial burdens that have been put upon them, inpatient services enjoy better prospects when it comes to profit and competitive advantages although inpatient units often cause extra costs for the public. Klaus Dörner: Die Gesundheitsfalle. München 2003, p. 48.

home, and pensioners, who are looking for new challenges. There are only a few reliable figures on the social background of volunteers. According to a rule of thumb, 80 - 90% of the volunteers are women in the later stages of their lives. A significant number of medical students and other young people, considering a career in health care, often work as volunteers to gain some valuable hands-on experience in the field of palliative care. [36]

Almost everywhere across Europe volunteers receive education and training before they start working in a hospice setting. As necessary as the preparation of volunteers seems, the professionalisation of volunteers does imply problematic features, as it alters the situation of the once independent informal carers. On one hand they are turned into semi-professionals, on the other hand the threat is imminent that they might drop to the bottom of the hierarchy within the team.

It is important to note that traditional care for the ill was organised in neighbourhoods and local self-administration. A few volunteers feel their part is marginalized and devaluated by medical dominated quality control. The short-term affront of volunteers could cost dearly, as it would require extraordinary efforts to win them back as a "social resource" but it looks likely that in future times a lot of social tasks cannot be carried out without the extensive help of volunteers.

4.8 Integrated palliative care pathways

Do **patients** have the **choice** between inpatient hospice, a hospital palliative care unit, a nursing home or home care to receive palliative care? These options seem to be highly relevant when it comes to the patients autonomy, but at the same time they are not available to most patients in Europe. With very few exceptions (for example, England and the Netherlands), the provision of specialist palliative care is not guaranteed on nation-wide scales. The integration into primary care structures is still fragmentary in most parts of Europe (see table 6). Therefore the implementation of palliative care pathways into existing health care structures seems to be desirable.

Dr Katalin Hegedus, President of the *Hungarian Hospice-Palliative Association* and member of the Board of Directors of the *European Association of Palliative Care*, calls for the need of **"complex services"** that offer inpatient, outpatient and home care service at the same time. [37] **"Complex services"** are patient-oriented services whose structures allow a "smooth transition" between the different internal settings for both patients and the palliative care team members. **Day care** can play an important part as it gives patients the first opportunity to become familiar with the caring team and vice versa. This eases the chances to overcome inhibitions often experienced by patients when external help is needed. Professional care by a **home care team** or the admission

[36] cp.: Barbara Whitewood: The role of the volunteer in British palliative care. In: *European Journal of Palliative Care*. 1999. Volume 6. Issue 2, p. 45. Elise Harvey: Why hospice volunteering? In: *Volunteering*. Number 32. November 1997, p. 11.

[37] Katalin Hegedus: VI. Hungarian Hospice-Palliative Congress. Hospice in Hungary 2004. Miskolc 23.04.2004.

to an **inpatient unit** at a later stage of the disease will not be as shocking and stressful for patients if they already know the surroundings and staff members. This also applies to the multi-professional team as it is still imperative that the longer a team cares for a patient, the more likely the realisation of holistic care becomes.[38]

Adequate care of the dying, on a large scale, can only be achieved when professionals in **primary care** receive basic education and training in palliative care. As John Ellershaw points out, "[...] one of the outstanding questions of our time has to be: Why has the model of best practice not been transferred from the hospice to hospital settings, and indeed to community and nursing home settings?"[39] The following statement by the British Department of Health exemplifies the importance of the care for the dying that has been expressed by other European governments in similar ways:

> Providing the best possible care of cancer patients remains of paramount importance. Too many patients still experience distressing symptoms, poor nursing care, poor psychological and social support, and inadequate communication from health care professionals during the final stages of an illness [...] The care for all dying patients must improve to the level of the best.[40]

Palliative care services can play an important role in this. Already hospices and palliative care units function as training and education centres, and as **"Centres of Excellence"**[41], that are willing to share and pass on their knowledge and skills to others. This is already practised in countries with broad service structures in place, as well as in countries where the development is in its early stages. In the latter countries it is quite common that palliative care team members give voluntary lectures for other health professionals or people interested in the topic (for example Denmark, Slovakia).

Most experts demand and actively support the **integration of palliative care into existing health care structures**. This is consistent with the approach followed by the founder of the modern hospice movement, Dame Cicely Saunders. According to international experts palliative care education at both undergraduate and postgraduate level for health professionals is essential to achieve a better care for the dying. **Integrative care pathways,** for example*The Liverpool Integrated Care Pathway for the Terminal/Dying Phase* (see country report England), are presented in this book. As the models are very complex, they can only be presented briefly. We hope to promote the international discourse and exchange of experiences, as sources for further reading are given to allow the reader to gain a more detailed view on the concepts presented here.

---

38 cp.: Johann Baumgartner et al.: Pilotprojekt "Stationäre Palliativbetreuung" in der Steiermark. Die wissenschaftliche Begleituntersuchung. Graz 1999, p. 160.

39 John Ellershaw/Susie Wilkinson: Care of the dying. A pathway to excellence. Oxford and New York 2003, p. xii.

40 Department of Health: The NHS cancer plan – A plan for investment, a plan for reform. London 2000. In: John Ellershaw/Susie Wilkinson: Care of the dying. A pathway to excellence. Oxford and New York 2003, p. xii. Cp. for example: Regierungserklärung Österreich 2003 - 2006 (The Austrian Government Declaration 2003 - 2006), p. 25. On the Internet: http://www.parlinkom.gv.at/v-klub/regerkl.pdf

41 The five *Centres of Excellence for Palliative Care* in Norway and the three evolving *Centers of Excellence in Palliative Care* in Netherlands are examples.

The provision of palliative care in **nursing homes** is still in its early stages in most European countries. The Netherlands lead the way in this field, after all 13 percent of the inpatient palliative care units are situated in nursing homes.[42] At this point, we would also like to refer to the country report on Norway where a role model of palliative care in a nursing home setting is introduced.

Regional or national information services could be vital to promote palliative care. So far only three countries (England, France and the Netherlands) dispose of services or centres that offer information to health professionals, volunteers, patients, relatives and interested people. The most famous information service is located at *St Christopher's Hospice* in London. Founded in 1977, *Hospice information* provides valuable information on hospice and palliative care services worldwide. Similar models exist with *Agora* in the Netherlands and the *Association François-Xavier Bagnoud* in France. Since 2003, the *International Observatory on End of Life Care* in Lancaster, England, provides research-based information about hospice and palliative care provision in the international context.

4.9 Palliative Care for everyone?

According to the *WHO*,cancer accounts for almost one fifth of the deaths in Europe.[43] Approximately 90 percent of the patients that receive palliative care are suffering from cancer. In the light of this plausible attention on cancer patients, the question arises whether this happens at the expense of other patient groups. Patients in palliative care institutions are rarely older than 70 years even though 90 percent of the dying are actually aged 70 or older. Do moribund patients with long-term illnesses (for example dementia or Alzheimer) disappear into the system of palliative care? Dame Cicely Saunders rightly points out that "people with a diagnosis other than cancer have similar distress, often for longer periods.[44] Therefore one of the main priorities for the future is to facilitate admission to palliative care and to intensify research for non-cancer patients, as "there is increasing evidence that patients with non-malignant conditions have palliative care needs at the end of life, but that few of these patients access specialist palliative care services, including those with multiple sclerosis (MS) and other neurological conditions."[45]Already there are studies that focus on other pa-

42 Elizabeth Davies/ Irene Higginson (Eds.): Better Palliative Care for Older People. Copenhagen 2004, 24. On the Internet: http://www.euro.who.int/document/E82933.pdf

43 http://www.euro.who.int/document/ehr/e76907gh.pdf

44 Dame Cicely Saunders: The evolution of palliative care. Reprinted from: The Pharos of Alpha Omega Alpha Honor Medical Society. Volume 66. Number 3. Summer 2003, p. 6.

45 http://www.kcl.ac.uk/depsta/palliative/research/neuro.html

tient groups, for example dementia[46] or multiple-sclerosis[47] patients, in the context of palliative care.[48]

5. Country rating

Table 6 represents a rating of current palliative care provision in the sixteen countries considering both quality and quantity of the services. The rating is based on the quantitative data available and on the 150 qualitatively drafted interviews with experts.[49]

We would like to stress that the rating is not a ranking of the countries which is why the countries are listed alphabetically. The table is intended to identify the strengths and weaknesses of palliative care in the respective countries. What are the areas that are largely well-developed? What are others that need more attention in the future? Where else can countries look to improve? The rating aims to enable the reader to identify leading countries or others in a similar position. One example could be the excellent integration of palliative care into primary care structures in the Netherlands. Experts from countries, who struggle in this area, could be inspired by models established in the Netherlands. This does not intend a process of standardisation as health care structures are diverse in each country but may deliver ideas that could be useful for other countries as well.

For the better understanding a brief explanation of the five categories:

Inpatient provision:

This category is largely based on the earlier table on inpatient hospice and palliative care beds in Europe (table 3). Whereas for some countries table 3 includes inpatient beds in nursing homes (i.e. Norway), the rating for inpatient provisions focuses on inpatient palliative care beds in voluntary hospices and hospital units. Taking into account the different situation in the countries, the rating considers the following qualitative and quantitative aspects: How many inpatient beds are available? How far is the inpatient provision balanced within the countries? Are well-educated and trained staff available in adequate numbers? Are multi-professional teams in place? Does the ratio of caring staff to patients and relatives give consideration to a patient-oriented care?

---

46 In this context the Dementia Services Development Centre at the University of Stirling in Scotland is worth mentioning. The centre is carrying out studies on palliative care concerning dementia patients. Interview with Andrew Langford, 17 March 2004, in London. Information can be accessed on the Internet: http://www.dsdc.stir.ac.uk

47 Currently a research project at the famous King's College in London is under way that focuses on the palliative care needs of patients with MS. Personal communication with MS Palliative Care Co-ordinator Carolin Seitz, 18.October 2004. On the internet: http://www.kcl.ac.uk/depsta/palliative/research/ms.html

48 In Italy Dr. Michele Gallucci set up an organisation called CARDEA Onlus, that aims to promote hospice and palliative care for *all* potential patient groups at the end of life.

49 Other important categories such as the funding of services or the role of volunteers have not been included in this rating but remain fundamental for the success of palliative care.

Outpatient and home care provision:

Day care, hospital mobile teams and consultation teams are considered in this category. The same questions for rating of inpatient provision structures are applied here: Quantity and quality of services, access, cooperation with other services etc.

Integration in primary health care structures:

Primary care structures considered here are: nursing and care homes, general practitioners, community and home care. How far is palliative care integrated in primary health care services? For example, is palliative care provided in nursing or care homes? Are regular care givers educated in palliative care? Do networks between specialist palliative care services and primary services operate? Are education and training opportunities offered to GP's and community nurses?

Training and education opportunities:

Public or private training and education opportunities in the respective countries do fall in this category. Is palliative medicine part of the medical curricula at university? How far is palliative care taught in education for nurses? Can doctors, nurses or other professions specialise in palliative care? Are there training and education opportunities outside university courses? Are interdisciplinary courses in palliative care provided?

Palliative care specialists:

Are well-educated and trained staff available in sufficient numbers? Do differences in numbers and education exist between the diverse professions involved? Is advanced training and further education on offer for carers in palliative care? Are predominantly multi-professional teams operating?

The rating system includes the following grades:

*****	nation-wide highly developed both quantitatively and qualitatively
****	pre-dominantly well developed on a nation-wide scale
***	a wide provision with palliative care with obvious (profound) regional variations
**	regional structures with highly evident differences in quality und quantity
*	development in its early stages, no overall provision structure, single initiatives and services
–	no services etc. on offer or known.

Country	Inpatient provision	Outpatient and home care provision	Integration in primary health care structures	Training and education opportunities	Palliative care specialists
Denmark	**	**	*	**	**
Germany	****	****	***	****	***
England	*****	****	****	*****	****
Estonia	*	**	-	-	*
France	***	***	***	****	***
Italy	****	***	****	***	***
Latvia	**	-	-	*	*
Lithuania	*	**	-	-	*
Netherlands	****	****	*****	*****	****
Norway	***	****	****	****	*****
Austria	****	****	***	****	***
Poland	****	****	**	****	**
Slovakia	**	**	-	**	*
Czech Rep.	***	**	-	***	**
Ukraine	**	*	-	**	*
Hungary	***	***	***	***	**

Table 6: Palliative Care country rating

6. Problems and threats within palliative care

Initially the hospice movement has, above all, presented itself as an example of humanitarian end-of-life care, and continuously distances itself from Euthanasia, just as it has been embedded in Euthanasia legislation in the Netherlands and in Belgium. The question arises whether the distinction between humanitarian end-of-life care and Euthanasia will remain intact. It is suspected that in practice the border between the two is already becoming unclear – for example in the confusing term passive Euthanasia or the possibility of a medically assisted suicide.

The European society – one could say – is about to find a new solution for the "problematic" act of dying: With Palliative care the wealth of regionally distinctive traditional ways and methods of dealing with the dying and death could disintegrate.[50] Palliative care responds to the perplexity surrounding eroding family ties, increasingly

[50] cp. most notably Philippe Ariès: Studien zur Geschichte des Todes im Abendland. München 1981; Louis-Vincent Thomas: Anthropologie de la mort. Paris 1975.

high-number of the elderly and – a particularly modern symptom – people's fear of pain. In contrast to former times, the latter one seems to have taken the place of the tribunal of god. It may be true that there is no other answer to the "problem of dying" in Europe than to spread palliative care. At the same time palliative care will have to deal with the looming threat of Europe-wide levelling of the industry. The current heightened Europe-wide discussion about "spirituality" in palliative care underlines this.[51] Without much doubt, the best medical and nursing care at the end of life remains somewhat inefficient if spiritual care is neglected. Then again, "good" spiritual care in a more and more secularised world is hard to achieve. Is it possible to manage the spiritual pain like physical aches? Will "spirituality" turn into a additive that will be dosed carefully when needed? Is it imaginable to instrumentalise spirituality detached from local and cultural relations in Europe? Will spirituality in the end be measured in Europe-wide quality standards?

The number of humanitarian questions that accumulate with the rising number of elderly people and the care of the dying also poses questions of economical issues. As funeral parlours make money with the death of people, "dying" is also set to become an interesting economic area. In the context of GATS (General Agreement on Trade in Services) the provision of health care services are considered goods that can be traded. Therefore, it is hard to rule out a palliative care-dumping. As a consequence, palliative care services could be forced to compete in a free market. Who offers the cheapest and best care for the dying?[52] Is it imaginable that costly dying will be outsourced? The once civil hospice movement could then degenerate to a company providing service for a set of clients culminating in luxury hospices for the rich and low-standard services for the poor.

7. Europe at the crossroads: between palliative care and Euthanasia

Euthanasia is on the agenda. On June 27 2004, the European Commission controversially discussed a conflicting report on a European law on Euthanasia presented by the Swiss liberal politician Dick Marty. The proposal was passed on to the Social Committee who is asked to submit a report that includes a different opinion within one year. Marty claims that although Euthanasia is prohibited in 45 member states of the European Commission, in practice it is a widespread phenomenon.[53] In 2001, 2054 reported cases of Euthanasia were counted in the Netherlands while estimations even assume a number of 3800. In case of legalisation, the *German Hospice Foundation* (*Deutsche Hospiz-Stiftung*)estimates 24,000 Euthanasia-casualties mainly due to economical reasons. Stein Husebø pointed out that if the Dutch legislation regard-

[51] Herbert Geschwind: Apects de la spiritulité en Médicine Palliative. Son rôle dans la pratique des soignants. Paris, 06 February 2004.

[52] Some hospice services offer "dying rituals" on their websites as part of their programme already.

[53] http://www.aerztezeitung.de29April2004.

ing Euthanasia were applied to the whole of Europe there would be around 250,000 cases of Euthanasia per year, of which 60,000 would be without the express consent of the patient. [54] At present Euthanasia is legalised in the Netherlands and Belgium,in Switzerland medically assisted suicide is possible. Visible tendencies point toward an extension of the laws currently in place:

- In the Netherlands new policy proposals regulating Euthanasia without the patients consent are currently discussed.
- In Belgium – initiated by Willem Distelmann, a medical ethicist at the *Free University of Brussels* – plans are discussed to extend the country's Euthanasia law to allow the procedure for children, starting at the age of 12, as well as dementia patients, who have completed a corresponding declaration of intention. [55]
- In Switzerland the Academy of Medical Sciences changed its guidelines for the care of dying patients. Physician-assisted suicide is now part of the medical treatment attendance.

On the other hand, there are critical voices within the European Commission that question the current development, Dr Peter Liese, the chairman of the Christian Democratic working group for bioethics in the European parliament, cautions against the establishment of Euthanasia. Instead he is calling for alternative treatment for people at the end of their lives in accordance with the Gatterer-report that proposed a fortification of the hospice movement and palliative medicine. [56]

8. Summary

Palliative care is, to a certain extent, disaster aid, Europeans no longer know how to deal with their dying. There is always the risk that technocratic solutions will find widespread acceptance in such situations. At the moment there is still a wealth of regionally distinctive traditional ways and methods of dealing with the dying and death. [57] Palliative care will have to deal with the question of how Europe-wide equalisation of the discipline, with the simultaneous elimination of all cultural differences, can be avoided. On one hand, it could mean that respect for cultural differences can be revived as a result of the debate; however, it could also mean that a process has now begun in which from the old religious ties a new therapeutical service is born,

---

54 It is true that the number of reported Euthanasia cases in the Netherlands goes down currently, nevertheless a study has found out that only a total of 54 percent of all Euthanasia cases had been reported. The Association of Physicians KMNG, who supports Euthanasia, admits that fewer and fewer doctors report cases of Euthanasia requested by terminally ill patients (Frankfurter Allgemeine Zeitung vom 09 July 2004).

55 cp. http://www.hz-online.de/index.php?mode (Pressehaus Heidenheim. 28 April 2004.)

56 http://www.kath.net from 29 April 2004. Council of Europe, Parliamentary Assembly: Protection of the human rights and dignity of the terminally ill and the dying. Doc. 8421. 21 May 1999.

57 This is best documented by Philippe Ariès: The Hour of our Death, New York 1981.

which considers itself to be a specialist or sub discipline within palliative care.[58] We should remember at this point that "dying" is something what "I" can do – along with running, thinking and talking.

Will palliative care be able to salvage the cultural and local peculiarities or – from a more pessimistic point of view – if it will turn out to be an "emergency solution" levelling the different cultural forms of dying. It remains to be seen whether Jacques Derridas words on the cultural diversities of dying describe the past or if they will also be appropriate for the future: Every culture has its own funeral ceremonies, its own representations of forms of death, its own ways of mourning and burial, its own evaluation of the price of existence and its own group or individual lives.[59]

Sources and literature

Ariès, Philippe: Studien zur Geschichte des Todes im Abendland. München 1981.

Ariès, Philippe: Die Geschichte des Todes. München 1999.

Baumgartner, Johann u.a.: Pilotprojekt "Stationäre Palliativbetreuung" in der Steiermark. Die wissenschaftliche Begleituntersuchung. Graz 1999.

Bioskop-AutorInnenkollektiv: "Sterbehilfe" Die neue Zivilkultur des Tötens? Frankfurt am Main 2002.

Clark, David Between hope and acceptance: the medicalisation of dying. In: British Medical Journal. Volume 324. 13. April 2002, p. 905 et seqq.

Clark, David/Wright, Michael: Transitions in End of Life Care: Hospice and Related developments in Eastern Europe and Central Asia. Buckingham 2003.

Commission of the European Communities. Communication from the Commission to the Council, the European Parliament, the Economic and Social Committee and the Committee of the Regions. The future of health care and care for the elderly: guaranteeing accessibility, quality and financial viability. 05 December 2001, p. 4. On the Internet: http://europa.eu.int/eur-lex/en/com/cnc/2001/com2001_0723en01.pdf

Council of Europe, Parliamentary Assembly: Protection of the human rights and dignity of the terminally ill and the dying. Doc. 8421. 21. May 1999.

Davies, Elizabeth /Higginson, Irene (Eds.): *Palliative Care – The Solid Facts. WHO* Regional Office for Europe. Copenhagen 2004.

Davies, Elizabeth /Higginson, Irene (Eds.): Better Palliative Care for Older People. Copenhagen 2004.

Derrida, Jacques: Aporien. Sterben – Auf die "Grenzen der Wahrheit" gefasst sein. München 1998.

Emanuel, E./Batin, B.: What are the Potential Cost Savings from Legalizing Physician-Assisted Suicide? In: New England Journal of Medicine. Volume 339. 1988, p. 167 - 172.

Dörner, Klaus: Der gute Arzt. Lehrbuch der ärztlichen Grundhaltung. Stuttgart 2001.

[58] c.p.: The still significant article by John McKnight: Professionelle Dienstleistung und entmündigende Hilfe, in: Ivan Illich et al.: Entmündigung durch Experten. Zur Kritik der Dienstleistungsberufe, Reinbek 1979, p. 37 - 56 (English: Ivan Illich, John McKnight et al.: Disabeling Professions, London 1977).

[59] Jacques Derrida: Aporien. Sterben – Auf die "Grenzen der Wahrheit" gefasst sein. München 1998, p. 48.

Dörner, Klaus: Die Gesundheitsfalle. München 2003.

Emnid-survey 2003: "Was denken die Deutschen über Palliative-Care?" ("What do Germans think of palliative care?"). On behalf of the Deutsche Hospiz Stiftung (German Hospice Foundation).

European Commission Community research: Promoting the Development and Integration of Palliative Care Mobile Support Teams in the Hospital. The fifth framework programme 1998 - 2002 "Quality of life and management of living resources".

European Economic and Social Committee. Plenary Assembly 20 and 21 March 2002. Hospice work – an example of voluntary activities in Europe. On the Internet: http://www.esc.eu.int/documents/summaries_plenaries/2002/synt_03_en.PDF

Francke, A.L. / Willems, D.L.: Palliatieve zorg vandaag en morgen. Feiten, opvattingen en scenario's. Maarssen: Elsevier gezondheidszorg, 2000. As cited by Ministry of Health, Welfare and Sport in the Netherlands: Palliative care for terminally ill patients in the Netherlands. Dutch Government Policy. The Hague 2003.

Fusco-Karmann, Claude/Tinini, Gianna: A review of the volunteer movement in EAPC countries. In: European Journal of Palliative Care. Vol. 8. No. 5/2001, p. 199 - 202.

Gronemeyer, Reimer: Kampf der Generationen. München 2004.

Hegedus, Katalin: VI. Hungarian Hospice-Palliative Congress. Hospice in Hungary 2004. Miskolc 23.04.2004.

Higginson, Irene: Palliative and Terminal Care. In: Stevens,A/Raftery,J (Eds.): *Palliative and Terminal Care Health Care Needs Assessment*. Oxford 1998, p. 1 - 45.

Husebø, Stein/Klaschik, Eberhard: Palliativmedizin. 3rd edition, Berlin et al. 2003.

Loewy, Erich H./Gronemeyer, Reimer (Ed.) in Zusammenarbeit mit Michaela Fink, Marcel Globisch und Felix Schumann: Die Hospizbewegung im internationalen Vergleich, Giessen 2000.

Loewy, Erich H./Gronemeyer, Reimer (Ed.) in Zusammenarbeit mit Michaela Fink, Marcel Globisch und Felix Schumann: Wohin mit den Sterbenden? Hospize in Europa – Ansätze zu einem Vergleich. Münster, Hamburg und London 2002.

Harvey, Elise: Why hospice volunteering? In: *Volunteering*. Number 32. November 1997.

Humbert, Vincent: Je vous demande le droit de mourir. Paris 2003.

Husebø, Bettina Sandgathe /Husebø, Stein: Die letzten Tage und Stunden. Oslo 2001.

Kampmann-Grünewald, Andreas: Solidarität oder "Sozialkitt"? Der Strukturwandel freiwilligen gesellschaft-lichen Engagements als Herausforderung christlicher Praxis. Mainz 2004.

Materstvedt, LJ/Kaasa, S: Euthanasia and physician assisted suicide in Scaninavia – with a conceptual suggestion regarding international research in relation to the phenomena. In: Palliative Medicine. Vol. 16. No.1/2002, p. 17 - 32.

McKnight, John: Professionelle Dienstleistung und entmündigende Hilfe. In: Illich, Ivan u.a.: Entmündigung durch Experten. Zur Kritik der Dienstleistungsberufe. Reinbek 1979, p. 37 - 56.

Nauck, Friedemann /Klaschik, Eberhard: The role of health policy in the development and organisation of palliative medicine. Nijmegen: Pallium Report 1998.

Parliamentary Assembly of the European Council. 10.09.2003. Doc. 9898. Report by Dick Marty, Switzerland. on the Internet:
http://assembly.coe.int/Mainf.asp?link=http://assembly.coe.int/documents/workingdocs/doc03/edoc9898.htm

Personal communication with MS Palliative Care Co-ordinator Carolin Seitz, 18 October 2004.

Saunders, Cicely/Kastenbaum, Robert (Eds.): Hospice Care on the International Scene. New York 1997.

Saunders, Cicely: The evolution of palliative care. Reprinted from: The Pharos of Alpha Omega Alpha Honor Medical Society. Volume 66. Number 3. Summer 2003.

ten Have, Henk (Eds.): Palliative Care in Europa: Concepts and Policies. Amsterdam 2001.

ten Have, Henk/Clark, David (Eds.): The Ethics of Palliative Care: European Perspectives. Buckingham 2002.

Thomas, Louis-Vincent: Anthropologie de la mort. Paris 1975.

van der Maas, P/Emanuel, L: Factual Findings. In: Regulating how we die. The ethical medical, and legal issues surrounding physician-assisted suicide. Edited by Emanuel, L. Cambridge MA, Harvard University Press. 1998. p. 151 - 174.

von der Heide, A/Deliens, L/Faisst, K/Nilstun, T/Norup, M/Paci, E/van der Wal, G/van der Maas,P.J.: End-of-life decision-making in six European countries: descriptive study. In: The Lancet. 17 June 2003.

Whitewood, Barbara: The role of the volunteer in British palliative care. In: *European Journal of Palliative Care*. 1999. Volume 6. Issue 2, p. 44 - 47.

Internet sources

Dementia Services Development Centre at the University of Stirling in Scotland: http://www.dsdc.stir.ac.uk

Katholischer Nachrichtendienst 29.04.2004.: http://www.kath.net

Official Homepage The European Court of Human Rights: The European Court of Human Rights (ECHR) has rejected a request for Euthanasia from Mrs Dianne Pretty http://www.euro-fam.org/scripts/spop/articleINT.php?&LG=EN&LJ=FR&XMLCODE=2003-03-27-2025

Population Division of the Department of Economic and Social Affairs of the United Nations Secretariat, World Population Prospects: The 2002 Revision Population Database: http://esa.un.org/unpp

Pressehaus Heidenheim. 28.04.2004. In: http://www.hz-online.de/index.php?mode

World Health Organization: http://www.who.int/cancer/palliative/definition/en/

Part Two – Country reports

The following country reports are all structured following the same pattern. With this, the schema must not be overseen that comparisons have been made between small countries, large countries, eastern and western countries to highlight the major differences. The state of statistics available vary enormously – the Italian Lombardy offers more palliative structure than all Baltic countries in total: this is why we are in danger of comparing apples with oranges. The structures are however comparable – also for the reason that palliative provisions in Europe are becoming more and more similar.

Austria

Marcel Globisch

1. General conditions

1.1 Demographics

- In 2000, the population of Austria numbered 8.1 million; 1.2 million higher than in 1950. According to predictions, the population will drop to 7.4 million by 2050.[1]
- Since the early to mid 1950s the average life expectancy of 65.7 years has risen about 13 years to 78.5 years of age. By 2050 another rise is expected to bring the average life expectancy at birth to 83.6.[2]
- In 1950, people 65 years or older in Austria constituted 10.1% of the population. In 2000, it was already 15.5% and is projected to grow to a remarkable 30.6% by 2050.[3]
- Similarly, people aged 80 years or older constituted 1.2% of the population in 1950. This grew to 3.5% in 2000 and is estimated to massively increase to 12.8% by 2050.[4]
- The older-person support ratio, the number of persons aged 15 to 64 years per older person over the age of 65, was 66.8% of the total population in 1950. In 2000, the support ratio had increased to 67.8%, but is expected to drop to 55.8% by 2050.[5]
- The results of a recent survey indicated "approximately 80% of all people in Austria wish to die at home or in familiar surroundings. Only 5% wish to spend their last hours in a nursing home, 6% in a hospital and another 7% say they do not care about their place of death.[6]

---

1 Population Division of the Department of Economic and Social Affairs of the United Nations Secretariat, *World Population Prospects: The 2002 Revision* and *World Urbanization Prospects: The 2001 Revision*. Official Homepage of the United Nations: http://esa.un.org/unpp

2 ibid.

3 ibid.

4 ibid.

5 ibid.

6 Paul M. Zulehner: Jedem seinen eigenen Tod. Für die Freiheit des Sterbens. Ostfildern 2001. In: Hospiz – und Palliativführer Österreich 2002. Vienna 2002, p. 6.

- In relation to the European Union's average mortality rate, Austria registered a faster decline in mortality (18%) between 1970 and 1995, with the reduction in cancer-induced mortality being the greatest. Whereas the number of deaths from cancer dropped by 17%, or from 228 to 189 per 100 000 population within 25 years, the decline in the EU average was much lower than this. [7]
- Another survey proves that in reality the numbers are almost reversed with around 70% of all Austrians dying in institutions in 2001. 55.3% die in hospitals and 11.6% in nursing homes. In fact, only 27% spent their last hours in familiar surroundings. [8]

1.2 Health care system

In 2001, total health care expenditure in Austria was 8% of GDP. [9] Austria's social insurance funds cover almost all labour force participants and retirees, with the exception of a few smaller groups within the population. Austrians cannot choose their social health insurance fund as they are assigned to social insurers according to their occupation or profession. Unemployment benefit applicants are automatically insured and fully entitled to all cash benefits and benefits in kind. Since health insurance coverage extends to the family members of compulsorily or voluntarily insured persons, 99 percent of the population have health insurance cover, and only 1% are without health insurance. [10]

In Austria patients are free to select between public and private hospitals. The daily rate in hospitals is 7.63 € [11], since 2002 the same applies for palliative care units in hospitals (Palliativstationen) which are regarded as acute units in hospitals (cp. 2.3. Legal regulations and funding).

2. Hospice and palliative care in Austria

2.1 History [12]

Until the end of the 1980's, individuals from different professional backgrounds were the only people who dedicated their time to spread the idea of hospices. [13] Similar to developments in many other European countries, nurses were particularly interested in caring for terminally ill and dying patients. [14] Physicians were a bit more reserved

---

7 European Observatory on Health Systems and Policies: http://www.euro.who.int/document/e72787.pdf

8 Statistic Austria. In: Hospiz – und Palliativführer Österreich 2002. Vienna 2002, p. 17.

9 World Health Organization: http://www.who.int/countries/aut/en/

10 European Observatory on Health Systems and Policies: http://www.euro.who.int/document/e72787.pdf

11 Bundesministerium für Gesundheit und Soziale Sicherung: Sozial-Kompass Europa. Soziale Sicherheit in Europa im Vergleich. Bonn 2003.

12 An extensive and excellent documentation of the history of the Austrian hospice movement can be found in: Anne Elisabeth Höfler: Die Geschichte der Hospizbewegung in Österreich. IFF-Palliative Care und organisationales Lernen. Kursbuch Palliative Care 2/2001. Vienna 2001.

13 ibid., p. 14.

14 ibid, p. 22.

in general, but death and dying were part of discussions among doctors – this can be illustrated in a conference on the topic held by the *Steirischen Ärztekammer* (Styria Medical Association) in 1979. [15] People of the early hospice days were inspired by foreign models like *St Christopher's Hospice* [16]in England, the first palliative unit in Germany set up at the University Clinic in Cologne, and lectures held by individuals such as Elisabeth Kübler-Ross. [17]

Initial efforts to build an inpatient hospice failed due to financial reasons, as the hospice concept was still relatively unknown – death and dying was taboo, as a quote by the director of the *Charity of the Archdiocese Vienna*, prelate Ungar, proves: "The *Wiener* do not want to know anything about dying." [18]

At the end of the 1980's the foundations for the first network of individuals, groups and initiatives were laid. In 1987 the Austrian section of the *IGSL (International Society for the care of the dying)* was founded. 35 people from different fields attended the constitutive session. Different working groups were set up with the aim to promote the hospice idea. The groups were focusing on the different areas: generation of new members/public relation; education and advanced training; research; voluntary hospices; palliative units in hospitals; pastoral care in hospitals; geriatric care; social and health policy; volunteers. [19] It is striking that from the beginning hospice advocates intended to re-integrate their idea of care of the dying into existing health care structures. [20] This approach has been followed until today by the Austrian hospice and palliative care experts. [21]

In the autumn of 1987 the *Charity of the Archdiocese Vienna* set out first plans for a home care hospice team. [22] However it took two years until the home care team started its work. Two physicians with special training in palliative medicine started as volunteers and later on were paid part-time. With the help of four diploma nurses, a coordinator and another assistant seriously ill patients were cared for in their homes. [23]

Two of the main problems in the beginning were the lack of patients, a problem that could be solved with rising recognition. The other, reliable funding, proved to be more difficult. To overcome the early financing worries, different potential sponsors

---

15 ibid, p. 14 et seq.

16 Similar to Germany, the documentary film by the Jesuit Reinhold Iblacker ("Noch 16 Tage") on *St Christopher's Hospice* had a major impact on the Austrian hospice movement.

17 Anne Elisabeth Höfler: Die Geschichte der Hospizbewegung in Österreich. IFF-Palliative Care und organisationales Lernen. Kursbuch Palliative Care 2/2001. Vienna 2001, p. 15 et seq.

18 ibid, p. 17.

19 ibid, p. 20.

20 ibid, p. 24.

21 Hospiz Österreich: Die letzten Schritte des Weges. Ansichten. Einsichten. Aussichten. Hospiz- und Palliativbetreuung in Österreich. Ein Arbeitspapier von Hospiz Österreich vorgestellt beim Hospizdialog am 13. Febr. 2004 im bm:gf. Zur Information von Politikern und Medienfachleuten. Wien Februar 2004.

22 Interview with Dr. Franz Zdrahal, 27 February 2004, in Vienna. cp. also: Anne Elisabeth Höfler: Die Geschichte der Hospizbewegung in Österreich. IFF-Palliative Care und organisationales Lernen. Kursbuch Palliative Care 2/2001. Vienna 2001, p. 24.

23 ibid.

were contacted to put the hospice idea on a more solid foundation. At the time, only the *Charity of the Archdiocese Vienna* assured the required financial support.[24]

Albeit the commitment shown by individual churches was eyed critically by the official Austrian church[25], the early hospice days were dominated by church initiatives (Charity, deaconry, religious orders).[26] In 1998, Pope Johannes Paul II visited the *CS-Hospice Rennweg* in Vienna. The Pope's visit not only attracted media coverage but was also regarded as a mark of recognition of the hospice care by the Catholic Church.[27]

The killing of seriously ill elderly people committed by care staff at the hospital in Lainz in 1988 caused a widely discussion about the conditions in hospitals for both carers and patients. A commission, called up by the Minister of Health of the time, Harald Ettl, recommended the implementation of hospice services as one measure to be taken.[28]

If not before the end of the Nineties the need for care inpatient of terminally ill patients was highly visible. As early as 1985 Dr. Franz Zdrahal was provided with ten beds for pain therapy treatment, mainly for cancer patients.[29] In September 1992 the congregation opened *St. Raphael hospice unit* as part of the *Department of Anaesthesia.* A year later it was incorporated as a subsection of the ward for Internal Medicine.[30]

As part of a model project in 1995, a inpatient hospice unit with a capacity of 20 beds was set up at the *Geriatriezentrum Wienerwald (GZW).* The hospice unit was the first of such kind within Vienna's *Krankenanstaltenverbandes.*[31] In autumn of the same year *Caritas Socialis* opened the inpatient hospice *CS-Hospiz Rennweg.* From the start, the 12-bedded hospice was part of a nursing and social centre. The building costs were covered by the municipality of Vienna.[32]

On the Initiative of the *Mobile Charity Hospice*, the first day care hospice was established within the nursing home St. Barbara, run by the *Charity of the Archdiocese Vienna*, in October 2000.[33]

Thanks to the ongoing efforts by head physician Dr. Marina Kojer, the first Austrian *Medical department for Geriatric Palliative Medicine* started its work at the *GZW* in December 2000.[34]

---

24 Anne Elisabeth Höfler: Die Geschichte der Hospizbewegung in Österreich. IFF-Palliative Care und organisationales Lernen. Kursbuch Palliative Care 2/2001. Vienna 2001, p. 25.

25 ibid, p. 26.

26 ibid, p. 25.

27 ibid, p. 26.

28 Prim. Dr. Erich Aigner. In: Anne Elisabeth Höfler: Die Geschichte der Hospizbewegung in Österreich. IFF-Palliative Care und organisationales Lernen. Kursbuch Palliative Care 2/2001. Vienna 2001, p. 27.

29 Interview with Dr. Franz Zdrahal, 27 February 2004, in Vienna.

30 Anne Elisabeth Höfler: Die Geschichte der Hospizbewegung in Österreich. IFF-Palliative Care und organisationales Lernen. Kursbuch Palliative Care 2/2001. Vienna 2001, p. 27.

31 ibid, p. 28.

32 ibid, p. 28 et seq.

33 ibid, p. 29.

34 ibid.

2.2 Hospice and palliative care services

In October 2002 there were 20 inpatient independent hospices or palliative care hospital units with a capacity of 151 beds (107 beds in the acute sector and 44 for long term care). In addition three day care hospices and 86 outpatient and home care services were operating. [35] Unfortunately there are no more recent nationwide statistics available. It is likely that the number of services has further grown within the past couple of years. It is estimated that the total number of inpatient palliative care beds in Austria is about 190 today.

The national hospice umbrella organisation *Hospice Austria* has set sufficient outpatient and home care as primary aims:

> In knowledge that most people wish to die at home, from the beginning the top priority of the hospice pioneers was to favour home care and outpatient services over inpatient units. Today several *Bundesländer* in Austria provide palliative care for patients and their relatives in their homes all over the country. [36]

Dr. Johann Baumgartner emphasises that one of the main targets is not to set up "professional dying centre" but to integrate palliative care into primary care structures. To achieve this, regulated education and training schemes in palliative care for the different professions involved, are of paramount importance. [37] *Hospice Austria* released a graded-concept of palliative care provision (Chart 1), which should guarantee good palliative care across the different care institutions and services already in place "as in future those services will continue to bear the major burden of care." [38]

The model includes the following components:

The main task of the *Hospizteam* (hospice team) is to support and relieve the family of the terminally ill person to enable patients to remain in their familiar surroundings as long as possible. The hospice team consists of qualified volunteers which works closely together with home care services. Volunteers work at the patients homes, in nursing homes and in hospitals. [39]

The interdisciplinary *Mobile Palliativteam* (mobile palliative team) advices and supports patients, relatives, doctors and nurses. In some cases the team also gives hands-on care. In addition the *Mobile Palliativteam* helps to coordinate the transitions between home and hospital care. [40]

The *Palliativkonsiliardienst* (advisory service) is situated in hospitals and mainly gives advice to doctors and nurses. The service is not so much aimed at the patients

---

35 Hospiz – und Palliativführer Österreich 2002. Vienna 2002, p. 52 - 55.

36 Hospiz – und Palliativführer Österreich 2002. Vienna 2002, p. 4.

37 Interview with Dr. Johann Baumgartner, 26 August 2003. in Graz.

38 Hospiz Österreich: Die letzten Schritte des Weges. Ansichten. Einsichten. Aussichten. Hospiz- und Palliativbetreuung in Österreich. Ein Arbeitspapier von Hospiz Österreich vorgestellt beim Hospizdialog am 13. Febr. 2004 im bm:gf. Zur Information von Politikern und Medienfachleuten. Vienna Februar 2004, p. 9.

39 ibid. p. 13.

40 ibid. p. 16.

<table>
<tr><th rowspan="2"></th><th rowspan="2">Traditionelle Dienstleister des Gesundheitswesen</th><th colspan="3">Hospiz- und Palliativbetreuung</th></tr>
<tr><th colspan="2">unterstützende Angebote</th><th>betreuende Angebote</th></tr>
<tr><td>im Akutbereich</td><td>Abteilungen, Stationen und Ambulanzen des Krankenhauses</td><td rowspan="3">Hospizteams</td><td>Palliativ-konsiliar-dienste</td><td>Palliativ-stationen</td></tr>
<tr><td>im Langzeitbereich</td><td>Senioren- und Pflegeheime</td><td rowspan="2">Mobile Palliativteams</td><td>Stationäre Hospize</td></tr>
<tr><td>zu Hause</td><td>Ärzte für Allgemeinmedizin, niedergelassene Fachärzte, Hauskrankenpflege, Heimhilfe, Sozialarbeit, Physiotherapie, ...</td><td>Tageshospize</td></tr>
</table>

Chart 1: Components of hospice and palliative care.
Courtesy of Hospiz Österreich. In: Hospiz Österreich: Die letzten Schritte des Weges. Ansichten. Einsichten. Aussichten. Hospiz- und Palliativbetreuung in Österreich. Ein Arbeitspapier von Hospiz Österreich vorgestellt beim Hospizdialog am 13. Febr. 2004 im bm:gf. Zur Information von Politikern und Medienfachleuten. Wien Februar 2004, p. 9.

and their relatives. The *Palliativkonsiliardienst* only advices the doctors and nurses in charge. The decisions are made by the latter. [41]

The *Tageshospiz* (day hospice) is catered to support the patient and his relatives to allow the patient to remain in their familiar surroundings as long as possible. The medical support is normally provided by doctors from the institution in which the day care unit is located in. In some cases qualified general practitioners or one of the *Mobile Palliativteams* give medical support. [42]

The *Stationäre Hospiz* (inpatient hospice) is a separate building or inpatient unit, that – depending on the organisation – is either independent, or situated in a nursing home or in a hospital. Seriously ill and dying patients with incurable diseases and limited life expectancy are admitted to the hospice. Those patients staying at the hospice neither need to be treated in hospital nor can be cared for at home anymore. Pain therapy, symptom control, palliative care, including psycho-social and spiritual care, are part of the offerings. The participation of qualified doctors is required. [43]

A *Palliativstation* (palliative ward or palliative care hospital unit) is a independent unit in a acute hospital. The patients suffer from a incurable and advanced illness. A

41 ibid. p. 19.
42 ibid. p. 21.
43 ibid. p. 23.

complex symptomatic, and intensive medical attendance require the patients stay in hospital. The aims of the interdisciplinary teams are to control the patients symptoms in order to admit the patient home or to another service. The *Palliativstationen* are required to work in line with the agreements laid down in the *Austrian hospitals plans (Österreichische Krankenanstaltenplan).*[44]

The Ministry of Health (*Bundesministerium für Gesundheit*) commissioned the Austrian Federal Institute for Health Care (*Österreichisches Bundesinstitut für Gesundheitswesen*) to develop definitions, quality criteria, requirement figures and guidelines for the implementation of the graded-concept. The preliminary draft of agreement § 15a says:

> In particular it is agreed to plan a nation-wide and equivalent provision of palliative and hospice care in line with the developed graded-concept. In terms of the requirement figures, the realisation of spanning hospice and palliative care provision on all levels of health care, that is in the acute and long term sector as well as in outpatient and home care, is to be ensured.[45]

2.3 Legal regulations and funding

The Austrian system differentiates between cases of nursing and treatment. The insurance company pays for hospital stays in cases of treatment. If the patient is classified as a nursing case, the occurring costs must be covered by the patient himself or with the financial support of relatives or social welfare. If a hospice operates on the basis of a nursing home, the patient must pay up to 80 percent of his income for his stay.[46]

There are neither contracts with sickness funds nor any standardised funding system in place for inpatient hospices, which leaves them rely on donations. In contrast, palliative care hospital units have been integrated in the *performance-oriented hospital financing system* established in 1997. Since 2002 the palliative care wards (*Palliativstationen*) are regarded as acute units in hospitals and with that, have been integrated into the health care system.[47] Unlike in hospices where patients have to pay up to 100 €per day, the hospital financing system is to the advantage of the patients who – for a limited period – only have to pay the daily hospital rate of 7.63 €.

Part of the new financing system is an implemented degression scheme. A maximum number of points are allocated for the first 14 days. Starting with the fifteenth day the daily rate – or the allocated points – decreases with every day until day 28 where only half the points are awarded for the treatment of a patient. From day 28 the number of points remains the same.

---

44 ibid, p. 26.

45 Vorentwurf § 15 a Vereinbarung, Seite 8: 2. ABSCHNITT, Artikel 3 (2).

46 Anne Elisabeth Höfler: Die Geschichte der Hospizbewegung in Österreich. IFF-Palliative Care und organisationales Lernen. Kursbuch Palliative Care 2/2001. Vienna 2001, p. 28; cp. also: Thomas Frühwald: Öbig-Konzept für eine stationäre palliativmedizinische Versorgung im österreichischen Krankenhaussystem. In: Wohin mit den Sterbenden? Hospize in Europa – Ansätze zu einem internationalen Vergleich. Edited by Reimer Gronemeyer/Erich H. Loewy: Münster 2002, p. 48; Interview with Dr. Johann Baumgartner, 26 August 2003, in Graz.

47 Email-Correspondence with Dr. Harald Retschitzegger, 23 September 2004.

The new has led to positive and negative consequences at the same time: Palliative care hospital units are endeavour to release patients as soon as their situation has been stabilised or improved.

For palliative care this funding system is not cost-covering as with this system financial reward is very much bound to the use of technical equipment. The fact that palliative care requires most of all a high number of staff to ensure the intensive communicative care, is not considered in the financing system in place. [48]

Moreover patients may have to be released to fulfil the financing system which can be difficult at times either because of lacking adequate palliative care provision structures, or due to financial problems of a patient who cannot afford to stay in a hospice or nursing home.

In this context is has to be noted that people in charge of hospital palliative care units try to allow people to stay longer in order to avoid cases of hardship "because in some cases we know that discharges are impossible." [49] At the same time the targeted limited lengths of stay can have positive consequences too as services, and health planers, are encouraged to explore new ways, for example to improve the provision of palliative care in the patients home. [50] In case of the hospital palliative care unit in Ried (*Palliativstation Ried*) this is exemplified in the fact that more than 40 percent of all patients are discharged home. [51]

As there is no funding system for voluntary hospices in place, only two independent hospices (in Graz and Salzburg) remain in Austria. Other "voluntary hospices" [52], as the one in Innsbruck, have been converted into hospital palliative care units (*Palliativstationen*). The average lengths of stay has gone down continuously in Innsbruck, before and after the transformation into a *Palliativstationen*. According to Dr. Elisabeth Medicus, the head doctor, there have been no changes since the transformation. [53] However a short length of stay remains problematic. The less time patients stay in a hospice, the more difficult successful palliative care becomes because a considerable amount of time is required to deliver palliative care, to control somatic symptoms and, most of all, to get to know the patient and his or her social environment. "Palliative care should begin as early as possible, for example before

---

48 Harald Retschitzegger: Von der Pionierphase in die tägliche Arbeit: Hospiz St. Vinzenz – Palliativstation am Krankenhaus der Barmherzigen Schwestern Ried im Innkreis. In: Katharina Heimerl/Andreas Heller: Eine große Vision in kleinen Schritten. Aus Modellen der Hospiz- und Palliativbetreuung lernen. Freiburg im Breisgau 2001, p. 145.

49 Email-Correspondence with Dr. Harald Retschitzegger, 23 September 2004.

50 ibid.

51 cp. Harald Retschitzegger: Von der Pionierphase in die tägliche Arbeit: Hospiz St. Vinzenz – Palliativstation am Krankenhaus der Barmherzigen Schwestern Ried im Innkreis. In: Katharina Heimerl/Andreas Heller: Eine große Vision in kleinen Schritten. Aus Modellen der Hospiz- und Palliativbetreuung lernen. Freiburg im Breisgau 2001, p. 145.

52 Although the hospice in Innsbruck has officially been transformed into a *Palliativstation* (hospital palliative care unit), it is still called a hospice.

53 Interview with Dr. Elisabeth Medicus, 28 August 2003, in Innsbruck.

a palliative surgery. Often one of the main deficits are late referrals into Palliativstationen."[54] A research study completed by a pilot project in Steyr "Inpatient palliative care" comes to similar conclusions.[55]

In July 2002, the *Familienhospizkarenz* (family rest period) was established in Austria. *Familienhospizkarenz* is a legal claim that allows employees a reduction, change or release of their usual working time in order to care for a dying relative. *Familienhospizkarenz* can be engaged by spouses, parents, children, grandchildren, adopted children, foster children, partner or siblings. Applications can be handed in as late as five days before the intended start if the rest period. The rest period lasts for three months and can be easily extended up to six months if required.[56] Dr. Baumgartner thinks the *Familienhospizkarenz* is a decent model as is not restricted to nursing duties. However Baumgartner critically marks that claims of *Familienhospizkarenz* remain problematic as people often cannot afford to cover the suspension of earnings.[57] Martin Böker, co-leader of the hospice in Salzburg, assumes that with the current conception, the rest period is normally only be used by women whose partner is employed and earning enough. Böker adds that he is not aware of anyone in Salzburg that has actually claimed Familienhospizkarenz up to now.[58]

In case of hardships applications for special support can be filed to the Federal Ministry for Social Security and Generations. There are 55 reports cases of which 39 have been accepted so that approximately 60 percent of the loss of income were covered.[59] In the second half of 2002 around 150 people made use of the family rest period.[60]

2.4 Organisations

Hospiz Österreich is the national umbrella organisation representing more than 100 home care, outpatient and inpatient services in Austria. *Hospiz Österreich* was founded in 1993 and is active on national and international level. Representatives from different professional backgrounds and the respective federal states are members of the organisation.[61] Network, quality assurance, support of new and existing services and education are the main fields of activities of *Hospiz Österreich*.[62]

54 Interview with Dr. Petra Dirschlmayer, 25 August 2003, in Ried.

55 Johann Baumgartner u.a.: Pilotprojekt "Stationäre Palliativbetreuung" in der Steiermark. Die wissenschaftliche Begleituntersuchung. Graz 1999, p. 160.

56 Information brochure *Familienhospizkarenz* by the Austrian Ministry for Family Affairs.

57 Interview with Dr. Johann Baumgartner, 26 August 2003, in Graz.

58 Interview with Martin Böker, 26 February 2004, in Salzburg.

59 Wolfgang Wiesmayr: Familienhospizkarenz: Erste Erfahrungen in: Hospiz Oberösterreich. Lebenswert – Informationen der Hospizvereine Oberösterreichs. Frühjahr-Sommer 2003. Linz 2003, p. 5.

60 ibid.

61 Hospiz – und Palliativführer Österreich 2002.Vienna 2002, p. 10. More information on *Hospiz Österreich* can be found at: http://www.hospiz.at

62 Anne Elisabeth Höfler: Die Geschichte der Hospizbewegung in Österreich. IFF-Palliative Care und organisationales Lernen. Kursbuch Palliative Care 2/2001. Vienna 2001, p. 29.

The ***Austrian Society for Palliative Care*** (***Österreichische Palliativgesellschaft***) was established in 1999. It is a independent and multi-professional organisation (e.g., physicians, nursing staff, psychologists, social worker and volunteers).[63]

2.5 Education and training of professional staff

The times when Austrian professionals had to go abroad to receive education and training in palliative care are long gone.[64] Today the national hospice umbrella organisation *Hospiz Österreich* plays a significant role providing education and training opportunities:

> In the ten years of its existence the umbrella organisation has accomplished impressive achievements. A standard curriculum for interdisciplinary education and training in palliative has been introduced with the umbrella organisation itself giving education to approx. people since 1998. The organisation also worked out quality criteria which serve as a solid foundation nationwide. By establishing a palliative care institution at the University Clinic in Graz a important university link has been set up.[65]

Sixty hours of palliative care are taught in the basic training of nurses. In addition there is the opportunity for nurses to participate in an 160-hour advanced training programme. Since the beginning of 2003 palliative medicine was implemented into the physicians' curriculum. However participation in the courses is voluntary.[66] There are plans for standardised curricula on a nationwide scale.

There are various interdisciplinary education and training opportunities on offer.[67] In 1998 the *Österreichische interdisziplinäre Palliativlehrgang* (Austrian interdisciplinary palliative course) was set up. Based on its model, regional courses are held in the different federal states (Vorarlberg, Salzburg, Upper Austria); a co-operation with *IFF* (Institute for Interdisciplinary Research and Education at the Universities of Klagenfurt, Vienna, Innsbruck and Graz). In 2000, the *Österreichische interdisziplinäre Palliativlehrgang* was accredited by the Austrian Ministry of Science as one of three modules of the university course palliative care. Successful participants graduate as *Masters of advanced studies in palliative care*. According to the Norwegian physician Stein Husebø, who is teaching palliative medicine in Bergen and Vienna, the inter-professional university course is unique worldwide.[68]

---

63 Information brochure *ÖPG*. More information on *ÖPG*: http://www.palliativ.at/

64 cp.: Anne Elisabeth Höfler: Die Geschichte der Hospizbewegung in Österreich. IFF-Palliative Care und organisationales Lernen. Kursbuch Palliative Care 2/2001. Vienna 2001, p. 22.

65 Press release by the Austrian Ministry of Health, 03 November 2003. In: http://www.bmgf.gv.at/cms/site/news_einzel.htm?channel=CH0089\&doc=CMS1067862515021

66 Interview with Dr. Johann Baumgartner, 26 August 2003, in Graz.

67 Detailed information on training and education opportunities in Austria can be accessed on the official websites of the two national umbrella organisations: http://www.palliativ and http://www.hospiz.net

68 Anne Elisabeth Höfler: Die Geschichte der Hospizbewegung in Österreich. IFF-Palliative Care und organisationales Lernen. Kursbuch Palliative Care 2/2001. Vienna 2001, p. 22.

2.6 Volunteers

With the transformation of voluntary hospices into hospital palliative care units (Palliativstationen) there an increasing trend towards professionalisation, which is highlighted in the standardised and obligatory education and training of volunteers established by *Hospiz Österreich* in 2002. In the first instance volunteers are interviewed by staff members in charge of the hospice or hospital palliative care unit before being permitted to take part in the *Befähigungskurs für Ehrenamtliche* (qualification course for volunteers) [69]:

> The course gives an introduction of at least 70 hours into hospice work. [70] [...] To obtain a certificate of competence, hospice volunteers should also receive sufficient practical experience [...] Practical experience of at least 40 hours is recommended. [71]

The course focuses on several topics that are divided into four categories (biographical, communicative, informative and spiritual). [72] The fee for the course is between €400 and €500. The absorption of costs in not regulated consistently. Whereas in Vorarlberg the expenses are covered by the federal state, [73] the volunteers in Ried pay the fee themselves. [74] As interviews with several experts show, there are divergent opinions on the extent of education and training courses for volunteers. All agree in the need to prepare volunteers for their work with terminally ill people and their relatives. However, there are different views on the complexity of such courses and the selection of volunteers in general. Dr. Johann Baumgartner is an advocate of a standardised education course for volunteers and thinks such courses are indispensable. [75] Karl Bitschnau bears in mind that courses for volunteers should not become too time-consuming. Bitschnau adds "that in palliative care learning by doing still is the best teaching method. The monthly meetings with volunteers are essential for the quality of care provided. The volunteers are encouraged to constantly reflect on their work. The participation in further training programmes is obligatory." [76] Dr. Medicus thinks that "that the volunteers must be familiar with the overall concept of hospice care. At the same time, in individual cases, a course should not become an obstacle for potential volunteers." [77] Dr. Medicus suggests that courses could be attuned to the actual work volunteers are supposed to do later: "If a volunteer intends to work in a office or in public relations, he or she might need a different education than someone directly

69 Hospiz – und Palliativführer Österreich 2002. Vienna 2002.

70 Dachverband Hospiz Österreich. Hospizbewegung/Palliative Care: Standards für die Befähigung ehrenamtlicher MitarbeiterInnen, p. 3. In: http://www.hospiz.at/pdf_dl/std_ea.pdf

71 ibid.

72 ibid, p. 5.

73 The volunteers have to work two years for *Hospice movement Vorarlberg* otherwise they have to pay back the money. Interview with MAS Karl Bitschnau, 29 August 2003, in Feldkirch.

74 Interview with Dr. Petra Dirschlmayer, 25 August 2003, in Ried.

75 Interview with Dr. Johann Baumgartner, 26 August 2003, in Graz.

76 Interview with MAS Karl Bitschnau, 29 August 2003, in Feldkirch.

77 Interview with Dr. Elisabeth Medicus, 28 August 2003, in Innsbruck.

involved with the patients."[78] Dr. Franz Zdrahal regards preparatory courses as sensible, but remains sceptical about a dogmatic compliance with regulations. He pleads for "possibilities to make exceptions when it comes to the selection of volunteers."[79]

2.7 Example

Palliative care unit at the Krankenhaus der Barmherzigen Schwestern Ried im Innkreis[80]

Organisation and funding[81]

The palliative ward is formally integrated in the department of anaesthesia and internal medicine at the hospital of the *Barmherzigen Schwestern Ried* (Merciful Sisters Ried) but operates independently. It is situated in a separate building next to the hospital.

80 percent of the building costs were covered by the Federal State Upper Austria, the remaining 20 percent paid by the *Barmherzigen Schwestern*. The running costs are covered through the *performance-oriented hospital financing system* (see 2.3.).

The professionals[82]

The interdisciplinary professional team includes three doctors, 13 diploma nurses, one physiotherapist, one clinical psychologist, one musical therapist and one spiritual adviser. If required, specialists from all other disciplines in the hospital can be called in.

Besides the care for ten beds in the palliative care unit, the doctors also give advice on symptom control, pain therapy or indication for patients treated in other hospital units. They are also available for telephone enquiries from resident doctors.

The volunteers

At the moment 19 women and one man are working as volunteers. The volunteers are trained and led by two diploma nurses. Before the volunteers start their work on the ward they have passed a education course in line with the standards set by the national hospice umbrella organisation *Hospiz Österreich*. Afterwards they are interviewed by

---

78 ibid.

79 Interview with Dr. Franz Zdrahal, 27 February 2004, in Vienna.

80 An extensive description of *Hospiz St. Vinzenz – Palliativstation* is available in Harald Retschitzegger: Von der Pionierphase in die tägliche Arbeit: Hospiz St. Vinzenz – Palliativstation am Krankenhaus der Barmherzigen Schwestern Ried im Innkreis. In: Katharina Heimerl/Andreas Heller: Eine große Vision in kleinen Schritten. Aus Modellen der Hospiz- und Palliativbetreuung lernen. Freiburg im Breisgau 2001, p. 143 - 153.

81 ibid.

82 Interview with Dr. Petra Dirschlmayer, 25 August 2003, in Ried; cp. also: Harald Retschitzegger: Von der Pionierphase in die tägliche Arbeit: Hospiz St. Vinzenz – Palliativstation am Krankenhaus der Barmherzigen Schwestern Ried im Innkreis. In: Katharina Heimerl/Andreas Heller: Eine große Vision in kleinen Schritten. Aus Modellen der Hospiz- und Palliativbetreuung lernen. Freiburg im Breisgau 2001, p. 146.

the coordinators. Not until then a decision is made whether the volunteer will become part of the team or not. The possible duties of volunteers include: walks with the patients, reading, doing handicrafts, painting and organisational tasks such as preparing the regular relatives meetings. [83]

Peculiarities [84]

The palliative ward is characterised by its homelike atmosphere, in particular by old furniture donated to the unit by a women who passed away. The premises are bright and welcoming, the doors of the staff rooms are usually open. The ten single rooms are equipped with television sets, spacious cupboards for the patients' clothes, and "special care" beds. Patients are entitled to arrange their room according to their wishes and needs. Personal belongings, such as carpets, paintings or stereos can be brought along to allow the patient to feel at home. For all rooms, there is the opportunity to move the patient outside in their bed or wheelchair. Thereby patients have the chance to spend some time in the beautifully arranged garden which many of them take. Relatives can stay over night in one of the guest rooms or alternatively in the patients room.

The palliative ward in Ried

The bath is equipped with a lift, cnabling to the patient to enjoy a relaxing bath. According to staff members, this is often very important for the patients. The bathroom is neatly arranged and maintained at a pleasant temperature. At the request of the patient, they can take a bath in special oils or flavours. Often the fragrance can be

[83] ibid.

[84] Observations made during the visit of the palliative care unit on 25 August 2003. cp. also Interview with Dr. Petra Dirschlmayer, 25 August 2003, in Ried.

smelt in the corridors, creating a familiar atmosphere for patients, staff members and visitors, as Dr. Dirschlmayer reports.[85]

The team in Ried has invented a form for the documentation of patients' progress. The form is filled out daily by all staff members directly involved with the patient. Several physical and psychological components are assessed and depicted. On the basis of the course, the patients' progress can be measured. This quality control fulfils two functions: it is a model for quality assurance as it provides evidence on which measures have been successful or not. On the other hand, it increases the satisfaction of staff members as the positive outcome of treatment measures becomes more visible.

Coffee mornings organised regularly are very good for patient morale and are attended by many relatives. In addition, memory books including all deceased patients are kept in the ward. Every patient is remembered by a photo and some words written by a staff member.

3. Summary

Major progress has been made in the provision with hospice and palliative care in Austria over the past ten years. The awareness for the need of good hospice and palliative care has risen in the last few years as can see on the basis of acts of parliament[86], the audit court report[87] and the government declaration in March 2003.[88]. Standardisation in many areas of hospice and palliative care has progressed considerably. Since December 2002 nationwide standards for caring staff (inpatient, outpatient and home care), social workers, and the selection and training of volunteers in palliative care have been in place. One of the positive consequences of this standardisation is the high level of qualification of both professionals and volunteers. At the same time, the question poses to what extent volunteers should be trained. People who have not attended the standardised "qualification" course are not "qualified" to work in palliative care services even when directly involved with patients and their relatives. But as some experts report, some services make exceptions to the rule and allow volunteers to do

---

85 Interview with Dr. Petra Dirschlmayer, 25 August 2003, in Ried.

86 http://www.parlinkom.gv.at/pd/pm/XXI/I/his/009/I00933_.html In: Hospiz Österreich: Die letzten Schritte des Weges. Ansichten. Einsichten. Aussichten. Hospiz- und Palliativbetreuung in Österreich. Ein Arbeitspapier von Hospiz Österreich vorgestellt beim Hospizdialog am 13. Febr. 2004 im bm:gf. Zur Information von Politikern und Medienfachleuten. Wien Februar 2004, p. 7.

87 Wahrnehmungsbericht des Rechnungshofes: Stationäre Palliativmedizinische Versorgung, p. 47. In: Hospiz Österreich: Die letzten Schritte des Weges. Ansichten. Einsichten. Aussichten. Hospiz- und Palliativbetreuung in Österreich. Ein Arbeitspapier von Hospiz Österreich vorgestellt beim Hospizdialog am 13. Febr. 2004 im bm:gf. Zur Information von Politikern und Medienfachleuten. Wien Februar 2004, p. 7. Im Internet: http://www.rechnungshof.at/Berichte/Steiermark/Steiermark_2003_1/Steiermark_2003_1.pdf

88 Regierungserklärung 2003 - 2006, p. 25. Im Internet einzusehen unter: http://www.parlinkom.gv.at/v-klub/regerkl.pdf In: Hospiz Österreich: Die letzten Schritte des Weges. Ansichten. Einsichten. Aussichten. Hospiz- und Palliativbetreuung in Österreich. Ein Arbeitspapier von Hospiz Österreich vorgestellt beim Hospizdialog am 13. Febr. 2004 im bm:gf. Zur Information von Politikern und Medienfachleuten. Wien Februar 2004, p. 7.

office work without having taken part in the training programme. A broad volunteer support is still indispensable and explicitly desired by all parties involved. However, it can be put into question whether the enormous time-consuming qualification course prevents some people from taking part because they cannot afford it. Will this increase the threat that voluntary commitment is the privilege of those people who can "afford" it? In order to prevent this from happening, the financial and social obstacles should be kept as low as possible, the ongoing professionalism of volunteers watched closely.

The advocates of the implemented standardisations see the introduction of the *performance-oriented hospital financing system* for hospital palliative care units as the main reason for the changes made. This brings along a more reliable and calculable funding system but at the same time requires the introduction of standards in order to prove that obligations involved have been met. [89] However the given budget only covers parts of the actual costs occurring. For that reason Martin Böker, administrative head of the *Helga Treichl Hospice* in Salzburg, rules out the possibility of the transformation of the hospice into a hospital palliative care unit "as to date there is no funding system in place that realistically covers the actual costs and additional expenses." [90]

The interviews with experts from Austria indicate that the hospice *movement* is still *developing*.

The efforts by different representatives from various backgrounds points out their endeavours to establish patient-oriented concepts that will also affect the Austrian health care system as a whole. *Hospiz Österreich* has developed a "vision" for the year 2010. Several Federal States have issued plans to improve hospice and palliative care. [91] The prospects look promising to offer "palliative and hospice care for all levels of health care, that is in short- and long term care, in outpatient and home care" [92] as targeted by the Austrian Health Ministry. The course is set to continue the improvement of the care of seriously ill and dying people in Austria.

Sources and literature

Baumgartner, Johann/ Wagner, Brigitte/ Krainz, Dieter: Pilotprojekt "Stationäre Palliativbetreuung" in der Steiermark. Die wissenschaftliche Begleituntersuchung. Graz 1999.

Bericht des Rechnungshofes, p. 47. Fürstenfeld. In: Hospiz Österreich: Die letzten Schritte des Weges. Ansichten. Einsichten. Aussichten. Hospiz- und Palliativbetreuung in Österreich.

89 Interview with Dr. Johann Baumgartner, 26 August 2003, in Graz.

90 Interview with Martin Böker, 26 February 2004, in Salzburg.

91 Examples are: Steyr (ÖBIG 2000), Vorarlberg (2002), Salzburg (2002), Upper Austria(2003), Burgenland (2003/2004). In: Hospiz Österreich: Die letzten Schritte des Weges. Ansichten. Einsichten. Aussichten. Hospiz- und Palliativbetreuung in Österreich. Ein Arbeitspapier von Hospiz Österreich vorgestellt beim Hospizdialog am 13. Febr. 2004 im bm:gf. Zur Information von Politikern und Medienfachleuten. Wien Februar 2004, p. 7.

92 Vorentwurf § 15 a Vereinbarung. Seite 8: 2. Abschnitt. Artikel 3 (2).

Ein Arbeitspapier von Hospiz Österreich vorgestellt beim Hospizdialog am 13. Febr. 2004 im bm:gf. Zur Information von Politikern und Medienfachleuten. Wien Februar 2004, p. 7.

Bundesministerium für Gesundheit und Soziale Sicherung: Sozial-Kompass Europa. Soziale Sicherheit in Europa im Vergleich. Bonn 2003.

Bischof, Hans-Peter/Heimerl, Katharina/Heller, Andreas (Ed.): Für alle die es brauchen. Integrierte palliative Versorgung – das Vorarlberger Modell. Vienna 2002.

Entschließungsantrag Nationalrat, Beschluss im Gesundheitsausschuss am 06.12.2001, als Vierparteienantrag im Nationalrat am 13.12.2001 beschlossen. In: Hospiz Österreich: Die letzten Schritte des Weges. Ansichten. Einsichten. Aussichten. Hospiz- und Palliativbetreuung in Österreich. Ein Arbeitspapier von Hospiz Österreich vorgestellt beim Hospizdialog am 13. Febr. 2004 im bm:gf. Zur Information von Politikern und Medienfachleuten. Wien Februar 2004, p. 7.

Frühwald, Thomas: Öbig-Konzept für eine stationäre palliativmedizinische Versorgung im österreichischen Krankenhaussystem. In: Wohin mit den Sterbenden? Hospize in Europa – Ansätze zu einem internationalen Vergleich. Hg. v. Reimer Gronemeyer/Erich H. Loewy: Münster 2002, p. 48 - 55.

Höfler, Anne Elisabeth: Die Geschichte der Hospizbewegung in Österreich. IFF-Palliative Care und organisationales Lernen. Kursbuch Palliative Care 2/2001. Vienna 2001.

Hospiz – und Palliativführer Österreich 2002. Vienna 2002.

Hospiz Österreich: Die letzten Schritte des Weges. Ansichten. Einsichten. Aussichten. Hospiz- und Palliativbetreuung in Österreich. Ein Arbeitspapier von Hospiz Österreich vorgestellt beim Hospizdialog am 13. Febr. 2004 im bm:gf. Zur Information von Politikern und Medienfachleuten. Vienna February 2004.

Husebø, Stein; Klaschik, Eberhard: Palliativmedizin. Berlin/Heidelberg 2003. 3rd edition.

Information brochure *Familienhospizkarenz* by the Austrian Ministry for Family Affairs.

Information brochure *ÖPG*.

Email-correspondence with Dr. Harald Retschitzegger, 23 September 2004.

Government declaration 2003 - 2006, p. 25. In: Hospiz Österreich: Die letzten Schritte des Weges. Ansichten. Einsichten. Aussichten. Hospiz- und Palliativbetreuung in Österreich. Ein Arbeitspapier von Hospiz Österreich vorgestellt beim Hospizdialog am 13. Febr. 2004 im bm:gf. Zur Information von Politikern und Medienfachleuten. Wien Februar 2004, p. 7.

Retschitzegger, Harald: Von der Pionierphase in die tägliche Arbeit: Hospiz St. Vinzenz – Palliativstation am Krankenhaus der Barmherzigen Schwestern Ried im Innkreis. In: Heimerl, Katharina/Heller, Andreas: Eine große Vision in kleinen Schritten. Aus Modellen der Hospiz- und Palliativbetreuung lernen. Freiburg im Breisgau 2001, p. 143 - 153.

Statistic Austria. In: Hospiz – und Palliativführer Österreich 2002. Vienna 2002.

Seniorenbericht 2000 – Bericht zur Lebenssituation älterer Menschen in Österreich. Vienna 2000.

Vorentwurf § 15 a Vereinbarung. Seite 8: 2. Abschnitt. Artikel 3 (2).

Wiesmayr, Wolfgang: Familienhospizkarenz: Erste Erfahrungen in: Hospiz Oberösterreich. Lebenswert – Informationen der Hospizvereine Oberösterreichs Frühjahr-Sommer 2003. Linz 2003.

Zulehner, Paul M.: Jedem seinen eigenen Tod. Für die Freiheit des Sterbens. Ostfildern 2001.

Internet sources

Dachverband Hospiz Österreich. Hospizbewegung/Palliative Care: Standards für die Befähigung ehrenamtlicher MitarbeiterInnen, p. 3. In: http://www.hospiz.at/pdf_dl/std_ea.pdf

Entschließungsantrag Nationalrat, Beschluss im Gesundheitsausschuss am 06.12.2001, als Vierparteienantrag im Nationalrat am 13.12.2001 beschlossen. http://www.parlinkom.gv.at/pd/pm/XXI/I/his/009/I00933_.html

European Observatory on Health Systems and Policies: http://www.euro.who.int/document/e72787.pdf

Helga Treichl Hospice Salzburg: http://www.roteskreuz.at/74.html

Official homepage Charity Austria: http://www.caritas.at/index.html

Official homepage Hospice Austria: http://www.hospiz.at

Official homepageDeaconry Austria: http://www.diakonie.at/

Official homepage Austrian IGSL: http://www.igsl-hospizbewegung.at/

Official homepage Austrian Society for Palliative Care: http://www.palliativ.at/

Official homepage Austrian Red Cross: http://www.roteskreuz.at

Population Division of the Department of Economic and Social Affairs of the United Nations Secretariat, *World Population Prospects: The 2002 Revision* and *World Urbanization Prospects: The 2001 Revision*. Official homepage der Vereinten Nationen: http://esa.un.org/unpp

Press release by the Austrian Ministry of Health, 03 November 2003: http://www.bmgf.gv.at/cms/site/news_einzel.htm?channel=CH0089&doc=CMS1067862515021

Government declaration 2003 - 2006. http://www.parlinkom.gv.at/v-klub/regerkl.pdf

Wahrnehmungsbericht des Rechnungshofes: Stationäre Palliativmedizinische Versorgung. http://www.rechnungshof.at/Berichte/Steiermark/Steiermark_2003_1/Steiermark_2003_1.pdf

List of interviews (in chronological order)

- Dr. Petra Dirschlmayer, Physician *Palliativstation* (Palliative care unit) *am Krankenhaus der Barmherzigen Schwestern Ried im Innkreis*, 25 August 2003
- Dr. Johann Baumgartner, Board member *Hospice Austria* and *Austrian Society for Palliative Care*, Coordinator *Palliativbetreuung Steyr* Graz, 26 August 2003
- Dr. Elisabeth Medicus, Medical director *Hospice Innsbruck*, 28 August 2003
- MAS Palliative Care Karl Bitschnau, Head *Hospice movement Vorarlberg* and Board member *Hospice Austria* Feldkirch, 29 August 2003
- Mag. Martin Böker, Administrative head *Helga Treichl Hospice* Salzburg, 26 February 2004
- Dr. Susanne Dretnik, Physician *Helga Treichl Hospice* Salzburg, 26 February 2004
- Karin Horwath, Nurse *Helga Treichl Hospice* Salzburg, 26 February 2004
- Dr. Franz Zdrahal, Medical director *Mobile Hospice teams Charity Archdiocese Vienna*, 27 February 2004

Czech Republic

Felix Schumann

1. General conditions

1.1 Demographics

- In 2000, the population of the Czech Republic numbered around 10.3 million. According to predictions, the population will drop to 8.4 million inhabitants by 2050.[1]
- The average life expectancy of 74.0 is expected to grow to 81.2 years of age by 2050, whereas the median age will rise enormously from 37.6 years in 2000 to 51.6 by 2050.[2]
- In 1950, people 65 years or older in the Czech Republic constituted 8.3% of the population. In 2000, it was already 13.8% and is projected to grow to remarkable 32.0% by 2050.[3]
- Similarly, people aged 80 years or older constituted only 1.0% of the population in 1950. That percentage grew in 2000 to 2.3 and is estimated to grow to 9.0 by 2050.[4]
- The number of persons aged 15 to 59 years per older person over the age of 60, was 69.8% of the total population in 2000 and is expected to drop to 54.8% by 2050.[5]
- In 2002 a total of 108.243 people died in the Czech Republic.[6] The most frequent causes of death were diseases of the circulatory system (57 152 cases) and tumours (28 893 cases).

1.2 Health care system

In the years 1990 and 1991 the liberalisation of the Czech insurance industry started, following the principles of de-Monopolisation, decentralisation and liberalisation. In

---

1 Population Division of the Department of Economic and Social Affairs of the United Nations Secretariat, *World Population Prospects: The 2004 Revision* and *World Urbanization Prospects: The 2003 Revision*. Official Homepage of the United Nations: http://esa.un.org/unpp

2 ibid.

3 ibid.

4 ibid.

5 ibid.

6 Czech Statistical Office: Statistical Yearbook of the Czech Republic 2003: http://www.czso.cz

this context the basic principle of the patients free choice was introduced into the health care system. Since then a general obligatory insurance is in place with people having the free choice between 27 health insurance funds. The number of health insurance funds has since then dropped to nine. Their financing is determined by law and is based on contributions and on the redistribution of these contributions. Health insurance contributions are based on a certain percentage of income (13.5%), paid by employers and employees in a ratio of 2:1 for the employed, by self-employed persons directly and by the state (through the Ministry of Finance) on behalf of the large non-waged population (this includes pensioners, students, all children, etc.).[7] As a result all citizens are compulsorily insured. Due to the restructure all Czechs have access to extensive medical provision, additional payments are rather scarce.[8] Districts and municipalities own most hospitals and clinics, with only a few small hospitals being truly private.[9] The number of hospital beds (860 per 100.000 inhabitants in 2002) is higher than the EU-average.[10] The number of physicians is below the EU-average (350 per 100.000 inhabitants in 2002).[11]

2. Hospice and palliative care in the Czech Republic

2.1 History

After the political changes at the end of 1980,s, many physicians and nurses had the opportunity to spend some time in different health care settings in Western Europe and North America. For some of them the contrast between the lamentable level of care for terminally ill in Czech Republic on one side, and the ideas and the reality of hospice and palliative care abroad on the other side, was striking and inspiring.[12] Dr Marie Svatosova played a crucial role in the popularisation of the concept of hospice care in the country. She organised hundreds of conferences for health care professionals and the general public to promote the hospice concept. She wrote and published two books on the concept of hospice care.[13] She was also actively involved in the set up of hospice services.

In 1992 the first palliative care unit opened in Babice. The 15-bedded unit was set up within a hospital for pulmonary diseases. The unit admitted patients with lung

---

7 European Observatory on Health Care Systems: Health care systems in transition. Czech Republic. Copenhagen 2000. http://www.euro.who.int/document/e70931.pdf

8 AOK-Bundesverband: Auch in Tschechien sollen Positivliste und Fallpauschalen Kosten senken: http://www.aok-bv.de/bundesverband/presse/presseservice/psgpolitik/index_02974.html

9 World Health Organization Regional Office for Europe: Highlights on Health in Czech Republic. Kopenhagen 2001, 28.

10 AOK-Bundesverband: Auch in Tschechien sollen Positivliste und Fallpauschalen Kosten senken: http://www.aok-bv.de/bundesverband/presse/presseservice/psgpolitik/index_02974.html

11 ibid.

12 Ondrej Slama: Palliative care in Czech Republic. Unpublished paper 2002.

13 ibid.

cancer in particular but also patients with other types of tumours. However, due to funding problems, this unit has been transformed into a long-term care unit. [14]

In 1995, initiated by Dr Marie Svatosova, the first free standing Czech hospice started its work in Cerveny Kostelec, located north-west of Prague. The hospice was strongly inspired by British models. [15]

Between 1996 and 2002 six further independent hospices were founded in Brno, Prague, Rajhrad, Litomerice, Plzen and Olomouc. The hospice in Brno was part of the *Comprehensive Oncological Institute* in Brno and had to be closed in 2001 because of funding problems.

In 2003 the Czech Republic has six hospices, with a total capacity of 185 beds. [16] Since 1995 an annual conference on the topic palliative medicine takes places in Brno, with 150 to 300 participants from different professional background (medicine, nursing care and social work). In 1998, Prof Dr Jiri Vorlicek from *University of Brno*, published a T*extbook of Palliative Medicine*, which is widely used by oncologists and other medical specialists. In the following year the *Czech Pain Society* set up a palliative medicine section.

In September 2001 the *Educational Institute of Palliative Medicine* was et up within *State Institute of Postgraduate Training and Accreditation in Medicine* in Prague. On a regular basis, it provides training courses in palliative medicine. In the same year, the *Scientific advisory board of the Ministry of Health* recommended to recognise "Chronic pain management and palliative medicine" as separate medical subspecialties. However no decision has yet been made on this issue. [17]

People working in palliative care show great interest in international contacts. Various partnerships or cooperation's with British hospices have been the outcome of those contacts. A lot of palliative care staff members from the Czech Republic have had the chance to visit Great Britain and the United States to take part in training courses. [18]

2.2 Hospice and palliative care services

In 2003 the Czech Republic has six hospices, with a total capacity of 185 beds: [19]
- Cerveny Kostelec (founded 1995) with 30 beds
- Plzen (1998) with 24 beds
- Prague (1998) with 25 beds
- Rajhrad (1999) with 50 beds
- Litomerice (2001) with 26 beds
- Olomouc (2002) with 30 beds.

---

[14] ibid.

[15] ibid.

[16] Czech hospices on the Internet: http://www.hospice.cz/hospice1/index1.php

[17] Ondrej Slama: Palliative care in Czech Republic. Unpublished paper 2002.

[18] Interview with Dr Ondrej Slama, 20 August 2003, in Brno.

[19] Czech hospices on the Internet: http://www.hospice.cz/hospice1/index1.php

All hospices are integrated into care facilities. There is one hospital mobile team in the Masaryk University Hospital, Brno, and two home care services that provide a comprehensive palliative care approach.[20] Some home care services in the Czech Republic provide palliative care. The *Klíček Foundation* plans the development of a children's hospice based on international role models near Prague.[21]

As one expert explains, most people in the countryside die among their families or their neighbours. However in the big cities, where the majority of the moribund lives alone or in nursing homes, most people die in hospitals or homes. All hospice units are either located in the suburbs or in close distance to the metropolitan area (Prague, Brno and Olomouc). The clients come from the cities and not from rural areas. The average length of stay in Czech hospices is 10 days.[22]

Outpatient and home hospice care hardly exist. One of the reasons for this is the lack of voluntary support in the hospice sector.

As the overview of the regional coverage of hospice beds in the Czech Republic shows (see table 1), the estimated need for 5 beds per 100.000 inhabitants is not covered in various regions of the country:

Region	Population (30.09.01)	Current capacity	Recommended capacity	Coverage with beds (in percent)
Moravia, Olomouc	1.917.020	30	96	31,3%
Middle Bohemia	1.131.839	No beds	57	0%
South Bohemia	630.138	No beds	32	0%
Usti Liberec	1.256.924	26	75	34,7%
Praha	1.172.893	26	59	44,1%
Hradec Kralove Pardubice	1.063.344	30	53	56,6%
Plzen Karlovy Vary	859.521	26	43	60,5%
Brno Zlin Vysocina	2.250.177	69	113	61,1%

Table 1: Regional coverage of hospice beds in the Czech republic (2003)[23]

[20] International Observatory on End of Life Care at Lancaster University: http://www.eolc-observatory.net/

[21] http://www.volny.cz/scrc2000/Czechnat/Klieek/Englishver/englishver.html

[22] Interview with Marie Samankova, 19 August 2003, in Prague.

Only two of the six hospices are carried by non-church organisations. Many physicians assume that the hospice concept and palliative medicine are religiously motivated. Some parts of the Czech population remain critical towards hospice initiatives as they fear that spiritual care could result in a Christian indoctrination at the deathbed. This scepticism towards a "dogmatic view of the world" has to be considered against the background of the times of political oppression, which is still in peoples mind. Their suspicion of a "conversion at the deathbed" results in a rather negative attitude towards hospice care. [24]

Another important topic is the information of patients on their diagnosis and state of health. Should the patient be informed in any case or should he not be bothered with the bad news. Czech physician's often share the paternalistic tradition, which clears the doctor from the basis principle of transparency because it "is dangerous for the patient if he is aware of his situation." Physicians defend their position by saying that patients do not want to know their diagnosis if they do not explicitly ask for it.

Generally Czech hospices, and doctors working in the field, not only do not share this opinion, but also follow an oppositional approach based on transparency and co-operation between the patient and staff members. In 2001, a law passed which gives patients the right, and doctors the obligation, to inform the patient about his health status. The new law points towards a more transparent and open relationship between the patient and physicians [25]

2.3 Legal regulations and funding

The terms 'hospice´ and 'palliative care´ are not mentioned in any legislative text. Palliative care services are recognised by Health Authorities and by Public Health Insurance as a form of nursing services. The financing from PHI is therefore insufficient and nowhere near adequate for these services to be able to fulfil their tasks. The PHI reimbursement represents on average only half of real total expenses. The remaining expenses are covered by subventions from the Ministry of Health (20 - 40%), local authorities (5 - 10%) and private donations. [26]

Similar to the non-existence of a clearly structured concept for hospice and palliative care, which gives account of the professions that should be involved and what their training should be, there is no adequate regulation for the daily rates in hospices. According to estimations 46.30 €per patient per day are necessary. However the health insurance companies only provide the daily rate of 30.90 €, the same amount which is given to residential care for the elderly. [27] In some hospices the patients and/or their

---

23 Source: Vaclav Filec: Prehled kapacity hospicovych luzek v Ceske republice dle kraju. 2002. Published at: http://www.hospice.cz/hospice1/data/kapacita2002.rtf Revision by Felix Schumann. Differences to the number of beds are due to different sources.

24 Interview with Dr Ondrej Slama, 20 August 2003, in Brno.

25 ibid.

26 International Observatory on End of Life Care at Lancaster University: http://www.eolc-observatory.net/

27 Interview with Marie Samankova, 19 August 2003, in Prague.

families are asked to contribute what they can and want or have to pay a fixed amount per day.[28]

2.4 Organisations

Association of Providers of Hospice Care (SPHP)

The National Hospice Umbrella Organisation *SPHP*, led by Marie Samankova in Prague, represents the hospices in negotiations with the Ministries and Health Insurance Companies.

Czech Pain Society

The *Czech Pain Society* strives towards the promotion of palliative medicine. It publishes its own journal called "Bolest" (English: pain).

2.5 Education and training of professional staff

In contrast to palliative medicine, pain therapy is approved as medical subspecialty. Therefore some activities in the field of palliative medicine took part in the context of pain departments. In September 2001 the *Educational Institute of Palliative Medicine* was et up within *State Institute of Postgraduate Training and Accreditation in Medicine* in Prague. Since 2003 courses in palliative medicine are compulsory for upcoming general practitioners. For all other disciplines participation in such courses is still voluntary. Most of the lectures take place in Prague or at *St. Joseph Hospice* in Rajhrad. The courses in Prague are held twice per year, with 40 - 50 participants. Courses for volunteers are given five teams a year in Rajrad, with 20 participants in each course. This means that around 200 people receive basic training in palliative care each year.[29]

The recognition of palliative medicine as a medical subspecialty would have very important consequences for the acceptance of palliative medicine within the medical, for nursing education and also for the funding of palliative care from Health Insurance Companies.

Palliative care courses are neither an integral part of the education curriculum for nurses, nor do specialist palliative care training courses exist. However several institutions offer course that last from one day to one week. Participation in these courses is voluntary. A lot of staff members received grants which allowed them to spend time in hospice and palliative care units abroad (i.e. England, USA, Germany)

2.6 Volunteers

Similar to other countries in Central- and Eastern Europe (i.e. Slovakia or Hungary), voluntary work has no tradition in the Czech Republic.[30] Nevertheless in the meantime

---

[28] International Observatory on End of Life Care at Lancaster University: http://www.eolc-observatory.net/

[29] Interview with Dr Ondrej Slama, 20 August 2003, in Brno.

[30] ibid.

every hospice has 20 to 25 volunteers. Volunteers have the chance to take out insurance for their duties.

In hospitals, and in institutions that care for handicapped people, voluntary commitment is also growing.[31] Problems occur when doctors and nurses regard the voluntary participation as a way of public control. For example nurses consider their working area as relatively autonomous. New staff members, such as volunteers, with no specific working duties, can thus create confusion in the rather rigid social hierarchy present in Czech hospitals.

In general, professional hospice staff members are very satisfied with their volunteers and regard the cooperation as fruitful.[32]

2.7 Examples

St. Joseph's Hospice

St. Joseph's Hospice in Rajhrad near Brno opened in 1999. It is run by the *Charity of Brno*. The 50-bedded, three floored hospice was converted from barracks. Most patients are admitted from hospitals in Brno or they come from their own homes. The multi-professional team includes four physicians, 20 nurses and 30 assistant nurses, 20 volunteers as well as psychologists, social workers and physiotherapists. On a weekly basis a multidisciplinary team meeting is held, where past proceedings are reflected and all aspects involving the care for the dying are discussed.[33]

St. Joseph's Hospice runs its own education centre, which is an integral part of the activities and the only training post for palliative care in Moravia. In coordination with the *Pain Clinic Brno* and postgraduate centre in Prague, palliative care courses for physicians and nurses are held.

The funding of the hospice is provided by the health insurance companies, the remaining funds are given by the *Charity* or the *Health Ministry*.[34] More money is required from the insurance companies to guarantee the long term funding.

The patient rooms usually have three beds, curtains can be raised to separate if necessary. The hospice chapel, attached to the building as a tower, is located on the ground floor.

When a patient has died, the team is anxious to provide silence. In case of a shared room, the curtains are raised. Sometimes a chaplain comes to see the dead person. Relatives and staffmembers stay in a circle around the, lid a candle. "When the patient is peaceful and without harm, it gives us strength", says the nurse Vladka Stastna. The constant care for the dying is guaranteed by staff members or relatives.[35] "We try to be with the patient until the very end", reports Vladka Stastna. The body of the dead person stays in the room for up to two hours. The person is washed and – after

[31] Interview with Marie Samankova, 19 August 2003, in Prague.
[32] Interview with Dr Ondrej Slama, 20 August 2003, in Brno.
[33] Interview with Dr Ladislav Kabelka, 21 August 2003, in Rajhrad.
[34] ibid.
[35] Interview with Vladka Stastna, 21 August 2003, in Rajhrad.

consultation with the family – clothed. Due to legal regulations the body has to be removed from the room after two hours and is then either handed to a funeral parlour, the cooling chamber or to the family. Sometimes the family decides to lay out their dead relative in the hospice's chapel. There, a candle is lit for the person.

The average length of stay in the hospice is one month.[36] Some patients stay half a year or longer in *St. Joseph's Hospice*.

Hospice Svaty Kopecek Olomouc

The hospice in Olomouc is situated close to the famous old pilgrimage church on the "holy mountain" in Svaty Kopecek, a suburb of Olomouc in the East of the Czech Republic. Originally the building was owned by the Catholic Church. After the Second world war it was devolved on the state and conversed into a pilgrim hostel.[37] After 50 years the *Statutory City of Olomouc* decided to transmit the object, which was in a bad state, free of charge to the ownership of *Archidiocesan Caritasy Olomouc* for the purpose of the hospice construction. The budget for the object reconstruction and the equipment was put together from different sources. The main funds were provided by the *Archdiocesan Caritasy Olomouc* and the *Ministry of Health*.[38] The rest was acquired from collections, benefit events, gifts, grants and other supports. Some of the donated money came from as far as Switzerland.

The new hospice started its work in 2002. Behind the dirt on the ceilings and walls, frescos and murals were found, which have been restored and give the hospice a special historical atmosphere. After the long and extensive restoration work, *Hospice Svaty Kopecek Olomouc* has been developed into an impressive and beautiful harbourage. On its backside it turns towards the pilgrimage church that, whereas the front, where the patients rooms are situated, offer a fantastic view of the panorama of the city of Olomouc.

60 percent of the funding comes from the health insurance companies, the rest is provided by the *Archdiocesan Caritasy Olomouc*, the Social Ministry and from patients contributions.[39] The team consists of three doctors, 12 nurses and 13 assistant nurses and volunteers.[40]

The hospice has two floors and a total of 30 beds. The average length of stay is 30 days. Most patients come from Olomouc or areas close by but some are admitted from more distant regions. The majority of the clients are cancer patients. They are admitted by general practitioners or from local hospitals. The hospice is endeavoured to present their work to the public and to inform about the possibilities of hospice work. This is achieved through events staged in the hospice as well as in cooperation with newspapers and radio. "However the best advertisement for hospice work is when

36 ibid.
37 Interview with Jana Vazanova, 22 August 2003, in Olomouc.
38 Hospice in Svatý Kopecek Olomouc. Unpublished paper.
39 ibid.
40 ibid.

patients and their families are satisfied and they tell others about the hospice" thinks the leader of the hospice, Jana Vazanova.

Entry of the Hospice Svaty Kopecek Olomouc

3. Summary

The funding of the six hospices from the health insurance companies works only partial. The remaining funds are provided by town councils, donators and institutions, mostly the Caritas. For the future a better cooperation between the different hospice services and initiatives seems to be desirable as this would facilitate the negotiations with health care authorities.

Czech hospices primarily orient towards England and Poland, where staff members have taken part in education and training courses. The experiences from abroad have been a major influence for their work. Various education and training opportunities are offered by Czech hospices and taken up by several professionals from the Czech Republic and the neighbouring countries, such as Slovakia.

For the future it looks likely that Euthanasia will become an urgent topic. Hospice experts, who strictly oppose the idea of Euthanasia themselves, assume a big potential for the acceptance of Euthanasia among physicians and parts of the population.

According to one expert, the main questions concerning palliative care in the Czech Republic are: [41]

- In how far will palliative medicine distinguish itself as a medical subspecialty or in how far should it be integrated into existing clinical medicine?

[41] Interview with Dr Ondrej Slama, 20 August 2003, in Brno.

- How can the provision of palliative care, the culture of care be improved in hospitals and nursing homes?
- How can hospice and palliative care be funded adequately, when health insurance companies only cover half of the expenses?

In addition, collective demands formulated by Czech experts are:[42]

- to improve the socio-cultural background of palliative care
- to improve the situation of the dying in long-term care units
- the introduction of effective, patient-centred funding

There is hope for a successful realisation of these demands in the foreseeable future if the public, experts and politicians work together.

Sources and literature

Clark, David/ Wright, Michael: Transitions in End of Life Care: Hospice and Related Developments in Eastern Europe and Central Asia. Buckingham 2002.

Hospice in Svatý Kopecek Olomouc. Unpublished paper.

Slama, Ondrej: Palliative care in Czech Republic. Unpublished paper 2002.

Internet sources

AOK-Bundesverband: Die EU-Beitrittsländer. Tschechische Republik: http://www.aok-bv.de/politik/agenda/euerweiterung/index_01458.html

Children's hospice initiative Klicek: www.volny.cz/scrc2000/Czech_nat_/Klieek/English_ver_/english_ver_.html

Czech hospices on the internet: http://www.hospice.cz/hospice1/index1.php

Czech Statistical Office: Statistical Yearbook of the Czech Republic 2003: http://www.czso.cz

EAPC-East Newsletter Nr. 17 – December 2003. Cited in: International Association for Hospice and Palliative Care: http://www.hospicecare.com/newsletter2004/january04/page6.html

European Observatory on Health Care Systems: Health care systems in transition. Czech Republic. Copenhagen 2000. http://www.euro.who.int/document/e70931.pdf

Filec, Vaclav: Prehled kapacity hospicovych luzek v Ceske republice dle kraju. 2002.
http://www.hospice.cz/hospice1/data/kapacita2002.rtf

International Observatory on End of Life Care at Lancaster University: http://www.eolc-observatory.net/

Population Division of the Department of Economic and Social Affairs of the United Nations Secretariat, *World Population Prospects: The 2004 Revision* and *World Urbanization Prospects: The 2003 Revision*. Official Homepage of the United Nations: http://esa.un.org/unpp

[42] EAPC-East Newsletter Nr. 17 – December 2003. Cited in: International Association for Hospice and Palliative Care: http://www.hospicecare.com/newsletter2004/january04/page6.html The following experts put the list together: Zdenek Bystricky, Zdenek Kalvach, Antonin Pecenka, Martina Spinkova and Ludmila Vostrakova.

World Health Organization Regional Office for Europe: Highlights on Health in Czech Republic. Copenhagen 2001: http://www.who.dk/

List of interviews (in chronological order)

- Marie Samankova, Head Hospice Umbrella Organisation *SPHP* Prague, 19 August 2003
- Dr. Ondrej Slama, Physician, *Pain Clinic Brno*, 20 August 2003
- Dr. Ladislav Kabelka, Phsician, *St. Joseph's Hospice* in Rajhrad, 21 August 2003
- Vladka Stastna, Nurse, *St. Joseph's Hospice* in Rajhrad, 21 August 2003
- Jana Vazanova, Head, *Hospice Svaty Kopecek Olomouc*, 22 August 2003

Denmark

Marcel Globisch

1. General conditions

1.1 Demographics

- In 1950, the population of Denmark was approximately 4.27 million. By 2000, the population had increased to 5.32 million. It is predicted that the population will be about the same in 2050 (5.27 million). [1]
- Since the early to mid 1950s the average life expectancy of 71.0 years has risen 6.6 years (2000 - 2005). By 2050 another rise is expected, increasing life expectancy to 81.4 years. [2]
- In 1950, people 65 years or older in Denmark constituted 9.1% of the population. By 2000, it was already 15.0% and is projected to grow to almost 25% by 2050. [3]
- Similarly, people aged 80 years or older constituted 1.2% of the population in 1950. By 2000, that figure had grown to 4.0% and is estimated to rise to 9.3% by 2050. [4]
- The older-person ratio, the number of persons aged 15 to 64 years per older person over the age of 65, was 64.6% of the total population in 1959. In 2000, this figure had grown to 66.7%. However, it is expected to drop significantly to 59.6% by 2050. [5]
- The cancer death rate is approximately 15,000 cancer-deaths per year [6], about the same as in the UK (2,800 per 1,000,000). [7]

---

1 Population Division of the Department of Economic and Social Affairs of the United Nations Secretariat. *World Population Prospects: The 2002 Revision* and *World Urbanization Prospects: The 2001 Revision*. Offizielle Homepage der Vereinten Nationen: http://esa.un.org/unpp

2 ibid.

3 ibid.

4 ibid.

5 ibid.

6 Kræftens Bekæmpelse (The Danish Cancer Society). Kræftdødsfald i Danmark (Cancer deaths in Denmark). 1998. In: Tove Bahn Vejlgaard: Educational needs in palliative care of doctors and nurses in a Danish county hospital and the related primary care. Dissertation project. Msc in Palliative Care. King's College London. London January 2002, p. 6.

7 Higginson I. Palliative and Terminal Care. In Stevens A, Raftery J, eds. *Palliative and Terminal Care Healthcare Needs Assessment*, pp 1 - 45. Oxford: Radcliffe Medical Press, 1998. In: Tove Bahn Vejl-

- In 1996, 49.7% of deaths from all causes occurred in hospitals. 24.5% occurred in nursing homes and 22.2% at home. The remaining 3.6%. of deaths in Denmark took place in a variety of other places. [8]

1.2 Health care system

The Danish healthcare service can be divided into 2 sectors: the Primary healthcare sector and the hospital sector. The primary sector deals with general health problems and its services are available to all. The hospital sector deals with medical conditions which require more specialised treatment, equipment and intensive care. In addition to the treatment of patients, both general practitioners and hospitals are involved in preventive treatment as well as in the training of health and medical research personnel. [9]

Like Denmark as a whole, the healthcare sector has 3 political and administrative levels: the State, the counties and the municipalities (national, regional and local levels). The healthcare service is organised in such a way that responsibility for services provided by the health service lies with the lowest possible administrative level. The 273 local authorities, together with the local authorities of Copenhagen and Frederiksberg, are local administrative bodies. Local authorities have a number of tasks, of which health represents a small part. In the health field, the local authorities are responsible for district nursing, public healthcare, school healthcare and child dental treatment. Local authorities are also responsible for the majority of social services, some of which (older people's homes, older people's housing) have to do with the healthcare service and are of great importance to its functioning. [10]

Running a hospital requires a larger population than that of the majority of local authorities. This responsibility lies with the 14 counties. However, hospitals in the local authorities of Copenhagen and Frederiksberg are run by a special administrative body: the Copenhagen Hospital Cooperation. The counties are also responsible for the practising sector; however, this responsibility lies with the local authorities in Copenhagen and Frederiksberg. The counties have wide-ranging powers to organise the health service for their citizens, according to regional requirements and resources, without the intervention of the government. [11]

The task of the state in healthcare provision is first and foremost to initiate, coordinate and advise. One of the main tasks is to establish the goals for a national health

---

gaard: Educational needs in palliative care of doctors and nurses in a Danish county hospital and the related primary care. Dissertation project. Msc in Palliative Care. King's College London. London January 2002, p. 6.

[8] Government paper. Help to live until you die. Report from a government working group about palliative care in the counties. May 2001.

[9] Information brochure Healthcare in Denmark: Ministry of the Interior and Health. 5th edition. 2002, p. 5.

[10] Information brochure Healthcare in Denmark: Ministry of the Interior and Health. 5th edition. 2002, p. 8 et seq.

[11] Information brochure Healthcare in Denmark: Ministry of the Interior and Health. 5th edition. 2002, p. 9.

policy. The Ministry of the Interior and Health, in its capacity as principal health authority, is responsible for legislation on healthcare. This includes legislation on health provisions, personnel, hospitals and pharmacies, medicinal products, foodstuffs, vaccinations, pregnancy healthcare, child healthcare and patients' rights. The Ministry of the Interior and Health legislation covers the tasks of the counties and the local authorities in the health area. The Ministry also sets up guidelines for the running of the healthcare service. A central provision requires that, every fourth year, the counties and the local authorities formulate a healthcare plan in order to improve the coordination and efficiency of the different administrative levels involved in healthcare. Moreover, the Ministry of the Interior and Health supports efforts to improve productivity and efficiency, for example by the sharing of experience and the professional exchange of information.[12]

The national healthcare system is financed via income taxes. The state, the county, and the municipality collect these for each taxpayer. The 14 counties in the country run and finance their own hospitals. If a patient needs a referral from one county to another, for more specialised treatment, for example, the home county has to pay the receiving county. Home care is run and financed by each of the 275 municipalities. General practitioners are working on an individual basis licensed by the state and are paid by the national health insurance. For the development of palliative care this means that although guidelines and recommendations should be followed, it is still at the level of each county to decide how to implement them in hospitals, and at the level of the municipalities when it concerns home care. Unlike the UK, there is no tradition of charity funded healthcare in the country, so all development emanates from within the national health system.[13]

2. Hospice and Palliative Care in Denmark

2.1 History

Care of the dying was a rather neglected issue in the Danish society until the mid eighties. The first national report concerning care of seriously ill and dying patients was published by the National board of health in 1986[14] inspired by the development of hospices in the UK. In 1992, the Danish Parliament signed into law the rules on "passive euthanasia". One of the implications of these rules is that the patient can

---

12 Information brochure Healthcare in Denmark: Ministry of the Interior and Health. 5th edition. 2002, p. 9 et seq.

13 Tove Bahn Vejlgaard: Educational needs in palliative care of doctors and nurses in a Danish county hospital and the related primary care. Dissertation project. Msc in Palliative Care. King's College London. London January 2002, p. 4.

14 Sundhedsstyrelsen (National board of health). Terminal pleje (terminal care). 1986. Copenhagen, Denmark, Sundhedsstyrelsen. In: Tove Bahn Vejlgaard: Educational needs in palliative care of doctors and nurses in a Danish county hospital and the related primary care. Dissertation project. Msc in Palliative Care. King's College London. London January 2002, p. 3.

reject treatment and can avoid being kept alive artificially. If life-prolonging treatment is futile the doctor must abide by the patient's wishes and stop therapy. [15]

St. Lukas Hospice, situated in Copenhagen, was the first hospice to open in Denmark, in 1992. It took three years to establish the second Danish hospice, St. Maria Hospice, in Vejle. Both are private institutions. In 1997, the first palliative care unit in a hospital was founded at Bispebjerg Hospital. It remains the only palliative care unit within a hospital setting in Denmark.

The board of health and the national institute for health systems has published two reports on palliative care over the years [16] and finally in 1999 produced national guidelines on palliative care. [17] The WHO's definition of palliative care was adopted in Denmark. All these publications are inspired by palliative care as it has developed in the UK.

The development of hospice and palliative care has been slow – as stated in the national cancer plan [18] – and differs between counties. Some counties in Denmark have not yet planned how to develop palliative care while others have made significant progress.

2.2 Hospice and palliative care provision

Currently there are six inpatient hospices and one palliative care unit in Denmark providing a total of 75 beds. According to the Ministry of the Interior and Health, two more hospices are planned. On the isle of Fyn the latest hospice started its work at the end of 2004 providing care for 12 patients. By December 2005, another 12 bed hospice will open in South Sjaelland while another 8-bed hospice is planned in North Sjaelland for 2006. [19]

According to Irene Higginson's widely approved study on palliative and terminal care healthcare needs, there is an estimated need for 50 specialist palliative care beds

---

15 http://etisk.inforce.dk/graphics/03_udgivelser/publikationer/ENG003.htm#3.3

16 Sundhedsstyrelsen (National board of health). Omsorg for alvorligt syge og døende (Care for seriously ill and dying patients). 1996. Copenhagen, Denmark, Sundhedsstyrelsen. See also: Busch CJ, Cramon P, Timm H, and Wagner L. Palliativ indsats i Danmark (Palliative care in Denmark). DSI 91.01. 1997. DSI – Institute for Sundhedsvæsen. In: Tove Bahn Vejlgaard: Educational needs in palliative care of doctors and nurses in a Danish county hospital and the related primary care. Dissertation project. Msc in Palliative Care. King's College London. London January 2002, p. 3.

17 Sundhedsstyrelsen (National board of health). Faglige retningslinier for den palliative indsats (Guidelines for palliative care). 1999. Copenhagen, Denmark, Sundhedsstyrelsen. In: Tove Bahn Vejlgaard: Educational needs in palliative care of doctors and nurses in a Danish county hospital and the related primary care. Dissertation project. Msc in Palliative Care. King's College London. London January 2002, p. 4.

18 Kræftstyregruppen (the cancer steering committee). Den nationale kræftplan (The National Cancer Plan). 149 - 151. 2000. Copenhagen, Denmark, Sundhedsstyrelsen. In: Tove Bahn Vejlgaard: Educational needs in palliative care of doctors and nurses in a Danish county hospital and the related primary care. Dissertation project. Msc in Palliative Care. King's College London. London January 2002, p. 7.

19 Interview with Jette Blichfeldt, 10 June 2004, in Copenhagen.

per million people.[20] In Denmark, this indicates a need for approximately 250 beds.[21] Despite three new hospices set to open within the next 11/2 years, Denmark would still only have some 91 inpatient beds.

Inpatient hospice and palliative care units

Name	Founded	Beds
St. Lukas Hjemmehospice, Copenhagen	1992	10
St. Maria Hospice, Vejle	1995	10
Palliative Care unit Bispebjerg Hospital, Copenhagen	1997	12
Diakonissestiftelsens Hospice, Copenhagen	1997	10
KamillianerGaarden Hospice, Ålborg	1999	12
Hospice Søholm,Århus	1999	11 [23]
Hospice Fyn, Fyn	2004	12

Table 1: Compiled by the collected data. Up to December 2004.

2.3 Legal regulations and funding

The development of palliative care in Denmark depends on the three different sectors in the Danish health system. Although government's guidelines and recommendations should be followed it is up to each individual county to decide how to implement the guidelines in hospitals and up to the municipalities to determine home care recommendations.

The national guidelines from 1999 make recommendations for the management of symptoms based on the four dimensional understanding of palliative care (psychological, physical, social and existential-spiritual aspects), on ethical issues, on the needs of carers etc. The recommendations also include a description of how to organise palliative care. This includes a description of patient-and-family-centred multidisciplinary care and the palliative specialist team that follows the patient as a link between primary care and hospital sector. The palliative team can work from a base with or without beds; in the latter case in the form of a palliative care unit or a hospice.[24]

20 Higginson I. Palliative and Terminal Care. In Stevens A, Raftery J, eds. *Palliative and Terminal Care Healthcare Needs Assessment*, pp 1 - 45. Oxford: Radcliffe Medical Press, 1998. In: Tove Bahn Vejlgaard: Educational needs in palliative care of doctors and nurses in a Danish county hospital and the related primary care. Dissertation project. Msc in Palliative Care. King's College London. London January 2002, p. 6.

21 Tove Bahn Vejlgaard: Educational needs in palliative care of doctors and nurses in a Danish county hospital and the related primary care. Dissertation project. Msc in Palliative Care. King's College London. London January 2002, p. 6.

24 Tove Bahn Vejlgaard: Educational needs in palliative care of doctors and nurses in a Danish county hospital and the related primary care. Dissertation project. Msc in Palliative Care. King's College London. London January 2002, p. 4.

In February 2000, the national cancer plan was published with recommendations for the future management of cancer in Denmark. The report assumes that palliative care in Denmark is less developed and that the counties and municipalities need to evaluate their efforts and be active in implementing the guidelines of the National board of health. Moreover it recommends that resources are allocated to education in palliative care and that specialist education should be established.[25]

In May 2001, the association of counties, association of communities and the health ministry published the report "Help to live until you die"[26]. The report described various palliative care initiatives in Denmark and concludes that the services differed a lot in organisation as well as quality around the country. It concludes that resources and efforts are needed at all levels to educate and train health staff and to implement the recommendations of the national board and the cancer steering group.[27]

Since July 2002, patients have been able to choose another option if the public hospital system is unable to offer examination and treatment within two months. The only exceptions would be where a medical assessment shows that the patient's condition will not worsen if he or she has to wait longer. It will be up to patients to decide where they receive treatment. A precondition for such a choice is that the patients have been examined and referred for treatment. It is then possible to receive treatment at public hospitals, private hospitals or hospitals abroad if necessary.[28] So far, five hospices are covered by the Hospital Care Act and thus considered as "free choice" institutions. The three are *St. Maria Hospice, St. Lukas Hospice, Diakonissestiftelsens Hospice, KamillianerGaarden Hospice* and the recently established hospice on the isle of Fyn.[29]

As Tove Vejlgaard points out:

> There is a major problem in the implementation of the guidelines because while the guidelines are very good, no one follows them. Guidelines are only good if they are implemented. Denmark is a case in point.[30]

---

25 Kræftstyregruppen (the cancer steering committee). Den nationale kræftplan (The National Cancer Plan). 149 - 151. 2000. Copenhagen, Denmark, Sundhedsstyrelsen. In: Tove Bahn Vejlgaard: Educational needs in palliative care of doctors and nurses in a Danish county hospital and the related primary care. Dissertation project. Msc in Palliative Care. King's College London. London January 2002, p. 5.

26 Amtsrådsforeningen (The association of Counties). Hjælp til at leve til man dør. (Help to live until you die). 2001. Copenhagen, Denmark, Amtsrådsforeningen. In: Tove Bahn Vejlgaard: Educational needs in palliative care of doctors and nurses in a Danish county hospital and the related primary care. Dissertation project. Msc in Palliative Care. King's College London. London January 2002, p. 5.

27 Kræftstyregruppen (the cancer steering committee). Den nationale kræftplan (The National Cancer Plan), p. 149 - 151. 2000. Copenhagen, Denmark, Sundhedsstyrelsen. In: Tove Bahn Vejlgaard: Educational needs in palliative care of doctors and nurses in a Danish county hospital and the related primary care. Dissertation project. Msc in Palliative Care. King's College London. London January 2002, p. 5.

28 http://www.stm.dk/publikationer/Regeringsgrundlag/reggrund\%20uk\%202001.html

29 Interview with Jette Blichfeldt, 10 June 2004, in Copenhagen.

30 Interview with Dr. Tove Vejlgaard, 08 June 2004, in Århus.

In 2004, the *Danish Society of Palliative Medicine (DSPaM)* and the cancer board set up another working group to establish common goals for the development of palliative care in Denmark. [31]

2.4 Organisations

Danish Hospice Forum

The Danish Hospice Forum is voluntary led by Ole Bang, a businessman from Ålborg. The forum promotes the hospice ethos on its own website, which gives information on the history of hospice movement, conferences and links to current services that offer palliative care in Denmark. Most Danish hospices are members of the forum.

Danish Society of Palliative Medicine

The *Danish Society of Palliative Medicine (DSPaM)* was founded in 2001. It is a purely medical organisation with no other professions involved. The DSPaM is a collective member of the European Association of Palliative Care and co-founder of the Nordic Specialist Course for Palliative Care which has been established with representatives from the other Scandinavian countries – Norway, Sweden, Finland and Iceland (see 2.5.).

The Association for Palliative Care

The *Association for Palliative Care* was founded in 1993. It is a multi-professional association. [32]

2.5 Training and education of professional staff

Doctors: On average, it takes to 61/2 years to complete the medical course at the three Danish universities (Copenhagen, Århus and Odense). [33] Until the introduction of the Nordic Course in 2003, there were essentially no education and training programmes in palliative medicine in Denmark. In her dissertation "Educational needs in palliative care of doctors and nurses in a Danish county hospital and the related primary care", Tove Vejlgaard refers to a report by the cancer steering group published in 2001:

In June 2001 the cancer steering group published a report with recommendations for the education of health staff in cancer treatment. It was concluded that very little teaching in oncology as such and none in palliative medicine was offered at any of the medical schools in Denmark [. . .] Palliative care was not specified in the survey, but in the theoretical courses for all fields, the specialty of oncology is so far the only to have a course in palliative medicine (3 day course) [. . .] The report recommends that

---

[31] Email from Dr. Tove Vejlgaard, 15 January 2004.

[32] Interview with Dr. Tove Vejlgaard, 08 June 2004, in Århus.

[33] http://www.aek.or.at/EUSTUDPPT/systeme.html

multidisciplinary courses in palliative care should be offered to health staff at regional levels. [34]

Of the approximately 15,000 doctors in Denmark, only about 12 work in the field of palliative care. These physicians specialise in family medicine, anaesthesiology, oncology, internal medicine or geriatrics. Four Danish doctors acquired the Diploma of Palliative Medicine from The University of Cardiff and one doctor completed the Masters course on Palliative Care at King's College in London.

Therefore, one of the first tasks of the Danish Society of Palliative Medicine, founded in June 2001, was to develop a common Nordic specialist course in palliative medicine. [35] Together with colleagues from the other Scandinavian countries the Nordic specialist course in Palliative Medicine was created in 2001 - 2002. Tove Vjelgaard, one of the founders of the Nordic Course, on the need of such a Scandinavian course:

> We were faced with a situation where new palliative care units and programmes might be established but without the appropriate medical staffing. We felt, if we want to bring this field further, we need doctors who have specialist training. Denmark is too small a country to be able to deliver what was necessary on its own, so we contacted the Norwegian, Swedish and Finish doctors and the one Icelandic one to establish the Nordic Course. [36]

The first course commenced in October 2003 and continues. Due to overwhelming interest and the many qualified applicants whom the organisers were unable to admit to the first course, a second course began in February 2005. Twenty nine applicants were admitted to the first course. Due to the restrictions, only six out of fifteen Danish applicants could join the course. The national associations consider and nominate students among the applicants from their respective countries. For the selection among qualified applicants it is taken into consideration where applicants are placed and their role or future role in the development of palliative care, aiming at an even and fair distribution within each country. [37] Health directors from the counties in Denmark were agreed on the importance of specialist training. As a rule, hospitals fund the tuition and boarding of Danish students.

The group decided to use the British Curriculum in Palliative Medicine, level C [38], as the basis for the course content, as more or less all current palliative medicine

---

34 Tove Bahn Vejlgaard: Educational needs in palliative care of doctors and nurses in a Danish county hospital and the related primary care. Dissertation project. Msc in Palliative Care. King's College London January 2002. S. 5f.

35 Tove Bahn Vejlgaard: Educational needs in palliative care of doctors and nurses in a Danish county hospital and the related primary care. Dissertation project. Msc in Palliative Care. King's College London January 2002. S. 12.

36 Interview with Dr. Tove Vejlgaard, 08 June 2004, in Århus.

37 Information paper Nordic Specialist Course.

38 Palliative Medicine Curriculum for Medical Students, General Professional training and Higher Specialist training. Association for Palliative Medicine of Great Britain and Ireland, 1991.

curricula are based on this. Attention was also paid to the EAPC Curriculum [39] and the Swedish Curriculum. [40] The course is aimed at doctors in the forefront of palliative medicine, who will play an important part in developing the field in their countries. Research is therefore an integral part of the specialist training, and a limited research project is included in the course.

Nurses: A specialist training course has been established for a limited number of nurses who have working experience from specialist palliative care. The course is organised by *The Danish Nurses' Organisation* and the first module commenced in October 2001. [41]

At a non-specialist level, there are no co-ordinated programmes but courses take place in various settings. Some courses have taken place within a private multi-professional association that was funded in 1993 with the purpose of supporting the development of palliative care in Denmark. [42]

The general training of nurses from the national nursing schools has been changed with a new executive order from March 2001. [43] Palliative care as such is not mentioned in the order but many objectives relating to understanding and managing serious illness, death and dying from different perspectives are set." [44]

2.6 Volunteers

It is difficult to get an exact picture of the state of volunteer support in palliative care in Denmark as there are no official statistics. According to the information and data collected from existing hospices, there are currently 116 volunteers working in this field. [45]

The comparatively low participation of volunteers is a result of what can basically be described as the non-development of a voluntary culture in Danish healthcare. As a representative of the Ministry of Interior and Health confesses: "In Denmark we do

---

39 Report and Recommendations of a Workshop on Palliative Medicine Education and Training for Doctors in Europe. European Association for Palliative Care (EAPC), 1993.

40 Svensk läroplan i palliativ medicin. Svensk Förening för Palliativ Medicin, 2001.

41 Tove Bahn Vejlgaard: Educational needs in palliative care of doctors and nurses in a Danish county hospital and the related primary care. Dissertation project. Msc in Palliative Care. King's College London. London January 2002, p. 13.

42 Tove Bahn Vejlgaard: Educational needs in palliative care of doctors and nurses in a Danish county hospital and the related primary care. Dissertation project. Msc in Palliative Care. King's College London. London January 2002, p. 13 et seq.

43 Undervisningsministeriet (The Ministry of Education). Bekendtgørelse om sygeplejerskeuddannelsen (Executive order on the nursing education). 232 af 30.03.2001. 2001. In: Tove Bahn Vejlgaard: Educational needs in palliative care of doctors and nurses in a Danish county hospital and the related primary care. Dissertation project. Msc in Palliative Care. King's College London. London January 2002, p. 14.

44 Tove Bahn Vejlgaard: Educational needs in palliative care of doctors and nurses in a Danish county hospital and the related primary care. Dissertation project. Msc in Palliative Care. King's College London. London January 2002, p. 14.

45 50 of those volunteers work at the KamillianerGaarden Hospice in Ålborg, another 32 in Vejle, 9 volunteers each at Hospice Søholm and St. Lukas as well as 16 at Bispebjerg Hospital.

not have a tradition of using volunteers in healthcare."[46] The reasons for a lack of volunteerism are manifold. The proportion of working women is very high, leaving little time to care for family and friends. There is a fear from workers' unions that volunteers may take away jobs from professional staff.[47] Scepticism often expressed by professional staff is also visible in the hospice sector. *Diakonissestiftelsens Hospice* has totally abandoned the option of using volunteers. Nurse Charlotte Kjaersgard on the reservations of using voluntary staff:

> We think it is not good for them [the patients – M.G.) to have contact with too many people coming and going [. . .] And sometimes people that have some problems themselves and maybe they haven't mourned enough and then they think if I'm volunteer at a hospice, I might get better. That is very selfish. And that's what we don't want.[48]

The nine volunteers who work at *Hospice Søholm* in Århus work only in the evening and during the daytime in the weekends. Whereas the acquisition of volunteers is quite easy, the definition of their field of activity is a bit more problematic. The Director of nursing, Jytte Husted, sums up the difficulties: "It is new for us to have so many volunteers, we only had three or four before. Our challenge right now is to learn how to use them."[49] The first Danish hospice, *St. Lukas Hospice* in Copenhagen, had to deal with similar problems in the start. As Jette Riis, Director of nursing of the home care team, recalls, the hospice choose not to use any volunteers in the first five years of existence as the professionals themselves had to find their way in the totally unknown field of hospice work at that time:

> If the professionals are not very confident in their own role, it is very difficult to see where the volunteers should be complementary. And so I think it was necessary to have this five years of experience doing hospice work in the Danish way before we opened up for volunteers. And when we did it, there were of course nurses especially saying, what are the volunteers here for?[50]

The resistance against volunteers is not solely restricted to professional staff. The following observations made by Jette Riis allow two interpretations. On one hand they corroborate the belief that there is no strong culture of volunteerism existing in Denmark but on the other hand, also show that is possible to convince people of the advantages of voluntary support:

"So there is a quite a bit of resistance but what we know is when we have convinced the patient that it is a good idea that the volunteer could be a good support for them,

46 Interview with Jette Blichfeldt, 10 June 2004, in Copenhagen. This was also expressed in other interview, amongst those: Interview with Helle Tingrupp, 11 June 2004, in Copenhagen.

47 Interview with Dr. Nan Sonne, 10 June 2004, in Copenhagen.

48 Interview with Charlotte Kjaersgard, 11 June 2004, in Copenhagen.

49 Interview with Jytte Husted, 09 June 2004, in Århus.

50 Interview with Jette Riis, 10 June 2004, in Copenhagen.

then we see that they are very happy."[51] Little by little, the initial scepticism has given way as volunteers are now regarded as an integral part of hospice work at *St. Lukas*.[52]

Great emphasis is placed upon the strict division of the range of activities of professional and voluntary staff members. This applies to all institutions that use volunteers in their team.

A basic training course is required by all hospices. The content and scope of the course varies from hospice to hospice. Most hospices offer training courses that touch the basics of the hospice philosophy and do not require a great amount of time.

An interview with Inge Thomsen, voluntary coordinator at *KamillianerGaarden Hospice*, also focused on the question of how much education volunteers need before they work in the field. Thomsen draws the attention to the perspective of patients and their relatives. She noticed that many patients and relatives appreciate having the chance to speak with quite normal, unprofessional people such as the volunteers.

"Indeed, there are subjects that some of them prefer to discuss with a volunteer"[53] Due to this, Inge Thomsen stresses that it is important to prepare volunteers for their work but not to train them like professionals:

> The volunteers are not semi-professionals, and therefore the training is not in nurse-related subjects. Of course we offer courses dealing with subjects as grief and bereavement, the hospice philosophy and so on. And of course it is good to have experience being together with serious ill or dying people, but we give priority to the personal qualities of the volunteers. Are you a person who can tolerate seeing and listening to a very ill person. Are you able to handle this or is it too much for you?[54]

The tasks carried out by volunteers are the same in most settings. Examples are: going for a walk with patients, shopping, setting the table, making coffee, washing the dishes, talking to the patients and/or relatives, sitting at his bedside (if required during the night).[55] Most importantly, the volunteers have no other obligations – in contrast to the professional staff – and can spend unhurried time with the patient.[56]

2.7 Example

KamillianerGaarden Hospice

Organisation and funding

KamillianerGaarden is a private hospice that was founded in 1999. It provides palliative care for 12 beds. Treatment of the patients is funded by the county. The

---

[51] Interview with Jette Riis, 10 June 2004, in Copenhagen.

[52] Interview with Jette Riis and Annedorte Friberg, 10 June 2004, in Copenhagen.

[53] Interview with Inge Thomsen, 07 June 2004, in Ålborg.

[54] Interview with Inge Thomsen, 07 June 2004, in Ålborg.

[55] Interview with Dr. Nan Sonne, 10 June 2004, in Copenhagen.; Interview with Jytte Husted, 09 June 2004, in Århus; Interview with Kirsten Justessen, 07 June 2004, in Ålborg. Interview with Inge Thomsen, 07 June 2004, in Ålborg.

[56] Interview with Jytte Husted, 09 June 2004, in Århus.

county gets one third of the money from the municipals. Additional funding comes from various charity events and donations.

Patients are normally admitted by general practitioners. Patients can be admitted for rehabilitation, symptom control or to give caring family members a rest before the patient returns back home. In 2003, a total of 290 applications were made for admission to the hospice. Due to capacity, only 176 could be accepted. The patients had to wait an average 5 days for admission to the hospice. In 2003, the average lengths of stay was 19 days. 73,9% of the patients died in the hospice.

At the same time, the hospice is the centre of palliative care in Northern Jutland. The community service serves to the citizens of Ålborg and the surrounding suburbs either in their own homes, in hospital or in nursing homes. The team collaborates with regular home care services, general practitioners, hospitals and with the so-called "palliative nurses", who are situated at local hospitals. These are in constant contact with the inpatient hospice team and deal with people at home or in hospital in their territory.

The hospice also acts as a education centre for both professionals and people interested in the field. For instance the "palliative nurses" receive their palliative care education in the hospice. Two months are spent working in the hospice and another four gaining valuable experience working with the team. In this way, a network of palliative care experts has been created that covers the whole county. Currently a new scheme is being developed by giving expertise and training to home care nurses in each district in the county. In this programme, home care nurses spend eight weeks in the hospice and another four weeks with the "palliation nurses". [57]

The whole network gives service to half of the patients dying from cancer in North Jutland. According to Kirsten Justessen, the Ministry of Interior and Health intends to extend this model to the whole of Denmark. [58]

The hospice would like to create a nurse research post but so far this has not been possible due to financial reasons. The hospice staff gives approximately 100 lectures and courses per year. Some of the lectures and courses are held on a voluntary basis by hospice staff members, others are part of their paid job. Kirsten Justessen on the importance of such educational programmes:

> We really try to share the knowledge that we have with as many people as possible. [The hosipice] should not only be a good place to die but also a place where we generate and spread knowledge. That is very important for us. [59]

Professionals

The professional inpatient hospice team includes a doctor, who is also working for the community service, nurses, a music therapist, a voluntary coordinator and a chaplain.

---

[57] Interview with Kirsten Justessen, 07 June 2004, in Ålborg.

[58] Interview with Kirsten Justessen, 07 June 2004, in Ålborg.

[59] Interview with Kirsten Justessen, 07 June 2004, in Ålborg.

The community service consists of two doctors, four nurses, a physiotherapist, a social worker, a chaplain and a psychologist.

In this specific circumstance the focus is set on members of two professions (a chaplain and a music therapist) who have not been central to the detailed descriptions of other hospice services portrayed in this book. Nevertheless, they are very important in the hospice context, especially at KamillianerGaarden Hospice.

One of the two doctors, Dr. Mona Kelm-Hansen, is currently taking part in the Nordic Specialist Course. Her colleague, Dr. Niels Brunsgaard, is an oncologist, with no formal education and training in palliative care. He had also applied for the Nordic Specialist Course but was rejected due to limited capacities and the regulation to only accept one doctor from the same hospice at a time. As there are no other training programmes available in Denmark, Dr. Brunsgaard acquired most of his knowledge in palliative care by attending conferences. He reports that a third medical post was set up at the hospice but nobody applied for the job.[60] The nursing staff has not changed in the five years of existence even though there are lots of nurses applying for a job at the hospice. However applications have to be rejected as there is no funding available for new staff.[61] The chaplain, Ole Raakjær, works part-time in the hospice and part-time in his parish. Raakjær talks about what he calls "the every-day-consciousness and the basic expectations to life" that human beings usually express: "The world is basically a safe place to live for me and my family. Life is meaningful, coherent and predictable. Children never die before their parents."[62] Some of these views do not apply in a hospice anymore as patients undergo a change and experience reality as the opposite to their basis expectations: "That we neither can control life nor future; that we don't have the power we think we have; that there is suffering and pain in the world and it can hit me and my family; that death is not just something that comes when you are old."[63] Raakjær thinks his job, and that of the whole team, is "to ensure, that, broadly speaking, there is room and space for thoughts and reflections on this existential and metaphysical shock [...] to offer the patient and relative a spiritual language in which his or her life can be interpreted." Raakjær believes that it is crucial to distinguish between problems and burdens because "problems can be solved but burdens must be carried". The spiritual and existential care is about the burdens and Raakjær thinks that is important not to let the patient alone in this difficult situation.

The existential questions often raised by patients are "does life has a meaning?", "what is the meaning of my life?" or "why me?". Raakjær considers that his role is not primarily to answer those questions but to encourage the patient to think about those questions himself.

Questions against the background of religious beliefs seem to be of particular interest in the context of terminal care. According to Raakjær, the attitude shown by

60 Interview with Dr. Niels Brunsgaard, 07 June 2004, in Ålborg.

61 Interview with Kirsten Justessen, 07 June 2004, in Ålborg.

62 Interview with Ole Raakjær, 07 June 2004, in Ålborg.

63 Interview with Ole Raakjær, 07 June 2004, in Ålborg.

many dying patients towards religious matters can be regarded as a reflection of the special role religious beliefs play in Denmark:

> If I ask them are you religious, they would say no I'm not religious but I believe in God, I believe in a higher power. It is very vague. It is not very dogmatic in the old philological way of thinking. It makes it sometimes very frustrating and also very exciting. [...] I think we are in a new era, a new period where many people are very interested in religious matters and very spiritual. [...] you can use the Christian language together with re-incarnation. [...] It is like a supermarket. You take a bit of everything, I wonder about this, what do you have on offer for me? I like the thought about heaven, I like the thought about re-incarnation. In the traditional way of thinking you cannot combine those things but for Danes it does not matter, that's the way I believe. [64]

27-year old music therapist Annette Majlund has been working at the hospice since early 2004. Music therapy is a crucial part of the multi-disciplinary hospice team in Ålborg. Majlunds predecessor, the German nun Marianne Bode, cared for 63 of the 176 patients in 2003. [65] Annette Majlund describes the possibilities of musical therapy in the care of dying patients:

> My function as a music therapist is to use music as a therapeutic tool to follow a patient through the process of dying [...]
>
> The closer we are to death, the more we prefer silence and inner peace. Some instruments and sounds, like the human voice and harp, are though allowed in this room [...]
>
> The sound of a humming voice is well known from our very beginning, it comforts us and can bring us a feeling of well being [...]
>
> The breathing is our life-line. It is the rhythm of our breathing that first of all creates the bodies own music as long as we are alive. Therefore music makes it possible to communicate with a human being until the very end. Furthermore we use our breathing to express ourselves when words are no longer able to come up. By listening carefully to a patients breathing, it is possible for me to be informed whether he or she is relaxed or anxious [...]
>
> Patients are usually referred to a music therapist following a team-evaluation of his or her symptoms. Music therapy is used in palliative care in situations where patients have difficulties in coping with the reality about a coming death, and therefore need help to create strategies to regain control over their lives. [66]

Annette Majlund often plays on a little harp whose gently sounds can be very comforting as the researcher himself experienced during a meditation session. Miss Majlund had proposed to do such a meditation in order to illustrate her work. As this was the fourth interview on the day with another to follow, the researcher had his doubts but in the end engaged with the proposal. The impact was quite impressive. Inside a few minutes, under the influence of the subdued music ("one tone at a time") played on

---

64 Interview with Ole Raakjær, 07 June 2004, in Ålborg.

65 KamillianerGaarden Annual report 2003. Ålborg 2003, p. 13.

66 Interview with Annette Majlund, 07 June 2004, in Ålborg.

the harp, the breathing calmed down and the researcher was able to part with his role as the interviewer.

Volunteers

The field of activity of the 50 volunteers at KamillianerGaarden is almost identical with the work done by volunteers in other Danish hospices as has been described already (see 2.6). It is worth pointing out that, since autumn 2003, volunteers in Ålborg also care for the patients in their own homes in the interests of supporting and relieving the caring relatives. [67] Kirsten Justessen clearly verbalises the standing of volunteers in her hospice: "They are a crucial part of the environment here." [68]

3. Summary

As there is no tradition of charity funded healthcare in the country, all development is coming from within the national health system. Through its practice, the hospice movement has undoubtedly contributed to eliminating some of the taboo perceptions surrounding death. It has become more acceptable to talk about death and has thus, in a certain sense, become easier to relate to the death process, in both personal and political contexts. [69] In Denmark only very few professionals have formal education and training in palliative care. In the case of doctors, no more than five own a degree in palliative medicine. The introduction of the *Nordic Specialist Course in Palliative Medicine* should lead to a major improvement in this particular area within the next few years. There are some examples like the model in North Jutland, where efforts have been made to educate general nurses in palliative care. The networks established should eventually contribute to better care for the dying in the primary care sector.

Despite the fact that only very few professionals have formal education in palliative care, new hospices have been established in the past few years, and others are currently planned. Most importantly doctors are concerned about the risk of developing 'restricted' models of palliative. As development is ongoing and as pressure on the counties to allocate resources to this development is growing, there is a risk that palliative care services could be started without the presence of professionals with sufficient knowledge, skills and experience and that such restricted services could exert undue influence on the standards for future development. The threat of ambitious local politicians who consider hospices as a matter of prestige is at hand as Dr. Brunsgaard critically notes:

Local politicians are trying to establish hospices. I think they are running into trouble. It is easy to build the house but to get the people to run it, to get the right spirit inside, that is maybe not

67 Interview with Inge Thomsen, 07 June 2004, in Ålborg.

68 Interview with Kirsten Justessen, 07 June 2004, in Ålborg.

69 http://etisk.inforce.dk/graphics/03_udgivelser/publikationer/ENG003.htm#3.3

so easy. I think it is most important that you have the people you need to run it. Doctors who take care of the patients and staff educated for this purpose. [70]

There are contrasting views on the current standard of palliative care in Denmark. Some experts contend that a distinctive feature for palliative care should be that it is thoroughly ‚patient centred‘, open minded and in a constant process of development, compared to the Danish health service as a whole. Patients and relatives are, for example, involved in the evaluation process at KamillianerGaarden, the better to improve the service. [71] Kirsten Justessen has found that people involved in the field of palliative care in Denmark are working very hard to improve care for the dying: "I have been in this field for only 11/2 years, but I have experienced a high level of professional commitment and eagerness to increase knowledge. We strive to have a scientific approach in spite of low funding." [72]

However, not all experts in the field are of the same view. One refers to the concept of "chronic niceness" established by the well-known English chaplain Peter Speck. According to Speck, "chronic niceness" is a phenomenon among people working in the field of palliative care that could prove to be a stumbling block for future developments. [73] One example which supports this point of view is the scrappy implementation of the excellent national guidelines and recommendations. Tove Vejlgaard believes that "the risk of developing restricted models of palliative care is present, and unfortunately several services of this kind have already been established." [74] Based on the observations made during my stay in Denmark, these concerns do appear to be valid, in some instances. Although all services visited undoubtedly deliver good care for the dying, some were not as ‚patient centred‘ as one might hope. In those cases, the influence of management is dominant with very few formal evaluations of patients' needs in place. This is strikingly apparent in the (non-)use of volunteers.

As discussed earlier, in Denmark there is no distinctive culture of volunteerism in the healthcare system. Although the government has expressed a wish for volunteers to play a bigger role [75], other contradictory statements suggest that there may not be much of an increase in volunteering in the palliative care sector. As one expert notes:

They [the government] don't think it is the job of the people to take care of their mother or father when they get old, they say we have institutions to do that and where we can visit our elderly relatives from time to time. I don't think that is a very good part of the Danish family policy but actually that's how it is.

---

70 Interview with Dr. Niels Brunsgaard, 07 June 2004, in Ålborg.

71 Interview with Kirsten Justessen, 07 June 2004, in Ålborg. Interview with Ole Raakjær, 07 June 2004, in Ålborg.

72 Email from Kirsten Justessen, 04 November 2004.

73 Peter Speck: Working with dying people – on being good enough. In: Anton Obholzer/Vega Zagier Roberts (eds). The Unconscious at Work: individual and organisational stress in the human services. London 1994.

74 Interview with Tove Vejlgaard am 08.06.2004 in Århus.

75 Interview with Jette Blichfeldt, 10 June 2004, in Copenhagen.

The question remains as to whether the lack of a culture of volunteerism is a phenomenon of the Danish society as a whole or if it is the result of a unreadiness among some professionals and politicians working in the healthcare sector. The examples of Ålborg and Vejle demonstrate that it is not due to a sheer lack of willing volunteers. Whether this is a local phenomenon is the question. One observation made during the visit of one hospice could be significant: In this particular hospice volunteers are only used in the late afternoon and in the evening. In a conversation with a patient, the lady expressed that she often feels lonely in the hospice. Having visited more than 30 hospices in Europe and having spoken to several patients, this was a rather unusual thing to hear from a hospice patient. On inquiry, one of the nurses told us that most of the volunteers have day jobs and therefore cannot care for the patients during day time. "At the request of the voluntary coordinator, young and communicative volunteers" are preferred. There is nothing wrong with using young and communicative volunteers. However this should not happen at the expense of the patients, whose interests should always come first, in keeping with hospice philosophy. Most patients do not care about the volunteers' age – they just want someone to talk to, at any time of the day if possible. Furthermore it is alarming that "old people" are excluded and young volunteers are preferred for their "better communication skills". Communication skills are not the exclusive preserve of "young" people. They are also a matter of personality and life experience.

For some time the different organisations of hospice and palliative care in Denmark have coexisted, rather than working together. However it was always beyond dispute that all parties share the desire to improve care for the dying. Together with the *Danish Society of Palliative Medicine*,the opportunity should be taken to establish a Danish model of hospice and palliative care developed by both health professionals and members of civil society who might be regarded as the advocates of patients. Recent developments indicate the willingness of all parties to merge their expertise and interests to better care for the dying in Denmark. If this trend continues, standards of palliative care in Denmark will continue to improve.

Literature and sources

Amtsrådsforeningen (The association of Counties). Hjælp til at leve til man dør. (Help to live until you die). Amtsrådsforeningen. Copenhagen 2001.

Busch CJ, Cramon P, Timm H, and Wagner L. Palliativ indsats i Danmark (Palliative care in Denmark). DSI – Institut for Sundhedsvæsen. DSI 91.01. 1997.

Higginson, Irene: Palliative and Terminal Care. In: A. Stevens, J. Raftery (Hrsg.). *Palliative and Terminal Care Healthcare Needs Assessment*, S. 1 - 45. Oxford 1998.

Information brochure: Healthcare in Denmark. Ministry of the Interior and Health. 5th edition. 2002.

KamillianerGaarden Annual report 2003. Ålborg 2003.

Kræftens Bekæmpelse (The National Board of Cancer). Kræftdødsfald i Danmark (Cancer deaths in Denmark). 1998.

Kræftstyregruppen (the cancer steering committee). Den nationale kræftplan (The National Cancer Plan). 149 - 151. Sundhedsstyrelsen. Copenhagen 2000.

Population Division of the Department of Economic and Social Affairs of the United Nations Secretariat. *World Population Prospects: The 2002 Revision* and *World Urbanization Prospects: The 2001 Revision.*

Speck, Peter: Working with dying people – on being good enough. In: Anton Obholzer/Vega Zagier Roberts (eds). The Unconscious at Work: individual and organisational stress in the human services. London 1994.

Sundhedsstyrelsen (National board of health). Terminal pleje (terminal care). Sundhedsstyrelsen. Copenhagen 1986.

Sundhedsstyrelsen (National board of health). Omsorg for alvorligt syge og døende (Care for seriously ill and dying patients). Sundhedsstyrelsen. Copenhagen 1996.

Sundhedsstyrelsen (National board of health). Faglige retningslinier for den palliative indsats (Guidelines for palliative care). Sundhedsstyrelsen. Copenhagen 1999.

Undervisningsministeriet (The Ministry of Education). Bekendtgørelse om sygeplejerskeuddannelsen (Executive order on the nursing education). 232 af 30.03.2001. 2001.

Vejlgaard, Tove Bahn: Educational needs in palliative care of doctors and nurses in a Danish county hospital and the related primary care. Dissertation project. Msc in Palliative Care. King's College London January 2002.

Internet sources

http://esa.un.org/unpp
http://www.aek.or.at/EUSTUDPPT/systeme.html
http://www.sanktlukas.dk/
http://www.sctmariahospice.dk/
http://www.stm.dk/publikationer/Regeringsgrundlag/reggrund\%20uk\%202001.html
http://etisk.inforce.dk/graphics/03_udgivelser/publikationer/ENG003.htm#3.3

List of interviews (in chronological order)

- Kirsten Justessen, Assistant matron, *KamillianerGaarden Hospice* Ålborg, 07 June 2004
- Ole Raakjær, Chaplain, *KamillianerGaarden Hospice* Ålborg, 07 June 2004
- Inge Thomsen, Voluntary coordinator, *KamillianerGaarden Hospice* Ålborg, 07 June 2004
- Annette Majlund, Music therapist, *KamillianerGaarden Hospice* Ålborg, 07 June 2004
- Dr. Niels Brunsgaard, Doctor, *KamillianerGaarden Hospice* Ålborg, 07 June 2004
- Dr. Tove Vejlgaard, Medical director, *St. Maria Hospice*; Board member *Danish Society of Palliative Medicine* Århus, 08 June 2004
- Jytte Husted, Director of nursing, *Hospice Søholm* Århus, 09 June 2004
- Dr. Nan Sonne, Doctor, Palliative Care unit *Bispebjerg hospital* Copenhagen, 10 June 2004
- Jette Riis, Director of the nursing home care team, *St. Lukas Hospice* Copenhagen, 10 June 2004

- Annedorte Friberg, Director of the nursing of the inpatient team at *St. Lukas Hospice* Copenhagen, 10 June 2004
- Jette Blichfeldt, *Ministry of Interior and Health* Copenhagen, 10 June 2004
- Helle Tingrupp, Leader, *Hospice Diakonissestiftelsens* Copenhagen, 11 June 2004
- Charlotte Kjaersgard, Nurse, *Hospice Diakonissestiftelsens* Copenhagen, 11 June 2004

England

Marcel Globisch

1. General conditions

1.1 Demographics

- In 2000 the population of Great Britain [1] numbered almost 59 million; 9 million higher than in 1950. The population is expected to continue to climb by some 7 million to 66 million inhabitants by 2050. [2]
- Since the first half of the 1950s the average life expectancy of 69.2 has risen about nine years to 78.2 years of age. By 2050 another rise is expected to bring the average age to 83. [3]
- In 1950, those aged 65 years or older in Great Britain constituted 10.7% of the population. In 2000, it had already reached 15.9% and is projected to grow to 23% by 2050. [4]
- Similarly, people aged 80 years or older constituted 1.5% of the population in 1950. That percentage grew in 2000 to 4.1 and is estimated to grow to 8.5 by 2050. [5]
- Demographic support ratios are used as indicators for the ratio of the working-age population to the non-working-age population. The older-person support ratio, the number of persons aged 15 to 64 years per older person (those over the age of 65), was 66.9% of the total population in 1950. In 2000, the support ratio decreased to 65.1%, and is expected to drop to 60.6% by 2050. A decline in birth rates continues to point towards an ageing British society. In the first half of the 1960s an average of 966,000 people were born each year. In 2005 this figure had dropped to 653,000 people. [6]

---

1 All demographic data by the United Nations apply to Great Britain. There are no separate stats available for England in the *World Population Prospects.*

2 Population Division of the Department of Economic and Social Affairs of the United Nations Secretariat, *World Population Prospects: The 2002 Revision* and *World Urbanization Prospects: The 2001 Revision.* Official Homepage of the United Nations: http://esa.un.org/unpp

3 ibid.

4 ibid.

5 ibid.

6 ibid.

- Around 520,000 people die each year in England. Cancer accounts for a quarter (130,000) of these deaths. Other terminal illnesses include coronary heart disease (22%), respiratory disease (16%) and cerebrovascular diseases, including stroke, (11%).[7]
- Over half of all patients wish to be cared for and to die at home. However, in 2000 67% of all deaths occurred in a hospital or similar inpatient NHS or non-NHS establishment. Only 19% occurred at home and 4% in hospices. The remaining 21% of deaths in England occur in a variety of other institutions (e.g. care homes, private nursing homes, etc.). In terms of cancer patients, only 25% realise this wish of dying at home. More than 50% die in NHS hospitals, 18% in hospices and the remaining 7% in other institutions (e.g. care homes).[8]

1.2 Health care system

Unlike other countries such as Germany, there is no compulsory health insurance in Great Britain. The health of the community is the responsibility of the National Health Service (NHS). The NHS is free of cost at the point of delivery to any resident of Britain. All taxpayers, employers and employees contribute to operational costs.[9]

The vast majority of people are seen by primary care services in the community. They remain the first points of contact most people have with the NHS. They cater to about 90% of patient contacts with the health service, at half the cost of hospital care. The government's long-standing policy is to build up and extend these services to relieve the more costly secondary care services of hospital and specialists.[10]

There are no fees to the patient for services provided by the NHS. The patient has the freedom to choose doctors and hospitals within the NHS subject to acceptance by the doctor in question. If patients cannot find a doctor willing to accept them, the Primary Care Trust will assign a patient to a doctor's list. There is no direct access to specialists; patients are admitted by the family doctor. The same procedure applies in most cases for hospital admissions. Normally family doctors select the hospital best suited to the patient's needs. Again, there is no charge for the patient except for if the patient asks for special amenities or treatment that is not clinically necessary.[11]

---

7 Health Select Committee. Hospices and Palliative Care. Memorandum from Department of Health. No. 7. Session 2003 - 04, p. 3.

8 Julia Addington-Hall: Care of the dying and the NHS. Briefing paper for Nuffield Trust. März 2003. In.: Health Select Committee. Hospices and Palliative Care. Memorandum from Department of Health. No. 7. Session 2003 - 04, p. 14.

9 cp. Federal Ministry of Health and Social Security: Sozial-Kompass Europa. Soziale Sicherheit in Europa im Vergleich. Bonn 2003.

10 http://elt.britcoun.org.pl/h_what.htm#NHS

11 http://www.europa.eu.int/comm/employment_social/missoc/2003/uk_part2_en.htm

2. Hospices and Palliative care in England

2.1 History

The modern hospice movement in England, as well as the rest of the world, is closely connected with Dame Cicely Saunders. In 1967, she founded St. Christopher's Hospice; the first modern hospice in the world. From her experience as a nurse, social worker, and doctor, Dame Cicely saw holistic palliative care as something that patients needed. However, it could not be created within the NHS at the time because neither the environment nor the willingness to deliver holistic and patient-centred care existed. [12] Nevertheless, she always envisaged that this model of care would be transferred back into the NHS. [13] Hospice Care was first developed in the UK by the *voluntary sector* [14], but is increasingly being provided within NHS hospitals and palliative care centres within the community.

Today her vision is a recognised and integral part of health provision. [15] At the same time, the term "palliative care" seems to be the more commonly used term by professionals, though it is still often synonymous with the more traditional expression "hospice care". ‚Hospice' institutions and ‚palliative care' institutions are referred to interchangeably, [16] which can be confusing at times for those observing the English system from outside. In contrast to Germany, where palliative wards and voluntary hospices represent two different concepts, there is no such strict division between palliative- and hospice-care inpatient services in England. The term "palliative wards" was not used by any of our experts. A so-called hospice can be located in a hospital building, an unthinkable scenario in Germany. [17]

Since 1987 health authorities in England have been required to make plans for palliative care provision; however, their record in doing so has been patchy. [18] In 1999 a

[12] Health Select Committee. Hospices and Palliative Care. Memorandum from Department of Health. No. 7. Session 2003 - 04, p. 4.

[13] Dame Cicely Saunders: The evolution of palliative care. Reprinted from The Pharos of Alpha Omega Alpha Honor Medical Society. Volume 66. Number 3. Summer 2003, p. 6.

[14] The *voluntary sector* includes all free-standing, independent hospices. Most of them are run by charities, i.e. Marie Curie, Sue Ryder. Although most of them receive money from the NHS, they count as non-NHS services.

[15] cp. et al.: Jane Seymour et al.: Palliative care and policy in England: a review of health improvement plans in 1999 - 2003. In: *Palliative Medicine*. 2002. Volume 16. Issue 1, p. 5.

[16] This can be exemplified by *St. John's Hospice* in London. On the organisation's website it is declared as a hospice (cp. http://www.hje.org.uk/hospice.html), whereas in the *Hospice Directory 2004* it is listed as *St. John's Palliative Care Centre* (cp. Hospice Directory 2004. Hospice and Palliative Care Services in the United Kingdom and Ireland. London 2004). However it has been recently recognised by the organisation that it is confusing to call themselves St John's Palliative care centre and Hospice. Therefore they are now called St John's Hospice. Personal E-mail correspondence with Melissa Reddish, 08 October 2004.

[17] Again the *St. John's Hospice* cites as an example. It is located in a hospital setting but bears the name hospice. But Melissa Reddish points out, "that it is an unusual situation at St Johns that the Hospice works alongside a private hospital. This has happened as part of a history specifically to this place and is not a common occurrence." Personal E-mail correspondence with Melissa Reddish, 08 October 2004.

[18] Jane Seymour et al.: Palliative care and policy in England: a review of health improvement plans in

survey of health authorities, commissioned by the Department of Health, showed wide regional variations between those with agreed and published plans. [19] The *Calman-Hine-Report* [20] released in 1995 was a very influential report. It represented a vision of what future cancer services should look like and helped bring about substantial change in the field. [21]

2.2 Hospice and Palliative Care Provision

Adult inpatient Units	Adult Units	NHS Units	Vol[299]	Beds	NHS Beds	Vol	Children	Beds
England	172	42	130	2637	490	2147	27	201

Table 1: Hospice and Palliative Care Services in England (January 2004) [22] [23]

Inpatient services

In England, there are a total of 172 adult units. Approximately 80% of the 2,637 specialist palliative care beds are in voluntary hospices; the remaining 20% are provided by the NHS. The average NHS percentage funding for this inpatient activity is currently just over 30%, the rest is provided by charitable means (see 2.3 Legal regulations and funding). [24] Hospital teams are fully paid by the NHS; there are no voluntary

1999 - 2003. In: *Palliative Medicine*. 2002. Volume 16. Issue 1, p. 5. cp.: Department of Health. HC (87) 4 (2). London 1987.

19 National Council for Hospice and Specialist Palliative Care Services The palliative care survey 1999. National Council for Hospice and Specialist Palliative Care Services London 2000. Zit. n.: Jane Seymour et al.: Palliative care and policy in England: a review of health improvement plans in 1999 - 2003. In: *Palliative Medicine*. 2002. Volume 16. Issue 1, p. 6.

20 The *Calman-Hine-Report* is available for download on the official website of the Department of Health: http://www.dh.gov.uk/assetRoot/04/01/43/66/04014366.pdf

21 Interview with Prof Alison Richardson, 18 March 2004, in London.

22 Hospice Directory 2004: Hospice and Palliative Care services in the United Kingdom and Ireland. London 2004, p. 145 et seq.

23 The voluntary units include 10 Marie Curie hospices with 244 beds and 6 Sue Ryder units with 113 beds. The remainder are independent local charities including 2 services exclusively for HIV/AIDS with 54 beds.

24 Andrew Hoy: Written Evidence to the House of Commons Health Committee regarding Palliative Care. 25.02.2004.

funded hospital teams. In addition, there are currently 27 paediatric units (201 beds) in England.

The differences between NHS and voluntary services are narrowing and merging. The ethos is similar in both sectors. The training of staff has increased in similarity regardless of whether they work for the NHS or non-NHS services. All staff, including nurses, doctors and allied healthcare professionals, undertake advanced training in Specialist Palliative Care.[25] Nonetheless, there are striking differences remaining. So far the voluntary sector has always benefited from the fact that whatever it could raise, it could spend. As a consequence, the voluntary sector has provided better quality buildings, staff and food, plus more pleasant surroundings and the like. "If you would put this into an analogy, one would say, that voluntary hospices provide Rolls-Royce service, while we – as an NHS unit – it's more like a Ford Focus service."[26]

However, *voluntary hospices* continue to rely enormously on public goodwill, which can be quite difficult as Andrew Langford points out. As the average NHS funding is just over 30%, the long-term financial status remains insecure.[27] Donations and legacies are still vital to the survival of the hospice community, accounting for 66% of total income in 1997.[28]

According to Dr Naysmith, normally the average length of stay in *voluntary hospices* is shorter compared to inpatient NHS-units.

> The voluntary sector is always very aware that it has to please the public from which they are subsidised. If the unit is always full and people only have a slight chance of getting into the hospice people will not want to donate their money. Therefore, it is better to serve as many patients as possible. Because of this voluntary hospices tend to be more careful about the people they admit and have a tendency not to admit people that might stay a long time.[29]

In contrast, NHS Palliative Care units have to reach a certain number of admissions per year set by the NHS to receive their funding. The targets are neither very demanding nor strict at the moment. For example, if there is a good reason to keep a patient for a period of three months because no other services are available, and they cannot be cared for at home either, the NHS normally would agree to the longer stay.[30] However, this could change in the near future as a new system of funding is discussed. Today a certain amount of money is paid per year by the NHS. The new system would see that the *NHS palliative care units* receive money per care episode. Dr Naysmith states: "Then I will also be driven that people won't stay too long because I won't have enough money to afford to keep them for a long time."[31]

---

25 Interview with Dr Anne Naysmith, 16 March 2004, in London. Interview with Andrew Langford, 17 March 2004, in London.

26 Interview with Dr Anne Naysmith, 16 March 2004, in London.

27 Interview with Andrew Langford, 17 March 2004, in London.

28 Avril Jackson/ Ann Eve: Hospice Care in Britain, 145. In: Dame Cicely Saunders/ Robert Kastenbaum (Ed.): Hospice Care on the International Scene. New York 2001; The continuing importance of legacies for the voluntary sector was also expressed by Dr John Ellershaw. Interview with Dr John Ellershaw, 22 March 2004, in Liverpool.

29 Interview with Dr Anne Naysmith, 16 March 2004, in London.

The government is trying to reduce the variation because at present across England one hospital might keep its patient for three days for a certain procedure, while another may keep the patient for ten days with no medical reason for that variation. With the new system, it will be uneconomical to keep the patient for ten days and drive everybody nearer to the average. [32]

Dr Naysmith prefers the old system because "it allows more flexibility and is more patient-centred." [33] Compared to *NHS* services, *Voluntary hospices*have more freedom. Amongst other areas, this can be seen in the use of more radical complementary therapies. Andrew Langford discussed the advantages of *voluntary hospices* relating to the use of complementary therapies; "the use of complementary therapies has become an integral part of most voluntary hospice services. In a society where there has been a boom in interest in complementary therapies the Specialist Palliative Care field has responded excellently in accessing and providing therapies patients now want as a part of their care package" [34]

But it is also important to point out that whereas there is clear evidence of patients and carers appreciating complementary services, there is much less clear evidence on their impact on outcomes at this time. [35] For that reason evaluative research of the cost effectiveness and safety of different complementary therapies in supportive and palliative care is needed. [36]

Patient statistics in 2002 [37]

- 42,000 new patients admitted to an inpatient unit
- 58,000 admissions
- 95% suffering from cancer
- 29,000 deaths occurred
- 13 days average stay in a hospice
- 150,000 patients seen by home care teams
- 3 - 4 months average length of home care
- 151,000 died of cancer in the UK

Care at home

There are currently 264 *Home Care teams* and another 81 *Hospice at Home services* that enable patients to stay at home longer, and often render admission to an inpa-

33 ibid.

34 Interview with Andrew Langford, 17 March 2004, in London.

35 Interview with Prof Alison Richardson, 18 March 2004, in London.

36 National Institute for Clinical Excellence: Guidance on cancer Services Improving Supportive and Palliative Care for Adults with Cancer – the Manual, London 2004, p. 155. Official homepage of the National Institute for Clinical Excellence. http://www.nice.org.uk/pdf/csgspmanual.pdf

37 Patients statistics apply for the whole UK. In: National Council for Hospice and Specialist Palliative Care Services: National Survey of patient activity data for Specialist Palliative Care Services for the year 2002 - 3.

38 Hospice Directory 2004: Hospice and Palliative Care services in the United Kingdom and Ireland. London 2004, p. 145 et seq.

	Home Care	Hospice at Home	Day Care	Hospital Support Nurses	Hospital Support Teams
England	**264**	**81**	**211**	**53**	**220**

Table 2: Community and Hospital Support Services (January 2004) [38]

tient unit unnecessary. Hospice and palliative care enable this for people by providing specialist advice and working along with GPs and district nurses. Many teams, often known as *Hospice at Home*, deliver extended palliative nursing, medical, social and emotional support in the patients' homes, as well as in nursing and elderly homes in order to support patients and their families. Care can be provided for crisis management or on a long-term basis. There are a wide range of different models of *Hospice at home*, varying from *rapid response teams* [39] offering specialist support, to the provision of less intensive, on-going support. Some teams are able to offer 24-hour access to care. *Marie Curie nurses*, for example, provide hands-on, round-the-clock nursing care for patients in their own homes. These nurses are usually requested by the district nurse. Many of the community nurse specialists in palliative care are *Macmillan nurses* whose services have been funded initially by the charity, *Macmillan Cancer Relief* (see 2.4. National organisations). [40]

Hospital-based services

Hospital services include Hospital Palliative Care Teams, Macmillan Support Services, and Symptom Control Team. They are advisory services working within a hospital setting providing symptom control, pain relief, and emotional support for patients and care givers, as well as education and support for staff. Some of the hospital teams include an entire team of doctors, nurses, social workers and chaplains, while others offer a single support nurse. [41]

Day care services

Day Care is provided by 211 services in England. Day care is a supplement to home care services that allows patients to continue living at home while maintaining contact with all the hospice facilities once or twice a week. Services may include medical and nursing care, spiritual support, physiotherapy, occupational therapy and comple-

---

39 For more information on *rapid response teams* see: Gerry King et al.: Dying at home: evaluation of a hospice rapid-response service. In: International Journal of Palliative Nursing. 2000. Volume 6. No. 6, p. 280 - 287.

40 Hospice Directory 2004: Hospice and Palliative Care services in the United Kingdom and Ireland. London 2004, p. vi.

41 ibid.

mentary therapies.[42] A wide range of creative and social activities is provided to give patients the opportunity to regain some element of control and confidence.[43] Patients also have the chance to meet other terminally ill patients who are in a similar situation and share their experiences, which can be very helpful in helping them to cope with difficult circumstances.[44]

2.3 Legal regulations and funding

National policy in relation to palliative care is set out in the *NHS Cancer Plan*[45] and in the *National Service Frameworks (NSFs)*[46]. Three of the four key aims of the *NHS Cancer Plan* (2000) are relevant to palliative care. These are:

1. To ensure people with cancer get the right professional support and care as well as the best treatments;
2. To tackle inequalities;
3. To build for the future through investments in the workforce and research.[47]

In order to achieve these targets, the *NHS Cancer Plan* provided *specialist palliative care* services with £50 Million pounds sterling for 2003.[48]

Estimates made by the *National Council for Hospice and Specialist Palliative Care Services (NCHSPCS)* for the year 2000 signified that total expenditure on *adult specialist palliative care services* was around £300 million; of this around £170 million was provided by the *voluntary sector* and £130 million was provided by the *NHS.* Around £215 Million was related to the provision of inpatient services managed by voluntary providers (£150 Million voluntary and £65 Million NHS) and a further £34 Million related to *NHS* managed services. *Community specialist palliative care service* expenses amounted to £37 Million and expenditures on *hospital specialist palliative care teams* amounted to £14 Million.[49]

---

42 Hospice Directory 2004: Hospice and Palliative Care services in the United Kingdom and Ireland. London 2004, vi.

43 Avril Jackson/ Ann Eve: Hospice Care in Britain, p. 147. In: Dame Cicely Saunders/ Robert Kastenbaum (Ed.): Hospice Care on the International Scene. New York 2001.

44 Interview with Sheena Boyd, 08 July 2003, in London.

45 The complete *NHS Cancer Plan* is available for download on the official website of the Department of Health: http://www.dh.gov.uk/assetRoot/04/01/45/13/04014513.pdf

46 *National Service Frameworks (NSFs)* set national standards and identify key interventions for a defined service or care group. More information on *NSFs* is available via: http://www.dh.gov.uk/PolicyAndGuidance/HealthAndSocialCareTopics/HealthAndSocialCareArticle/fs/en?CONTENT{_}ID=4070951\&chk=W3ar/W

47 Health Select Committee. Hospices and Palliative Care. Memorandum from Department of Health. No. 7. Session 2003 - 04, p. 6.

48 Department of Health: Action to ensure £50 million investment in palliative care delivers the best services for patients. 23.12.2002. Reference number 2002/0531.

49 Health Select Committee. Hospices and Palliative Care. Memorandum from Department of Health. No. 7. Session 2003 - 04, p. 5.

Average funding by the NHS for voluntary hospices is currently just over 30%.[50] NHS bodies are able to make arrangements with voluntary hospices for the provision of services by the voluntary bodies on particular terms and conditions. These provisions enable an NHS body to enter into arrangements with a hospice on such terms as may be agreed for the hospice to provide services which would otherwise be available on the NHS, or which it is desired should be provided to NHS patients by the hospice.[51]

The Department of Health announced a central budget for specialist palliative care provision from 2003 - 2006 to tackle the inequalities in access to specialist palliative care and to enable the NHS to make a more realistic contribution to the costs of hospices in providing agreed levels of service.[52] According to Dr John Ellershaw, Medical Director at the Marie Curie Centre, Liverpool, "there are plans the government is working out, as to how much core services should cost for palliative care patients, and it is thought that that may well be more than 70 or 80% of our running costs. In 2008 there will be new funding mechanisms that may give hospices more money."[53]

At the moment voluntary hospices are funded by a broad sheet agreement. As stated by Andrew Langford, Managing Director at the *Trinity Hospice* in London, the new system could work out well for the voluntary sector:

> It will be very interesting. I personally think that we might be better off. At the moment we get thirty percent of our funding from the NHS, that's based on 80 percent occupancy. This year we've been running at about 90 percent occupancy but we didn't get any more money from the NHS so we have exceeded their targets. I think if we can continue in that way, and we were funded on what we do rather than an agreement, we come out of it quite well [...] I think it will be a lot fairer way of funding services.[54]

Four years ago the *National Institute for Clinical Excellence (NICE)* was asked by the Department of Health to develop guidance on *Supportive and Palliative Care Services for Adults with Cancer*. This was completed in March 2004.[55] Relevant professional and patient stakeholders were involved in the development process of the 209-page document, and Professor Alison Richardson chaired the guidance development group. Recommendations were made on a total of thirteen topics:

- Co-ordination of care,
- User involvement in planning, developing and evaluating services,

---

50 Andrew Hoy: Written Evidence to the House of Commons Health Committee regarding Palliative Care. 25.02.2004.

51 Health Select Committee. Hospices and Palliative Care. Memorandum from Department of Health. No. 7. Session 2003 - 04, p. 50.

52 Department of Health. Planning and funding specialist palliative care provision 2003/04 - 2005/06. http://www.dh.gov.uk/assetRoot/04/06/08/61/04060861.pdf

53 Interview with Dr John Ellershaw, 22 March 2004, in Liverpool.

54 Interview with Andrew Langford, 17 March 2004, in London.

55 National Institute for Clinical Excellence: Guidance on Cancer Services Improving Supportive and Palliative Care for Adults with Cancer – the Manual, London 2004. The complete document is available for download: http://www.nice.org.uk/pdf/csgspmanual.pdf

- Face-to-face communication,
- Information,
- Psychological support services,
- Social support services,
- Spiritual support services,
- General palliative care services; including care of dying patients,
- Specialist palliative care services,
- Rehabilitation services,
- Complementary therapy services,
- Services for families and carers, including bereavement care,
- Research in supportive and palliative care plus current evidence and recommendations for the direction and design of future research. Professor Richardson talks about the impact of the NICE-guidance:

> The *NICE-Guidance* is a must-do. It is given to all the chief executives, to the hospitals, to the health authorities, you have to implement it [...] It's a must-do for voluntary hospices as well if they want NHS money [...] Based on the guidance a standards document is developed against which services are then assessed. That's a bit like a stick [...]. And again, if hospices wish to maintain income that is the NHS part of the money, they will have to deliver to those standards. [56]

However, the guidance is not a standard document outlining how particular services should look, rather it outlines what the core of any service should be. For example, it states there should be inpatient beds, but it does not say whether they should be in a hospice or in a hospital. In addition, no firm recommendations are given concerning palliative day care services because there is not enough evidence at present. The guidance makes statements about education but it is not a standard document. It is the responsibility of the professional and statutory bodies to ensure services resemble a certain form. [57]

2.4 Organisations

Help the Hospices [58] *(HTP)* is a national charity for the hospice movement which was founded by the Duchess of Norfolk, in 1994. *HTP* supports hospices throughout the UK through grant-aid, training, education, information, national fundraising and advice. *HTP* runs an extensive central training programme, offers subsidies to hospices for educational programmes and provides individual bursary awards for hospice staff. Through the *Independent Hospice Representative Committee HTP* gives voice to the common interests and concerns of independent hospices. In addition, HTP is facilitating the development of a UK network of organisations and individual supporting services overseas through the UK Forum for hospice and palliative care worldwide. In

56 Interview with Prof Alison Richardson, 18 March 2004, in London.

57 ibid.

58 More information: http://www.helpthehospicep.org.uk/

the future this will include a funding structure to support hospices overseas, developing training and education for international staff and advocacy programmes.

Hospice information[59] *(HI)* is a joint venture between the *St Christopher's Hospice* and *HTP*. *HI* is a worldwide resource for professionals and the public which encourages sharing of information and experience amongst those involved in hospice and palliative care. *HI* offers a comprehensive enquiry service, website and statistical information. The publications include UK and International Directories, a range of electronic news bulletins, quarterly magazines, listings of educational and job opportunities as well as a range of practical advice and information leaflets and reports. Avril Jackson, Information Officer at *HI*, underlines the importance of an information service such as *HI*: "I think very strongly that in any country where you've got a hospice and/or palliative care movement that is evolving, information should be a crucial part of your strategy."[60] *HI* runs aprofessional database that includes 100 professionals who are willing to work as volunteers in developing countries in order to share their knowledge in palliative care.

Macmillan Cancer Relief[61] *(MCR)* is a UK charity that works to improve the quality of life for people living with cancer and their families. *MCR* funds *Macmillan* nurses and doctors, who specialise in cancer care. It builds cancer care units for inpatient and day care and gives grants to patients in financial need. *MCR* also funds a medical support and education programme to improve doctors' and nurses' skills in cancer care.

Marie Curie Cancer Care[62] *(MCCC)* provides ten inpatient centres in Great Britain; more than 2,800 Marie Curie nurses care for people in their own homes. MCCC also has a Research Institute and an Education Service for health professionals involved in cancer and palliative care.

The ***National Council for Palliative Care***[63] acts as the co-ordinating and representative organisation for hospice and palliative care in England, Wales und Northern Ireland. It represents the views and interests of hospice and palliative care services to government, health authorities, the media and statutory and voluntary national agencies. It provides advice and supports the sharing of knowledge, information and experience. The *National Council for Palliative Care* is actively involved in the making of clinical guidelines in Palliative Care – for example, the *NICE-Guidance on Supportive and Palliative Care Services for Adults with Cancer*. It also publishes a quarterly magazine, *Information Exchange*, and a series of occasional papers.

Sue Ryder Care[64] runs 18 centres in the UK that provide care for patients and residents with many different disabilities and diseases. Each care centre specialises to meet the needs of the local community. Services include long-term care, respite care,

---

59 More information on the work of hospice information: http://www.hospiceinformation.info/
60 Interview with Avril Jackson, 15 March 2004, in London.
61 More information via: http://www.macmillan.org.uk/
62 More information on: http://www.mariecurie.org.uk/
63 More information via: http://www.ncpc.org.uk/
64 More information available on: http://www.suerydercare.org/

specialist palliative care, rehabilitation, day care and domiciliary care. Six of those inpatient services are hospices.

2.5 Education and training of professional staff

When Dame Cicely Saunders established *St Christopher's Hospice,* and later*Hospice Information*, one of her founding principles was to regard the hospice as a place where people could learn and share their experiences, a place where education, training and research take place "to raise standards generally and also to stimulate others to think about these problems."[65] Today, many hospices in England, in fact all over the world, follow these principles:

> Like many hospices we regard education as a large part of our role. Not only to provide services for patients that need them, we also spend a lot of time training primary care staff, staff from hospitals and others.[66]

Doctors: In 1996 a document was published by the general medical council which identified core objectives of training within the medical undergraduate education framework. One of these is the care of the dying. In Liverpool, undergraduate medical students spend one month of their undergraduate training in palliative care.[67]

Only a few general practitioners (GPs) received formal education in palliative medicine.[68] The *Gold Standards Framework (GSF)*[69] is one of several models that aim to enhance the quality of palliative care services provided by GP practices.[70] It is already being implemented in 500 practices across Great Britain.[71]

The Gold Standards Framework[72][73] aims to improve the quality and organisation of palliative care provided by the whole primary care team by developing the practice-based organisation

65 cp. Dame Cicely Saunders: Watch with me. Inspirations for a life in hospice care. Sheffield 2003, p. 2 et seq.

66 Interview with Andrew Langford, 17 March 2004, in London.

67 Interview with Dr John Ellershaw, 22 March 2004, in Liverpool.

68 Interview with Dr Anne Naysmith, 17 March 2004, in London.

69 Keri Thomas: The Gold Standards Framework in community palliative care. In: *European Journal of Palliative Care* Volume 10. Number 3. 2003, p. 113 - 115. cp. also: The Macmillan Gold Standards Framework Programme in http://www.macmillan.org.uk/showdocument.asp?id=271

70 There are several articles that look into the role of GP's in palliative care: cp. et al.: Department of Health: Quality Standards in the Delivery of GP Out of Hours Services London June 2002; Barbara Hanratty: Palliative care provided by GPs: the carer's viewpoint. In: *British Journal of General Practice*. Volume50. No. 457. London 2000, p. 653 - 654; Catherine Shipman et al.: Building bridges in palliative care: evaluating a GP Facilitator programme. In: *Palliative Medicine* 2003. Number 17, p. 621 - 627; Catherine Shipman et al.: How and why do GPs use specialist palliative care services? In: *Palliative Medicine 2002*. Volume 16. Issue 3, p. 241 - 246.

71 Health Select Committee. Hospices and Palliative Care. Memorandum from Department of Health. No. 7. Session 2003 - 04, p. 7.

72 Keri Thomas: Caring for the Dying at Home. Companions on a journey. Oxford 2003. In: National Institute for Clinical Excellence: Guidance on Cancer Services Improving Supportive and Palliative Care for Adults with Cancer – the Manual, London 2004, p. 122.

73 Keri Thomas: The Gold Standards Framework in community palliative care. In: *European Journal of Palliative Care.* Volume 10. Number 3. 2003, p. 113 - 115. cp. also: The Macmillan Gold Standards

of care of dying patients. The framework focuses on seven key tasks – optimising continuity of care, teamwork, advanced planning (including out-of-hours), symptom control, and patient, carer and staff support. Early evaluation data are becoming available [74], with findings confirming an increase in patients dying in their preferred place and improved quality of care as perceived by the practitioners involved. [75] [76]

An evaluation in England found that one of the strengths of the programme was the enhancement of GPs' positive attitudes towards specialist services, improving communication between primary care and specialist palliative care. [77] Since April 2004 a new contract between GPs and the NHS has been introduced that should also contribute to the willingness of GPs to improve their skills in the care of the dying. The contract states: "they have to perform palliative care, and are not allowed to opt out of it. They can opt out of most things but not palliative care. But they only have to do it between 9am-5pm from Monday to Friday. [78]

In England, the Royal College of Physicians is the medical college responsible for the speciality of Palliative Medicine. The medical speciality is relatively young, receiving formal recognition in 1987. A palliative medicine training programme lasts four years. [79]The government recognises that the current numbers of palliative medicine practitioners is inadequate in relation to demands on the service and it is also unevenly distributed across the country. [80] The Government's workforce census showed 155 consultants in September 2002 in the UK. [81] In written evidence given to*House of Commons,* Dr Andrew Hoy asserts there are at least 100 posts unfilled in England alone. [82] However, based on the number of specialist registrars currently

---

Framework Programme in http://www.macmillan.org.uk/showdocument.asp?id=271. NHS Modernisation Agenciep. Cancer Services Collaborative. http://www.modern.nhp.uk/cancer

74 NHS Modernisation Agency and Macmillan Cancer Relief: *Gold Standards Framework: interim evaluation report.* Unpublished. January 2003. In: National Institute for Clinical Excellence: Guidance on Cancer Services Improving Supportive and Palliative Care for Adults with Cancer – the Manual, London 2004, p. 122.

75 Nigel King et al.: *Gold Standards Framework. Phase 2: Qualitative case study evaluation – final report.* Primary Care Research Group. School of Human and Health Sciences. University of Huddersfield. 2003. In: National Institute for Clinical Excellence: Guidance on Cancer Services Improving Supportive and Palliative Care for Adults with Cancer – the Manual, London 2004, p. 122.

76 National Institute for Clinical Excellence: Guidance on Cancer Services Improving Supportive and Palliative Care for Adults with Cancer – the Manual, London 2004, p. 122.

77 Catherine Shipman et al.: *Building Bridges: The Macmillan GP Facilitator Programme in Palliative Care: an evaluation. Report to Macmillan Cancer Relief.* London. Department of Palliative Care & Policy, King's College. 2001.In: National Institute for Clinical Excellence: Guidance on Cancer Services Improving Supportive and Palliative Care for Adults with Cancer – the Manual, London 2004, p. 122.

78 Interview with Dr Anne Naysmith, 17 March 2004, in London.

79 ibid.

80 Health Select Committee. Hospices and Palliative Care. Memorandum from Department of Health. No. 7. Session 2003 - 04, p. 10.

81 ibid.

82 Hoy, Andrew: Written Evidence to the House of Commons Health Committee regarding Palliative Care, 25.02.2004. cp. et al. Interview with Dr Anne Naysmith, 17 March 2004, in London.

in training and the age profile of the existing consultant workforce, the number of consultants is expected to grow substantially over the next few years. [83]

Nurses: Between 1997 and September 2002 there was a net increase in nurses working in the NHS of 50,000. According to a government paper, this increase will enable the recruitment of additional district nurses, plus those on wards caring for patients with terminal illness, cancer site specific specialists and palliative care nurse specialists. [84] However, Dr Naysmith says that it will take "many years before we have an increased number of doctors and nurses to provide a decent service. [85]

In 2002 a study was released that dealt with care for terminally ill patients from the district nurse's perspective. [86] [87] Kerri Wright has stated that district nurses view themselves as having a central and valued role in terminal care, yet studies have highlighted concerns that they may not have the necessary skills to provide effective terminal care." [88] At the moment, palliative care is only taught to a small amount in the general training for nurses. [89] Thus Wright believes that changes have to be made in this area:

> This study has highlighted how important the relationship between the district nurse and the terminally ill client and carer is in both identifying and meeting their needs at home [...] the importance of formal structures to be put in place within palliative care and district nurse training to allow the opportunity and skills for this relationship to be fostered and developed. [90]

Consequently £6 million has been allocated between 2001 and 2006 as part of the NHS Cancer Plan to improve the training of district nurses in relation to palliative care. Early indications are that this funding has enabled the participation of 10,000 nurses and other health care professionals in continuing professional development programmes and that it has been very well received. A formal evaluation is currently in progress. [91]

Macmillan specialist palliative care nursing services were first established in Great Britain in 1975. Today there are more than 2,000 Macmillan nurses in the UK who

---

83 Health Select Committee. Hospices and Palliative Care. Memorandum from Department of Health. No. 7. Session 2003 - 04, p. 10.

84 ibid. p. 10 et seq.

85 Interview with Dr Anne Naysmith, 17 March 2004, in London.

86 Kerri Wright: Caring for the terminally ill: the district nurse's perspective. In: *British Journal of Nursing*. 2002. Volume 11. No. 18.

87 Another article that concentrates on the role of *district nurses* caring for dying patients is: Lynne Hughes: Palliative Care in the Community. *Primary Health Care*. Volume 14. Nr. 6. July 2004, p. 27 - 31. The article is available for download: http://www.nursing-standard.co.uk/archives/phc_pdfs/phcvol14-06/phcv14n6p2731.pdf

88 Kerri Wright: Caring for the terminally ill: the district nurse's perspective. In: *British Journal of Nursing*. 2002. Volume 11. No. 18, p. 1180.

89 Interview with Ann Lee and Averil Parry, 26 March 2004, in Taunton.

90 Kerri Wright: Caring for the terminally ill: the district nurse's perspective. In: *British Journal of Nursing*. 2002. Volume 11. No. 18, p. 1185.

91 Health Select Committee. Hospices and Palliative Care. Memorandum from Department of Health. No. 7. Session 2003 - 04, p. 7.

deliver palliative care to patients with cancer.*Macmillan nurses* have specialised in *Cancer Care* und *Palliative Care*, their role is that of a nurse specialist, thus they are also known as *specialist palliative care nurses* or*clinical nurse specialists in palliative care*. *Macmillan nurses* play a significant role in palliative care services in hospice, community and hospital settings across Great Britain. More than two-fifths of cancer patients who died in Great Britain in 1995 were estimated to have received support from *Macmillan specialist palliative care nurses*.[92] Therefore *Macmillan nurses* are often synonymous with the nursing care of the dying in the public's eye.[93]

All *Macmillan nurses* are Registered Nurses with at least five years' experience, including two or more years in cancer or palliative care. They also attend specialist courses in managing pain and other symptoms, and in psychological support. Part of their role is to share their expertise with colleagues, to help improve standards of care, and to co-ordinate care between the hospital and the patient's home.[94] Melissa Reddish, *Clinical Nurse Specialist* in Palliative Care,sees *Macmillan nurses* as the link between the community and the hospice.[95] Usually they do not provide practical care although some nurses undertake a more hands-on role.[96] The role of the district nurse and Macmillan nurse has often become confused. An interview study of 43 terminally ill patients in 1996 found that emotional support was only associated with the Macmillan nurses and that clinical care alone was connected with the role of the district nurses.[97]

2.6 Volunteers

In January 1999, there were 236 specialist palliative care inpatient services using volunteers in Great Britain.[98] This figure alone indicated that volunteers are an integral part of British hospice and palliative care, whether they are working directly with patients and their relatives, or giving other essential support, such as raising money.[99] However, hospice services starting in other countries who find it rather difficult to attract and work with volunteers should view Great Britain's example as encouraging, because it was not easy in the early days. This fact was outlined in a paper by Sheila

92 Julie Skilbeck et al.: Clinical nurse specialists in palliative care. Part 1. A description of the Macmillan Nurse Caseload. *Palliative Medicine*.2002. Volume 16. Issue 4, p. 285 - 296. In: Jessica Corner et al.: *Journal of Advanced Nursing*. March 2003. Volume 41. Issue 6, p. 562.

93 Interview with Prof Alison Richardson, 18 March 2004, in London.

94 Official Homepage of the Macmillan Cancer Relief Organisation: http://www.macmillan.org.uk/aboutmacmillan/disppage.asp?id=358

95 Interview with Melissa Reddish, 08 July 2003, in London.

96 Interview with Prof Alison Richardson, 18 March 2004, in London.

97 Gunne Grande et al.: What terminally ill patients value in the support provided by GP's, district nurses and Macmillan nurses. In: *International Journal of Palliative Nursing*. 1996. Volume2, Issue 3.p. 138 - 143. Cited as in.: Kerri Wright: Caring for the terminally ill: the district nurse's perspective. In: *British Journal of Nursing*. 2002.Volume 11. No. 18, p. 1180.

98 Barbara Whitewood: The role of the volunteer in British palliative care. In: *European Journal of Palliative Care*. 1999. Volume 6. Issue 2, p. 44.

99 ibid.

Hanna, the first voluntary service organiser at St Christopher's Hospice, in 1975: "the use of volunteers in this field was nebulous and I felt myself groping very much in the dark." [100]

Every palliative care organisation in the UK is different, and so is the involvement of volunteers, which varies from one hospice to the next – it is dependent on the local population of recruits. [101] The volunteers work in a variety of roles in different places: inpatient settings, day care, the patient's home, supporting outpatient clinics, driving and helping family and friends in their bereavement. [102]

Screening and support of volunteers

The growing importance of the volunteer worker in English hospice and palliative care services is also highlighted by the existence of voluntary services managers [103], who are now employed as members of staff. The voluntary service manager is accountable for the department and has to adhere to an annual budget, policies, and procedures. They have the significant task of balancing the needs of the organisation, the team and individual volunteers. A Government report in 1996, *Making a Difference: Strengthening Volunteering in the NHS*, clearly supports the engagement of voluntary service managers: "Trusts with voluntary services managers reported far more volunteer involvement than those without." [104]

Training and education

Similar to the various ways volunteers are integrated in palliative care services, the education and training of volunteers differs from one hospice to the next. It can be seen as a basic principle that volunteers in almost all services are trained before they start their work. An ongoing in-service training programme is also common in most services. Usually the volunteer and the hospice service sign an agreement in which the rights and duties of both parties are identified. [105]

Great emphasis is placed on the education and training of volunteers who work in bereavement services. These volunteers undergo extra training programmes, learning to support family and friends through their bereavement. Some hospices train their volunteers to become bereavement counsellors. [106]

---

[100] The paper was written in 1975 for a presentation at a conference in New York and provides an interesting insight into the first eight years of St Christopher's volunteers. We are much obliged to Denise Brady and the staff at St Christopher's library for giving us access to this and many other papers, articles and books in their exceptional library.

[101] ibid. p. 44, 47.

[102] ibid. p. 44.

[103] Derek Doyle has published a very interesting and helpful handbook for *volunteer service managers* in hospice and palliative care. Derek Doyle (Ed.): Volunteers in hospice and palliative care. A handbook for volunteer service managers. Oxford 2002.

[104] *Making a Difference: Strengthening Volunteering in the NHS*, NHS Executive, 1996. In: Barbara Whitewood: The role of the volunteer in British palliative care. In: *European Journal of Palliative Care*. 1999. Volume 6. Issue 2, p. 47.

[105] ibid., p. 45.

[106] ibid.

The essential role of volunteers within palliative care services is also emphasised in the *NICE-Guidance* on *Supportive and Palliative Care.* [107] According to NICE, it is recommended that those programmes that offer bereavement services using volunteer support workers should ensure mechanisms for recruiting, training, supervising and managing volunteers are in place. [108]

Social background of volunteers

There has been little research on the social background and motivation of volunteers. A cross section of people from 18 to 80 offer their services, a large proportion of those who are accepted are retired. [109] In her article on the role of volunteers in British palliative care, Barbara Whitewood reveals that young volunteers are often looking for hands-on experience in the hospice before enrolling in a university course in medicine. [110] Elise Harvey comes to a similar conclusion: "The young people coming forward are often looking for work-experience before embarking on a career within medical/caring professions and the experience is usually of a ‚hands-on' nature [...] [111]

2.7 Example

Marie Curie Hospice in Liverpool

According to Dr John Ellershaw "the population and the activity of the *Marie Curie Hospice* is quite representative of most voluntary hospices in the UK." The hospice was founded in 1994 in Liverpool and is one of ten hospices provided by the national cancer charity *Marie Curie Cancer Care.* It is located in the quiet suburb of Woolton, approximately 25 minutes from the centre of Liverpool. The*Marie Curie Centre (MCC)*, like many palliative care centres and hospice units, developed from a hospice on the hill outside the mainstream NHS into a specialist palliative care unit working in a multi-professional way. Today the hospice has 30 in-patient beds, a day therapy unit, complementary therapy and lymphodoema clinics among its services.

Organisation and funding

The inpatient unit is divided into two wards of 15 beds. Half of the rooms are four bedded bays, the rest are single-bed rooms. According to the English average, 95% of the patients cared for are suffering from terminal cancer. The average length of stay is 13 days, demonstrating its work as an acute unit. The majority of the admissions are from the community; 50% die at the centre and the other 50% are discharged

[107] Barbara Whitewood: The role of the volunteer in British palliative care. In: *European Journal of Palliative Care.* 1999. Volume 6. Issue 2, p. 47.

[108] National Institute for Clinical Excellence: Guidance on Cancer Services Improving Supportive and Palliative Care for Adults with Cancer – the Manual, London 2004, p. 162.

[109] Barbara Whitewood: The role of the volunteer in British palliative care. In: *European Journal of Palliative Care.* 1999. Volume 6. Issue 2, p. 45.

[110] ibid.

[111] Elise Harvey: Why hospice volunteering? In: *Volunteering.* Number 32. November 1997, p. 11.

back into the community. As Dr Ellershaw points out, "this is an important message. Many hospices are seen as places where people die, whereas more commonly one in two patients are discharged back into the community."[112] The average occupancy is approx. 80%; again, close to the national average.[113]

The day care service provides space for 10 patients and is open 4 days a week. It is providing a service for quite a fixed population, sometimes over quite a long period of time. Day care patients can visit a doctor as well as having complementary therapies.

The outpatient department is regarded as a very important part of service development. It is a cost-effective way of delivering multi-professional specialist palliative care to patients needs to be evaluated and developed further. At the *MCC* Liverpool, there are over 2,500 outpatient episodes each year, much more than in most other outpatient units in the country.[114] Approximately one third of these are medical outpatients, the others comprise of specialist lymphoedema services, physiotherapy, occupational therapy, social work, welfare rights and complementary therapies including aromatherapy, massage and reflexology. Dr John Ellershaw speaks about the advantages of the outpatient department:

> The patients can access the multi-professional team, come here and go home again. So it sends a message back to the community that you can come to the centre as an out-patient. But there are also patients that know the centre and have been so if they get ill at home and might be admitted into the hospice the fear isn't there because they know the environment, it takes down the barriers, that is important to access more patients.[115]

At the *MCC* Liverpool there is an expanding education programme, and last year 1,500 people attended courses at the centre. The centre is currently involved in the development of the undergraduate palliative care medical curriculum, which is tremendously important if the knowledge, skills, and attitudes of the doctors of tomorrow are to be improved. We have an active research interest group and the centre is involved in projects linked with the University of Liverpool and national multi-centre research initiatives. It is important to underpin our practice of palliative medicine with evidence-based research.

All care provided at the hospice is free of charge to patients and their families. The hospice gets roughly 52% of their funding from charitable sources, of which a large proportion is provided by the *Marie Curie Cancer Charity*. Legacies are an important element for the funding of the hospice. Other charitable funds are local fundraising activities, people doing sponsored walks or runs, coffee mornings or other fundraising events. Big supermarkets or large manufacturing companies make contributions,

---

[112] http://www.hospice-spc-council.org.uk/publicat.ons/partnerp.doc/partn013.htm

[113] Interview with Dr John Ellershaw, 22 March 2004, in Liverpool.

[114] ibid.

[115] Interview with Dr John Ellershaw, 22 March 2004, in Liverpool. Similar observations have been made in other hospices, i.e. at the day care centre at *St. John's Palliative Care Centre* in London. Interview with Sheena Boyd, 08 July 2003, in London.

as donators from various backgrounds underline the broad public acceptance of the hospice. [116]

Compared to other hospices the *MCC* receives a quite large percentage of money from the NHS, approx. 48%. [117]

The professionals

The multi-professional team includes doctors, nurses, social workers, occupational therapists, physiotherapists, chaplains, a lymphoedema practitioner, a welfare rights officer, a children's counsellor, and the appointment of a psychologist is planned. There are also a variety of complementary therapies in addition to these services.

Most of the nurses won't have formal palliative care qualifications before they start working at *MCC*, hence their first year is to receive training experience on the ward. At the education centre based in the *MCC* staff members have access to higher-level courses in order to complete a diploma or masters degree.

The volunteers

There are 130 volunteers working at the *MCC*, and two full-time voluntary coordinators select, educate and supervise them. The volunteers receive an introduction to the philosophy of the *MCC* and some training before they begin duties on the wards. The extent of the training depends on what volunteers want to do. "Volunteers who want to be bereavement counsellors have to be trained in that role because they perform one-to-one counselling roles. They need to know how to do it, so their training is more formalised." [118]

The volunteers decide in which areas they want to work; whether they want to be involved with patients and relatives or not. They work on reception, do some work on the wards and help giving out meals and drinks. They also support day therapy, outpatients and work in the administration department. The bereavement service is delivered mainly by volunteers but it is supervised and the education is provided by the social work department. They do not contribute to nurse care. [119]

The majority of the volunteers are retired. Most are females although there are quite a number of male volunteers who contribute to the service as well. [120]

Rituals

When a patient has died, the hospice is keen not to admit a new patient back into that bed the same day. Often the relatives come back on to the ward the next day "so it wouldn't be helpful to have someone else in the bed in which their relative

[116] Interview with Dr John Ellershaw, 22 March 2004, in Liverpool.
[117] ibid.
[118] ibid.
[119] ibid.
[120] ibid.

just died." [121] Exceptions have to be made sometimes when a very ill and demanding patient is admitted into the hospice and there aren't other beds available. [122]

There is no ritualisation around the bed itself. However, there are other ways in which patients are remembered in the hospice. In the chapel there is a tree where people can leave messages on the leaves for those who passed away in the hospice. They are remembered in a memoriam book. [123]

Specific issues

The Liverpool Integrated Care Pathway for the Dying Patient [124]

The Specialist Palliative Care Team based at the Royal Liverpool University Hospitals, together with the Team at the *MCC* Liverpool established the *Liverpool Care Pathway (LCP)* Project. The aim for the project was to translate Hospice care into the acute sector and develop outcome measures at the end of life.

The *LCP* empowers doctors and nurses to deliver high quality care to dying patients and their relatives. The *LPC* is a multi-professional project that incorporates evidence-based practice and national guidelines related to the care of the dying into clinical practice. The scheme promotes the education and empowerment role of the Specialist Palliative Care Team to bridge the theory practice gap. It provides demonstrable outcomes to support clinical governance. The *LCP* was awarded Beacon Status in the category Palliative Care in September 2000 [125] and has been well reviewed not only in England [126] but also in the Netherlands, where a *LPC* related programme has been established at the *Daniel de Hoed Clinic* in Rotterdam. "It's a sensible framework. Palliative Care needs to be wherever the patient is. So you can have a fantastic hospice service but you are only be accessed by a minority of patients." [127]

3. Summary

England is the mother country of the hospice movement and provides a role model for hospice and palliative care worldwide. Palliative care has been firmly established in English society and the formal health system. There is a strong supply of Palliative care services around the country; however, there are variations in the levels of provision between the regions in relation to inpatient beds and specialist workforce

[121] ibid.

[122] ibid.

[123] ibid.

[124] A detailed elaboration of the Liverpool Care Pathway Project can be found in: John Ellershaw/ Susie Wilkinson: Care of the Dying. A pathway to excellence.Oxford 2003.

[125] http://www.lcp-mariecurie.org.uk/about/default.asp

[126] Compare also Nice Guidance Key Recommendation 14: "In all locations, the particular needs of patients who are dying from cancer should be identified and addressed. The Liverpool Care Pathway for the Dying Patient provides one mechanism for achieving this." In: National Institute for Clinical Excellence: Guidance on Cancer Services Improving Supportive and Palliative Care for Adults with Cancer – the Manual, London 2004, p. 15.

[127] Interview with Dr John Ellershaw, 22 March 2004, in Liverpool.

availability. The high number of vacant consultant posts is a huge problem. However there are various of Government policy initiatives to overcome those deficits.

As in other European countries, palliative care is still pre-dominantly provided for cancer patients with 95% of the patients suffering from this disease. [128] However recent developments show efforts are being increased to make palliative care available to a larger number of non-cancer patients as well. Providing care for a wider group of terminally ill patients could mark a new milestone for palliative care in England, and the effects of such an achievement cannot be underestimated as the nation still sets the tone for the development of palliative care in Europe. It became very obvious in the interviews with experts from the other 15 countries portrayed in our project that they still look to England when it comes to planning and running palliative care services. Excellent concepts like the *Liverpool Integrated Care Pathway for the Dying Patient* have been adopted by others in Europe.

The highly developed specialist palliative care services, and the integration of palliative care into existing health structures have led to a major improvement in the care for the dying. Hospices, such as St. Margaret's Hospice in Taunton, function as education centres and give their expertise to other health care professionals. [129] As a result health care professionals, in both primary and secondary care, are much better trained in palliative care, although there is still the need to improve the quality and numbers of trained staff as recent initiatives indicate.

Professional services for the care of the dying are very much needed because England has one of the highest proportions of female labour participation in Europe so there are relatively few women at home who can be carers. [130] Especially in big cities like London, people often live isolated and without family support. [131] However, some professionals working in the field still believe that families play a constant part in the care of the dying and that this is often underestimated. [132] Their contribution is vital as this community service is an area that is not as highly developed as inpatient care. One-to-one care at home is very expensive because of the relatively high wage rates of nurses. [133]

The implementation of the *NICE-Guidance* should result in a further enhancement of palliative care services. Professionals from both primary and secondary health care sectors seem to be willing to improve the care of the dying. Experts agree that professionals, nurses in particular, still acknowledge their work with dying people as something very important and special. [134] Nonetheless some experts have expressed concerns that death and dying is increasingly taking a back seat in relation to pallia-

---

[128] Jane Seymour et al.: Palliative care and policy in England: a review of health improvement plans in 1999 - 2003. In: *Palliative Medicine*.2002. Volume 16. Issue 1, p. 9.

[129] Interviews with Anne Lee and Averil Parry, 26 March 2004, in Taunton.

[130] Interview with Dr Anne Naysmith, 17 March 2004, in London.

[131] Interview with Dr Philip Jones, 08 July 2003, in London.

[132] Interview with Suzie Croft, 08 July 2003, in London.

[133] Interview with Dr Anne Naysmith, 17 March 2004, in London.

[134] Interview with Prof Alison Richardson, 18 March 2004, in London; Interview with Andrew Langford, 17 March 2004, in London; Interviews with Anne Lee and Averil Parry, 26 March 2004, in Taunton.

tive care. This cannot solely be due to the fact that palliative care takes place earlier in the course of the disease today. Andrew Langford recalls a meeting of a several years ago, where the development of a strategy for palliative care throughout London was discussed; he made an interesting observation:

Of the people involved in this, the majority of us wanted to re-focus on one of the primary aims of palliative care which was the care of the dying and best possible death that we could possibly offer to people. And it was interesting that once we were talking a lot about actable palliative care, better access, better provision of services, that we felt very strongly what had to be in the strategy was a re-emphasis on the care of the dying and that it is still a very important and integral part of palliative care. [135]

A statement made by Julia Addington Hall, Professor of End of Life Care, underlines this: "Getting it right for dying patients is the hallmark getting it right for other patients too." [136] Dame Cicely Saunders reminds us that the care for the dying should not be neglected:

We must not forget that all our patients are eventually going to die and we must not so much concentrate on quality of life up to dying that we forget the actual problem of the dying, the last days and weeks, the families, the bereavement and so on. We will look for quality of life in our day care centre but even our day care patients will die eventually. [137]

Sources

Addington-Hall, Julia: Care of the dying and the NHS. Briefing paper for Nuffield Trust. March 2003. Cites as in.: Health Select Committee. Hospices and Palliative Care. Memorandum from the Department of Health. No. 7. Session 2003 - 04.

Bundesministerium für Gesundheit und Soziale Sicherung: Sozial-Kompass Europa. Soziale Sicherheit in Europa im Vergleich. Bonn 2003.

Department of Health: HC (87) 4 (2). London 1987.

Department of Health: Quality Standards in the Delivery of GP Out of Hours Services. London June 2002.

Doyle, Derek (Ed.): Volunteers in hospice and palliative care. A handbook for volunteer service managers. Oxford 2002.

Ellershaw, John/ Wilkinson, Susie: Care of the Dying. A pathway to excellence.Oxford 2003.

Grande, G/ Todd, C/ Barclay, S/ Doyle, J: What terminally ill patients value in the support provided by GP's, district nurses and Macmillan nurses. In: *International Journal of Palliative Nursing*. 1996. Volume2, Issue 3.138 - 143. Cited as in.: Wright, Kerri: Caring for the terminally ill: the district nurse's perspective. In: *British Journal of Nursing*. 2002.Vol. 11. No. 18, p. 1180 - 1185.

---

[135] Interview with Andrew Langford, 17 March 2004, in London.

[136] The Nuffield Trust for Research and Policy Studies in Health Services. The press release from 17 March 2003 is available for download: http://www.nuffieldtrust.org.uk/press/docs/careofdyingii-draftpressrelease1jtfinal.doc.

[137] Interview with Dame Cicely Saunders, 16 March 2004, in London.

Hanratty, Barbara: Palliative care provided by GPs: the carer's viewpoint. In: *British Journal of General Practice*. Volume50. No. 457. London 2000, p. 653 - 654 et seq.

Harvey, Elise: Why hospice volunteering? In: *Volunteering*. Number 32. November 1997.

Health Select Committee. Hospices and Palliative Care. Memorandum from Department of Health. No. 7. Session 2003 - 04.

Hospice Directory 2004: Hospice and Palliative Care services in the United Kingdom and Ireland. London 2004.

Hoy, Andrew: Written Evidence to the House of Commons Health Committee regarding Palliative Care. 25.02.2004.

Hughes, Lynne: Palliative Care in the Community. *Primary Health Care*. Volume 14. No. 6. July 2004, p. 27 - 31.

King, Gerry; Mackenzie, Jillian; Smith, Hezel; Clark, David: Dying at home: evaluation of a hospice rapid-response service. In: International Journal of Palliative Nursing. 2000. Volume 6. No. 6, p. 280 - 287.

King, N/ Bell, D/ Martin, N/ Farrell, S: *Gold Standards Framework. Phase 2: Qualitative case study evaluation – final report.* Primary Care Research Group. School of Human and Health Sciences. University of Huddersfield. 2003.

National Council for Hospice and Specialist Palliative Care Services. The palliative care survey 1999. National Council for Hospice and Specialist Palliative Care Services. London 2000. In:Seymour, Jane/Clark, David/Marples, Racheal: Palliative care and policy in England: a review of health improvement plans in 1999 - 2003. In: *Palliative Medicine*.2002. Volume 16. Issue 1, p. 5 - 11.

National Council for Hospice and Specialist Palliative Care Services. National Survey of patient activity data for Specialist Palliative Care Services for the year 2002 - 3.

National Institute for Clinical Excellence: Guidance on cancer Services. Improving Supportive and Palliative Care for Adults with Cancer – the Manual, London 2004.

NHS Modernisation Agency and Macmillan Cancer Relief: *Gold Standards Framework: interim evaluation report.* Unpublished. January 2003. In: National Institute for Clinical Excellence: Guidance on cancer Services. Improving Supportive and Palliative Care for Adults with Cancer – the Manual, London 2004.

Saunders, Cicely: The evolution of palliative care. Reprinted from The Pharos of Alpha Omega Alpha Honor Medical Society. Volume 66. Number 3. Summer 2003, p. 4 - 10.

Saunders, Cicely. Watch with me. Inspirations for a life in hospice care. Sheffield 2003.

Seymour, Jane/Clark, David/Marples, Racheal: Palliative care and policy in England: a review of health improvement plans in 1999 - 2003. In: *Palliative Medicine*.2002. Volume 16. Issue 1, p. 5 - 11.

Shipman, C/ Thompson, M/ Pearce, A/ Addington-Hall, J: *Building Bridges: The Macmillan GP Facilitator Programme in Palliative Care: an evaluation. Report to Macmillan Cancer Relief.* London. Department of Palliative Care & Policy, King's College. 2001. In: National Institute for Clinical Excellence: Guidance on cancer Services. Improving Supportive and Palliative Care for Adults with Cancer – the Manual, London 2004, p. 122.

Shipman, C/ Addington-Hall, J/ Barclay, S/ Briggs, J/ Cox, I/ Daniels, L/ Millar, D: How and why do GPs use specialist palliative care services? In: *Palliative Medicine 2002*. Volume 16. Issue 3, p. 241 - 246.

Shipman, C/ Addington-Hall, J/ Thompson, M/ Pearce, A/ Barclay, S/ Cox, I/ Maher, J/ Millar,

D. Building bridges in palliative care: evaluating a GP Facilitator programme. In: *Palliative Medicine* 2003. Number 17, p. 621 - 627.

Skilbeck, J/ Corner J/ Bath,P./ Beech, N/ Clark, D/ Hughes,P/ Douglas, H.R/ Halliday, D/ Haviland, J/ Marples, R/ Normand, C/ Seymour, J/ Webb, T: Clinical nurse specialists in palliative care. Part 1. A description of the Macmillan Nurse Caseload. *Palliative Medicine*.2002. Vol. 16. Issue 4, p. 285 - 296. In: Corner J/ Halliday, D/ Haviland, J/ Douglas, H.R/ Bath,P./ Clark, D/ Normand, C/ Beech, N/ Hughes,P/ Marples, R/ Seymour, J/ Skilbeck, J/ Webb, T: *Journal of Advanced Nursing*. March 2003. Volume 41, Issue 6, p. 562.

The Nuffield Trust for Research and Policy Studies in Health Services. Press release 17.03.2003.

Thomas, Keri: The Gold Standards Framework in community palliative care. In: *European Journal of Palliative Care.* Volume 10. Number 3. 2003, p. 113 - 115. cp. et al.: The Macmillan Gold Standards Framework Programme in http://www.macmillan.org.uk/showdocument.asp?id=271; http://www.modern.nhs.uk/cancer.

Thomas, Keri: Caring for the Dying at Home. Companions on a journey. Oxford 2003. In: National Institute for Clinical Excellence: Guidance on cancer Services. Improving Supportive and Palliative Care for Adults with Cancer – the Manual, London 2004.

Whitewood, Barbara: The role of the volunteer in British palliative care. In: *European Journal of Palliative Care*. 1999. Volume 6. Issue 2, p. 44 - 47.

Wright, Kerri: Caring for the terminally ill: the district nurse's perspective. In: *British Journal of Nursing*. 2002.Vol. 11. No. 18, p. 1180 - 1185.

Internet sources (in chronological order of appearance)

Population Division of the Department of Economic and Social Affairs of the United Nations Secretariat, *World Population Prospects: The 2002 Revision* and *World Urbanization Prospects: The 2001 Revision*. Official United Nations Homepage. http://esa.un.org/unpp

Official Homepage of the Macmillan Cancer Relief Organisation. The Macmillan Gold Standards Framework Programme. http://www.macmillan.org.uk/showdocument.asp?id=271

Official Homepage of St. John's Palliative Care Centre. http://www.hje.org.uk/hospice.html

Expert Advisory Group on Cancer [The Calman-Hine-Report]. A policy framework for commissioning cancer services: a report by the expert advisory group on cancer to the chief medical officers of England and Wales. Department of Health and the Welsh Office. London 1995. Official homepage of the Department of Health. http://www.dh.gov.uk/assetRoot/04/01/43/66/04014366.pdf

National Health Service Cancer Plan. Official homepage of the Department of Health. http://www.dh.gov.uk/assetRoot/04/01/45/13/04014513.pdf

National Service Frameworks. Official homepage of the Department of Health. http://www.dh.gov.uk/Home/fs/en

Department of Health: Action to ensure £50 million investment in palliative care delivers the best services for patients. 23.12.2002. Reference number 2002/0531.Official homepage of the Department of Health. http://www.dh.gov.uk/PublicationsAndStatistics/PressReleases/PressReleasesNotices/fs/en?CONTENT_ID=4026007&chk=zvLhrh

Department of Health. Planning and funding specialist palliative care provision 2003/04 - 2005/06. Official homepage of the Department of Health. http://www.dh.gov.uk/assetRoot/04/06/08/61/04060861.pdf

Official homepage of Help the Hospices. http://www.helpthehospices.org.uk/
Official homepage of Macmillan Cancer Relief Organisation. http://www.macmillan.org.uk/
Official homepage of Marie Curie Cancer Care. http://www.mariecurie.org.uk/
Official homepage of National Council for Palliative Care. http://www.ncpc.org.uk/
Official homepage of Sue Ryder Care. http://www.suerydercare.org/
The Macmillan Gold Standards Framework Programme. A programme for community palliative care. http://www.macmillan.org.uk/showdocument.asp?id=271
National Institute for Clinical Excellence: Guidance on cancer Services. Improving Supportive and Palliative Care for Adults with Cancer – the Manual, London 2004. Official homepage of the National Institute for Clinical Excellence. http://www.nice.org.uk/pdf/csgspmanual.pdf
NHS Modernisation Agencies. Cancer Services Collaborative. http://www.modern.nhs.uk/cancer
CancerBACUP. Helping people live with cancer. Anne Naysmith: You can choose (no) treatment. http://www.cancerbacup.org.uk/News/Newsletter/Issue47/Opinion
http://www.nursing-standard.co.uk/archives/phc_pdfs/phcvol14-06/phcv14n6p2731.pdf
http://www.nuffieldtrust.org.uk/press/docs/careofdyingii-draftpressrelease1jtfinal.doc

List of interviews (in chronological order)

- Dr Philip Jones
  Medical Director, *St. John's Palliative Care Centre*
  London, 08 July 2003
- Melissa Reddish
  Clinical Nurse Specialist in Palliative Care, *St. John's Palliative Care Centre*
  London, 08 July 2003
- Sheena Boyd
  Leader Day Care Centre, *St. John's Palliative Care Centre*
  London, 08 July 2003
- Suzie Croft
  Social worker, *St. John's Palliative Care Centre*
  London, 08 July 2003
- Avril Jackson
  Information officer, *Hospice Information*
  London, 15 March 2004
- Dame Cicely Saunders
  Founder/President, *St Christopher's Hospice*
  London, 16 March 2004
- Dr. Anne Naysmith
  Consultant in Palliative Medicine, *Pembridge Palliative Care Centre*
  London, 16 March 2004
- Andrew Langford
  Director of Patient Services, *Trinity Hospice*
  London, 17 March 2004
- Prof. Alison Richardson

Professor in Cancer and Palliative Nursing Care, *The Florence Nightingale School of Nursing and Midwifery*
London, 18 March 2004

- Dr. John Ellershaw
  Medical Director, *Marie Curie Centre Liverpool*
  Liverpool, 22 March 2004
- Ann Lee
  Nursing Director, *St. Margaret's Hospice*
  Taunton, 26 March 2004
- Averil Parry
  Lecturer in Palliative Care, *St. Margaret's Hospice*
  Taunton, 26 March 2004

Estonia

Michaela Fink

1. General conditions

1.1 Demographics

- In 2000, the Estonian population totalled 1,37 million. According to UN-predictions, it is expected to be only half as much, 657,000 inhabitants, by 2050. [1]
- Since the early to mid 1950s the average life expectancy of 65.3 has risen to 71.7 years of age in 2000. By 2050 another rise is expected bring the average life expectancy at birth to 79.4. [2]
- In 1950, people 65 years or older in Estonia constituted 10.6% of the population. In 2000, it was already 15.1% and is projected to grow to remarkable 31.2% by 2050. [3]
- Similarly, people aged 80 years or older constituted 1.8% of the population in 1950. That percentage grew slightly in 2000 to 2.6 and is estimated to grow to 9.3 by 2050. [4]
- The number of people aged 15 to 59 years per older person over the age of 60, was 60.8% of the total population in 2000 and is expected to drop to 44.0% by 2050. [5]
- The median age is will rise from 37.9 years in 2000 to 52.3 by 2050. [6]
- The annual mortality rate is expected to rise from 13,6 per 1000 inhabitants between 2000 - 2005 to 17,8 per 1000 inhabitants by 2045 - 2050. [7] The main causes of death are cardiovascular diseases. [8]
- 80 percent of all cancer patients in Estonia die at home, 20 percent spend their last few hours in hospitals. [9]

---

1 Population Division of the Department of Economic and Social Affairs of the United Nations Secretariat, World Population Prospects: The 2002 Revision Population Database: http://esa.un.org/unpp (medium variant).

2 ibid.

3 ibid.

4 ibid.

5 ibid

6 ibid.

7 ibid.

8 International Observatory of End of Life Care: http://www.eolcobservatory.net/global_analysis/estonia_epidemiology.htm

9 Interview with Heli Paluste, 20 February 2004, in Tallinn.

1.2 Health care system

Reforms to the Estonian public health care system came into effect after the country became independent in 1991. Health care provision and insurance are the responsibility of the Ministry for Social Affairs. The total health care expenditure was 5.5 percent in proportion of the GDP in 2002. In Estonia compulsory health insurance has been established. It is administered by the Central Sickness Fund and 17 regional sickness funds. The source of income of health insurance is 13 percent of the social tax or 13 percent of the employee's gross salary paid by the employer. By that 70 percent of the total health care costs are covered. Another 12 percent are covered by additional payments and 13 percent funded through additional state allowances. Other costs are balanced out by international subsidies. In order to establish a more efficient planning and coordination for the future, there are plans to reduce the number of sickness insurance funds.

About 95 percent of the Estonian population has health insurance. All persons are entitled to receive emergency care even if they have no health insurance. The non-working spouses of insured persons and all children up to 18 years of age are also covered without paying contributions as are full-time students and pregnant women. Despite the reformation of the health care system, the informal payment of medical and care service is still common similar to other Eastern European countries. [10]

2. Hospice and palliative care in Estonia

2.1 History

In 1997, Vaino Ratsep set up the first home care service at the cancer centre in Tallinn. This service can be seen as the root of the Estonian hospice movement. Since that time a growing network of outpatient provision has been developed under the leadership of the Estonian Cancer Society. [11]

2.2 Hospice and palliative care services

Currently there is only one inpatient hospice operating in Estonia. In 2002, an inpatient unit for dying patients was set up inside the Protestant-Lutheran hospital in Tallinn. Another hospice for HIV/Aids patients is planned in Narva. [12] Some other in-

---

10 cp. Official AOK-Website: http://www.aok-bv.de/politik/agenda/euerweiterung/index_01459.html cp. also: Official Homepage Estonian Ministry of Social Affairs: http://www.sm.ee/gopro30/Web/gpweb.nsf/pages/healthpolicy0006

11 Interview with Dr. Vahur Valvere, 20 February 2004, in Tallinn. Cp. also: David Clark/ Michael Wright: Transitions in End of Life Care. Hospice and related developments in Eastern Europe and Central Asia. Buckingham, Philadelphia 2003, p. 56.

12 Russians make up 28 percent of the population in Estonia, in some areas even 90 percent are of Russian nationality. A similar situation applies for Narva where Russians are not very well integrated into the Estonian society because of linguistic and social differences. Correspondingly problems such as unem-

stitutions – most notably cancer centres and some smaller hospitals in urban areas – provide inpatient and home care.

Estonia has many nursing homes and extended outpatient care provision structures for cancer patients. Almost every city has one or two cancer centres providing palliative care services at the patients homes. In 2003, a total of 15 such services were in place. [13] They are all part of the cancer society which negotiates and agrees contracts with sickness insurance funds.

It is planned to transform a lot of the small hospitals, in particular those in rural regions, into services that are capable to provide palliative care. The meagre equipped hospitals have serious financial problems and face the threat of closing. According to government representatives these hospitals are suited for the care of the dying because medical expenses are lower for this patient groups than for regular hospital clients. That way, and mainly for reasons of economy, new provision structures for terminally ill patients will develop.

Currently, there are no voluntary hospices due to a lack of private sponsors and volunteer support. [14]

In 2003, a total of 1123 beds for *long term medical* and *nursing care*, including palliative care beds, exist in Estonia. The estimated need however is 2000 beds (10 beds per 1000 inhabitants aged 65 years or older). In 2003, 10.071 of the total 38.859 patients seen by home care teams were cancer patients.

The network for chronically ill and high-maintenance patients includes:

- geriatric units in hospitals (2 beds per 1000 inhabitants aged 65 years or older)
- hospitals for the chronically ill, nursing homes and hospices (10 beds per 1000 inhabitants aged 65 years or older)
- home care
- day care
- Old people's homes (20 beds per 1000 inhabitants aged 65 years or older) [15]

2.3 Legal regulations and funding

There is no legislation regulating palliative care in Estonia. The costs are covered by the sickness insurance funds modelled on the accounting system in place for long term care. However experts complain that the provision with palliative care is much more expensive than the money paid by the sickness insurance funds. Due to this, patients are forced to pay the remaining cost themselves. The patient's proportion differs in the regions and institutions: Patients receiving palliative care at the cancer centre in Tallinn pay a daily rate of approximately 25 Estonian crowns (approx. 1.60 €) in

ployment, drug usage and alcoholism are widespread among the Russian population in Estonia. Hence the high HIV-infection rate could be linked to destructed social conditions. Interview with Dr. Jelena Leibour, 20 February 2004, in Tallinn.

13 Interview with Dr. Vahur Valvere, 20 February 2004, in Tallinn.

14 ibid.

15 The stats were generously made available by the Estonian Ministry of Social Affairs.

the first ten days of their stay. Patients provided with outpatient care have to pay a one-time fee of 15 Estonian crowns (approx. 0.95 €). [16] For one day at the hospice unit at the Protestant-Lutheran hospital in Tallinn the patients are demanded to give 74 Estonian crowns (approx. 4.79 €). [17] As the average pension in Estonia is only 96 € per month, most people can not afford to stay in the hospice.

2.4 Organisations

The *Estonian Cancer Society* is actively involved in the promotion of palliative care. There is no national palliative care organisation at present.

2.5 Education and training of professional staff

Education and training offers are very scarce in Estonia. Normally doctors and nurses receive education in palliative care in the neighbouring countries or through cooperation with palliative care services from abroad. The professional staff at the Protestant-Lutheran hospital in Tallinn was trained by experts from a Norwegian nursing school. The *Finnish Cancer Society* and the *University of Tampere* have funded palliative care courses in Estonia in the past. [18]

2.6 Volunteers

The collaboration of volunteers is not very common in Estonia. As in the other Baltic countries, the economical situation of most inhabitants is one of the main reasons for the lack of voluntary commitment. Most people work very hard and do not have much of any spare time that could be dedicated to voluntary work. Generally there is virtually no tradition of voluntary work in the public sector. Voluntary support rather takes place in the context of what can be called neighbourhood communities. Voluntary work in general has a negative connotation which goes back to the times of the Soviet occupation when people were often forced to give "voluntary" services. [19]

2.7 Examples

Palliative care at the Tallinn Cancer Centre

The cancer centre in Tallinn is situated in a hospital. It offers outpatient and home care palliative care for cancer patients in the terminal phase of their illness. It is one of two

[16] Interview with Dr. Vahur Valvere, 20 February 2004, in Tallinn. According to the Estonian Ministry of Social Affairs in Tallinn patients generally do not have to pay for home care.

[17] Interview with Dr. Jelena Leibour, 20 February 2004, in Tallinn.

[18] cp. David Clark/ Michael Wright: Transitions in End of Life Care. Hospice and related developments in Eastern Europe and Central Asia. Buckingham, Philadelphia 2003, p. 57.

[19] Interview with Dr. Vahur Valvere, 20 February 2004, in Tallinn. Information on the cancer centre can be found on the Internet: http://www.regionaalhaigla.ee

cancer centres in the city and provided care for a third of the total population. The second, smaller cancer centre in Tallinn belongs to *Tartu University Clinic*.

The public budget of the cancer centre is limited so that patients have to cover additional costs themselves. The team is led by director Vahur Valvere and consists of nurses, physiotherapists, two oncologists and one collaborator who works as a psychologist and social worker. A very few number of volunteers are also part of the team.

The home care team at the cancer centre is part of the Estonian Cancer Society, which is also headed by Valvere. It was founded in 1997 by Prof. Vaino Ratsep, the leader of the Cancer Society at that time.

In the near future, a consulting service for patients and relatives offering medical education, prevention and psychological advice is in planning. There are also plans to set up an inpatient hospice unit with 10 beds.

Hospice unit at the Protestant-Lutheran hospital in Tallinn

The first and only hospice in Estonia is located within the *Protestant-Lutheran hospital* in Tallinn. The service was set up in October 2002 and consists of special units for geriatric care, long term care and hospice care. In most cases the hospice patients – the majority of them are Estonian and Russian – are admitted from the nearby cancer centre. In future, the acceptance of HIV/Aids patients is in planning. Dr. Jelena Leibour, the Medical director of the unit, reports that often patients do not know they are admitted into a hospice. A lot of the doctors avoid telling the truth by not talking to the patient about the diagnosis.

The hospice provides care for 10 beds (5 double rooms). The team consists of three nurses, one social worker, a chaplain and some students who do their hands-on training at the hospice. Two times a week four volunteers (two men and two women) support the service. Volunteers do not have any formal training. However they are instructed by the hospice's chaplain. The volunteer's work is organised by the chaplains sister. The training of the nursing staff was provided by experts of a nursing school in Oslo.

The hospice is a run by the Protestant-Lutheran church and has an agreement with the sickness insurance funds to receive public funding for the patients. Only the Medical Director of the hospice is paid by the church.

The sickness insurance fund pays a daily-rate of 310 Estonian crowns per patient for the first two months of the stay. The hospice itself has to cover 50 percent of all costs whereas the patients have to pay 73 Estonian crowns per day, adding up to 2200 per month (approx.140.58 €). In case of very short stays, the patients are not asked to pay any fees. The average length of stay is four weeks.

3. Summary and outlook

In view of the urgency of the demographic changes in the Estonian society, the need of palliative care increasingly comes into the field of vision of health care experts.

the hospice in Tallinn

Those have set objectives for the near future that would improve the situation of palliative care in Estonia: sickness fund insurances should cover hundred percent of the occurring costs, national legislation and the expansion of existing provision structures, especially home care. The integration of palliative care as a obligatory part into the Medical Curriculum is also regarded as a priority. So far the lack of commitment shown by politicians and financial problems have limited the progress of palliative care in Estonia.

Sources and literature

Clark, David/ Wright, Michael: Transitions in End of Life Care. Hospice and related developments in Eastern Europe and Central Asia. Buckingham, Philadelphia 2003.

Internet sources

AOK-Bundesverband Official website: http://www.aok-bv.de/politik/agenda/euerweiterung/index_01459.html

Estonian Ministry of Social Affairs: http://www.sm.ee/gopro30/Web/gpweb.nsf/pages/healthpolicy0006

International Observatory of End of Life Care: http://www.eolc-observatory.net/global_analysis/estonia_ epidemiology.htm

Population Division of the Department of Economic and Social Affairs of the United Nations Secretariat, World Population Prospects: The 2002 Revision Population Database: http://esa.un.org/unpp

List of interviews (in chronological order)

- Heli Paluste (Chief Specialist) *Health Care Department Estonian Ministry of Social Affairs* Tallinn, 20 February 2004
- Dr. Vahur Valvere (Director and Chief of *Medical Oncology North-Estonian-Regional Hospital Cancer Center and Chairman of the Board Estonian Cancer Society) Cancer Centre Tallinn*, Tallinn, 20 February 2004
- Dr. Juhataja Helena Leibour (Hospice leader) *Hospice at the Protestant-Lutheran Hospital*, Tallinn, 20 February 2004

France[1]

Michaela Fink

1. General conditions

1.1 Demographics

- In 2000, the population of France numbered 59.3 million. According to predictions, the population will rise to 63.1 million inhabitants by 2050.[2]
- In the same time the average life expectancy of 79.4 is expected to grow to 84.8 years of age by 2050, whereas the median age will rise from 38.0 years in 2000 to 45.5 by 2050.[3]
- In 1950, people 65 years or older in France constituted 11.4% of the population. In 2000, it was already 16.3% and is projected to grow to 27.1% by 2050.[4]
- Likewise, people aged 80 years or older constituted 1.7% of the population in 1950. That percentage grew in 2000 to 3.9 and is estimated to grow to 10.9 by 2050.[5]
- The number of persons aged 15 to 59 years per older person over the age of 60, was 60.5% of the total population in 2000 and is expected to drop to 51.2% by 2050.[6]
- The annual crude death rate is expected to rise from 9.4 per 1000 inhabitants between 2000 - 2005 to 12.5 per 1000 inhabitants by 2045 - 2050.[7]
- Around 550.000 people die in France annually. According to estimations, between 150.000 to 200.000 of those cases are in need of palliative care. 142.000 people die of cancer diseases each year.[8]

---

1 Translated by Larissa Budde.

2 Population Division of the Department of Economic and Social Affairs of the United Nations Secretariat, *World Population Prospects: The 2004 Revision* and *World Urbanization Prospects: The 2003 Revision*. Official Homepage of the United Nations: http://esa.un.org/unpp

3 ibid.

4 ibid.

5 ibid.

6 ibid

7 ibid.

8 cp. Anna Simon: Palliativarbeit und Hospizbewegung in Frankreich. In: Die Hospiz-Zeitschrift. Fachforum für Hospizarbeit: Hospiz und Palliative Care international. Hg. v. Bundesarbeitsgemeinschaft Hospiz. Edition 14. 4. year 2002/4, p. 9.

- 70 percent of the population wish to die at home. In reality however 70 percent die in institutions and only 30 percent at home. [9]

1.2 Health care system

The Social Insurance System (*Sécurité Sociale*) (founded in 1946) includes health insurance, annuity insurance and family insurance. The main department, the *Régime Général,* is responsible for insurance within the *Sécurité Sociale* and offers insurance cover to employees in industry, trade, service and similar employments. 80% of the population are insured with this company which serves as base for the social security. The National Health Insurance companies (CNAMTS, *Caisse Nationale d'Assurance Maladie des Travailleurs Salariés*) manage the health insurance, which is a part of the *Sécurité Sociale*. The health insurance is financed mainly by social contributions gained from wages and income and from the general social tax (CSG) on capital yields. For health services there is a compensation of expenses: the patient receives a certificate of treatment, which he hands in to the insurance company. He is then refunded his expenses according to the contribution rates fixed by the state. The remaining costs the patient has to pay themselves if they do not have an additional insurance. Depending on national and regional agreements the principle of advance payment may be disregarded, especially in the case of great expenses as a hospital stay may cause. The rate of refunded costs takes into account the financial situation of the patient, so that even a complete reimbursement of expenses is possible. [10]

Around 10% of the gross inland product is devoted to the health sector. The national health insurance of France was able to present a nearly balanced account from 1999 to 2001. Since there was a considerable deficit in the health budget in 2003, a reduction of health services is being discussed currently, for example the introduction of surgery fees and increased prime costs in the case of hospital stays.

2. Hospice and palliative care in France

2.1 History

Following the loss of both her children as well as her husband in 1835 Jeanne Garnier as a 24 year old widow started to visit poor people in a house in Lyon which was called *Le Calvaire*. Together with other widows she founded the *Association des Dames du Calvaire* in 1842. The foundation made it their business to support and accompany terminally sick people.

---

[9] Lucien Neuwirth: Les soins palliatifs et l'accompagnement à domicile: Des concepts désormais très bien définis. Rapport d'information sur les soins palliatifs et l'accompagnement. Rapport d'information 207 (98 - 99). Commission des affaires sociales: http://www.senat.fr/rap/r98-207/r98-207.html

[10] cp. information on the Health System on the internet pages of the French embassy in Germany: http: //www.botschaft-frankreich.de

In 1874 Aurélle Jousset founded the *Oeuvre du Calvaire* and a hospice in the Rue Léontine, Xvième arrondissement, in Paris.

In 1880 the hospice – called *Maison Médicale des Dames du Calvaire* – was moved to the Rue de Lourmel 55, XVième arrondissement.

In 1971 the foundation, since then called *Maison Médicale Jeanne Garnier*, was officially recognised as a part of the public hospital system. In 1994 the house was completely renovated. Consisting of 81 beds it is one of France's largest Palliative Care institutions.

In 1974 Dr. Balfour Mount founded the first *Unité de soins palliatifs* (USP) in the *Royal Victoria Hospital* in Montréal, Canada. His experience rests on his work in London's St.-Christopher-Hospice. Mount used the term *Soins palliatifs* (Palliative Care), since hospice was rather negatively connoted in the French-Canandian language-use. A great number of French nurses went to Canada to train for Palliative Care there. The term *Soins palliatifs* is also used in France.

The modern hospice movement – *Le mouvement de soins palliatifs* – started with the public debate about the dishonouring treatment of the dying and death in the hospitals at the end of the 70s. *Associations de soins palliatifs* emerged, which took part in the ethic debates. Up to the present the ASP's more than the churches speak out against euthanasia and useless therapies at the end of life. One of the first *Associations de soins palliatifs* drew up a *Charte des soins palliatifs et de l'accompagnement* (Chart of Palliative Care), in which this opinion is substantiated and to which they continue to appeal to.[11]

In 1983 the charitable organization JALMALV (*Jusqu'à la mort accompagner la vie*) was founded.

In 1984 the *Association pour le développement des soins palliatifs* (ASP) was founded in Paris. Since 1995 ASP is called ASP-Fondatrice (ASPF) and is an *Association* of the UNASP (*Union nationale des associations pour le développement des soins palliatifs*).

In 1986 a ministerial circular was published, the so-called *Circulaire Laroque*, which is regarded as the political article of foundation for the Palliative Care in France. The text defines Palliative Care and discloses the recommendations of a committee of experts on the improvement of the care for the dying in hospitals. This multi-disciplined committee was set up by the health minister of that time. The text also includes drafts on possible structures of care, the appeal to found Palliative Care facilities, and it defines the responsibilities of the Palliative Care in nursing, teaching and science.

The first *Unité de soins palliatifs* was founded in France in 1987 by the initiative of Dr. Maurice Abiven and with the support of the *Association pour le développement de soins palliatifs* (ASP) in the *Hôpital de la Cité Universitaire* in Paris. Following that, similar formations succeeded this foundation, especially the *Équipes mobiles*.

[11] Before the end of 2004 a law still prohibiting euthanasia but also restricting useless therapies at the end of life is expected to be released by the French government.

In 1990 existing organisations like JALMALV and UNASP founded the SFAP (*Société française d'accompagnement et de soins palliatifs*) to unite all of France's *Associations de soins palliatifs* under that name. Doctors, nurses and other professionals are also members of the SFAP, which serves as the main negotiator with the health politicians and the representatives of the health insurance fund. 15.000 single members and 150 hospice initiatives belong to the SFAP today.[12] 74% of all *Associations de soins palliatifs* are members of the SFAP.[13]

On the grounds of the hospital reform of 1991 the Palliative Care became an important part of public hospitals.

On behalf of the Health Ministry Dr. Henri Delbecque presented a report on the current state of development of the Palliative Care in France in 1993.[14]

In 1999 Lucien Neuwirth wrote the report of the *Commission des affaires sociales* of the senate of Palliative Care in France.[15] In the same year Bernard Kouchner (*Secrétaire d'état à la santé*) developed a plan for the advance of Palliative Care intended to run for three years, which received considerable financial aid by the health Ministry. The *Conseil économique et social* presented a report on Palliative Care in 1999 as well.[16]

A law guaranteeing every human the right to Palliative Care at the end of their life became effective on June the 9th (n° 99 - 477).

Currently the *Programme national de développement des soins palliatifs 2002 - 2005*, under the auspices of the Health Ministry and supported by a number of experts and organisations of Palliative Care is at work, with the aim to improve the care at home, to increase the integration of Palliative Care into the Health System, and to further the reception of Palliative Care within relevant kinds of jobs.[17]

---

12 cp. online http://www.sfap.org (Adhérents) – In 2000 the SFAP published an up-to-date guide, Le répertoire de soins palliatifs en France, including addresses of Palliative Care Institutions in France. cp. also http://www.sfap.org/modules.php?ModPath=dep\&ModStart=dep. The homepage of the English information service *Hospice Information* also offers a collection of addresses concerning the international hospice movement: http://www.hospiceinformation.info. A specially voluminous collection of addresses can be accessed via the homepage of the *Association française d'information funéraire*: http://www.afif.asso.fr/francais/conseils/conseil48.html. Finally, the French centre of documentation of Palliative Care, the *Association Francois-Xavier Bagnoud*, offers a wealth of information and addresses on the Internet: http://www.cdrnfxb.org/index.php

13 Les associations de bénévoles a fin 2002. A statistic of the SFAP + CNAM (03.09.2003). – Today, a number of experts of the *Associations soins palliatifs* criticise that the SFAP had turned into an organisation dominated by medical experts.

14 Henri Delbecque:Les soins palliatifs et l'accompagnement des malades en fin de vie. La documentation française. Paris 1993.

15 Lucien Neuwirth: *Les soins palliatifs et l'accompagnement à domicile*: http://www.senat.fr/rap/r98-207/r98-207.html

16 Donat Decisier: L'accompagnement des personnes en fin de vie. Rapport du conseil économique et social. Éditions des journaux officiels. Paris 1999.

17 cp. the programme national de développement des soins palliatifs 2002 - 2005, Ministère de l'emploi et de la solidarité, Ministère délégué à la santé: http://www.sante.gouv.fr

In 2003 Marie de Hennezel presented a report on behalf of the Health Ministry, in which she described the current situation of the *Soins palliatifs* and offered recommendations on the improvement of existing support structures. [18]

2.2 Hospice and palliative care services

In France there are hardly any inpatient hospices that are independent of the hospital. The few existing ones are medical institutions and run by doctors and managers (for example the *Maison Médicale Jeanne Garnier* in Paris or the *Rivage* in Versailles).

In French the word "hospice" signifies an obsolete term for hospital. Therefore the term *Soins palliatifs* (Palliative Care) is preferred, as it includes the medical as well as the psycho-social and spiritual care of the dying. The support structures of the *Soins palliatifs* include:

- *Unités de soins palliatifs* (USP). These are palliative units within hospitals run by doctors. A multi-disciplinary team which includes volunteers, cares for the patients in medical and psycho-social respect. The number of beds in the USP's varies between 3 and 81. Generally though, there are 10 - 12 beds per unit, and one to each room. The average time the patients stay there is 23 days. [19]
- *Équipes mobiles de soins palliatifs* (EMSP). The *Équipes mobiles de soins palliatifs* are mobile, multi-disciplined advisory services, active within the hospital, which currently spread explosively in France – these do not take over any nursing care services and provide solely psycho-social and palliative-medical instruction. They also include volunteer workers.
- *Réseaux de soins palliatifs* are multi-disciplinary home-care services, serving in a coordinating function between the hospital and other outpatient services. The psychologically and palliative-medically schooled team of a *Réseau* does not take over any nursing cares either, and supports patients and families by offering advice. Public nursing care services provide care for the patients, and these are paid by the health insurance fund (comparable to the German welfare centres). Medical care at home is provided by the family doctors. Often patients are taken into a *Réseau* after their release from hospital.
- *Hospitalisation à domicile* (HAD): The so-called "hospital at home" is not specifically meant for the *Soins palliatifs*. The palliative-medical activities of a HAD are restricted to the treatment of pains. The team includes the personnel of the respective hospital unit (nurses, physiotherapists etc.) and the patient's family doctor.

---

18 Fin de vie et accompagnement. Rapport Marie de Hennezel. A summary of that report can be viewed on the homepage of the Health Ministry: http://www.sante.gouv.fr/htm/actu/hennezel/sommaire.htm. Concerning the history of the *Soins palliatifs* in France see for example Le historique de soins palliatifs en France on the homepage of the *Association Francois-Xavier Bagnoud*: http://www.cdrnfxb.org/index.php; or Anna Simon: Palliativarbeit und Hospizbewegung in Frankreich. In: Die Hospiz-Zeitschrift, p. 9 - 13; und Bernard Wary: Le mouvement palliatif français, petitehistoire et évolution. In: Revue JALMALV N° 69. Juni 2002, p. 9 - 15.

19 État des lieux national des structures de soins palliatifs: Enquête auprès des acteurs de terrain. SFAP. November 2003, p. 15: http://sfap.org/article.php?sid=39

- *Associations de soins palliatifs* (ASP) are societies advancing the concept of the *Soins palliatifs* and organizing the work of volunteers in Palliative Care. The *Associations* recruit and train volunteers, and coordinate work with medical institutions like public and private hospitals, clinics or *Réseaux de soins palliatifs,* so that volunteers can support dying people in cooperation with the *Équipes mobiles*, the teams of the *Unités de soins palliatifs* and others. The patients attended to by volunteers of the *Associations* are supposed to be in palliative-medical care at the same time. The volunteers visit the patients only in agreement with the doctor responsible for the particular patient.[20] The *Associations* are active locally, but tend to be organised in regional or national societies as well. They generally consist of volunteers as well and employ only few paid members in the administration.
- In addition *soins palliatifs* includes pain centres (*Centres de la douleur*), advisory centres as well as education programmes (*Diplômes universitaires de soins palliatifs (DUSP)* and *Diplômes inter-universities de soins palliatifs* (DIUSP).
  Presently 225 EMSP, 78 USP with 772 beds, 93 RSP and 175 ASP exist in France.[21]

2.3 Legal regulations and funding

The law issued on June 9th 1999 (No 99 - 477) served to legally fix Palliative Care with the French Parliament. According to this law every human has a right to Palliative Care at the end of his life. Furthermore, this law obligates hospitals and clinics to afford access to appropriate pain therapy and Palliative Care. Part of the legal procedure is the obligation of the Palliative Care institutions to offer of support by volunteers, though these have to be members of one of the *Association de soins palliatifs.*[22]

The Health Ministry's three-year-programme of 1999 and the *Programme national de soins palliatifs 2002 - 2005* also determine the financial support of the Palliative Care by the French government. The health insurance bears the cost of nursing care and since 1999 also gives financial support concerning publicity work and the training of volunteers. As the terms have to be negotiated anew each year it is not possible to predict how long this support will yet continue.[23]

---

[20] Interview with Jean-Pierre Greiveldinger (UNASP), 01 October 2003, in Paris. – About the structures of *Soins palliatifs*: Anna Simon: Palliativarbeit und Hospizbewegung in Frankreich. In: *Die Hospiz-Zeitschrift*, p. 11.

[21] État de lieux national des structures de soins palliatifs: Enquête auprès des acteurs de terrain. SFAP. November 2003, p. 15: http://sfap.org/article.php?sid=39 – These figures diverge from those lately released by the Health Ministry in the *Programme national de développement des soins palliatifs 2002 - 2005*. For the year 2001 this already lists 265 EMSP and 122 USP with 1040 beds, but only 30 RSP. cp. *Programme national de développement des soins palliatifs 2002 - 2005*. Ministère de l'emploi et de la solidarité. Ministère délégué à la santé. p. 11. – The centre of documentation *Francois-Xavier Bagnoud* lists 122 USP with 1040 beds and 265 EMSP for February 2002: http://www.cdrnfxb.org/content/view/106/

[22] cp. the homepage of the Health Ministry, which provides all relevant legal texts for the *Soins palliatifs*: http://www.sante.gouv.fr/htm/dossiers/palliatif/index.htm – see also http://usp-lamirandiere.com

[23] The Health Insurance bears 75 % of the costs for training of the volunteers.

Relatives of seriously ill patients may claim three month of unpaid leave – this opportunity, however, remains reserved for those people financially able to do so.

Both *Unités de soins palliatifs,* die *Équipes mobiles de soins palliatifs* and *Hospitalisation à domicile* are institutions of hospitals and financed by the respective budgets. The health insurance provides complete payment of the nursing care costs. [24] The average daily costs arising for a *Unité de soins palliatifs* per day and patient amount to 356 €, whereas the cost arising per day and patient during a stay within general hospital amount to 760 €. The daily cost for outpatient care amounts to about 175 €. [25]

The *Réseaux de soins palliatifs* receives national support. The French version of social insurance provides a special budget for network care, which pays the employed workers of the *Réseau.* The global amounts for this have to be negotiated anew annually. On the whole, the financial situation of the *Réseaux de soins palliatifs* is neither sufficiently secured nor regulated, so that the help of volunteers remains a main part of the *Réseaux.* [26] The *Associations de soins palliatifs* are supported by volunteers and donations.

2.4 Organisations

The *Société française d'accompagnement et de soins palliatifs (SFAP)* serves as parent organisation of the French Palliative Care. The *Union nationale des associations pour le développement des soins palliatifs (UNASP)* and the *Association jusqu'à la mort accompagner la vie (JALMALV)* are the two largest organizations of volunteers in Palliative Care work. All three organisations have their head office in Paris. The *Association Pierre Clément* in Strasbourg is smaller, yet still extremely engaged.

2.5 Education and training of professional staff

Seminars in palliative medicine and pain therapy are mandatory for French workers [27], yet there is no standardised provision and control for the organisation of such seminars in regards to content and duration – both are left to the universities. [28]

Those who wish to work for Palliative Care have to specialise in this field. For that purpose a number of universities offer so-called *Diplômes universitaires de soins palliatifs* (DUSP). These are post-graduate training sessions which run parallel to the

24 cp. the organistation of the soins palliatifs: http://www.doctissimo.fr/html/sante/mag_2000/mag1208/dossier/soins_palliatifs/sa_3004_loi_soins_palliatifs.htm

25 cp. Structures de soins palliatifs: État de lieux et perspectives. Association Francois-Xavier Bagnoud: http://www.cdrnfxb.org/content/view/106/

26 cp. Anna Simon: Palliativarbeit und Hospizbewegung in Frankreich. In: *Die Hospiz-Zeitschrift.* p. 12.

27 cp. 1. Circulaire DGES-GGS n 15. 09.05.1995. Ministère de l'enseignement supérieur et de la recherche et du ministère de la santé relative aux enseignements de 1er et 2ème cycles des études médicales. – 2. Arrêtés du 4 mars 1997 relatifs à la deuxième partie du deuxième cycle des études médicales. Journal officiel de la république française. 26 March 1997. Article 7, p. 4685 und Article 1, p. 4686.

28 cp. Anna Simon: Palliativmedizin im europäischen Vergleich: Frankreich. In: Thieme. Zeitschrift für Palliativmedizin: http://www.thieme.de/abstracts/palliativmedizin/abstracts2000/daten/pl_2.html

job over one or two years. The *Diplôme inter-universitaire de soins palliatifs* (DIUSP) was introduced in 1999 and serves as training with nationally similar content.[29] Several hospitals also offer training programs for Palliative Care.

2.6 Volunteers

The participation of volunteers in Palliative work is legally regulated in France. Institutions like the *Unités de soins palliatifs* are obliged to offer palliative support by volunteers. However, in several cases this is not possible as there are not enough volunteers or doctors refuse to coordinate their work with volunteers. Each volunteer working for a *Soins palliatifs* has to be a member of an *Association de soins palliatifs* and has to complete a training programme within an *Association.* The regulation of content is nationally standardised: the training consists of a practical part serving as an introduction to the work and a theoretical part treating mainly psychological problems. The relevance of medical and nursing care knowledge is restricted to instances where decisions concerning the intervention of a doctor or a nurse have to be made. The volunteers themselves are not allowed to render nursing care services. The duration of the trainings is similar at all *Associations.*

Towards the end of 2002 the 58 *Associations* of JALMALV counted 1127 volunteer members; the *Associations* of UNASP had 1427 and the remaining 66 *Associations* in France counted 1615 volunteer members. This amounts to about 4169 volunteers who were active within the *Soins palliatifs* at the end of 2002.[30] The greatest part of those volunteers are women between 50 and 70 years, even though a growing number of young people, employees and men engage themselves. Private experiences with sickness, dying and death tend to be the reasons for their commitment.

The volunteers' task is only to be there and to listen. It is easily imaginable that this strict regulation is impossible to keep without conflicts. On the one hand it is difficult for the hard pressed professionals to do without the help of volunteers in their nursing care services; on the other hand the female volunteers often happen to be retired nurses who find it hard to accept the boundaries of their job. Additionally, rivalry for the patient may arise: doctors and nurses, who for themselves would wish for more time for a private talk with the patient must watch the volunteers form strong bonds with them. Finally, the presence of volunteers often serves as incense as they glimpse a great deal of everyday work in the hospital, which is often regarded as supervision by doctors and nurses. For these reasons the volunteer helpers often are not called to the patient until too late. Nevertheless by now there are several hospital doctors working closely together with the EMSP and the ASP.

---

29 cp. ibid.

30 cp. Les associations de bénévoles a fin 2002. A statistic of SFAP + CNAM (03.09.2003). Received from Jean-Pierre Greiveldinger (UNASP, Paris).

2.7 Examples

The Union nationale des associations pour le développement de soins palliatifs (UNASP)

The *Union Nationale des associations pour le développement des soins palliatifs* in Paris is, besides JALMALV, the largest organisation of volunteers for Palliative Care in France. Towards the end of 2002 the UNASP included 51 *Associations des soins palliatifs* (ASP) with 1427 volunteer workers.[31] Besides the recruitment and training of volunteers, who work in the *Unités de soins palliatifs* as well as in the house, education of the public and of the professionals – through literature and congresses – make up the main tasks of the organisation. The UNASP serves as representative for the *Associations* to the public, to the health insurance, and to the SFAP. The UNASP also supports the *Associations* and develops training programmes for Palliative Care.

The volunteers of the *Associations* visit the patients once a week, for about four hours. They do not render nursing care services and have no medical training. Their task is to be there for the sick patient and to take strain off the relatives. In the outpatient sector family doctors, nurses or relatives approach the UNASP; in the inpatient sector this is done by the doctors and nursing personnel of the *Unités de soins palliatifs*. Most of the patients who are cared for at home simultaneously receive pain therapy by a palliative-medical professional of one of the EMSP.

Churches and local shops support the search for volunteers by displaying brochures. In the provinces regular events take place, for example in cinemas. "In the hospitals the UNASP-brochures are not happily received", says Jean-Pierre Greiveldinger, director of the UNASP: "Several doctors do not wish to hear of death and dying, after all their success rests with saving the health of their patients". It is hard to find an open ear in cities like Paris. Yet the demand for care is great. The criteria volunteer helpers must match remain strict nevertheless: the applicants have to be responsible, must be capable to work in a team, and they must not suffer from a terminal sickness themselves. They must be able to listen and to put personal wishes aside while dealing with the sick people. "What does it mean to listen?" – This question lies at the core of the training which every volunteer has to go through. This takes seven evenings, distributed over seven months. About 25% of the applicants continue after that. The volunteers are cared for by a psychologist. The UNASP works solely with volunteers and is kept up by support of membership rates and donations.[32]

The Association JALMALV-Strasbourg

Besides the UNASP JALMALV is the second most important organisation of volunteers for Palliative Care in France. JALMALV means *Jusqu,à la mort accompagner la vie - Accompanying life until death* . 61 *Associations* of France belong to the JALMALV. In the Alsace the organization is present in Colmar and in Strasbourg.

[31] ibid.

[32] Interview with Jean-Pierre Greiveldinger and Claude Reinhart, 01 October 2003, in Paris.

Recruiting and training of volunteers, advice in *Soins palliatifs* and support for relatives, as well as providing a 24-hours Telephone-service and mourning groups make up the main activities of JALMALV-Strasbourg. The organisation cares for an average of 40 - 50 patients, mainly cancer patients. Excluding the only full-time office-workers all 35 members – 31 women and 4 men between 40 and 70 years – are volunteers. A completed training is required to work for JALMALV-Strasbourg. The volunteers are trained in conversation, especially in non-verbal communication, and in psychology. Death and mourning are also talked about. This is succeeded by an introduction to the practical work: the new workers accompany experienced members to the *Unités de soins palliatifs* of the hospitals, they accompany the *Équipes mobiles de soins palliatifs* and visit the patients at home. The training is completed after one year. The participation in regular group meetings which discuss personal fears, conflicts and mourning is mandatory for the volunteers. The so-called *Groupes de paroles* take place once a month under the supervision of a psychologist.

Brigitte Grosshans holds the office of president of JALMALV-Strasbourg for about 10 years now. The trained nurse cares for dying people at home and simultaneously she works for the *Association* on a voluntary basis. She is responsible for the organization. During the interview with Brigitte Grosshans the volunteer Mireille Ochsenbein is present as well. She tells of her experiences with relatives, and of the dealings of the families with the dying:

Many families are afraid, and panic when the end approaches. They don't know what will happen, because they have no experience with death. Often they don't know what to do with the dead body. This is of course also a result of the disappearance of religious ties and duties. The outpatient team then assumes a critical advising function. Real complications arise when the relatives refuse to acknowledge that the patient will die, or when they are simply unable to address openly what everyone knows anyway. ‚Just don't say anything!', – that is what we often hear. But there are other stories as well: there once was a patient who knew he might suffocate in the end drew up a decree together with the Équipe mobile and his family regulating that no re-animating measures should be taken in the case of threatening asphyxiation. Of course it is terrible for the relatives to let the patient die in such a way.

You live with the families through all things, good and bad. And death is experienced in very different ways. They say there are several stages of dying, at the end of which stands the consent to the end. My experience is that there are different stages in dealing with the approaching death: there are denial, struggle, depression and consent, but there is no fixed order.

And the families: many have never seen a dead body before. In the media death is ever-present, but not in private life. We are no longer allowed to grow old and die. [33]

Jalmalv Strasbourg, Brigitte Grosshans, Reimer Gronemeyer, Mireille Ochsenbein

The Association Pierre Clément in Strasbourg

The *Association Pierre Clément*, another volunteer organisation for Palliative Care, was founded in 1985 by Jeanne Andrée Chausson. At that time Madame Chausson was a nurse and cared for a nineteen-year-old cancer patient – Pierre Clément. As the doctors could do nothing more for him and the hospital wanted to send him home the young nurse took the patient into her home and cared for him until his death one and a half years later. On his death-bed Pierre Clément asked Madame Chausson to do what she had done for him for others as well, and she built the first small *Unité de soins palliatifs* in the Alsace (in Hagenou). At the same time she founded the *Association Pierre Clément* and initiated a training for volunteer helpers. By now Jeanne Andrée Chausson works in the sector of nursing care training. Her husband, Maurice Chausson, currently holds the office of president of *Pierre Clément*.

Not counting two office workers who are paid by the health insurance all 116 members of *Pierre Clément* are volunteers. The engagement and training of volunteers is supervised by a psychologist and three pedagogues. It takes seven month and consists of two daylong meetings per month during the first eight weeks, of consecu-

33 Interview with Brigitte Grosshans (Director) and Mireille Ochsenbein (Volunteer), *Association JALMALV- Strasbourg*, 29 September 2003, in Strasbourg. For purposes of summary the words of Mrs. Ochsenbein have not been quoted exactly. For information on the *Association Jalmalv* see http://www.jalmalv.org

tive practical work as well as further meetings each month. The organisation subsists mostly on membership rates of the volunteers and other members, and on donations.

Especially old people and cancer patients are cared for by the *Unités de soins palliatifs*, in nursing homes and at home. 24 volunteers take turns in being present all day in the palliative wards in Hagenou. They work as much as they wish, there is no strict regulation of working hours. There is a large work schedule pinned to the office wall where everyone can enter his name to work when and as long as he wishes. The hours of attending to the patients the volunteers coordinate directly with the patient and the families. The average amounts to two hours per week. In the case of home care two volunteers attend to one patient together since the care for a patient in the familiar surroundings generally demands more workers:

> Families tend to draw the volunteers into the nursing care, which is not permitted. Of course this can't be complied with always. Many patients in the nursing homes suffer from dementia. It is obvious that you can't sit and listen alone, but have to help with eating and with other things. If a nurse is present the volunteers are allowed to help with nursing services as well. [34]

New voluntary helpers are won especially with the help of advertisements and lectures. The surrounding villages display advertising posters. The most important prerequisites to work for the organisation are considered to be reliability, psychological endurance, and the skill to hold oneself back in interaction with the patient. Great attention is paid to prevent missionary advances towards patients by volunteers who are themselves religious. They are supposed to talk from person to person, says Eliane Veidh, the director. The volunteers are mainly women who themselves have experience with sickness and death of people close to them. Nevertheless it is extremely hard to win enough volunteers, says Mrs. Veidh. The demand for Palliative Care here is great as well.

The average duration patients are cared for is varying. One patient has been cared for more than 10 years. The families of deceased patients are supported for a long time afterwards still. Once a month they meet with a psychologist of the *Association*.

The Association François-Xavier Bagnoud in Paris

The *Association François-Xavier Bagnoud* was founded in 1992 in Switzerland, and since 1997 it is present in Paris as well. Beside other humanitarian projects – especially aid projects concerning HIV/AIDS – the *Association* FXB engages in Palliative Care, developing and initiating programmes for Palliative Care and trying to alert the public to the topic; there is a 24-hour telephone-service offering advice to the public and to professionals of the health sector. AFXB also serves as the national centre for documentation of the *Soins palliatifs* in France, running a national, partly international, library. Further activities include science and training in Palliative Care as well as the home care for dying people and their families. A mobile, multi-disciplinary team working like one of the *Réseau de soins palliatifs* and caring for an average

[34] Interview with Eliane Veidh and Maurice Chausson, 10 October 2003, in Strasbourg.

of 30 patients at home and in hospital belongs to the centre for outpatient palliative care as well. The team coordinates the work of both nurses and doctors and provides palliative-medical advice. The founder of the AFXB, Albina du Boisrouvray, began to build up the outpatient service in a time when Palliative Care was supported by the state only within hospitals.

The help of volunteers is an important part of the AFXB. The volunteers are drawn from other *Associations* like JALMALV, and work in the library or in a mobile team. AFXB also receives financial support by the state, especially for the training of volunteers.[35]

The Association RIVAGE and the Unité Claire Demeure in Versailles

The *Association* RIVAGE (engl. shores) was founded in 1990 and trains about 20 volunteers each year, who then care for patients in the *Maison de Santé de Claire Demeure* and at home. *Claire Demeure* is a medical institution for geriatric long-term care and Palliative Care. The house was founded in 1971 by nuns and was extended in 1991. Of the 64 beds 48 are reserved for geriatric care, 16 for Palliative Care. On the whole 56 volunteers work for at least 4 hours per week in the *Unité de soins palliatifs,* in the 7 interdisciplinary *Équipe Groupes* of the outpatient palliative care and bereavement support. The average duration of the patients' stay in the *Unité* amounts to 25 days. The health insurance bears the cost for the stay for about three to four month. In case of longer stays the terms have to be negotiated anew or the patient is further cared for at home.

Claire Demeure is a private institution, which receives public money since it is regarded as a hospital service. The financial support consists of national subsidies (50%), membership rates (25%) and donations (5%). The remaining 20% are compensated by the help of volunteers. The health insurance bears 75% of the costs for the training of the volunteers in the A*ssociation.*[36]

The Maison Médicale Jeanne Garnier in Paris

The *Maison Médicale Jeanne Garnier* was originally an institution for poor, cancer or Aids patients. Today the inpatient units mainly admit cancer patients. Patients suffering from chronical pain receive pain therapy on an outpatient basis. The number of Aids infections has receeded, since HIV/Aids has become more of a chronic sickness thanks to modern medicines. 20% of the patients are admitted directly from their homes, but the greater part comes from hospital. The average age is 60 years, the average duration of stay amounts to two to four weeks, sometimes even three to four months.

The building of the house was financed by a private foundation of wealthy widows – the *Association des Dames du Calvaire*. The running costs are paid by the social

---

35 Interview with Dr. Alina Salomovichi, 03 October 2003, in Paris.

36 Interview Christiane Blanc-Chaudier, Marie Quinquis, Phillipe Vrouvakis and the volunteer Pia Neyret, 02.10.2003 in Versailles. The Association is online on http://www.association-rivage.com.

insurance funds. As the national support does not cover all costs *Jeanne Garnier* continues to be supported by the *Dames du Calvaires*, who have founded a number of further institutions for seriously ill people in France.

With 81 beds the *Maison Jeanne Garnier* is the largest *Unité de soins palliatifs* in France and one of the few *Unités*, which are not integrated into a hospital. [37] The best-known are the *Unités de soins palliatifs* and the *Équipes mobiles de soins palliatifs* in hospitals. As a mobile service the latter is of course considerably cheaper than inpatient units.

The interdisciplinary team includes doctors, nurses, psychologists, physiotherapists, a priest and 110 volunteers. The volunteers work in the *Maison Médicale Jeanne Garnier* and in a nursing home, the *Résidence Aurélle Jousset*, which is located in the same building.

The volunteers are trained in the house. At first the accompany one of the experienced volunteers for three days. Following a period of reflection the interested applicants may decide on the training. The volunteers should be sensitised to the needs of the patients. They are being prepared to cooperate with the psychologist caring for the personnel and the families of the patients during their time of mourning.

The rooms are single rooms which provide an additional bed each for a relative. For the time of the final days a special family room is provided. The relatives tend to make use of these offers especially during the last days of a patient. Some families travelling from further away often stay for longer. One woman for example lived there for six months until the death of her husband. [38]

3. Summary

Palliative Care is a powerful movement in France. It is carried out by the *Associations de soins palliatifs* (Non-governmental-organisations for Palliative Care) and their 4169 voluntary members, by the *Réseaux de soins palliatifs* (outpatient nursing care services) and by the public hospital institutions like the *Unités de soins palliatifs* (Palliative wards) and the *Équipes mobiles de soins palliatifs* (multi-disciplinary advisory services). Inpatient institutions independent of the hospital are scarce. The few existing ones are generally led by doctors and managers and serve as medical institutions for terminally sick patients.

The development of palliative home care is an important part of the *Programme national de développement des soins palliatifs 2002 - 2005* of the Health Ministry. On the one hand the outpatient/home care is cheaper than the inpatient care and on the other hand most people wish to die at home and still be treated professionally. The

---

[37] *Jeanne Garnier* is a *Maison Médicale* – therefore, a medical institution – and cannot be compared to an inpatient hospice as it is known in Germany.

[38] Interview with Monsieur Philippe Mazeron, 01 October 2003, in Paris. The institution is online at http://www.jeanne-garnier.org

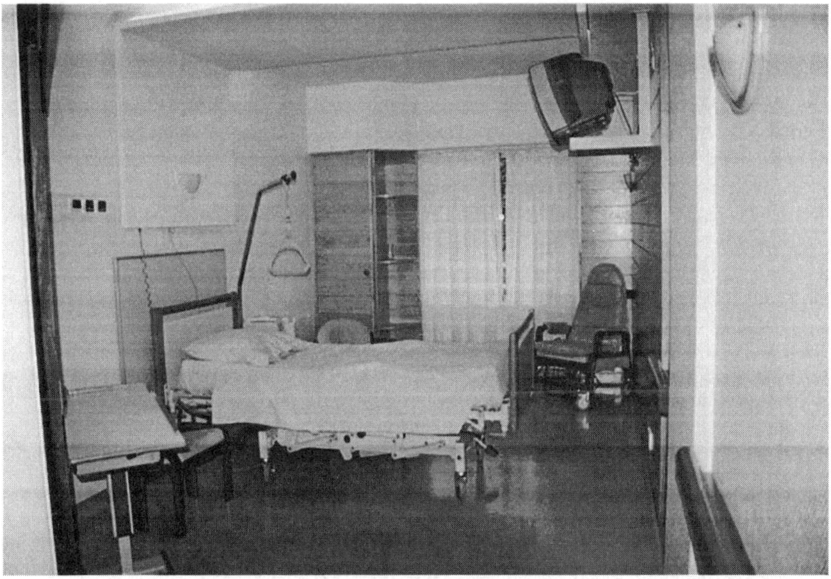

Room in the Maison Médicale Jeanne Garnier, Paris

cooperation of state, pubic health institutions and the powerful movement of the *Associations de soins palliatifs* becomes ever more important therefore. The problem with that is – and that goes for other European countries as well – that the family bounds become ever more instable, local bounds fray and the demands of flexibility and mobility of the job market continue to grow – the home care in familiar surroundings becomes less and less possible. Therefore inpatient support structures remain a necessary feature and also an urgent one.

Sources and literature

Association Francois-Xavier Bagnoud: Trame du dossier de demande d'autorisation d'une structure d'hospitalisation à domicile spécialisée en soins palliatifs. Paris 2000.

Blanchet, Veronique: Soins Palliatifs: Réflexions et pratiques. Paris 2000.

Circulaire DGES-GGS n 15. 09.05.1995. Ministère de l'enseignement supérieur et de la recherche et du ministère de la santé relative aux enseignements de 1er et 2ème cycles des études médicales. – 2. Arrêtés du 4 mars 1997 rélatifs à la deuxième partie du deuxième cycle études médicales. Journal officiel de la république française from 26 March 1997, article 7, p 4685 and article 1.

Decisier, Donat: L'accompagnement des personnes en fin de vie. Rapport du conseil économique et social. Éditions des journaux officiels. Paris 1999.

Delbecque, Henri:Les soins palliatifs et l'accompagnement des malades en fin de vie. Ministère de la santé et de l'action humanitaire. La documentation française. Paris 1993.

Desfosses, Gilbert: Unité de soins palliatifs avec lits et EMSP: Évolution des concepts. In: JALMALV 1996 n°44. p. 23 - 29.

Fernand-Bechmann, Dan.: Le métier de bénévole. Paris 2000 (Ethnolosociology).

Gomas, Jean Marie: L'organisation des soins palliatifs à domicile. La revue du praticien. Médicine générale. 1998 Tome 12, n°431.

Kermarec, Jean: Soins Palliatifs: Objectifs et réalisations de l'association pour le développement des soins palliatifs. In: Bull. Acad. Natle. Med. 1996 Vol. 180 n°8, p. 1951 - 1965.

Lassaunière, Jean-Michel: Guide pratique de soins palliatifs: Aspects médicaux. Paris 2000.

Lassaunière, Jean-Michel: Guide pratique de soins palliatifs: Aspects psycho-sociaux. Paris 2001.

Le Boucher d,Herouville, Christine: Équipes mobile de soins palliatifs. Une structure originale qui répond à un besoin spécifique. Réflexion menée à partir d'observations cliniques.Paris 1992.

Le développement des soins palliatifs. Ministère de l'emploi et de la solidarité. In: SFAP: Jounées nationales des équipes mobiles. Montpellier 2001.

Le répertoire des soins palliatifs en France. Paris 2000 (Edition à societé française d'accompagnement et de soins palliatifs).

Salamagne, Michèle: Hospice in France. In: Hospice Care on the International Scene. Ed. by Cicely Saunders/Robert Kastenbaum. New York 1997. p. 130 - 143.

Salamagne, Michèle: Accompagner jusqu'au bout de la vie: Manifeste pour les soins palliatifs. In: Récherches morales. Hg.v. Dr. Michèle Salamagne-H. / Emmanuel Hirsch. Paris 1992.

Sebag-Lanoe, Renée: Mourir accompagne. Paris 1984.

SFAP/CNAMS: Les associations de bénévoles a fin 2002. Statistics. 03.09.2003.

SFAP: Etat de lieux des structures de soins palliatifs: Enquête auprès des acteurs de terrain. November 2003. p. 15: http://sfap.org/article.php?sid=39

Simon, Anna: Palliativarbeit und Hospizbewegung in Frankreich. In: Die Hospiz-Zeitschrift. Fachforum für Hospizarbeit: Hospiz und Palliative Care international. From the Bundesarbeitsgemeinschaft Hospiz. Edition 14. 4. year 2002/4. p. 9 - 13.

Soins palliatifs à domicile: Expérience de l'équipe d'hospitalisation à domicile de Grenoble. In: Revue JALMALV n°20 1990. p. 23 - 26.

Tavernier, Monique: Les soins palliatifs. Paris 2000.

Wary, Bernhard: Le mouvement palliatif française. Petite histoire et évolution. In: Revue JALMALV n°69 June 2002. p. 9 - 15.

Internet sources

Hennezel, Jean Marie: Fin de vie et accompagnement. (Summary: http://wwwsante.gouv.fr/htm/actu/hennezel/sommaire.htm)

Le historique de soins palliatifs en France. Association François-Xavier Bagnoud: http://ww.cdrnfxb.org/index.php

Neuwirth, Lucien: Rapport d'information sur les soins palliatifs et l'accompagnement. Rapport d'information 207 (98 - 99). Commission des affaires sociales: http://www.senat.fr/rap/r98-207/r98-207.html

Organisation des soins palliatifs: http://www.doctissimo.fr/html/sante/mag_2000/mag1208/dossier/soins_ palliatifs/sa_3004_loi_soins_palliatifs.htm

Programme national de développement des soins palliatifs 2002 - 2005. Ministère de l'emploi et de la solidarité. Ministère délégué à la santé: http://www.sante.gouv.fr

Simon, Anna: Palliativmedizin im europäischen Vergleich: Frankreich. In: Thieme. Zeitschrift für Palliativmedizin: http://www.thieme.de/abstracts/palliativmedizin/abstracts2000/daten/pl_2.html

Structures de soins palliatifs: ètat de lieux et perspectives. Association Francois-Xavier Bagnoud: http://www.cdrnfxb.org/content/view/106/

Population Division of the Department of Economic and Social Affairs of the United Nations Secretariat, World Population Prospects: The 2002 Revision Population Database: http://esa.un.org/unpp

Periodicals

JALMALV
Revue de la Fédération JALMAV (Jusqu'à la mort accompagner la vie) 12, Hector Berlioz, 38000 Grenoble

Études sur la mort
Éditions l'esprit du temps – B.P. 107 - 33491 Le Bouscat cedex

ASP Liaisons
ASP Fondatrice pour le développement des soins palliatifs – 44, rue Blanche, 75009 Paris

Lettre de la SFAP
Société française d'accompagnement et de soins palliatifs. 106, Avenue Emile Zola, 75015 Paris

UNASP Actualites
Union nationale des associations pour le développment des soins palliatifs. 44, rue Blanche, 75009 Paris

Bibliography on the Internet

Association François-Xavier Bagnoud:
http://www.cdrnfxb.org/pdf/ouvrages.pdf (approx. 500 pages)

Information on the Internet

Association François-Xavier Bagnoud: http://www.cdrnfxb.org/index.php

Le répertoire de soins palliatifs en France. Paris 2000 (SFAP, Société française d'accompagnement et de soins palliatifs): http://www.sfap.org/modules.php?ModPath=dep&ModStart=dep

Association française d'information funéraire: http://www.afif.asso.fr/francais/conseils/conseil48.html
Hospice Information: http://www.hospiceinformation.info

List of interviews (in chronological order)

- Brigitte Grosshans (Director), Mireille Ochsenbein (Volunteer) *JALMALV-Strasbourg* Strasbourg, 29 September 2003
- Dr. Noëlle Vescovali (Director)
  Réseau de soins palliatifs à domicile Le Pallium
  Institut de promotion de la santé
  Trappes, 30 September 2003
- Dr. Aude Le Divenah (Responsible for Palliative Care)
  Ministére de la santé
  Direction de l'hospitalisation et le l'organisation des soins
  Paris, 30 September 2003
- Jean-Pierre Greiveldinger (Director)
  Claude Reinhart (Vizepräsident UNASP, Präsident ASP-Fondatrice)
  Union nationale des associations pour le développement de soins palliatifs (UNASP)
  Paris, 01 October 2003
- Philippe Mazeron (Director of Administration)
  Maison Médicale Jeanne Garnier
  Paris, 01 October 2003
- Christiane Blanc-Chaudier (President),
  Marie Quinquis (Vice president), Pia Neyret (Volunteer),
  Philippe Vrouvakis (Director OIDR)
  Association RIVAGE and *Maison Claire Demeure*
  Versailles, 02 October 2003
- Dr. Alina Salomovichi (Director of Palliative Care Centers)
  Centre de ressources national François-Xavier Bagnoud (CDRN FXB)
  Fondation Croix Saint Simon
  Paris, 03 October 2003
- Dr. Luc Plassais (leading Doctor)
  Unité de soins palliatifs, Hopital Cognacq-Jay
  Paris, 06 October 2003
- Dr. Michèle Salamagne, Dr. Sylvain Pourchet (leading Doctor)
  Unité de soins palliatifs, Hopital Paul Brousse
  Paris, 06 October 2003
- René-Claude Baud (Responsible for training)
  Association Albatros
  Lyon, 08 October 2003
- Jean-Louis Béal (Medical director),
  Veronique Alavoine (Psychologist)
  La Mirandière (USP)
  Association Jean-Pierre Pere

Quetigny, 09 October 2003

- Eliane Veidh (Director),
  Maurice Chausson (President)
  Association Pierre Clément
  Strasbourg, 10 October 2003

Germany

Felix Schumann

1. General conditions

1.1 Demographics

- In 2000, Germany's population totalled 82.3 million. Predictions indicate that the population will drop to 78.7 million inhabitants by 2050. [1]
- In the same time the average life expectancy of 78.6 is expected to grow to 83.7 years of age by 2050, whereas the median age will rise from 40.0 years in 2000 to 47.4 by 2050. [2]
- In 1950, people 65 years or older in Germany represented 9.7% of the population. In 2000, it was already 16.4% and is projected to grow to a remarkable 28.4% by 2050. [3]
- Similarly, people aged 80 years or older represented 1.0% of the population in 1950. That percentage grew in 2000 to 3.5% and is estimated to grow to 12.2% by 2050. [4]
- The number of people aged 15 to 59 years per older person over the age of 60, was 61.1% of the total population in 2000 and is expected to drop to 50.1% by 2050. [5]
- The annual mortality rate is expected to rise from 10.3% per 1000 inhabitants between 2000 - 2005 to 14.9 per 1000 inhabitants by 2045 - 2050. [6]
- Only 10% of all people die at home whereas 80 percent spent the last days of their lives in institutions. [7]
- As reported by the Federal Statistical Office, a total of 393,800 people – nearly every second person – died of a systemic circulatory disease, 210,000 of malignant neoplasms, 53,600 of diseases of the respiratory system, 41,800 of diseases of the

---

1 Population Division of the Department of Economic and Social Affairs of the United Nations Secretariat, *World Population Prospects: The 2004 Revision* and *World Urbanization Prospects: The 2003 Revision*. Official Homepage of the United Nations: http://esa.un.org/unpp

2 ibid.

3 ibid.

4 ibid.

5 ibid

6 ibid.

7 Klaus Dörner: Der gute Arzt. Lehrbuch der ärztlichen Grundhaltung. Stuttgart 2001, p. 97 et seqq.

digestive system, and 34,300 died an unnatural death e.g. poisoning or injuries in 2002.[8]

1.2 Health care system

Employers and employees each pay half of the latter's health insurance contributions. These vary from company to company and in 2002 stood on average at 14 percent of gross earnings.[9]The share of patients additional contributions are continuously growing. Almost everyone living in Germany has health insurance. Some 88 percent belong to a statutory health scheme and around nine percent are privately insured.Up to a certain level of income, all employees are obliged to join one of the over 315 statutory health insurance schemes. Persons earning a higher gross amount than this are free to join a private scheme if they so desire. Subject to certain conditions, the statutory system also covers pensioners, the unemployed, trainees and students.[10] 2.3 percent of the population have other insurance (for example welfare recipients), only 0,1 - 0,3 percent of the total population has no health insurance at all.[11]

The total health care expenditure was 11.2 percent in proportion to the GDP in 2002[12], which means that Germany ranks second in that category worldwide behind the United States of America. At the moment, cost-saving measures and structural reforms to the German social and health care system dominate public debate. The introduction of practice and prescription fees in 2004 are two examples of the current process of transformation.

The poor economic situation (decreased revenues) and the demographic development (increased expenditure) have put pressure on the German Health planers to reform the social and health care system.[13] The emphasis is placed on integrative concepts. Hospice and palliative care services can play a significant part in this process of transformation. In light of the reforms, especially the new *Hospital Financing Act*, the need for voluntary hospices will continue to rise. Hospitals will aim to admit terminally ill and dying patients into hospices even though it might only be for a few days.[14]

Only a few years ago, hospices [. . .] were regarded as the mischief's of the Health care system." [. . .] Today they could function as beacons. Integrative health care provision and effective case

[8] Official Homepage Federal Statistical Office Germany: http://www.destatis.de/presse/englisch/pm2004/p0410092.htm

[9] Official Homepage Ministry of Health and Social Security: http://www.bmgs.bund.de/eng/gra/index.php

[10] Official Homepage Ministry of Health and Social Security: http://www.bmgs.bund.de/eng/gra/index.php

[11] WIKIPEDIA, die freie Enzyklopädie: http://de.wikipedia.org/wiki/Gesundheitssystem

[12] Official Homepage Federal Statistical Office Germany: http://www.destatis.de/basis/e/gesu/gesugra2.htm

[13] Official Homepage Ministry of Health and Social Security: http://www.bmgs.bund.de/downloads/DieReformenglish.pdf

[14] Rochus Allert: Hospize und die Gesundheitsreform 2004. In: Die Hospiz-Zeitschrift 21. 6. Jahrgang 2004/3, p. 6.

management, which were intended by the Health Care Reform Act, have already been realised here. [15]

2. Hospice and palliative care in Germany

2.1 History

In 1971, Jesuit Father Iblacker's documentary film "Noch 16 Tage ... eine Sterbeklinik in London" (16 days to go ... a dying clinic in London) was shown on German television for the first time. Iblacker reports on the work at *St Christopher's Hospice* in London, the first hospice of modern times. The TV audience were presented with the opportunity to take a close look at the life of dying patients, spending the last few weeks and days in the hospice. In the film the patients express their wishes and fears. The staff are also portrayed with their tasks and principles. In hindsight, Pater Iblacker's intention was to promote the work at *St Christopher's* as a kind of role model for future services in Germany. At the time however, the documentary had counterproductive effects: The title "Sterbeklinik" [16] ("Dying clinic") was confusing for the audience and resulted in expressed rejection of the hospice concept by a majority of the viewers, which continued to dominate the public discussion in the seventies. In the "century of ignorance" [17], there was no noteworthy development of hospice and palliative care in Germany.

During the eighties, described as the "century of the pioneers", [18] the public took little notice of hospice care as tempered discussions on Euthanasia are held. The German pioneers are predominantly inspired by hospice care from England. [19] Key dates in the eighties are: [20]

- 1983 The first German *Palliativstation* (palliative ward) opens at the *University Clinic Cologne*
- 1985 Foundation of *Christophorus Hospice Society* in Munich
- 1986 Establishment of *IGSL-Internationale Gesellschaft für Sterbebegleitung und Lebensbeistand* in Bingen (International Society for the Care of the Dying and Life Support)

---

15 Petra Weritz-Hanf: Hospiz als Lernmodell für Gesundheitssystem und Gesellschaft. In: Die Hospiz-Zeitschrift 21. 6. Jahrgang 2004/3, p. 9.

16 As Seitz/ Seitz show in their excellent study, the television channel ZDF decided – against the will of Father Iblacker – to translate the term hospice with dying clinic to gain more publicity for the programme. Cp. Dieter Seitz/ Oliver Seitz: Die moderne Hospizbewegung in Deutschland auf dem Weg ins öffentliche Bewusstsein: Ursprünge, kontroverse Diskussionen, Perspektiven. Herbolzheim 2002, p. 143.

17 Dieter Seitz/ Oliver Seitz: Die moderne Hospizbewegung in Deutschland auf dem Weg ins öffentliche Bewusstsein: Ursprünge, kontroverse Diskussionen, Perspektiven. Herbolzheim 2002, p. 137.

18 ibid., p. 138.

19 Johann-Christoph Student (ed.): Das Hospiz-Buch. Freiburg im Breisgau 1999, p. 41.

20 cp. Dieter Seitz/ Oliver Seitz: Die moderne Hospizbewegung in Deutschland auf dem Weg ins öffentliche Bewusstsein: Ursprünge, kontroverse Diskussionen, Perspektiven. Herbolzheim 2002, p. 347, p. 138.

– 1986 Opening of the first German hospice in Aachen

The origins of hospice work in Germany have Christian roots with three Catholic priests being responsible for early developments.[21]

Similar to other European countries the nationwide development of hospice and palliative care services started in the nineties. In this "century of establishment"[22] for the first time inpatient services grew considerably. In 1990 there were only three inpatient hospices and three hospital palliative care units, whereas numbers had grown substantially in 1999 counting 65 inpatient hospices and 55 hospital palliative care units.[23] Key milestones in the nineties:[24]

- 1992 Foundation of *Bundesarbeitsgemeinschaft Hospiz e.V. zur Förderung von ambulanten, teilstationären und stationären Hospizen und Palliativmedizin (BAG)* (The German Hospice Umbrella Organisation). This national organisation includes all *LAG's*, the sixteen *Länder* (state) hospice organisations.
- 1994 Formation of *DGP-Deutsche Gesellschaft für Palliativmedizin* (German Society for Palliative Medicine)
- 1995 The *Deutsche Hospiz Stiftung* (German Hospice Foundation) starts its work
- 1995 Development of guidelines for hospice care, recommendations for the education and training of volunteers by the *BAG*[25]
- 1998 General agreement on the type and scope, and quality assurance for inpatient hospice care between insurance funds, *BAG* and charities[26]
- 1999 Establishment of the first *Chair of Palliative Medicine* at the University of Bonn

Besides the inpatient services, professional[27] or voluntary run home hospice services provide care for the dying. The voluntary teams were a key factor for the development of the German hospice movement in the nineties. From this, a voluntary civil movement was dedicated to improve the situation of the dying. The voluntary *BAG* represents the hospice movement in the public and also in discussions with policy makers and health care authorities.

The hospice movement has positioned itself as

(...) a civil movement of volunteers and professionals, who are dedicated to improving the situation of dying people and their relatives in every aspect, including medical ones. Alongside

21 cp. Johann-Christoph Student (ed.): Das Hospiz-Buch. Freiburg im Breisgau 1999, p. 39.

22 Dieter Seitz/ Oliver Seitz: Die moderne Hospizbewegung in Deutschland auf dem Weg ins öffentliche Bewusstsein: Ursprünge, kontroverse Diskussionen, Perspektiven. Herbolzheim 2002, p. 139.

23 Stein Husebø/ Eberhard Klaschik (eds.): Palliativmedizin. Berlin et al. 2003, p. 6.

24 cp. Dieter Seitz/ Oliver Seitz: Die moderne Hospizbewegung in Deutschland auf dem Weg ins öffentliche Bewusstsein: Ursprünge, kontroverse Diskussionen, Perspektiven. Herbolzheim 2002, p. 347.

25 Bundesarbeitsgemeinschaft Hospiz e.V. zur Förderung von ambulanten, teilstationären und stationären Hospizen und Palliativmedizin (BAG): http://www.hospiz.net/bag/index.html

26 ibid.

27 Dieter Seitz/ Oliver Seitz: Die moderne Hospizbewegung in Deutschland auf dem Weg ins öffentliche Bewusstsein: Ursprünge, kontroverse Diskussionen, Perspektiven. Herbolzheim 2002, p. 347.

pain therapy; palliative nursing, psychosocial and spiritual care are the characteristics part of hospice care.[28]

The following overview gives an account of the progress being made thanks to the efforts of both volunteers and professionals in the last few years:

Development of home care services:[29]

- 1996: 451 home care services
- 2001: 927 home care services
- 2004: 1310 home care services

Development of inpatient hospice and palliative care services:[30]

- 1996: 30 hospices, 28 palliative care hospital units
- 2001: 95 hospices, 74 palliative care hospital units
- 2004: 116 hospices, 92 palliative care hospital units[31]

Key dates this century:

- 2002 Palliative medicine was integrated into the *Approbationsordnung* (examination regulations) for physicians as an optional exam subject[32]
- 2002 General agreement on the promotion of home care, considering the orientation, quality and scope of services, between insurance funds, the *BAG* and charities
- 2003 Establishment of the second *Chair of Palliative Medicine* at the University Clinic in Aachen
- 2004 Release of the handbook *Sorgsam (careful). Qualitätshandbuch für stationäre Hospize (Quality handbook for inpatient hospice care)* for the assurance of quality standards in inpatient hospices

In contrast to other European countries, the hospice movement and palliative medicine in Germany have developed independently into different fields. The division between the two concepts is visible in the main organisations *DGP* and *BAG*, which have developed contradicting models of provision. On one side, the *DGP*, represents the mainly professional medical side, in the structural form of hospital palliative care units (Palliativstationen). On the other side, the *BAG* represents hospice care predominantly carried out by volunteers, in independent inpatient hospices and different forms of home care services. To a large extent the developments of the two concepts have been independent from the other.[33] There are various reasons for this:

a) Physicians
   - Argue that they are not adequately integrated into hospice initiatives

---

28 Gerda Graf: Die Hospizbewegung in Deutschland. In: Qualifizierte Begleitung von Sterbenden und Trauernden. Ed. by Werner Burgheim. Merching 2003.

29 Bundesarbeitsgemeinschaft Hospiz e.V. zur Förderung von ambulanten, teilstationären und stationären Hospizen und Palliativmedizin (BAG): http://www.hospiz.net/bag/index.html

30 ibid.

31 Deutsche Gesellschaft für Palliativmedizin: http://www.dgpalliativmedizin.de/

32 Bundesministerium der Justiz (ed.): Bundesgesetzblatt Jahrgang 2002 Teil I Nr. 44, ausgegeben zu Bonn am 3. Juli 2002: Approbationsordnung für Ärzte vom 27. Juni 2002.

33 Stein Husebø/ Eberhard Klaschik (eds.): Palliativmedizin. Berlin u.a. 2003, p. 5.

- Object "the insufficient presence of doctors in German hospices [. . .], which will subsequently result in inadequate symptom control, particularly a lack of pain therapy in the case of incurable dying patients" [34]

b) Hospice lobbyists
   - Complain about "medical dominance" in the care of dying [35] and
   - fear the medicalisation of dying.

Beyond all the disputes and competition going on, there are cases where the two groups involved are willing to cooperate in order to improve the situation of the dying.

2.2 Hospice and palliative care services

For hospice work in Germany the basic principle "home care comes before inpatient care" applies:

> The emphasis of hospice work is to provide care at the patients or his families home to enable the dying person a life in dignity and self-determination until the very end [. . .] Besides home hospice care and the care of the dying in nursing homes, a limited number of inpatient hospices are necessary. The aim of inpatient hospice care is to offer care (palliative medicine and nursing care) in order to improve life quality of the dying person, which will not affect their dignity and also rules out active Euthanasia. [36]

In 2004 there were 1310 hospice home care services. [37] In order to understand the different concepts and grades of hospice home care, the nationwide model *Definitionen und Qualitätskriterien ambulanter Hospizarbeit der BAG und LAG Hospiz* (Definitions and quality criteria of hospice home care by the BAG and LAG Hospices) is presented in detail: [38]

a) Outpatient [39] hospice initiatives and hospice groups (760 in 2002) [40]
   Tasks:
   - Education and public relations and/or
   - Psycho-social support by specially educated hospice volunteers and/or
   - Bereavement support

b) Outpatient hospice services (AHD, 170 in 2002) [41]
   Tasks (in addition to 1):

---

[34] ibid., 6.

[35] Dieter Seitz/ Oliver Seitz: Die moderne Hospizbewegung in Deutschland auf dem Weg ins öffentliche Bewusstsein: Ursprünge, kontroverse Diskussionen, Perspektiven. Herbolzheim 2002, p. 203.

[36] Bundesarbeitsgemeinschaft Hospiz e.V. zur Förderung von ambulanten, teilstationären und stationären Hospizen und Palliativmedizin (BAG): Rahmenvereinbarung nach § 39a Satz 4 SGB V über Art und Umfang sowie zur Sicherung der Qualität der stationären Hospizversorgung vom 13.03.1998, i. d. F. vom 09.02.1999. http://www.hospiz.net/bag/index.html

[37] Bundesarbeitsgemeinschaft Hospiz e.V. zur Förderung von ambulanten, teilstationären und stationären Hospizen und Palliativmedizin (BAG): http://www.hospiz.net/bag/index.html

[38] ibid.

[39] Outpatient in German hospice settings mainly refers to home care provision.

[40] ibid.

[41] ibid.

- Psycho-social advice
- Terminal care, bereavement support, support for relatives
- Organisation and coordination of volunteer education courses
- Public relations

Standards:
- Qualified staff (at least 10 trained, standby volunteers; at least 0,5 full time, specially trained qualified coordinators)
- Hospice office
- Availability during office hours

c) Outpatient hospice and palliative care advisory services (AHPB, 50 in 2002)[42]
Tasks (in addition to 1 and 2):
- Advice on palliative care treatment and consistent consultation with attending physicians and care services involved
- Mediation of further help

Standards:
- High professional psycho-social advice
- At least 0,5 full-time palliative care staff members

d) Outpatient hospice and palliative care service (AHPP, no stats available)
Tasks (in addition to 1, 2 and 3):
- Palliative care provision in close collaboration with attending physicians
- Basic care if needed
- Where applicable instruction of relatives in palliative nursing measures

Standards:
- Qualified staff (at least three full-time palliative care staff members)
- 24 hour care
- Adequate equipment
- Link to a palliative medicine consultation service

Inpatient hospices in Germany are independent services which provide palliative care for patients with incurable diseases in the latter stages of their lives. They are small institutions, normally with a maximum 16 beds. The hospices are characterised by a familiar atmosphere, the rooms are constructed for the special needs of terminally ill patients. Inpatient hospices utilise equipment which guarantees the provision of good palliative care, including the different aspects (medical, nursing, social and psycho-social). A substantial proportion of the occurring costs are covered through additional payments by the patients, donations and various voluntary commitments. Inpatient hospices regard themselves as part of a health care network in the regional health and social system. They is also an integral element of outpatient voluntary hospice services providing care at the patients home.[43] In addition, there are also out-

[42] ibid.

[43] Bundesarbeitsgemeinschaft Hospiz e.V. zur Förderung von ambulanten, teilstationären und stationären Hospizen und Palliativmedizin (BAG): Rahmenvereinbarung nach § 39a Satz 4 SGB V über Art und Umfang sowie zur Sicherung der Qualität der stationären Hospizversorgung vom 13.03.1998, i. d. F.

patient services on offer, for example day care services, which provide palliative and social care in outpatient settings in order to relieve and support relatives and enable patients to remain in their familiar circumstances for as long as possible. The outpatient services are a supplement to the home care hospice services as well as integral parts of inpatient hospices.[44]

According to the *BAG Statistics 2002* (Frame of survey: 24 percent of all German hospices) the average length of stay in inpatient hospices in 2002 was 28 days. 93 percent of all patients were diagnosed with cancer. The reasons for admission were: Insufficient nursing care (68 percent), relatives unable to cope (58 percent), pain (37 percent), other somatic problems (27 percent), the patients desire to die in a hospice (27 percent). The average age of people who died in hospices was 70 years.[45]

A *Palliativstation* is a department in a hospital or affiliated to a hospital. It specialises in the treatment and care of patients with an incurable, progressive and advanced illness with limited life-expectancy. A multidisciplinary team working in a *Palliativstation* consists of qualified physicians, nurses, social workers, spiritual advisors, psychologists and other complementary therapists. The professional staff are supplemented by volunteers. The *Palliativstation* works as part of a network with medical centres, hospital departments, general practitioners, home nursing services, hospice home care services and inpatient hospices. It's aim is to alleviate illness- and therapy related pain and, if possible, to stabilise the condition of the patient in order to discharge them.[46]

In September 2004 there were 116 inpatient hospices (1045 beds) and 92 *Palliativstationen* (743 beds) in Germany.[47] In total, 208 inpatient services provide palliative care with a total capacity of 1788 beds. This means there are approximately 22 hospice and palliative care beds per one million habitants.

The levels of provision of inpatient hospices, *Palliativstationen* and outpatient or home care services vary strongly throughout the various states: A sufficient number of inpatient, outpatient *and* home care services exist in North Rhine-Westphalia, Baden-Wuerttemberg and Bavaria, in the new states, such as in Saxony or Thuringia, the provision of home care services is well-developed, whereas the inpatient sector is comparatively small due to a lack of financial resources.[48] Home and outpatient hospices services, inpatient hospices and *Palliativstationen* in Germany are liable to accredited quality standards.

In many places efforts are made to integrate palliative care into regular health care. One example for nursing and care homes is the department for elderly people at

---

vom 09.02.1999. Published at: http://www.hospiz.net/bag/index.html

44 ibid.

45 Bundesarbeitsgemeinschaft Hospiz e.V. zur Förderung von ambulanten, teilstationären und stationären Hospizen und Palliativmedizin (BAG): http://www.hospiz.net/bag/index.html

46 Deutsche Gesellschaft für Palliativmedizin: Definitionen der Deutschen Gesellschaft für Palliativmedizin (Stand: 31. Oktober 2003). Veröffentlicht unter: http://www.dgpalliativmedizin.de/

47 Deutsche Gesellschaft für Palliativmedizin: http://www.dgpalliativmedizin.de/

48 Interview with Gerda Graf and Christine Pfeffer, 07 July 2004, in Niederzier.

the *Innere Mission Munich,* which was set up as a pre-operating study in 2000. The projects *"Leben bis zuletzt – Palliativbetreuung in den Alten- und Pflegeheimen der Inneren Mission München"* aim to implement basic features of the hospice concept into the five care und nursing homes of the institution.[49] Several home care nursing services offer care for the dying provided by trained palliative care staff.

The cooperation between health care providers such as hospitals, nursing services and general practitioners has long been suggested by scientific studies.[50] However many intra and inter-institutional questions concerning training, funding and cooperation remain to be solved.

2.3 Legal regulations and funding

A number of legal requirements rule home, outpatient and inpatient hospice care in Germany. Amongst those, § 39a SGB V (Social Code Book V (Statutory Health Insurance) is of great importance. It defines the right to inpatient, outpatient and home hospice care. The allowances amount provided by sick insurances depends on the requirements set in § 39a. Under the rules of Social Code Book XI (Statutory Long-term Care Insurance) §§ 72, 75, 80, 80a nursing care funds are only allowed to pay services if a care contract has been agreed with the running institution. Frame contracts as well as care quality standards etc. are regulated by these paragraphs.[51]

In Germany there is a "dual" funding system in place for inpatient hospices. On the one hand it is covered by the already mentioned SGB V §39a and its frame contracts and on the other hand there is also a relation to the Social Code Book XI. The daily rate for inpatient hospices ranges between 210 and 300 €per patient. In line with § 2, para. 3 of the general agreement, benefits for hospice care are limited to four weeks.

For hospices the regulation applies that 10 percent of the budget has to be financed from own resources (donations, member fees etc.). Sometimes it proves to be difficult to raise the required 10 percent. Remaining costs have to be covered by the patients themselves. In this system, the share of insurance funds is higher than in nursing homes. In some cases this leads to re-admissions into nursing homes due to financial reasons. It also occurs that hospices are chosen for cost-saving reasons as families or social assistance authorities have to pay less than in nursing homes precisely because insurance funds allow higher benefits in hospices.

There is no such legislation for *Palliativstationen.* On the level of funding the *Hospital Financing Act* applies. According to Gerda Graf, the leader of the German

[49] This is i.e. documented in: IFF – Palliative Care und Organisationsethik (ed.): "Leben bis zuletzt". Palliativbetreuung in den Alten- und Pflegeheimen der Inneren Mission München. BewohnerInnenbefragung im Alten- und Pflegeheim Ebenhausen. Dokumentation. Wien 2002.

[50] For example in the Bielefeld study on home care services in North-Reine Westphalia: Michael Ewers/ Doris Schaeffer (eds.): Palliativ-pflegerisch tätige Hausbetreuungsdienste in NRW. Ergebnisse der Begleitforschung. Bielefeld 2003.

[51] Interview with Gerda Graf and Christine Pfeffer, 07 July 2004, in Niederzier.

hospice umbrella organisation *BAG Hospiz*, today, palliative medical provision in Palliativstationen is in most cases better than in hospices. But Graf also notes that psychosocial and spiritual care tend to be more enhanced in hospices.

There are problems at the crossover point between hospices and *Palliativstation*. *Palliativstationen* first and foremost are assigned to pain treatment, the average length of stay is only 9 days. Often patients are transferred to other departments after successful pain treatment – sometimes into hospices. As has been mentioned before, the average length of stay in hospices is 28 days, considerably longer than in *Palliativstationen*.

As an example, the final invoice of a small hospice in K. will be portayed here:

In 2003, the costs per day for all services performed in the hospice (nursing care, accommodation and food) capital expenditures were 281,47 € per bed. In line with the national general agreement, the institution has to cover 10 percent of these costs itself, which means 28,14 € in case of hospice K.

The remaining 253,32 € are covered by

Health insurance as per § 39a SGB V as benefits / allowances	142,80 €	142,80 €	142,80 €
Nursing care insurance	Care Grade I 33,63 €	Grade II 42,04 €	Grade III 47,07 €
A total of	176,43 €	184,84 €	189,87 €
Remaining contribution for the patient	76,89 €	68,48 €	63,45 €

If a patient is not able to cover the remaining costs himself, an application for social welfare is made.

A hospice can be founded by everyone. In contrast to other countries such as Italy, it does not necessarily have to be physician setting up a hospice. The nursing staff have to be educated in palliative care, there are also facility guidelines that have to be met. Single rooms are compulsory and the size of the rooms have to be designed in line with the *Heimbaumindestverordnung*, rules relating to the construction of care and nursing homes. The cooperation with a hospice home care service is also a precondition in order to guarantee integrated care.

The hospice movement in Germany is not only supported by political institutions but also because it represents a cost saving alternative to a hospital stay. However it remains unclear how palliative care in Germany will be financed in the future. In 2002, only 0.1 percent of the total amount of 142 billion € spent by the health insurance companies was used for palliative and hospice care provision. Calculations by the *German Society for Palliative Medicine* (*Deutsche Gesellschaft für Palliativmedizin*) indicate that a nationwide provision for palliative care would cost approximately 650 million € (approx. 0.45 percent of the total health expenditure in Germany in 2002).[52] Already many hospice and palliative care services are seriously underfunded. Whereas

[52] Frankfurter Allgemeine Zeitung, 23 September 2004.

in Great Britain annually approximately 300 million €is raised by donations, only around 20 million € is donated for hospice care in Germany each year. [53]

2.4 Organisations

The *Bundesarbeitsgemeinschaft Hospiz (BAG)* was founded in 1992. It is the nationwide representation of interests for the hospice movement in Germany. [54] The executive board is working on a voluntary basis. Amongst the members are home care, outpatient and inpatient hospice services, *Palliativstationen*, the 16 *Landesarbeitsgemeinschaften Hospiz* (the 16 hospice organisations from the 16 different states) as well as other hospice organisations. The *BAG*'s agenda is:

- the development and promotion of the hospice idea
- to represent the views and interests of their members to Government, Health Authorities and statutory and voluntary organisations
- to promote the cooperation between hospice initiatives and care services for dying people
- to provide education and training opportunities
- to support research into hospice related topics

The *BAG* does not run hospices itself. Their leader, Gerda Graf, emphasises the *BAG*'s intention to continue their work on a voluntary basis in the future.

The *Deutsche Hospiz Stiftung (German Hospice Foundation)* was founded in 1995. It lobbies for the rights of seriously ill and dying patients. The foundation currently has 55.000 members and sponsors. The staff consists of approximately 20 employees from different professional backgrounds who support and advise hospice projects. [55]

The *German Society for Palliative Medicine (Deutschen Gesellschaft für Palliativmedizin – DGP)* was created in 1994. It is a foundation of consultants in palliative medicine. The *DGP* is the most important force for the establishment of palliative medicine in the German health care system and scientific research. Since 2000, the *DGP* has published the Journal for Palliative Medicine (*Zeitschrift für Palliativmedizin*). [56]

2.5 Education and training of professional staff

In 2001, 20 institutions provided training and education in palliative care meeting the criteria set by *BAG* and *DGP*. [57] These are academies, hospices, palliative centre and

---

53 ibid.

54 More information on the BAG can be found on the official homepage: http://www.hospiz.net/bag/index.html

55 More information on the German Hospice Fundation at: http://www.hospize.de/

56 More information on the DGP can be found on the official homepage: http://www.dgpalliativmedizin.de/

57 Bundesarbeitsgemeinschaft Hospiz e.V. zur Förderung von ambulanten, teilstationären und stationären Hospizen und Palliativmedizin (BAG): http://www.hospiz.net/bag/index.html

training centres, which offer education and advanced training in various areas such as palliative medicine, palliative nursing care, supervision, bereavement courses designed for coordinators, spiritual advisors, staff from professional psycho-social background or volunteers. Many courses are rooted in the *Basis Curriculum for Palliative Care* (M. Kern, M. Müller, K. Aurnhammer) from 1996. According to legal regulations, the curriculum functions as the standard for leading nursing staff members. A nurse in charge, and also their deputy working in a German hospice, are required to have a taken part in a training course in palliative care (at least 160 hours). It is also compulsory to have further training which concentrates on the role as a leader of a team (at least 460 hours). Nurses in senior positions, who do not meet those criteria at the start of their work, have to take part in such training programmes within a period of five years. [58]

Today there are neither specialist palliative care nurses nor consultants in palliative medicine in Germany. On June 27th 2002 the new *Approbationsordnung* (examination regulations) for physicians became effective. In the second paragraph of the examination regulations it is said that "the exam tasks (...) should include one or various aspects: (...) amongst others the treatment of long term ill patients, incurable and dying patients, pain treatment and palliative medicine." [59] This offers the possibility to integrate palliative medicine as a optional subject in the medical curriculum. [60]

In 2003 palliative medicine was introduced as further training for physicians. [61] Further training should include: [62]

- 12 months at an authorised advanced training institution or to be subsituted pro rata by 120 hours of case seminars and inclusive supervision
- 40 hours advanced training in palliative medicine

There knowledge, experiences and skills in

- communication with long term ill or dying patients and their relatives
- advice and support of patients and their families
- the identification of curative, casual and palliative measures and provisions
- identification of pain causes and treatment of acute and chronic pain situations
- symptom control, i.e. dyspnea, nausea, emisis, obstipation, obstruction, ulcer wounds, anxiety, amentia, depression, insomnia.

---

58 Bundesarbeitsgemeinschaft Hospiz e.V. zur Förderung von ambulanten, teilstationären und stationären Hospizen und Palliativmedizin (BAG): Rahmenvereinbarung nach § 39a Satz 4 SGB V über Art und Umfang sowie zur Sicherung der Qualität der stationären Hospizversorgung vom 13.03.1998, i. d. F. vom 09.02.1999. http://www.hospiz.net/bag/index.html

59 Bundesministerium der Justiz (ed.): Bundesgesetzblatt Jahrgang 2002 Teil I Nr. 44, ausgegeben zu Bonn am 3. Juli 2002: Approbationsordnung für Ärzte vom 27. Juni 2002, p. 31.

60 Deutsche Gesellschaft für Palliativmedizin: Grundlagen der Palliativmedizin. Gegenstandskatalog und Lernziele für Studierende der Medizin, p. 3. Veröffentlicht unter: http://www.dgpalliativmedizin.de/

61 Bundesärztekammer (Arbeitsgemeinschaft der Deutschen Ärztekammern): (Muster-) Weiterbildungsordnung gemäß Beschluss 106. Deutscher Ärztetag 2003 in Köln. http://www.dgpalliativmedizin.de/

62 Deutsche Gesellschaft für Palliativmedizin: Definitionen der Deutschen Gesellschaft für Palliativmedizin (Up to 31 October 2003). http://www.dgpalliativmedizin.de/

– the treatment and care of seriously ill and dying patients should be acquired.[63]

2.6 *Volunteers*

Volunteers are still the pillar of the German hospice movement. 95 percent of hospice work is carried out by volunteers.[64] According to the *BAG* website in May 2005 approximately 80 000 volunteers are committing their time to hospice services.[65] The motives for the strong dedication in the hospice movement are predominantly personal experiences with death and dying but also the desire for a meaningful role.[66] The field of activities for volunteers working in inpatient hospices, hospital palliative care units and outpatient or home care hospice services vary from institution to institution. The volunteers – on the whole, women aruond retirement age – do not undertake nursing or medical care duties. They provide help in all other areas of hospice care. Often the professional background plays an important part defining the kind of commitment.[67] The tasks range from psycho-social and spiritual care provided for patients and their relatives to secretary or administrative work. The volunteers are prepared for their work in education courses. The courses are designed to enable the volunteer to care for the patients in a self-confident and responsible way. During the course volunteers should learn to discover and explore their own abilities and limitations and receive education in communication with seriously ill and dying patients[68] Further training courses and continuous supervision for the volunteers are also regarded as essential elements of voluntary hospice work.

2.7 *Examples*

Hospiz am St. Elisabeth Krankenhaus Halle (Saale)

The hospice in Halle, located in a part of former Eastern Germany, provides
- home care: psycho-social care, crisis intervention, on demand spiritual care. The home care service is free of charge. An average of 40 patients are cared for.

---

63 Bundesärztekammer (Arbeitsgemeinschaft der Deutschen Ärztekammern): (Muster-) Weiterbildungsordnung gemäß Beschluss 106. Deutscher Ärztetag 2003 in Köln, p. 163. http://www.dgpalliativmedizin.de/

64 Werner Burgheim: Hospizarbeit auf dem Weg zur Professionalisierung. In: Qualifizierte Begleitung von Sterbenden und Trauernden. Ed. by Werner Burgheim. Merching 2003, p. 2.

65 Bundesarbeitsgemeinschaft Hospiz e.V. zur Förderung von ambulanten, teilstationären und stationären Hospizen und Palliativmedizin (BAG): http://www.hospiz.net/bag/index.html

66 cp. Dorothea Razumovsky: Der Aspekt der Freiwilligkeit. In: Wohin mit den Sterbenden? Hospize in Europa – Ansätze zu einem Vergleich. Ed. by Reimer Gronemeyer/ Erich H. Loewy, in cooperation with Michaela Fink, Marcel Globisch, Felix Schumann. Münster 2002, p. 233.

67 cp. Wirtschafts- und Sozialausschuß, Stellungnahme zum Thema ‚Hospizarbeit als Beispiel für freiwillige Tätigkeit in Europa‘: http://europa.eu.int/eur-lex/pri/de/oj/dat/2002/c_125/c_12520020527de00190028.pdf.

68 ibid., p. 6.

- day care: patients, that can still be cared for at home, can receive additional nursing care and choose between other offers from areas that include communication, creative work, social and spiritual care.
- inpatient hospice: the hospice is a small institution with a familiar atmosphere. It offers eight single rooms equipped with shower and toilet, telephone and television. The rooms can be individually arranged to the patients wishes and needs, family and friends are welcome to visit at any time of the day. The stay in the hospice is not limited, a short term stay is also possible. The patients are cared for by general practitioners and – if necessary – by medical specialists. The funding is based on the legal regulations with health insurance companies who pay a lump sum (Care Grade 2). Health insurances in the old *Bundesländer* (states) pay more than those in the parts of Eastern Germany. The additional costs are covered by a pool of donators and also by monetary fines. The patients are asked – if they can afford – to pay 10 €per day to allow the hospice to make replacement investments. The average length of stay is between 29 - 30 days. All eight beds are usually occupied.

The different services rely on the help of volunteers. They support the nursing staff, transport patients and their relatives, are on the telephone or are involved in public relations. Between 50 - 60 volunteers work for the hospice. The preparatory course for volunteers lasts 90 hours.

Hospice services in Halle started their work in 1985. The hospice is situated next to *St. Elisabeth-Hospital.* A palliative care unit is located in the same house. Heinrich Pera presumes that the hospital palliative care unit will experience great difficulties in the near future as a result of health care reforms. The new concept intends to shorten the average stay in hospitals to 3 - 5 days, whereas the adjustment of pain therapy treatment averagely requires between 10 - 14 days. It is therefore impossible to get pain under control within 3 - 5 days.

Heinrich Pera, who was one of the main initiators of the Eastern German hospice movement and sadly passed away last year, considered home care services to be of preference over inpatient units. Inpatient hospices only make sense when they operate within existing home care and outpatient structures. However Pera feared that many new inpatient hospices could develop without proper planning as inpatient units are visible for everyone and therefore easier to realise when it comes to acquiring funding and public support. Pera regarded day care as an important opportunity for cancer patients who can be cared for at home. These patients do not receive funding from the special care health insurance company.

Inpatient hospices have to deal with financial problems as well. Health insurance companies for example do not pay for artificial respiration as this is seen as a life-prolonging treatment which classifies the patient as a non-hospice client. Ongoing negations point towards an agreement that health insurance companies are willing to pay when a patient is able to breathe six hours per day without artificial assistance.

The Hospice in Halle

The hospice in Halle, kitchen and common room/ (l.) Heinrich Pera, (r.) Reimer Gronemeyer

The hospice in Halle is mainly providing care for cancer patients. The number of cancer diseases in the region is comparatively high, probably a result of the close proximity to hte chemical industry in Bitterfeld. A high number of children are suffering from cancer there. The hospice in Halle also functions as an education centre, providing seminars and advisory service. The education and training opportunities on offer draw a lot of interest from people from Eastern European countries. [69]

Hospice Speyer [70]

Since 1989 the deaconess Speyer had been considering whether to build a hospice on their premises. After seven years of planning, the hospice was opened in February 1996 under the responsibility of the deaconess. The following targets were set for the hospice:

- To take the wishes of dying patients seriously and – if possible – to grant them
- To guarantee high quality pain therapy and symptom control
- To care for people who suffer from loneliness and face imminent death in a dignified way.

The hospice provides hospice care in seven single rooms. The rooms have separate living and sleeping areas and a bathroom with shower and toilet. In addition, the hos-

69 Further information on the hospice in Halle can be accessed at: http://www.hospiz-halle.de/

70 The description relies on interview conducted by David Distelmann. David Distelmann: Hospize in Rheinland-Pfalz. Eine empirische Studie, Gießen 2004 (Thesis at Justus-Liebig-University Giessen).

pice offers a large living room, a dining room and kitchen, a highly modern bathroom, a silent room and relatives can stay overnight. Care is provided by a multi-professional team.

The daily rate per guest is 244,45 €. In line with the contract for hospices in Germany, the hospice has to cover 10 percent of the actual costs by donations. The patients have to pay 77,00 €per day. If the patient is not able to provide the required funds, the social welfare office sometimes bears the costs. The remaining is mostly covered by the standard and special care health insurance companies although the benefits vary depending on the level of care the patient requires. However the hospice still relies on the financial support of the running institution – the deaconess Speyer – and a pool of sponsors and donators as the incomes from patients and health insurances do not cover all costs. "Without a powerful institution hospice work is impossible, at least not to the high level of provision in our service with nine established posts and several other staff members", argues the hospice leader Miss Schultheis.

The deceased remain – in line with the hospice concept – one day in their room to allow relatives and the caring team enough time to say goodbye. The occurring costs have to be covered the running institution. With 80 cases each year, they add up considerably.

The professional team consists of 12 employees of which nine hold an established post. The hospice staff include most of all qualified nursing staff. The leader of the hospice, Miss Schultheis, is also a nurse. A spiritual advisor, a social worker and a psychologist are also part of the staff members. A number of volunteers and external staff (Physiotherapist, supervisor) complete the team. The ratio of nursing staff to patients is 1,2:1 (nine nurses to seven patients).

Generally all guests (patients) are accepted at the hospice, no matter what their religious or cultural background may be. However Muslim guests are rather uncommon. In the rare cases when Muslims are admitted into the hospice, it is often because they are suffering from an infection that does not allow home care.

The guests are allowed to bring personal belongings and even pets. People, who are admitted to the hospice, suffer from incurable diseases, some of them live alone or cannot be cared for at home because of their advanced illness. The hospice also allows relatives, who care themselves for their sick family member, to take a valuable break. A guest can only be admitted to the hospice at their own request. The age of patients varies from 30 to 90 years. Before being admitted to the hospice, a staff members pays a visit to the patients home or hospital. Most hospice patients suffer from cancer in the final stage.

The occupancy rate is between 80 and 90 percent. The last statistics that give insight into the lengths of stay date back to the year 2000. 95 percent of the admitted patients died in the hospice that year, of which

- 31 percent died in the first week of their stay,
- 14 percent in the second week,
- 12 percent after three weeks of admission,

The Hospice in the Wilhelminenstift, Speyer

- 9 percent after four weeks,
- 16 percent after spending 2 months in the hospice,
- 8 percent after three months,
- 6 percent stayed for as long as six months,
- 3 percent died in the hospice after staying six to twelve months.
- and 1 percent had been there for more than a year.

The selection of staff proves to be difficult "as a lot of people want to work in this field, who are looking for something, trying to find things out for themselves" as Miss Schultheis points out. All staff members are asked to participate in a course on palliative care. In addition further training programmes are offered by the deaconess. Volunteers begin their work by participating in a basic seminar, where they are educated and supervised.

Besides the deaconess Speyer runs a hospital palliative care unit, which has slightly different aims than the hospice. There, patients don't necessarily have to be in an advanced stage of their illness.

The hospices is doing a lot of public relation work. Lectures and charity events are held in the hospice. The German television channel *ZDF* broadcasted a church service that was staged in the hospice.

The hospice works closely with the home care hospice service in Speyer, which is run by the ecumenical welfare centre in Speyer.

Hospice Association Alsfeld

The *Alsfelder Hospizverein* (Alsfeld Hospice Association) was founded in 2001 by Dr Johannes Pfann, a anaesthesist in a hospital in Alsfeld. His intention was to improve the care for dying people at home as in fact 83 percent currently die in institutions in the Vogelsberg area. But the offer provided was rejected by the population in the rural small town and its surrounding villages. People were too timid to accept help offered by strangers. Instead the 8 volunteers of the hospice initiative now care for dying people in the Alsfeld hospital and two nursing homes. New volunteers are recruited through lectures which are advertised in the local newspaper. "In the beginning we just accepted everyone but now we have certain criteria", reports Dr Pfann. People, who are seriously ill themselves or have lost a relative within the past six months, are not allowed to volunteer. The training of volunteers consists of 11 sessions. In the beginning personal experiences with death and dying are exchanged. The following sessions deal with the hospice idea and the history of the hospice movement, the role of volunteers, communication, nursing care, basic medical questions, the care for seriously ill gerontopsychiatric patients, courses of diseases, pain therapy, social work and legal aspects of hospice work, last wills of patients, parting and bereavement, the search for meaning, religion as well as rituals and burial. In the last class, the volunteers are asked to decide on the areas of their future involvement.

In most cases, the *Hospizverein (Hospice Association)* is called upon by nursing staff from nursing homes. At the time of the interview, three patients were being cared for. Volunteers visit the patients 2 - 3 a week. They talk to them and their relatives, read out loud to them, sing and pray together, listen to music and act as mediator between care services, the church and doctors. They relieve families but are not allowed to take over nursing care duties.

In 2003 a house was offered as a donation to the *Hospizverein* but eventually had to be rejected due to the inability to acquire the funding for further costs. Currently an outpatient and an inpatient pain unit have been set up in the Alsfeld hospital. At the end of 2004 a series of concerts, art exhibitions and lectures on the topic hospice took place in the hospital. [71]

3. Summary

A survey of 398 people in various German cities results in 56 percent of respondents being aware of the term "hospice work" but only 2 percent know about "palliative medicine". [72] This shows that the German public only gradually noticing hospice and palliative care. However the rising number of newspaper reports, television documentaries and public events, indicate that public interest on the topics death, dying, hospice and palliative care are currently growing.

In Germany home care hospice services, inpatient hospices and hospital palliative care units work together in an integrated system of provision. Nevertheless there are striking regional differences in the state of provision which leaves Germany still far from a nationwide provision with palliative care. It is therefore one of the main tasks to establish a stronger network of all types of services all over the country. For example in the near future a concept concerning hospice work in nursing homes will be discussed in order to find ways to ensure quality of services. The target is to develop a model similar to the existing quality handbook for inpatient hospices.

The hospice movement is becoming increasingly under the pressure from professionalisation. Its strength however is its psycho-social and spiritual care of the patients. Palliative care hospital units are under threat of the possible introduction of the case fees amendment act. Their strong point – in contrast to inpatient hospices – is the excellent palliative medical treatment. It would be desirable to see both sides improving their rather weak areas in the best interest of the patient without losing their initial identity. In Bavaria for instance, the hospice movement actively promoted palliative medicine as a specialty. [73] The experience of other countries such as England and the

---

71 Interview with Dr Johannes Pfann, 07 April 2004, in Alsfeld.

72 Frankfurter Allgemeine Zeitung, 23 September 2004.

73 Kittelberger, Frank: Hospizarbeit in Bayern. Eine Studie der Hospizbewegung in Bayern zur Orientierung kirchlichen Handelns. München 2000, p. 41.

Netherlands shows how important the cooperation of different types of institutions and services is for adequate care of dying patients.

Sources and literature

Bundesarbeitsgemeinschaft Hospiz e.V./ Deutscher Caritasverband e.V./ Diakonisches Werk der EKD e.V. (Ed.): SORGSAM. Qualitätshandbuch für stationäre Hospize. Wuppertal 2004.

Burgheim, Werner (Ed.): Qualifizierte Begleitung von Sterbenden und Trauernden. Merching 2003.

Burgheim, Werner: Hospizarbeit auf dem Weg zur Professionalisierung. In: Qualifizierte Begleitung von Sterbenden und Trauernden. Ed. by Burgheim, Werner. Merching 2003.

Dreßel, Gudrun/ Erdmann, Bernadett u.a.: Sterben und Tod in Thüringen. Ergebnisse einer sozialwissenschaftlichen Repräsentativbefragung. Friedrich-Schiller-Universität Jena 2001.

Dörner, Klaus: Der gute Arzt. Lehrbuch der ärztlichen Grundhaltung. Stuttgart 2001.

Everding, Gustava/ Westrich, Angelika (Ed.): Wüdig leben bis zum letzten Augenblick. Idee und Praxis der Hospiz-Bewegung, 2. erweiterte Auflage. München 2000.

Ewers, Michael/ Schaeffer, Doris (Ed.): Palliativ-pflegerisch tätige Hausbetreuungsdienste in NRW. Ergebnisse der Begleitforschung. Bielefeld 2003.

Feigs, Christine Ursula: Aspekte ehrenamtlicher Mitarbeit im Hospiz, dargestellt am Beispiel der Hospizdienste Lahn-Dill gGmbH. Gießen 2003 (Examensarbeit).

Graf, Gerda: Die Hospizbewegung in Deutschland. In: Qualifizierte Begleitung von Sterbenden und Trauernden. Ed. by Burgheim, Werner. Merching 2003.

Gronemeyer, Reimer/ Loewy, Erich H. (eds.) in cooperation with Michaela Fink, Marcel Globisch, Felix Schumann: Wohin mit den Sterbenden? Hospize in Europa – Ansätze zu einem Vergleich. Münster 2002.

Heller, Andreas (ed.): Kultur des Sterbens. Bedingungen für das Lebensende gestalten. Freiburg 2002.

Husebø, Stein/ Klaschik, Eberhard (eds.): Palliativmedizin. Berlin u.a. 2003.

IFF – Palliative Care und Organisationsethik (ed.): "Leben bis zuletzt". Palliativbetreuung in den Alten- und Pflegeheimen der Inneren Mission München. BewohnerInnenbefragung im Alten- und Pflegeheim Ebenhausen. Dokumentation. Wien 2002.

Kittelberger, Frank: Hospizarbeit in Bayern. Eine Studie der Hospizbewegung in Bayern zur Orientierung kirchlichen Handelns. München 2000.

Loewy, Erich H./ Gronemeyer, Reimer (eds.) in cooperation with Michaela Fink, Marcel Globisch, Felix Schumann: Die Hospizbewegung im internationalen Vergleich. Gießen 2001.

Müller, Monika/ Kessler, Gera (eds.): Implementierung von Hospizidee und Palliativmedizin in die Struktur und Arbeitsabläufe eines Altenheims. Eine Orientierungs- und Planungshilfe. Bonn 2000.

Pera, Heinrich: Sterbende verstehen. Ein praktischer Leitfaden zur Sterbebegleitung, 4. Auflage. Freiburg 1995.

Pfeffer, Christine: Brücken zwischen Leben und Tod. Eine empirische Untersuchung in einem Hospiz. Köln 1998.

Razumovsky, Dorothea: Der Aspekt der Freiwilligkeit. In: Wohin mit den Sterbenden? Hospize in Europa – Ansätze zu einem Vergleich. Ed. by Gronemeyer, Reimer/ Loewy, Erich H. in Zusammenarbeit mit Michaela Fink, Marcel Globisch, Felix Schumann. Münster 2002.

Rest, Franco: Sterbebeistand, Sterbebegleitung, Sterbegeleitung, 4. Auflage. Berlin/Köln 1998.

Sabatowski, Rainer/ Radbruch, Lukas u.a.: Palliative Care in Germany – 14 years on European Journal of Palliative Care 2 (1998), p. 52 - 55.

Sabatowski, Rainer u.a.: Hospiz- und Palliativführer 2003. Stationäre und ambulante Palliativ- und Hospizeinrichtungen in Deutschland. Neu-Isenburg 2002.

Seitz, Dieter/ Seitz, Oliver: Die moderne Hospizbewegung in Deutschland auf dem Weg ins öffentliche Bewusstsein: Ursprünge, kontroverse Diskussionen, Perspektiven. Herbolzheim 2002.

Sterben hier und anderswo. Kulturelle Aspekte der Sterbebegleitung. Dokumentation der 7. Fachtagung des Landes Hessen zur Verbesserung der Sterbebegleitung in Marburg am 13.11.2002.

Student, Johann-Christoph (ed.): Das Hospiz-Buch. Freiburg im Breisgau 1999.

Student, Johann-Christoph (ed.): Sterben, Tod und Trauer. Handbuch für Begleitende. Freiburg 2004.

Wilkening, Karin/ Kunz, Roland: Sterben im Pflegeheim. Perspektiven und Praxis einer neuen Abschiedskultur. Göttingen 2003.

Winkel, Heidemarie: Das Recht auf den eigenen Tod. Erfurt 2002.

Periodicals

Bundes-Hospiz-Anzeiger

Die Hospiz-Zeitschrift. Fachforum für Hospiz- und Palliativarbeit

Zeitschrift für Palliativmedizin

Internet sources

Bundesärztekammer (Arbeitsgemeinschaft der Deutschen Ärztekammern): (Muster-) Weiterbildungsordnung gemäß Beschluss 106. Deutscher Ärztetag 2003 in Köln. Veröffentlicht u.a. unter: http://www.dgpalliativmedizin.de/

Bundesarbeitsgemeinschaft Hospiz e.V. zur Förderung von ambulanten, teilstationären und stationären Hospizen und Palliativmedizin (BAG): http://www.hospiz.net/bag/index.html

Bundesarbeitsgemeinschaft Hospiz e.V. zur Förderung von ambulanten, teilstationären und stationären Hospizen und Palliativmedizin (BAG): Rahmenvereinbarung nach § 39a Satz 4 SGB V über Art und Umfang sowie zur Sicherung der Qualität der stationären Hospizversorgung vom 13.03.1998, i. d. F. vom 09.02.1999. Veröffentlicht unter: http://www.hospiz.net/bag/index.html

Bundesarbeitsgemeinschaft Hospiz e.V. zur Förderung von ambulanten, teilstationären und stationären Hospizen und Palliativmedizin (BAG): Rahmenvereinbarung nach § 39a Abs. 2 Satz 6 SGB V zu den Voraussetzungen der Förderung sowie zu Inhalt, Qualität und Umfang der ambulanten Hospizarbeit vom 03.09.2002. Veröffentlicht unter: http://www.hospiz.net/bag/index.html

Bundesministerium der Justiz (ed.): Bundesgesetzblatt Jahrgang 2002 Teil I Nr. 44, ausgegeben zu Bonn am 3. Juli 2002: Approbationsordnung für Ärzte vom 27. Juni 2002.
Deutsche Gesellschaft für Palliativmedizin: http://www.dgpalliativmedizin.de/
Deutsche Gesellschaft für Palliativmedizin: Grundlagen der Palliativmedizin. Gegenstandskatalog und Lernziele für Studierende der Medizin. Veröffentlicht unter: http://www.dgpalliativmedizin.de/
Deutsche Gesellschaft für Palliativmedizin: Definitionen der Deutschen Gesellschaft für Palliativmedizin (Stand: 31. Oktober 2003). Veröffentlicht unter: http://www.dgpalliativmedizin.de/
Hospizverein Alsfeld e.V.: http://www.vogelsbergkreis.de/invos/1hos_als.htm
Official Homepage Federal Statistical Office Germany: http://www.destatis.de/presse/englisch/pm2004/p0410092.htm
Official Homepage Ministry of Health and Social Security: http://www.bmgs.bund.de/eng/gra/index.php
Population Division of the Department of Economic and Social Affairs of the United Nations Secretariat, World Population Prospects: The 2002 Revision Population Database: http://esa.un.org/unpp
WIKIPEDIA, die freie Enzyklopädie: http://de.wikipedia.org/wiki/Gesundheitssystem
Wirtschafts- und Sozialausschuss. Stellungnahme zum Thema ‚Hospizarbeit als Beispiel für freiwillige Tätigkeit in Europa': http://europa.eu.int/eur-lex/pri/de/oj/dat/2002/c_125/c_12520020527de00190028.pdf

List of interviews (in chronological order)

- Heinrich Pera, Head, Hospice in Halle and Prof Dr Linhaard Otto, Doctor (retired), Hospice in Halle, 22 July 2003 (Interview: Reimer Gronemeyer, Michaela Fink)
- Ms Krahe, *Hospice St. Martin* Koblenz, 30 March 2004 (Interview: David Distelmann)
- Rita Schultheis, Leader, *Hospice Wilhelminenstift Speyer*, 31 March 2004 (Interview: David Distelmann)
- Barbara Mutschler, Nurse in charge, *Christophorus Hospice Mainz*, 02 April 2004 (Interview: David Distelmann)
- Dr Johannes Pfann, Doctor, *Alsfeld hospital*, 07 April 2004 (Interview: Michaela Fink)
- Gerda Graf, Voluntary head, *Bundesarbeitsgemeinschaft Hospiz e.V. zur Förderung von ambulanten, teilstationären und stationären Hospizen und Palliativmedizin (BAG)* and Christine Pfeffer, Sociologist, collaborator *Bundesarbeitsgemeinschaft Hospiz e.V. zur Förderung von ambulanten, teilstationären und stationären Hospizen und Palliativmedizin (BAG)* Niederzier, 07 July 2004

Hungary

Marcel Globisch

1. General conditions

1.1 Demographics

- In Hungary an *aging process* of society can be observed, although it nevertheless progresses markedly slower there than in Western Europe and also in comparison with some countries in Eastern Europe.
- In the year 1950 the population count of Hungary totalled 9.3 million. In 2000 10.0 million people lived in Hungary. By 2050 the population is estimated to fall to around 7.6 million [1].
- The average life expectancy has risen from 63.6 years (1950 - 1955) to 71.9 (between 2000 - 2005) years. By 2050 another rise is expected to bring the average age to 79.3 years [2]. The comparatively low life expectancy can be ascribed above all to Hungary having the highest cancer rates Europe-wide [3].
- In 1950, people aged 65 years or older constituted 7.3 % of the population. In 2000 it was already 14.6 % and is projected to grow to 28.8 % by 2050 [4].
- Similarly, people aged 80 years or older constituted 0.8 % of the population in 1950. That percentage grew in 2000 to 2.5 and is estimated to grow to 7.6 by 2050 [5].
- In 1950, the working-age population (15 - 64 years) made up 67.6 % of the entire population. In 2000 that percentage had minimally risen to 68.4 %. For the future, a rapid decrease to 57.2 % in the year 2050 is expected [6].
- In 2003, 132.833 people died in Hungary; 33.537 of these died of cancer. In the same year 2.203 patients received care by Palliative Care institutions [7].

---

1 Population Division of the Department of Economic and Social Affairs of the United Nations Secretariat. *World Population Prospects: The 2002 Revision* and *World Urbanization Prospects: The 2001 Revision*. Official homepage of the United Nations: http://esa.un.org/unpp

2 ibid.

3 Imre Rodler / Gabor Zajikás: Hungarian Cancer Mortality and Food Availability Data in the Last Four Decades of the 20th Century. In: Annals of Nutrition & Metabolism. Vol. 46 No. 2. 2002, p. 49 - 56.

4 ibid.

5 ibid.

6 ibid.

7 Katalin Hegedus: VI. Hungarian Hospice-Palliative Congress. Hospice in Hungary 2004. Miskolc 23.04.2004.

1.2 Health Care System

During communist times, health care was the responsibility of the state and was administered through a hierarchical model which was highly centralized. Following a reformation in 1993, the Hungarian healthcare system today is principally a comprehensive, compulsory, employment-based national health insurance scheme that provides near universal coverage both in terms of treatment and in terms of population, with nearly all citizens receiving care whether or not they contribute.

The management and supervision was delegated to a self-governed committee. The compensation of the providers falls within the responsibility of the National Fund and is mainly contribution orientated. Excepting additional payment for medication or medical care is free.[8]

Compared to the western European population, the Hungarian population is in poor physical condition, the quota of deaths by cancer (342.5 per 100.000) is the highest in relation to other countries of Eastern Europe or Central Asia[9]. In 2002 the permission of general medicine surgeries was agreed on within the scope of a ten-year program for the reformation of the health system. With the enacting of a new law in 2003 the way was cleared for a large-scale privatisation of the health system (including the hospitals). Special care is given to the foundation of institutions for home and outpatient care as well as the advancement of private health insurances and nursing institutions as an alternative to the current inefficient health system, which is characterized by too many hospitals.[10] According to the OECD, for the year 2000, Hungary maintained 6.5 hospital beds per 1000 inhabitants. With that Hungary together with Germany and the Czech Republic leads the world count.[11] Astonishing is the comparatively low number of employees in the hospital sector and the number of full-time workers employed per bed. In Hungary this figure lies visibly below the UN-average (0.8 to 2.0).

One may not understand the Eastern European health care system without confronting a phenomenon called tipping. The informal payment of medical and care services was tolerated in Hungary at the time of Communism and still remains an integral part of the health system, as statistics of the *European Observatory on Health Care Systems* prove. In 1997 the share of costs the patients had to pay amounted to

---

8 cp.: Eva Orosz/ Andrew Burns: Organisation for Economic Co-operation and Development. The Health Care System in Hungary. Economics Department Working Papers No. 241. The text can be accessed on the internet:
http://www.olis.oecd.org/olis/2000doc.nsf/4f7adc214b91a685c12569fa005d0ee7/c125685b0057c558c12568cf00330dd9/\$FILE/00076478.PDF

9 David Clark/ Michael Wright: Transitions in end of life care. Hospice and related developments in Eastern Europe and Central Asia. Buckingham 2003:60.

10 cp.: Complete monitoring report of the preparation of Hungary for the membership within the EU, p. 10. In: http://www.mfa.gov.hu/NR/rdonlyres/38C506FC-02D5-417F-B62B-5CD6101ED9C2/0/cmr_hu_final_de.pdf

11 Bundeszentrale für politische Bildung (German Federal Organisation for Political Education): http://www.bpb.de/popup_druckversion.html?guid=MPPBS3

17.4%.[12] So-called informal payments to doctors and nurses constitute 8% of that.[13] This practice has existed since the early years of Communism when the salaries of physicians were held at an artificially low level. The practice that has penetrated into all aspects of patient-physician relationship is still present. It discriminates between rich and poor and divides physicians beyond the possibility of reconciliation. Thus, the medical profession is divided, the patients are uncertain whom to pay, when and how much, and are exposed to the mercy of the system. The legal status of tipping is controversial. Although tipping as a form of bribery is an illegal and punishable act, it is a common knowledge that a tip given after medical treatment is a sign of gratitude and not against the actual law.[14] The practice of "gifts" is so common in Hungary that many Hungarians regard it as a national tradition rather than a case of severe bribery.[15] Hospice workers refuse these "gifts" as they argue that financial reasons should play no part in the treatment of patients. This paradigm of equality of patients and the renunciation of illicit money tends to cause conflicts between the workers in Hungarian hospitals who wish to retain the old structures[16].

2. Hospice and palliative care in Hungary

2.1 History

Dr Alaine Polcz, a psychologist who has been working with dying children for 40 years, and Dr Katalin Muszbek, psychiatrist and head of a psycho-oncology hospital team, established the Hungarian Hospice Foundation in 1991.[17]

In the first instance, international contacts were established to become acquainted with the hospice idea. The *Hungarian Soros Foundation* supported the first hospice initiative.[18]

The concept of hospice was completely unknown to the public, the approach to death and dying a taboo[19]. Consequently the *Hungarian Hospice Foundation's* main concern was to bring this new form of care for the dying into the public and to enlist relevant social instances for support. A first project was launched in the *National Institute of Oncology.* A number of doctors, physiotherapists and volunteers had worked

12 European Observatory on Health Care Systems: Healthcare systems in transition – Hungary. Kopenhagen 1999, 25. In: http://www.who.dk/document/e68317.pdf

13 ibid.

14 Imre Szebik: Masked ball: ethics, laws and financial contradictions in Hungarian health care. In: *Science and Engineering Ethics*. Vol. 9. Issue 1. 2003, p. 109 - 24.

15 Complete monitoring report of the preparation of Hungary for the membership within the EU.p. 17. In: http://www.mfa.gov.hu/NR/rdonlyres/38C506FC-02D5-417F-B62B-5CD6101ED9C2/0/cmr{_}hu{_}final{_}de.pdf

16 Interview with Barbara Kallo on August 12th 2004 in Budapest. Interview with Dr Csaba Simkó and Kamilla Bánkút, 14 August 2003, in Miskolc.

17 Interview with Dr Katalin Muszbek, 12 August 2004, in Budapest.

18 Katalin Hegedus: Hospice movement in Hungary and experiences with hospital supportive teams: V Symposium – Hospice and Palliative Care. 21.03.2002.

19 Interview with Dr Katalin Muszbek, 12 August 2004, in Budapest.

in foreign hospices. They started the first home care hospice team in Budapest, which attended to 65 terminally ill cancer patients and their families in its first year. The *Hungarian Hospice Foundation* became an example for further hospice teams which were formed in Hungary during the following years [20].

In 1993 the *Semmelweis University of Medicine* organised a 24-hour course with the title "Ethical and psychological problems of death and dying. For the dignity of the dying and death". 100 - 120 participants regularly attended this course, and in 1994 further lectures on the same topic were offered. [21]

In a declaration of the Ministry of Health and Social Welfare in December 1993 the necessity of the integration of hospice work and Palliative Care into the health system was stated. This led to a considerable rise in the number of organisations founding hospice and palliative units as well as home care teams. The *Hungarian Soros Foundation,* the communities and the Ministry of Social Welfare supported these services with grants.

In 1995 the 19 Hospice and Palliative organisations formed the Hungarian Hospice-Palliative Association to state theirinterests and legally protect the name hospice from misuse [22]. The members also agreed that people who wish to engage themselves in hospice work have to pass a basic course spanning 40 hours before taking up their position. Additionally their continued participation in educational arrangements became obligatory. [23]

Today the umbrella organisation, the Hungarian Hospice-Palliative Association, arranges regular meetings where the hospice workers can exchange ideas. Since early 1997 annual national hospice congresses are held. The 10th anniversary of the Hungarian hospice movement in 2001 was organised [24] by the *Ministry of Health,* and the *Hungarian Hospice Foundation* was chosen NGO (non-governmental organisation) for the year 2002. [25] Both facts are further indicators for the growing acceptance of the hospice concept and its representatives in the Hungarian society.

2.2 Hospice and palliative care provision

In April 2005 Hungary had 11 inpatient hospice and palliative care units with 143 beds. Most of those 143 beds were situated in hospital settings. A further 46 beds exist in nursing homes. Additionally 2 day care centres, 5 hospital teams, and 15 hospice home care teams provide palliative care.

---

20 Katalin Hegedus: Hospice movement in Hungary and experiences with hospital supportive teams: V Symposium – Hospice and Palliative Care. 21.03.2002.

21 ibid.

22 David Clark/Michael Wright: Transitions in the end of life care. Hospice and related developments in Eastern Europe and Central Asia. Buckingham 2003, p. 65.

23 Katalin Hegedus: Hospice movement in Hungary and experiences with hospital supportive teams: V Symposium – Hospice and Palliative Care. 21.03.2002

24 ibid.

25 http://www.hospicehaz.hu/eng/rolunk-alap.html

Since their foundation in 1991, these hospice services have cared for 12.913 patients in all, for 2203 of these in the year 2003.[26] Compared to the year 2001 more than 600 additional patients were cared for, which accounts for a rise of 27.4%[27]. 89% of these patients suffered from cancer. The average duration of medical attention is 29.4 days[28]. The statistic mainly refers to forms of organisation, which provide hospice- or palliative care services. Regrettably there is no separate listing of the different types of organisations available. In 2004 the following personnel were working in Hungarian hospices: 33 physicians, 184 nurses, 27 physiotherapists, 20 psychologists and mental health experts, 19 priests, 15 social workers, 9 dieticians, 17 administrators/co-coordinators, 6 occupational therapists, 7 bereavement counsellor, 1 Bach flower therapist, 2 masseur and 121 volunteers.[29]

The inpatient units are located within hospitals as chronic departments, yet they operate in separate buildings, as in the case of the *Semmelweis Hospital* and the *Szt. László Hospital*. While the hospice in Miskolc is lea by a doctor[30], the hospice attached to the *Szt. László Hospital* is under the direction of a head nurse. Doctors from other hospital departments take over the medical care but are not continually present within the hospice.[31] Unfortunately Hungary's only paediatric hospice unit in *Bethesda Children's Hospice* was closed in February 2004 due to the reorganisation of paediatric oncology units in Budapest in February.[32]

Name:	Founded in:	No. of beds
Gyula, Pándy K. Hospital Hospice Department	1994	20
Budapest, Szt. László Hospital Hospice Department	1995	10
Miskolc, Semmelweis Hospital Erzsébet Hospice Home	1995	20
Pécs, Merciful Hospice	2004	18
Baranya County Hospital	2004	15
Heves County Hospital	2004	10
Komárom County Hospital	2004	10
Nagykanizsa, City Hospital	2004	10
Budapest, MÁV Hospital	2004	10
Budapest, Jewish Charity Hospital	2004	10
Budapest Hospice House	2005	10

Table 1. Inpatient Hospice and palliative care units

26 Katalin Hegedus: VI. Hungarian Hospice-Palliative Congress. Hospice in Hungary 2004. Miskolc 23.04.2004.

27 cp.: Katalin Hegedus: Hospice movement in Hungary and experiences with hospital supportive teams: V Symposium – Hospice and Palliative Care. 21.03.2002

28 Katalin Hegedus: VI. Hungarian Hospice-Palliative Congress. Hospice in Hungary 2004. Miskolc 23.04.2004.

29 ibid.

30 Interview with Dr Csaba Simkó, 14 August 2003, in Miskolc.

31 Interview with Zsóka Kelemen, 13 August 2003, in Budapest.

32 Email from Dr Andrea Bekesi, 15 October 2004.

Hospice care in nursing homes is only at its early stages. At present 4 homes exist where patients are cared for by hospice care teams. In Hajdúböszörmény 15 hospice beds are integrated, whereas the nursing homes in Sóstó and Tatabánya care for 5 hospice patients each, 4 further hospice beds are located in the nursing home in Pécs. [33]

There are also *hospital teams* whose main duty is to provide medical advice for terminally ill cancer patients in basic medical care, in hospitals and nursing homes. [34] Currently 5 such teams work in the following institutions: *Jewish Charity Hospital*, Budapest; *"Life for years" Foundation*, Dombóvár; *Satisfaction Hospice Foundation*, Budapest; *Hungarian Hospice Foundation*, Budapest; *Baranya County Hospital*, Pécs. Day care facilities exist in *St. Margit Hospital* in Budapest as well as in the *Erzsébet Hospice* in Miskolc. [35]

According to the Guidelines of the *Hungarian Hospice-Palliative Association*,home care hospice teams are expected to provide the patients with similar palliative care treatment as in hospital departments. The guarantee of a 24-hour care is desirable. [36] While the home care teams are responsible for the basic nursing care and physiotherapeutic treatment the multi-disciplinary teams solely attend to dying patients. The staff members have passed a hospice course and co-operate with other hospice services. [37]

Name:	Founded in:
Hungarian Hospice Foundation (Budapest)	1991
Hospice Foundation of Szombathely	1992
Satisfaction Hospice Foundation (Budapest)	1993
Miskolc, Erzsébet Hospice Foundation	1994
Debrecen, Spital Hospice	1994
Kecskemét, "Embracing Hands" Foundation	1995
Székesfehérvár, Help Bt	1995
Nagymaros, Pax Corporis Foundation	1995
Pécs, Social Net Association	1996
Óbuda-Békásmegyer Home Care Service	1998
Nyírtelek, Nursing Association	1998
Ruzsa, Bánfi Home Care Service	1999
Kaposvár, Nevitt Cindy Home Care Service	1999

33 Katalin Hegedus: VI. Hungarian Hospice-Palliative Congress. Hospice in Hungary 2004. Miskolc 23.04.2004.

34 Katalin Hegedus / Ildiko Szy (ed.): Hungarian Hospice Foundation/ Semmelweis University: Palliative Care of Terminally Ill Cancer Patients. Professional guidelines. 2nd improved and extended edition. Budapest 2002, p. 10.

35 Katalin Hegedus: VI. Hungarian Hospice-Palliative Congress. Hospice in Hungary 2004. Miskolc 23.04.2004.

36 Katalin Hegedus / Ildiko Szy (ed.): Hungarian Hospice Foundation/ Semmelweis University: Palliative Care of Terminally Ill Cancer Patients. Professional guidelines. 2nd improved and extended edition. Budapest 2002, p. 10.

37 Katalin Hegedus: VI. Hungarian Hospice-Palliative Congress. Hospice in Hungary 2004. Miskolc 23.04.2004.

Szeged, Hospice Foundation	2002
Pécs-Baranya Hospice Foundation	2004

Table 2. Hospice home care teams

2.3 Legal regulations and funding

Inpatient units are financed according to the hospital budget as chronic departments. In correspondence with the regulation of *special home care* the home care hospice teams receive support by the compulsory sickness insurance. A decree, which decides the financing of home care, was accordingly passed in 1996. This regulation provided the basis for the development of home care services. 300 home care services operate currently, among them 15 hospice teams. This account system covers only the functions of nurses and physiotherapists.[38] Therefore the hospice services are only able to survive with the help of funds and donations. Various organisations have engaged themselves in the hospice and palliative care system, among them the *Hungarian Soros Foundation, Phare (European grants for Eastern European Countries)* and the *Open Society Institute.*[39]

As part of the new *Health Care Act*, a new paragraph (article 99) was decreed in 1997, which legally defines the principles of *hospice care*:[40]

1. The care for dying patients (hereafter *hospice care*) is aimed at the psychical and mental care and the nursing of persons suffering from terminal illnesses. The aim of hospice care is the improvement of their quality of life, the reduction of pain and the protection of their dignity until the end.
2. In order to achieve the aims formulated in paragraph 1 the "patients are entitled to have their pain controlled, physical and mental sufferings ceased and they have the right to have with them their relatives and other persons in close emotional relationship"
3. Whenever possible, *hospice care* should be granted within the home of the patient and within the familiar environment.
4. *Hospice care* includes the psychosocial support of the family of the dying patient during the period of illness and after the patient's death.

National guidelines for *hospice-* and*palliative care* were developed by hospice and health experts and were initially published in 2000 and 2002 by the *Hungarian Hospice-Palliative Association*. These guidelines – approved of by the Health Department – were sent to all Hungarian hospitals.[41]

---

[38] Katalin Hegedus: Hospice movement in Hungary and experiences with hospital supportive teams: V Symposium – Hospice and Palliative Care. 21.03.2002

[39] ibid.

[40] ibid.

[41] Katalin Hegedus / Ildiko Szy (Ed.): Hungarian Hospice Foundation/ Semmelweis University: Palliative Care of Terminally Ill Cancer Patients. Professional guidelines. 2nd improved and extended edition. Budapest 2002.

On April 29th of this year, clear legal structures and financing guidelines for *hospice care* were decided on by the National Health Insurance and the Health Department. Hospice care therefore is an integral part of the health system. In September 2004, a 2-year model program started in the course of which the National Health Insurance will pay altogether 300 million Hungarian Forint to 21 home care services and 9 inpatient hospital departments which offer hospice care for patients and their families. [42] A lot of the existing inpatient and home hospice services applied, and also some "normal" hospital departments and home care services, who suited the application's requirements, for example they had nurses trained in hospice care or the service had a quality control system. Some of the other old hospices did not apply, but they continue their hospice work on the basis of other support. The application was very difficult for some services, because of the requirements. As a result, in addition to the existing Gyula, Miskolc and Pécs hospice inpatient centres, some other hospitals recieved financial support, that where not hospices before. Amongst those are Baranya County Hospital, Heves County Hospital, Komárom County Hospital, Zala County Hospital, and in Budapest, the MÁV Hospital. Most of the "new hospices" started their hospice work in autumn 2004. Thus the number of hospice beds in Hungary climbed considerably to 143 beds within a very short period of time. It is the same situation with the home care hospices, there are some new services supported by the NHIF. By taking this measure it is hoped to increase the number of people who have access to hospice care. A congress held by the *Hungarian Hospice Foundation*, the National Health Insurance and the *Open Society Institute* took place in April with the aim to map out the financing and a national strategy for hospice work. The conference advised to have 70% of the arising costs for at least half the people needing hospice care covered by the national social insurance until 2009. [43]

The Hungarian tax system contains a paragraph allowing citizens to assign 1% of their salary to the support of social organisations, churches and foundations, which increasingly benefits hospice institutions. Through advertising campaigns covering all media social organisations attempt to reach the largest possible number of people. The *Hungarian Hospice Foundation* has taken advantage of this fact. The institution in Budapest is an outpatient hospice service and in the near future will open the first independent inpatient hospice as well as a day care hospice. On the level of fundraising the *Hungarian Hospice Foundation* is already an exceptional case and can call the largest advertising campaign in the Hungarian health system its own, a campaign by now known beyond the Hungarian border. [44] Dr Katalin Muszbek, head of the institution, reports severe difficulties in the past in acquiring donations for the hospice service. [45] This was changed by the personal experience of the famous Hungarian ac-

42 Email from Dr Katalin Hegedus, 16 October 2004.

43 cp.: Official homepage of the Hungarian Hospice Foundation: http://www.hospicehaz.hu/eng/rolunkhir.html

44 Interview with Dr Katalin Muszbek. In: Pol.it. The Italian on line psychiatric magazine. http://www.pol-it.org/ital/psico-oncologia/katalineng.htm

45 Interview with Dr Katalin Muszbek, 12 August 2003, in Budapest.

tor Kata Dobó. During her last days the *Hungarian Hospice Foundation* had cared for Kata Dobó's grandmother, who suffered from cancer disease The positive personal experience with the hospice service prompted Dobó to become involved with the organisation. With help from the widely known advertising agency McCann-Erickson Budapest the *Hungarian Hospice Foundation* launched a large scale TV campaign. Dobó and two other famous personalities advertised for donations to the hospice. The well-produced spots were broadcast during prime time and produced pioneering effects. Donations have increased many times since the first serial – at the moment the second serial is broadcast. As *Programme Manager* Melinda Szöllösi reports questionnaires prove that since the TV campaign the familiarity with and acceptance of hospice services have increased enormously. [46]

2.4 Organisations

The ***Magyar Hospice-Palliativ Egyesület (Hungarian Hospice-Palliative Association)*** [47], as the national "umbrella" association,was founded in 1995 and represents the interests of 28 Hungarian hospice- and palliative institutions in, for example, negotiations with the Hungarian health Department. The Association initiated and coordinated of elaboration of the legal background of the Hungarian hospice-palliative care: Hospice and patient's right chapters of the Health care act (1997) and the National Guidelines (2002).

The Association started an offensive and successful media campaign with human rights and patients rights organisations in March 2003 to initiate a parliamentary examination in this field. Four questions were addressed officially to the Parliament to examine:

1. Are there enough available modern treatments, medicines and trained specialists in the institutions caring for dying patients?
2. Is there enough psychical care and information for terminal patients?
3. Are there enough palliative care services?
4. Is there good-quality care in the chronic departments and institutions?

After one year of this initiative and Parliament examination process the Ministry of Health accepted the Minimum Standards (2004) and the Health Care Insurance Fund started to finance the palliative care in Hungary. [48]

Since 1999 this organisation has been a member of the *European Association of Palliative Care* and is supported by the *Open Society Institute* in New York. [49]

46 Interview with Melinda Szöllösi, 12 August 2003, in Budapest.

47 For further information see: http://www.hospicehaz.hu/eng/rolunk-hir.html

48 Email from Dr Katalin Hegedus, 16 October 2004.

49 David Clark/ Michael Wright: Transitions in end of life care. Hospice and related developments in Eastern Europe and Central Asia. Buckingham 2003, p. 65

2.5 Professionals

A national training program for *Palliative Care*, organized by the Hungarian Hospice-Palliative Association, was accredited by the Health Department and includes a basic course spanning 40 hours as well as an advanced course of the same duration. Since 1994 more than 3000 people have participated in these courses. [50] Nine textbooks, a number of specialised literature and the *Kharon Thanatological Revue* were published. Curricula, guidelines and standards for palliative care (for example WHO- standards) have been translated into Hungarian.

Additionally a one-year post-graduate educational program for nurses (possibilities of graduation: trained hospice nurse, coordinator) exists, which, following a law decreed in June 2001 by the Ministry of Health, began in March 2002. [51]

While the readiness of the nurses concerning hospice- and palliative care seems rather distinct and corresponding courses are quite frequented, the attitude of the doctors is marked by reserve, ignorance and fears. What both professions often have in common is a lack of knowledge about hospice care, as proved by research conducted by the Institute of Behavioural Sciencesat the*Semmelweis University of Medicine*. 182 nurses, 288 students of medicine and 124 doctors were questioned about their attitude towards and knowledge about death and dying. The results go along with comparative questionnaires conducted in other countries. [52] 40,8% of the interviewees have never, during their practice or training, spoken to a dying patient about other things than purely medical concerns. About 40% of the interviewees did not know what to do with the term *hospice care* though they were given opportunities, which should have made finding an answer easier for them. [53] The reasons for this ignorance are obvious: in the course of the training for nurses spanning a whole 4600 hours only 33 hours were devoted to the treatment of the topics death and dying, for the medical students the time amounted to 34 hours by a total of 7000 hours.

A statement by Dr Katalin Muszbek summarises the importance of education and advanced training for the professionals in the area of hospice- and palliative care:

> Being fit for work in hospice care means having acquired its philosophy, being ready to work in a team and take part in extension trainings [. . .] Continuative education and the mental care of our staff is highly important, since burnout is a constant danger our colleagues have to face. Extension trainings and professional programmes help keep their knowledge and skills fresh and applicable, they help maintain high professional quality as well as reinforce their original motivation and a sense of competence. [54]

[50] Katalin Hegedus: VI. Hungarian Hospice-Palliative Congress. Hospice in Hungary 2004. Miskolc 23.04.2004.

[51] Katalin Hegedus: Hospice movement in Hungary and experiences with hospital supportive teams: V Symposium – Hospice and Palliative Care. 21.03.2002

[52] Katalin Hegedus and others: Attitude of Nurses and Medical Students toward Death and Dying. Poster for the 7th Congress of the European Association for Palliative care. Palermo. Italy 2001.

[53] ibid.

[54] Interview with Dr Katalin Muszbek. In: Pol.it. The Italian on line psychiatric magazine. http://www.pol-it.org/ital/psico-oncologia/katalineng.htm

2.6 *Volunteers*

Currently only 121 volunteers work in the Hungarian hospice- and palliative system [55], compared to the international figure a strikingly small number. Up until now, the reasons for this have not been researched. There are two possible main reasons for the lack of voluntary engagement: for one, Hungary's socialistic past where voluntary structures were not supported and consequently hardly existed. For another, the misuse of donated money by so-called charity organisations in post-socialistic Hungary proves to be a hindrance for those organisations who wish to work on an voluntary basis. The *voluntary* office therefore is seldom regarded or perceived as an *honour*. [56] In the institutions we visited especially religious people engaged themselves in voluntary hospice work. [57]

In the guidelines *Palliative Care of Terminally Ill Cancer Patients*,the work of the volunteers is defined in a separate chapter. [58] The selection of volunteers is supposed to begin with a personal conversation. After completion of a further undefined *hospice training* the volunteer is supposed to be introduced to the hospital work. After a three-month stay in the hospice section of the hospital assignment to the home care service is considered. The volunteers are supposed to support the patients, their relatives and the institution. They are assigned a vital role in the hospice work:

> Voluntary work is a significant contribution from an economical point of view. Voluntary work is a key-issue expressing civil commitment, trust, mutuality and solidarity among people. [59]

2.7 *Example* [60]

Erzsébet (Elisabeth) Hospice Foundation in Miskolc

Organisation and funding

In 1994 the *Erzsébet (Elisabeth) Hospice Foundation* in Miskolc began to care for terminally ill patients. In 2002 151 patients were cared for in their own homes. [61] The foundation also supports the *Erzsébet Hospice* , which is integrated into the *Semmelweis Hospital* in Miskolc and cares for about 320 - 350 patients each year. [62]With financial help from a foundation in the Netherlands, the number of beds in the inpatient

---

55 Katalin Hegedus: VI. Hungarian Hospice-Palliative Congress. Hospice in Hungary 2004. Miskolc 23.04.2004.

56 Interview with Barbara Kallo, 12 August 2003, in Budapest.

57 Interview with Dr Katalin Hegedus and Annamaria Köszegi, 11 August 2003, in Budapest. Interview with János Magyar, 14 August 2003, in Miskolc.

58 Katalin Hegedus / Ildiko Szy (ed.): Hungarian Hospice Foundation/ Semmelweis University: Palliative Care of Terminally Ill Cancer Patients. Professional guidelines. 2nd improved and extended edition. Budapest 2002, p. 10.

59 ibid., p. 62.

60 Additional detailed examples of hospice services in Hungary can be found in: David Clark/ Michael Wright: Transitions in end of life care. Hospice and related developments in Eastern Europe and Central Asia. Buckingham 2003, p. 195 - 214.

61 Statistics of the Erzsebet Hospice. Miskolc 2003, p. 24. Unpublished document.

62 Interview with Dr Csaba Simkó, 14 August 2003, in Miskolc.

hospice increased to 20 and a possibility of a day care hospice established. Unfortunately the day care department is not running at the moment. Currently more than 400 terminally ill cancer patients are being cared for per year – in Hungary's third largest city housing about 180.000 inhabitants. This number amounts to 60% of the terminally ill cancer patients concerned.[63]

The *Training and Resource Centre for Palliative Care* is an important part of the *Erzsébet Hospice Foundation.* More than 1.500 professional workers have been trained there, among them doctors, nurses, social workers, psychology students, so-called *mental hygiene students* as well as clergy. Other hospice institutions, like the *Jewish Charity Hospital hospice mobile team* in Budapest also send their members to Miskolc for their training.[64] In 2000 the achievements of the training centre were honoured by the *Open Society Institute* and the title "Educational and Training Centre" conferred. The main part of the home care hospice team's work is still financed by donations, funds and charity performances. The acquisition of donation money proves to be difficult as a tradition of donations does not exist and the people in and around Miskolc have their own financial problems to cope with.[65] Up to February 2004 the health insurance companies thought the home care in Miskolc sufficiently extended and they hold that other medical services already do the same work as the hospice service, so they refused to pay for the outpatient hospice teams.[66] Now the hospice home care service also received money from the health insurance for the nursing activities in Miskolc. Dr Csaba Simkó: "Furthermore there is a new nationwide trend in the financing of hospices in Hungary nowadays. In this new system money will be paid not only for the nursing care but also for the physician's, physiotherapist's and dietician's visits too."[67]

The care for one patient within the inpatient hospice is estimated at 7400 Hungarian Forint per day. So far the Health insurance paid 3400 Forint, the remainder was provided by the hospital. This way the hospital lost 30 million Forint (about 100 000 Euro) by financing the hospice unit.[68] In the new financing system the hospital will get 1.8 x 3900 Forint for a hospice bed per day. It will cover 75% of the costs.[69] The average stay within inpatient care is about 18 days.

The professional team of the inpatient hospice

The hospice employs 2 doctors, 15 nurses, 1 physiotherapist (part-time) and 1 voluntary coordinator who is a trained nurse as well. A protestant pastor works part-time in the hospice, a catholic priest comes at least twice a week. The greater part of the workers has received their training in the training centre of the *Erzsébet Hospice Foun-*

63 www.eapceast.org/upload/Elizabeth%20Hospice%20Hungary.doc
64 Interview with Dr Katalin Hegedus, 11 August 2003, in Budapest.
65 Interview with Dr Csaba Simkó, 14 August 2003, in Miskolc.
66 ibid.
67 Email from Dr Csaba Simkó, 17th October 2004.
68 Interview with Dr Csaba Simkó, 14 August 2003, in Miskolc.
69 Email from Dr Csaba Simkó, 17th October 2004.

dation. The team is not supervised. Earlier attempts failed "because of the poor care of one psychologist. Neither is supervision desired by the workers." [70]

The voluntary team of the hospice

The 12 volunteers (11 women, 1 man) are chosen, trained and supervised by a voluntary coordinator. In choosing the voluntary workers, attention is paid to the applicants not having suffered a death in their family in the last two years and that they themselves and no family member suffer a terminal illness at the moment of their application. A minimum age of 18 years is also required. [71] Before taking up work, the volunteer has to pass a training program. Special emphasis is placed on the psychological training of the volunteers. [72] For instance, the phases of the dying process are treated by Dr Elisabeth Kübler-Ross. Further aspects of training include communication, basic care and physiotherapy. Towards the end of the course the volunteers are taken along to visit patients to get an impression of the daily work. The volunteers themselves decide on their field of activity. 30% of this consists of nursing care, which initially caused conflicts with the professional nursing team. By now though, the relationship is perceived as very good. One indication for this is the communal use of the changing room by professionals and volunteers alike, which is rather uncommon by Hungarian standards. [73] The voluntary workers confirm that, describing the relationship to the nurses in the hospice as "very good. Compared to the nurses in the hospital these nurses are glad for our support" [74]. In addition to the improved relationship to the nurses Kamilla Bánkúti emphasises the fact that in the hospice no "gifts" by the patients are accepted and all are treated as equal. She comes to the hospice for 3 to 6 hours once a week to attend to the patients. She "converses with patients", takes them for walks, runs errands or helps distributing meals. [75] Like almost all volunteers in Miskolc she is very religious and is a member of the Roman Catholic church. In isolated cases voluntary coordinator János Magyar observes the risk of missionary ardour in religious volunteers. The training therefore clarifies that the initiative for prayer has to come exclusively from the patient and not from the voluntary. As in the case of the professionals there is no supervision, but once a month a meeting with the voluntary coordinator is held.

Specific issues

In all the conducted interviews a marked delimitation from the habits in Hungarian hospitals can be observed. The handling of the deceased patients is very dignified and ritualised. "We try to treat the dying just as it would happen if they were at home". [76] After the patient's death their body remains in the bed for 2 to 4 hours. In front of the

70 Interview with Dr Csaba Simkó, 14 August 2003, in Miskolc.
71 Interview with János Magyar, 14 August 2003, in Miskolc.
72 Interview with Dr Csaba Simkó, 14 August 2003, in Miskolc.
73 Interview with János Magyar, 14 August 2003, in Miskolc.
74 Interview with Kamilla Bánkúti, 14 August 2003, in Miskolc.
75 ibid.
76 Interview with Dr Csaba Simkó, 14 August 2003, in Miskolc.

nurses' room and in the patient's room a candle is lit and flowers for decoration are placed. The bed of the deceased patient remains vacant for at least one day, sometimes for even 48 hours. This is regarded as a symbolic gesture of respect for the dead. Sometimes team members, especially the nurses, also attend the funeral. [77]

3. Summary

In the course of its ten year history, the Hungarian hospice movement has been able to count a number of remarkable successes its own. Within the *Hungarian Hospice-Palliative Association* national hospice services are now organised and speak with one voice. A law for hospice- and palliative care has been established within the National Health Act. These shortly decided agreements with the compulsory sickness fund and the Ministry of Health are expected to guarantee the hospice services are able to operate on a financially secure basis in the future. After 13 years of lobbying, publicity and educational work, numerous advertising campaigns and the organisation of charity events to spread the hospice philosophy hospice work now is no longer a movement but an integral part of the health system.

Hospice services can draw from nursing personnel trained in standardised national basic and advanced courses and possessing at least basic knowledge of Palliative Care. The post-graduate course founded in 2002 will soon produce disciplinary specialised hospice nurses. Textbooks and teaching aids for hospice- and palliative care are available in Hungarian.

While the hospice and palliative training for nurses is expanding, the medical section states a severe shortage of doctors with palliative knowledge. Palliative care content hardly exists within the medical curriculum, though – if only sporadically –, there is some interest in the matter within the medical profession, as an integrative model in Miskolc shows, which tries to impart palliative care knowledge to resident doctors. [78] The integration of hospice structures into the existing frame of the health system still remains underdeveloped. At present, exist only two services in Hungary exist, which Katalin Hegedus defines as *complex services.* [79] This includes institutions which have established inpatient as well as outpatient and home care facilities and also operate as training and educational centres. The existing complex services *Hungarian Hospice Foundation* and *Erzsébet Hospice* will shortly be followed by a third such institution. Further educational work will be necessary to soften the stiffened structures of the current health system and to increase the still low acceptance of multi-disciplinary teams. Within the inner hospice structures this aim has obviously been reached. In the conducted interviews the interviewees repeatedly point out the conducive team structures and accentuate these as an asset towards other institutions. [80] The refusal of bribery

---

77 Interview with Annamária Breznai, 14 August 2003, in Miskolc.

78 Interview with Dr Csaba Simkó, 14 August 2003, in Miskolc.

79 Katalin Hegedus: VI. Hungarian Hospice-Palliative Congress. Hospice in Hungary 2004. Miskolc 23.04.2004.

80 for example: Interview with Nóra Ferdinandy, 12 August 2003, in Budapest.

and the explicit delimitation from the institution hospital is also mentioned in several interviews.[81]

Another deficit is the lack of inpatient hospice units in the medical faculties' clinical field where they would be necessary for the research and education in pain and symptom management. A few experts critically remark on the lack of suitable quality control and evaluation of hospice institutions. Dr Andrea Bekesi, head doctor of the only children hospice in Hungary, supports the importance of formal evaluations. For her it would be confirmation enough when the parents of deceased children return to express their thanks for the care their child received. In this way, they would give back much more than an evaluation certifying successful work. The indicator for successful work would be the continued contact with the family members and their positive reaction: "That's what I call success!"[82]

Hungary's socialistic past has prevented a tradition of donations or voluntary offices to arise. Yet the current development gives cause for hope, as the successful advertising campaign of the *Hungarian Hospice Foundation* shows. Chances are good that especially the terminally ill cancer patients will continue to profit from the pioneering work done by exceptional personalities like Dr Katalin Hegedus, Dr Katalin Muszbek and Dr Alaine Polcz.

Sources and Literature

Clark, David/ Wright, Michael: Transitions in end of life care. Hospice and related developments in Eastern Europe and Central Asia, Buckingham 2003.

Hegedus, Katalin: Legal and ethical elements of hospice-palliative services in Hungary. *Progress in Palliative Care* 8 (1) 2000, p. 17 - 20.

Hegedus, K., Pilling, J., Kolosai, N. and Bognár, T: Attitude of Nurses and Medical Students toward Death and Dying. Poster for the 7th Congress of the European Association for Palliative Care, Palermo, Italy, 2001.

Hegedus, Katalin: Hospice movement in Hungary and experiences with hospital supportive teams: V Symposium – Hospice and Palliative Care, 21.03.2002.

Hegedus, Katalin: VI. Hungarian Hospice-Palliative Congress. Hospice in Hungary 2004. Miskolc 23.04.2004.

Hegedus, Katalin/Szy, Ildiko (Ed.): Hungarian Hospice-Palliative Association: Palliative Care of Terminally Ill.

Cancer Patients. Professional guidelines. 2nd improved and extended edition. Budapest 2002.

Information brochure Jewish Social Support Foundation 2001 - 2002. Budapest 2002.

Rodler, Imre/ Zajkás, Gabor: Hungarian Cancer Mortality and Food Availability Data in the Last Four Decades of the 20th Century. In: Annals of Nutrition & Metabolism. Vol. 46. No. 2. 2002, p. 49 - 56.

Statistics of the Erzsébet Hospice. Miskolc 2003. Unpublished document.

[81] One of numerous examples is the interview with Edit Szigeti, 12 August 2003, in Budapest.

[82] Interview with Dr Andrea Bekesi, 15 August 2003, in Budapest.

Szebik, Imre: Masked ball: ethics, laws and financial contradictions in Hungarian health care. In: *Science and Engineering Ethics*. Vol. 9. Issue 1. 2003, p. 109 - 24.

Internet sources

Official Homepage of the United Nations: http://esa.un.org/unpp

Orosz, Eva / Burns, Andrew: Organisation for Economic Co-operation and Development. The Health Care System in Hungary. Economics Department Working Papers No. 241. Available online: http://www.olis.oecd.org/olis/2000doc.nsf/4f7adc214b91a685c12569fa005d0ee7/c125685b0057c558c12568cf00330dd9/\$FILE/00076478.PDF

Complete monitoring report of the preparation of Hungary for the membership within the EU.p. 10. In: http://www.mfa.gov.hu/NR/rdonlyres/38C506FC-02D5-417F-B62B-5CD6101ED9C2/0/cmr_hu_final_de.pdf

Bundeszentrale für politische Bildung: http://www.bpb.de/popup_druckversion.html?guid=MPPBS3

European Observatory on Health Care Systems: Healthcare systems in transition – Hungary. Copenhagen 1999. In: http://www.who.dk/document/e68317.pdf

Official Homepage of the Hungarian Hospice Foundation: http://www.hospicehaz.hu/

Official Homepage of the Hungarian Hospice/Palliative Association http://www.hospice.hu

Interview with Katalin Muszbek. In: Pol.it. The Italian on line psychiatric magazine. http://www.pol-it.org/ital/psico-oncologia/katalineng.htm

www.eapceast.org/upload/ Elizabeth%20Hospice%20Hungary.doc

List of interviews (in chronological order)

- Dr Katalin Hegedus, Leader Hospice Programme of the Jewish Support Foundation, President Hungarian Hospice-Palliative Association, Member of the Board of Directors EAPC Budapest, 11 August 2003
- Monika Veress, Nurse at Jewish Charity Hospital Budapest, 11 August 2003
- Annamária Köszegi, Social worker at Jewish Charity Hospital Budapest, 11 August 2003
- Dr Katalin Muszbek, Leader of the Hungarian Hospice Foundation Budapest, 12 August 2003
- Edit Szigeti, Head nurse of the Hungarian Hospice Foundation Budapest, 12 August 2003
- Barbara Kalló, Social worker of the Hungarian Hospice Foundation Budapest, 12 August 2003
- Melinda Szöllösi, Programme Manager of the Hungarian Hospice Foundation Budapest, 12 August 2003
- Nóra Ferdinandy, Physiotherapist of the Hungarian Hospice Foundation Budapest, 12 August 2003
- Zsóka Kelemen, Deputy head nurse at the Hospice of Szt. László Hospital Budapest, 13 August 2003
- Dr Csaba Simkó, Medical director at the Erzsébet Hospice Miskolc, 14 August 2003
- János Magyar, Voluntary coordinator at the Erzsébet Hospice Miskolc, 14 August 2003

- Annamaria Brezna, Physiotherapist at the Erzsébet Hospice Miskolc, 14 August 2003
- Kamilla Bánkúti, Voluntary worker at the Erzsébet Hospice Miskolc, 14 August 2003
- Dr Andrea Bekesi, Medical director of Bethesda Children's Hospice Budapest, 15 August 2003

Italy [1]

Reimer Gronemeyer

1. General Conditions

1.1 Demographics

- With 57.7 million inhabitants Italy is the "oldest" country in Europe. [2] In Italy the ageing process of society is even more dramatic than in other European countries:
- In 2000, the population of Italy totalled 57.7 million; 10 million higher than in 1950. According to predictions, the population will drop to 50.9 million by 2050. [3]
- In particular the *number of people of great age* has increased: In Italy there were 24,000 people at the age of 85 and older in 1871. In 1991 there were 412,000. By 2015 3,591,000 Italians will be 75 years and older. [4] In 2001 18.2% of the Italians were 65 years and older, 4.1% 80 and older. [5]
- The *death rate* in Italy will rise from 10.9 persons per 1000 inhabitants (in the years from 2000 to 2005) to 18.9 per 1000 inhabitants by 2050 (Medium estimation of the United Nations).
- The *Italian family* shrinks: 23% of the Italians are single, 20% of the couples do not have any children: So the dependency on home and inpatient services will probably increase.
- Approximately 300,000 people a year need a *treatment for chronic pain* in Italy. Of this number 140,000 are terminally ill tumour patients. [6] Every year, 160,000 Italians die of cancer.

---

1 Translated by Natalie Butz.

2 The age index 127.0 for Italy is calculated by the population "65 years and older" divided by the population "0 - 14 years". In comparison: Albania's index is 17.4, for France it is 85.7, and for Germany 103.5.

3 Population Division of the Department of Economic and Social Affairs of the United Nations Secretariat, World Population Prospects: The 2002 Revision and *World Urbanization Prospects: The 2001 Revision.* Official Homepage of the United Nations: http://esa.un.org/unpp

4 Source: For 1871, 1931, and 1991: Istat, Censimenti della popolazione; for 2015: Lo Conte e Sorvillo (2001) (Information of the Ministero del Lavoro e delle Politiche Sociali, October 30, 2003)

5 Source: Elaborazione dati Istat, 2002.

6 http://www.kwsalute.kataweb.it/Notizia/0,1044,2729,00.html

- More than 70% of Italians *die in institutions* – in hospitals, old people's and nursing homes. [7]

1.2 Health Care System

In the European Union almost half of the expenses on social security account for the "ageing and surviving dependents". Italy ranks first in this category with 63%. [8] The "Servizio Sanitario Nazionale" (the national health service) has existed since 1978. Contributions are not charged at all, the state finances the health care with taxes. Sometimes additional payments are necessary. Since the nineties the health service has been regionalised; as a consequence the north-south divide increased. In addition conservative governments – Lombardia – rather support the private sector, left-wing governments – Tuscany – rather back the health service organised by the state. "Actually the state guarantees an extensive care, but in practice the private sector flourishes." [9] Approximately one third of the health care of the citizens is actually done by the private sector – also because of long waiting periods in the state-run programs. The result is a two-class medical sector. Even the organisation of home nursing services is arranged differently according to region.

2. Hospice and palliative care in Italy

2.1 History

Palliative care developed late in Italy, compared to other European countries. [10] In 1987, there was only one Palliative Care Service, in 1999 there were just five. This fact is connected with two things: firstly, on the one hand the Italian family has been comparatively long intact, and on the other hand Italy has a strong tradition of voluntary help in hospitals and at home. The term "cure palliative" has gained acceptance in the meantime, although in Italy the word "palliativo" means "senseless", or "unnecessary". In Italy Palliative Care has specially been made public by the Fondazione Floriani, which was founded in Milano in 1977 to support Palliative Care in Italy. Vittorio Ventafridda can be seen as the spiritual father of this movement. In 1993 he defined

- treatment for pain,
- psychological and spiritual help in the face of death,
- multi disciplinary, and

---

7 EoLo – the project EoLo (End of Life in Ospedale) is financed by the Region Lombardia and the Associazione Cremonese per la Cura del Dolore. http://www.istituto.org/it/

8 Sozialkompass Europa, 2000, p. 123.

9 Michael Braun: Warten oder selber zahlen. Das Gesundheitswesen in Italien, in: Dr. med. Mabuse 148, March/April 2004, p. 18 - 20.

10 Though Michele Gallucci refers to Dr. Giuseppe del Chiappa's book "Discours de la morale du médecin", which created a basis for palliative medicine already in 1852.

– support of relatives

as general conditions for Palliative Care in Italy.

In 1999 this basis was replenished and broadened by the twelve point "Carta die diritti di merenti" ("Charter of rights of dying people"), which was published by Fondazione Floriani as well.

The activities of the Sue Ryder Foundation belong to the early steps in the direction of Palliative Care. Approximately ten thousand out of the three million inhabitants in Rome died every year in the eighties. Six thousand of them were suffering from cancer, seventy per cent of those died in hospitals. Therefore an aid programme for the domestic care of severely ill cancer patients was established in 1984. Due to the decreasing willingness and ability of the families to care for the dying persons, Sue Ryder expanded its activity in the nineties, and primarily tried to include volunteers. Beside doctors, nurses and psychologists, fifty volunteers currently participate in the domestic services, which are offered twenty-four hours a day.

The first Italian hospices were the Hospice Domus Salutis in Brescia, the Hospice of the Clinica Capitanio and the Hospice Pio Albergo Trivulzio in Milan. [11]

2.2 Hospice and Palliative Care Services

Between 241,000 and 286,000 people in Italy need Palliative Care every year, most of them are cancer patients. Since 1999, the Italian Ministry of Health is supporting the organisation of linked up care systems. It recommends following services:
- Out-patient care (Assistenza ambulatoriale)
- Integrated home care (Assistenza Domiciliare Integrate)
- Integrated specialised home care (Assistenza Domiciliare Specialistica)
- Hospital care or day hospital
- In-patient Palliative Care

The Italians make a distiction between Hospice Residentale (In-patient hospice outside hospitals) and Hospice Hospitaliero (hospice within hospitals). Even the independent hospices get money from the Servizio Sanitare Nationale, the national health service. The Società Italiana di Cure Palliative defines hospice as a "struttura sanitaria residenziale" (in-patient health structure), where Palliative Care is offered. The hospice is seen as an alternative to domestic care, if a temporary or permanent care at home is not possible. Due to Furio Zucco's statement, President of the Federazione Cure Palliative, Palliative Care Services and family doctors do not work well together. Sixty per cent of the patients taken care of by Palliative Care Services come from hospitals. [12]

It is quite difficult to give exact numbers about Palliative Care offers in Italy. The several regions deal differently with definitions and numbers, the dissociation between

---

[11] Giovanni Zaninetta: Gli Hospici in Italia: Una via ‚Latina' alle Cure Palliative? http://oasinforma.com/art/art-zaninetta.htm

[12] Furio Zucco at the congress "The International Meeting of Hospices", ANTEA Hospice, Rome, November 6 - 7, 2003.

geriatric and palliative care is not always clear, the state facilities and the private ones are sometimes put together, sometimes not. Nonetheless, there is no doubt that in Italy – as in other countries as well – alongside state facilities, 120 non-profit organisations endeavour to provide Palliative Care, where volunteers play an extremely important role. [13]

According to information from the Ministry of Health, there are 194 Palliative Care offers in Italy in 2004, which includes 2133 beds. So, according to the Ministry, the scheduled standard of 0.4 to 0.5 beds for 10,000 inhabitants is fulfilled. But this data only refers to the offer supported by the national programme. The actual number of beds is – according to the Ministry of Health – higher, because the regions have partly established Palliative Care Services by themselves. There are 46 in-patient hospices at national level financed by the state, which can only be found in the north of Italy. [14]

Michele Galluci includes the charitable facilities and so counts 168 centres of Palliative Care and 152 outpatient services in 2001, which are run by charitable organisations. In September 2002 there are – according to Gallucci – 184 hospices with 2003 beds, which are financed by the state. While the Ministry of Health counts the state facilities, Gallucci adds the services and institutions, which work charitably but are financed with money from the state. [15]

The *Osservatorio Permanente Cure Palliative* [16], published by Oscar Corli, gives a regular and very detailed overview of the development of Palliative Care in Italy. This source counted 220 palliative care units (in hospitals, hospices and palliative care home care programmes). 19 of those 220 services are situated in local hospitals. According to Corli there are 80 hospices with a total number of 791 beds. Corli does not include palliative wards in his calculations. [17]

According to Corli 64.4 per cent of all Palliative Care Structures can be found in the northern provinces, 18.6 per cent within the centre, 10.6 per cent in the south, and 6.4 per cent on the islands. 45 per cent of the Palliative Care Structures are state-owned, 33 per cent are run by charitable organisations, 12 per cent are private, and 10 per cent are established by religious institutions. [18]

With regards to Palliative Care, Lombardia is clearly the region with the most provisions – which is hardly surprising according to the financial situation. Lombardia

---

13 Written message by Oscar Corli, 18 October 2004. Furio Zucco: Le Organizzazzioni Non Lucrative (Onlus): da pomotorici a garanti delle Leggi. In: Il Movimento Hospice e le Cure Palliative, congress in Milan, October 27, 2000, organised by Fondazione Floriani, http://www.fondazionefloriani.org/pagchi.htm/

14 Ministry of Health http://ministerosalute.it/dettaglio/pdAtuPerTuDettaglio/

15 Interview with Michele Gallucci in Milan, June 30, 2004, cf. also Michele Gallucci: Les soins palliatifs en France et à l'etranger, Paper for the French Ministry of Health, December 12, 2002.

16 Oscar Corli (Ed.): Le Unità di Cure Palliative e le Organizzazioni Non Profit, latest edition, http://www.osservatoriocurepalliative.org/pub/

17 Personal correspondence with Oscar Corli, 18 October 2004.

18 Simona Zazzetta in a report to the X. congress of the Società Italiana per le Cure Palliative, Milan, March 2003, http://www.dica33it./argomenti/

is Italy's economic centre. There is data of domestic Palliative Care in Milan and the province for 2003. Palliative Care comprises according to that:
- 29 full-time doctors
- 31,5 part-time doctors
- 44 full-time nurses
- 25 part-time nurses
- 15 psychologists
- 21 social assistants
- 115 volunteers
- 24590 doctor's visits
- 35394 nurse's visits
- 1335 home visits by psychologists – beside care by the Palliative Care Team
- 392 sick persons who were visited by volunteers who made 3045 home visits
- 2789 patients cared altogether; 1957 persons were looked after until the end
- 35.2 days as an average time of care [19]

The typically Italian regional differences for are shown in several ways: there are for example in Lombardia 25 palliative sections ("hospice wards") in hospitals. In contrast the domestic care in Emila Romagna is much more distinctive.

The previous concentration of Palliative Care on cancer patients should be overcome in Italy in the future: Because of that, Dr Michele Gallucci founded in 2004 an organisation called CARDEA Onlus, which wants to work whole-heartedly for hospice services and Palliative Care at the end of lives of every illness. Incidentally, there is a growing interest – according to Michele Gallucci – in foundations of private hospices, which are financed by money from the state, inheritances and fund-raising-activities. A directly economic interest of the operators is – according to Michele Gallucci – at times perceptible. Especially in the region Latium the government gives money to private people to establish hospices, which is at times tantamount to outsourcing of palliative patients. The catholic church has a stake in a considerable number of hospices and hospice services. It has to be mentioned, that hospices can be a temporary place of residence. Approximately 30 per cent of the patients consult a hospice because of special complications, in order to return to the domestic care afterwards.

2.3 Legal regulations and funding [20]

With the law no. 39, September 28, 1999, the Italian government established the "Programma nazionale per la realizzazione di strutture per le cure palliative" (national pro-

[19] Data compiled by the Fondazione Floriani and the Lega Italiana contro i Tumori, paper handed over by Michele Gallucci at the interview in Milan, June 29, 2004.

[20] cf. above all Ministero della Salute – Direzione generale della programmazione sanitaria, dei livellli di assistenza e dei principi etici di sistema, 27 maggio 2004. (http://www.ministerosalute.it/dettaglio/; cf. also Furio Zucco/Annette Welshmann: The National Health Service and the care for the dying, in: European Journal of Palliative Care, 2001, 8 (2), p. 61 - 65.

gramme to realise structures of Palliative Care).[21] This was the first extensive impetus to answer the problems of care of the severely ill. The regions and the autonomous provinces were at the same time requested to pass appropriate programmes. This happened in 2001 and 2002. The Italian regions passed programmes regarding Palliative Care. The programmes had to be connected centrally and regionally with the Piano Sanitario Nazionale of 1998 - 2000. The patients in the final stages of cancer should receive special attention, as well as it is requested to put the dignity of the dying people and their quality of life in the centre of attention. At the same time it expresses the need to work towards a network of care structures. Domestic care is privileged: Hospices do only take over, if domestic care is not possible. The principle of hospices is: easy technology, but care on the highest level. Altogether 206.604.967 Euros were granted for the regions in 1998 - 1999 and 2000 - 2002. Amongst other things the number of hospices in Italy should increase to 184 hospices by this way – obviously a successful impetus.

During the first phase just a fraction of the approved money was withdrawn. 22 of the 134 financed services were realised, and 13.675.103 Euro were withdrawn of the first approved part of 132.476.875 Euros.[22]

With the order DPCM 20 the structural preconditions which are in force for hospices were formulated in detail on March 21st, 2000. These in turn should take effect in the regional programmes. In its guidelines, the ministry complies with the suggestions, which were made by the Società Italiana di Cure Palliative.[23] On April 12th, 2002, the minister of health summoned a committee with the task to support Palliative Care at home and in hospitals ("cure palliative in ospedale e a domicilio"). In Lombardia, a decree about the co-ordination of structures of Palliative Care had been passed already on November 30th, 1998. In the following of the national decree, there was a whole host of different regionally individual rulings.[24] The national health plan 2003 - 2005 gives Palliative Care priority.

The relevant Italian committees and organisations reject a law on euthanasia. The Società Italiana Cure Palliative and the Federazione Cure Palliative requested the Council of Europe together with other organisations in a statement on January 20th, 2004, highlight their opinions not to legalise euthanasia.[25] Currently the legal situation is – according to Michele Gallucci – as follows: The doctor always decides about the treatment of the unconscious patient.[26] The patient's instruction is only valid as long as the patient is conscious. There are several opinions in Italy about Palliative Care

[21] The law does not say anything about hospices, but only about in-patient centres for Palliative Care.

[22] Ibid.

[23] Società Italiana di Cure Palliative and Federazione Cure Palliative Onlus: Proposta di requisiti minimi technologici, strutturale e organizzativi per l'accreditamento delle unità di cure palliative e delle organizzazioni non profit, n.p., n.d.

[24] Raffaella Speranza: La tutela del modello hospice alla luce delle normative regionale e nazionali. In: Il Movimento Hospice e le Cure Palliative, congress in Milan, October 27, 2000, organised by Fondazione Floriani, http://www.fondazionefloriani.org/pagchi.htm/

[25] http://www.sicp.it/news/2004/

[26] Interview with Michele Gallucci, Milan, June 30, 2004.

and euthanasia. Some people say, Palliative Care prevents euthanasia, others say, it is exactly the preparation for that (Michele Gallucci).[27]

As an example the calculation of a new hospice shall be described which was planned in a building whose structures go back to the XIV. century. In 2000, the Hospice Cascina Brandezzata was planned for twelve beds in Milan. The costs of the re-building, the fittings etc. amounted to 3.470.000.000 Lira (approx. 1.7.000.000 Euro). That means that approx. 140.000 Euro have to be invested in every bed.[28]

2.4 Organisations

The *Fondazione Floriani* is the centre of many activities in the field of Palliative Care in Italy. Fondazione Floriani was founded in 1977 with the intention to support Palliative Care in Italy. A survey of the public awareness of Palliative Care which was carried out for the Fondazione showed, that 36 per cent of those questioned knew, what Palliative Care is.[29] Part of the Fondazione is the Fandazione Floriani Bibliotheca as well as domestic care services (see below). It is the umbrella organisation of the training association SIMPA and SICP.[30]

The *Società Italiana di Cure Palliative* (SICP) was founded in 1986. It represents the branch of Palliative Care. It organises the annual congresses to develop Palliative Care in Italy, and published among other things two brochures – together with the Federazione Cure Palliative: "Proposta di requisiti minimi tecnologici, strutturali e organizzativi" (Suggestions for technical and structural minimum requirement of Unità Cure Palliative's accreditation and the one of non-profit organisations). Besides: Linee guida per le organizazzioni senza fini di Lucro per le cure palliative, which states the work of the volunteers more precisely.[31]

Federazione Cure Palliative, Onlus[32], and president Furio Zucco, work closely together with the Società Italiana di Cure Palliative, and unites nationally the non-profit organisations which concern themselves with Palliative Care. (fedcp@tin.it and http://www.fedcp.org).

The *Istituto Maestroni* is a research institute for Palliative Medicine. It was founded in 1998 by the Fondazione Floriani, Milan, and the ACCD (Associazione Cremonese per la Cura del Dolore), Cremona. Currently two projects are primarily carried out: Since 1993, the project "Staging" has endeavoured to classify cancer patients according to quality of life. For this STAS, developed by Irene Higginson, was

---

27 Ibid.

28 Bruno Andreoni: Il progetto Hospice "Cascina Brandezzata", in: Il Movimento Hospice e le Cure Palliative in Italia, congress in Milan, October 27, 2000.

29 G. Di Mola/G.Ventafridda e.a: Indagine sulla conoscenza delle cure palliative nella popolazione Italiana, in: Rivista Italiana di Cure Palliative 1, 2001, p. 15 - 18.

30 http://www.fondazione.floriani.org

31 http://www.sicp.it

32 ONLUS is the Italian term for non-profit organisations (Organizzazioni Non Lucrative di Utilità Sociale).

used basically. The project EoLo (End of Life in ospedale) concerns itself with the situation of dying persons in hospitals. [33]

Lega Italiana per la Lotta contro i Tumori. [34]

The Italian branch of the *EAPC* (European Association for Palliative Care), Director Franco di Conno. The Italian EACP belongs to the field of the *Instituto Nazionale per lo Studio e la Cura die Tumori*, Milan.

Società Assistenza Malato Oncologico Terminale S.A.M.O.T.

There are more institutions involved with Palliative Care and hospice services. They are partly mentioned in section 2.7 (Caritas Ambrosiana, Fondazione Moschino, Fondazione Don Carlo Gnocchi, Sue Ryder Italia, Antea).

2.5 Education and training of professional staff

S.I.M.P.A., the Scuola Italiana di Medicina e Cure Palliative, has existed since 1989. Together with the Fondazione Floriani, it offers a "Master Di Secondo Livello In Cure Palliatiave", which can be received at the Università dell'Insubria di Vareseor the Università degli Studi di Milano (Dr Michele Gallucci is the principal). [35]

Apart from this, the "Scuola di Formazione e Aggiornamento in Medicina Palliativa" was founded in Milanand also the "Scuola Paradigma". There is the "Centro Studi Pallio" in Turin, in Rome ANTEA offers with "Formad" a training of Palliative Care. S.A.M.O.T. organises courses of Palliative Care in Palermo.

2.6 Volunteers

Volunteers play quite an important role in Italy, according to Michele Gallucci, they are less accepted in the south of Italy than in the north, because there the family is still considered to be responsible originally. But there are volunteers in hospices and palliative sections in the south, but rarely in the domestic care. An important person for the activity, the organisation, and the training of volunteers in Italy is Claude Fusco Karmann [36]. She is the chairwoman of Milan's section "Italian League against cancer". Ms Fusco Karmann leads the training of the volunteers who want to support Palliative Care. 700 volunteers work for the League in the region of Milan. The volunteers are meticulously chosen, they have to fulfil the criteria as follows:

- They have to be between 18 and 65 years old.
- Students and trainees who want to become nurses, psychologists or doctors are not accepted as volunteers.

---

33 http://www.fedcp.org

34 http://www.legatumori.mi.it

35 Cf. also Carlo Peruselli: Le Scuole di medicina palliativa in Italie und: Flavio Cruciatti/Massimo Monti: I programmi di formazione ed educazione permanente interna, esterna e tutoriali in Hospice, both in: Il Movimento Hospice e le Cure Palliative in Italia, congress in Milan, October 27, 2000.

36 Cf. among others the interview with Claude Fusco Karmann in: Innovations in: End-of-Life Care, An International Journal of Leaders in End-of-Life Care. http://www2.edc.org/lastacts/archives/

- Volunteers should not apply if one of their relatives is suffering heavily from cancer at the time of application.
- Volunteers should offer to give up half a day, two times a week or one long evening.
- Anyone who got over suffering from cancer should not become a volunteer.

Mostly 200 of 400 applicants are left over who will then be invited to an MMPI-Interview (Minnesota Multiphasic Personality Inventory). The interview takes approximately one hour. In this way those who want to solve personal problems or people who are hypochondriacs are sorted out. Only the ones who are driven by the spirit of solidarity should become volunteers.

87 per cent of the volunteers are women, 22 per cent are men. 45 per cent of the volunteers are between 40 and 50 years old. Mostly they are women whose children are grown-up, and men who are retired (These men are often not older than 50 years in Italy.) The training courses take 32 hours; 100 to 130 people take part every year.

Apart from this volunteer organisation of Milan, there are a lot of locally supported trainings and activities. In Brescia (Domus Salutis, see below 2.8), the VAD (Volontari Assistenza Domiciliare) takes part in the domestic care. But this organisation does not take on the job of the care in a narrower sense. The service is free of charge.

The Fondazione Floriani, Milan, plays a very important role in the training of volunteers as well.

2.7 Examples

There is a large variety of Palliative Care in Italy. To fulfil this variety, the different forms should be the centre of attention: hospices in hospitals, a hospice incorporated into a nursing home, a private hospice, a church hospice, and a hospice which started as a place of admission for AIDS patients.[37] It has to be mentioned that the Fondazione Floriani has organised a complex network of domestic care in Lombardia. Together with the "Lega italiana per la lotta contro i tumori", a "Unità di Cure Palliative Domiciliari" which consists of nurses, doctors, social assistants, psychologists, and volunteers, is carried on in many places. The service works among others in Milan, Monza, Desio, Lecco, Merate, Vimercate, and Cremona.

Hospiz Casa di Cura Columbus, Milan[38]

The hospice Casa di Cura Columbus has existed since 2001. It is situated in a big hospital with a view of a nice park. There are 15 double rooms for one patient and a relative. The team consists of nurses, doctors, psychologists and volunteers. The four doctors work on other wards as well. The staff are paid from the budget of the health authority of the state. The patients come from the whole of the province. Dr. Tansini, an internist, laments the small number of hospices. The average stay in the hospice

[37] Of course this is just a small selection. So it can only be mentioned that there is a small oncological Palliative section in the military hospital in Rome (Policlinico Militare di Roma Celio) (Interview with the head physician Dr Astorre, Rome, November 04, 2003.).

[38] Interview with Dr Tansini, 29 June 2004, in Milan.

lasts 20 days. Only cancer patients for whom therapy is not possible anymore, and whose relatives are not able to guarantee domestic care, are accommodated. The average age is 68 years. Since 2001, the hospice has taken care of 250 patients. Relatives can stay overnight and attend the meals. The patients do not pay any contributions. The patients know where they are, but do not want to speak about it generally. They talk to nurses, doctors, volunteers or relatives differently about their situation. According to Dr Tansini, no one asks for active euthanasia. For these patients, anger or denial of the approaching death is generally over.

An expert for communication and a doctor teach volunteers in the hospice. The volunteers, most of them women, come once a week. They talk to the patients, help with the meals, and do office work.

The mortuary is used as the room to say goodbye. Generally no priest is asked to come, because otherwise the approaching death would be obvious.

Hospice Istituto Geriatrico, Milan[39]

This hospice of ten beds which was founded in 2004 is part of a big nursing home[40] consisting of 510 beds including a rehabilitation ward. The patients are generally oncological patients. One relative can stay overnight in the patient's room and attend meals. The patients do not pay any contributions. Mostly the patients come from nursing homes, their life expectancy amounts to three to four months. The average stay in the hospice lasts 30 days. There are also patients who have their pain controlled, and who are sent home again afterwards. Experience shows that the treatment lasts nine days. Six trained nurses, eight unskilled nurses, one psychologist, one social worker and one honorary worker are part of the team. The social worker and the psychologist are just partly there. They are paid by the Ministry of Health.

The patients do not necessarily get to know that they are in a hospice, usually they will be told if they ask the doctors. In the house there are no hints showing that the place is a hospice.

There is an exactly established procedure of admission, which mainly includes a questionnaire, which is completed with the help of the relatives. The criteria is as follows:

The patient has to

- suffer from an illness of terminal stage,
- be an inhabitant of Lombardia,
- be older than twenty years,
- agree to his admission or – if that is not possible – one of the relatives has to do so.

The questionnaire contains details about the person and the family. As motives for the admission the following can be marked with a cross: control of the symptoms, difficulties with coping everyday life (autonomy), the patient lives on his own, or the family is not able to help, difficulties with the organisation of the domestic situation.

---

39 Interview with doctor Dr.essa Paola Zinna and volunteer Massimo Marconi, 29 June 2004, in Milan.

40 In Italy the nursing home is called RSA Residentia Sanitaria Assistentiale.

Before listing medical steps the question is: has the patient been informed about the kind of his complaint and the prognosis? If not, the reason has to be explained. Did the patient take part in the decision about his admission? If not, the reason has to be clarified as well.

Hospice ANTEA, Rome[41]

The private hospice Antea was founded in 1988 by Guiseppe Casale. Casale is not a doctor. ANTEA includes an in-patient hospice and out-patient domestic care. Altogether there are 13 doctors, 25 nurses, two physiotherapists, one social worker and sixty volunteers involved. The hospice itself consists of ten beds and takes care of approximately 100 patients at the same time.

The training ("formazione") of the volunteers is neither religious nor denominationally orientated and takes place twice a week for a duration of three months. The subjects range from "History of Palliative Care" to the question "What can be done for the patients?" the volunteers do the shopping, help the families, listen to them and talk to the patients and their relatives.

Every room is furnished in a way that relatives can stay overnight. Some of the patients are only accommodated temporarily – e.g. if the family needs a break of the care. The average stay of the patients lasts 45 days. The state pays for accommodation in a hospice for not more than six months. Currently the state pays for fifty of the patients, the other fifty have to be financed with money from donations. The staff of the ANTEA hospice is paid by money from the state. The law of 1999 made a government support possible. In November 2003, ANTEA organised an international hospice congress in Rome, whose aim it mainly was – according to the head – to develop nationwide comparable quality standards.

Hospice Domus Salutis, Brescia[42]

The hospice Domus Salutis belongs undoubtedly to the most impressive hospices in Europe. The house is an independent building inside a hospital run by catholic nuns. An oval building with two floors with 29 beds in single rooms. Entering the entrance hall made of glass one passes a big portal framed by two pillars, which bear a monumental inscription: "Hospice", artificial ponds and sculptures on both sides. There is a well cared for garden inside the inner courtyard, a sophisticated atmosphere inside the rooms, each with a bathroom and a spare bed for relatives, who want to stay with the patient. There are day rooms for the relatives, and a room to say goodbye in the basement which looks like a chapel. A team experienced in Palliative Care looks after the patients. The staff shall improve the patients' quality of life, control the symptoms, and create a human-familiar surrounding. The average stay lasts 19 days. The costs are

41 Based on the interview with Giuseppe Casale, Claudia Monti, and Raffaela Dobrina, 05 November 2003, in Rome and documents of the ANTEA hospice, among others the quarterly published periodical ANTEA, Atti di Vita.

42 Interview with Giovanni Zaninetta, 05 August 2003, in Brescia.

250 Euro per day. Tumour patients are predominant here as well. Dr. Zaninetta, head of this institution, supposes that the number of hospices in Italy will grow quickly. Most of the people want to die at home, but it is often impossible. The familiar conditions rather get worse, so more in-patient institutions have to be expected.

Hospice Domus Salutis, Brescia

From here, thirty patients can be looked after at home (according to the concept "Integrated domestic care"). Volunteers go on a training course of twenty hours before they start working. There is also a day hospital and an out-patient treatment belonging to Domus Salutis.

Hospice di Abbiategrasso (Provinz Milano)[43]

In 1994, this hospice was opened for AIDS patients. It can be found in a Art Nouveau villa in a large garden in the centre of Abbiategrasso. In 2000, twelve guests could be accommodated. Recently cancer patients were accommodated as well. Relatives can stay in the hospice. There is a chapel, a day room for guests and visitors, a room for physiotherapy, a room to dine, and a room for recreating activities.

The team consists of one physician of Palliative Care, a psychologist, an teacher (for creative and rehabilitating activities), a person for spiritual questions (assistente

[43] Hospice di Abbiategrasso: Carta die Servizi, http://www.netsys.it/hospice

Hospice Domus Salutis, Brescia

spirituale), a person for the administration, six nurses, four persons of extra staff (ausiliari socio-assistenziali – ASA). The team meets once a week for discussions, further education and supervision. Every year, there are 2650 hours of professional care, and 1116 hours of care by the volunteers per patient. The volunteers work in the kitchen, do the ironing, support the nurses during their night shifts and at the weekends. There are approximately 100 volunteers.

3. Summary

The development of Palliative Care in Italy runs in similar patterns and with comparable concepts as in the rest of Europe. The special features arc:

- There is an extreme ageing of society in Italy.
- According to that, the costs of the olderlies' health is very high.
- There is a North-South divide of the Palliative Care in Italy: Especially the care in Lombardia is much more closely structured than in the south of Italy.
- In-patient hospices are sooner enlarged compared to other countries, whereat economic incentives play an important role
- The main focus of Palliative Care is with cancer patients

- The governmental health insurance (SSN) pays for the stay in a hospice or the domestic care for maximum of six months.
- Since 1999, there has been a law in Italy in respect of Palliative Care which makes a financing with state-run funds possible.
- The head of every hospice has to be a doctor.

Sources and Literature

Andreoni, Bruno: Il progetto Hospice "Cascina Brandezzata", in: Il Movimento Hospice e le Cure Palliative in Italia, congress in Milan, October 27, 2000, arranged by the Fondazione Floriani, Milan. http://www.fondazionefloriani.org/pagchi.htm.

Baraldi, Giulia: La qualità della pRomaessa. Viaggio di un' assisstente sociale nelle cure palliative, Milan 2001. (Interviews with dying persons and their relatives, published by the Congregazione Ancelle della Carità, Domus Salutis).

Bundesministerium für Gesundheit und Soziale Sicherung: Sozial-Kompass Europa. Soziale Sicherheit in Europa im Vergleich. Bonn 2003.

Cattagni, Federica: Ed è subito sera. La vita accanto a chi muore, Milano 1999. (Dissertation published by the Congregazione Ancelle della Carità, Domus Salutis.)

Corli, Oscar: Le Unitá di Cure Palliative e le Organizzazioni Non Profit nell'Italia del 2000, Milan 2000.

Corli, Oscar: Palliative Care in Italy in the new millennium, in: European Journal of Palliative Care, 2001, 8 (2), p. 58 - 60.

Comitato Etico presso la Fondazione Floriani: Carta dei Diritti dei Morenti, Milan 1997.

Contini, Enzo: Il movimento "hospice": le sue origini e la sua filosofia, in: La voce dell'ANAPACA, April 1999.

Creton, Giovanni: The Ryder Italia Experience in Rome. In: Cicely Saunders/Robert Kastenbaum (Ed.): Hospice Care on the International scene. New York 1997, p. 151 - 157.

Cruciatti, Flavio/Monti, Massimo: I programmi di formazione ed educazione permanente interna, esterna e tutoriali in Hospice, beides in: Il Movimento Hospice e le Cure Palliative in Italia, congress in Milan, October 27, 2000.

Curare quando non si può guarire, in: Quaderni di Cure Palliative, 1, 1993, p. 11 - 14.

Di Mola, Giorgio/Ventafridda, Vittorio and M.T.Crisci: Indagine sulla conoscenza delle cure palliative nella popolazione Italiana, in: Rivista Italiana di Cure Palliative 1, 2001, p. 15 - 18.

Fusco-Karmann, Claude/Tinini, Gianni: A review of the volunteer movement in EAPC countries, in: European Journal of Palliative Care, 2001; 8; p. 199 - 202.

Il Movimento Hospice e le Cure Palliative. Mete raggiunte e prospettive future. Atti del Convegno organizzato dalla Fondazione Floriani, Milan, October 27, 2000, (www.fondazionefloriani.org/paghi.htm/).

Nicoscìa, Salvatore: Il movimento Hospice in Italia: un decennio a fianco del malato e del morente. VIII. Congresso di Cure Palliative. Genova 1997.

Peruselli, Carlo: Le Scuole di medicina palliativa in Italie in: Il Movimento Hospice e le Cure Palliative in Italia, congress in Milan, October 27, 2000.

Pomposini, Rita: Struttura per cure palliative: l'importanza dell'hospice, in: Assistenza Anziani, vol. 2, n.1, 2004, p. 18 - 21.

Population Division of the Department of Economic and Social Affairs of the United Nations Secretariat, World Population Prospects: The 2002 Revision Population Database: http://esa.un.org/unpp

Privitera, Salvatore: Palliative Care in Italy, in: Henk ten Have/ Rien Janssens (Eds.): Palliative Care in Europa. Concepts and Policies, Amsterdam etc. 2001, p. 99 - 108.

Toscani, Franco: Palliative care in Italy: accident or miracle?, in: Palliative Medicine 2002, 16, p. 177 - 178.

Speranza, Raffaella: La tutela del modello hospice alla luce delle normative regionale e nazionali, in: Il Movimento Hospice e le Cure Palliative in Italia, congress in Milan, October 27, 2000.

Zucco, Furio: Le Organizzazzioni Non Lucrative (Onlus): da pomotorici a garanti delle Leggi. In: Il Movimento Hospice e le Cure Palliative, congress in Milan, October 27 2000.

Zucco, Furio/Welsman/Anntte: The National Health Service and the care for the dying, in: European Journal of Palliative Care, 2001, 8 (2), p. 61 - 65.

Periodicals

Quaderni die Cure palliative, since 1993, continued with the subtitle Rivista di Medicina de Dolere e trattamento dei sintomi.

La Revista Italiana di Cure Palliative, since 1999, the official journal of the Società Italiana di Cure Palliative.

Bibliography

Most important source in Italy is: Biblioteca di Cure Palliative Fondazione Floriani: www.fondazione.floriani.org/Biblioteca.htm

Congress

At the congress "The International Meeting of Hospices" in Rome, November 6 - 7, 2003, it was possible to interview some of the participants. Almost every Italian expert of Palliative Care was there. The presentations of the congress are part of this paper.

Internet Sources

Osservatorio Permanente Cure Palliative
c/o Formenti – Grünenthal

Direzione Marketing Area Dolore
http://www.osservatoriocurepalliative.org/pub/

Hospice Italiani, Azienda Ospedaliera "G.Salvini"
Milan, in corporation with
Federazione Cure Palliative (Onlus)
http://www.aogarbagnate.lombardia.it/

Ministero della Salute
Hospice
http://www.cerca.ministerosalute.it/motorericerca/servlet/

Hospice Information: http://www.hospiceinformation.info

Internet addresses:

http://www.kwsalute.kataweb.it/Notizia/0,1044,2729,00.html
http://ministerosalute.it/dettaglio/pdAtuPerTuDettaglio/
http://www.osservatoriocurepalliative.org/pub/
http://www.istituto.org/it/ist_eolo.asp
http://www.dica33it./argomenti/
http://www2.edc.org/lastacts/archives/
http://www.netsys.it/hospice
http://www.fondazionefloriani.org/paghi.htm/

List of interviews (in chronological order)

- Dott. Giovanni Zaninetta, Direktor
  Casa di Cura Domus Salutis Hospice,
  Brescia, 05 August 2003

- Dr.ssa Adriana Turriziani, Primario Hospice
  Hospice Oncologico Villa Speranza
  Università Cattolica Sacro Cuore
  Rome, 04 November 2003

- Dott. P. Astorre, Colonello
  Policlinico Militare di Roma Celio,
  Rome, 04 November 2003

- Dott. Guiseppe Casale, Director
  Claudia Monti, Director

Raffaella Dobrina, nurse
Antea Hospice,
Rome, 05 November 2003

- Dott. Guiseppe Tansini
  Casa di Cura Columbus
  Dipartimento Oncologico
  Hospice
  S. Francesca Cabrini,
  Milan, 29 June 2004

- Dr. ssa Paola Zinna and
  Massimo Marconi, volunteer
  Hospice Istituto Geriatrico
  "Piero Radaelli"
  Dr. Georgio Casale, Director
  Milan, 29 June 2004

- Dott. Michele Gallucci
  S.I.M.P.A., Milan
  Milan, 30 June 2004

Latvia

Michaela Fink

1. General conditions

1.1 Demographics

- In 2000, the Latvian population totalled 2,37 million. According to UN-predictions, it is expected to total only 1,33 million inhabitants by 2050.[1]
- Since the early to mid 1950s the average life expectancy of 66.0 has risen five years to 71.0 years of age. By 2050 another rise is expected bring the average life expectancy at birth to 79.1.[2]
- The median age is will rise from 37.8 years in 2000 to 53.0 by 2050.[3]
- In 1950, people 65 years or older in Latvia constituted 11.2% of the population. In 2000, it was already 15.1% and is projected to grow to 30.8% by 2050.[4]
- Similarly, people aged 80 years or older constituted 1.9% of the population in 1950. That percentage grew a little to 2.6 in 2000 and is estimated to grow to 9.6 by 2050.[5]
- The annual mortality rate is expected to rise from 13,6 per 1000 inhabitants between 2000 - 2005 to 17,9 per 1000 inhabitants by 2045 - 2050.[6]
- The main causes of death in Latvia are diseases of the circulatory system, cancer, and external causes; the incidence of tuberculosis has been increasing since 1989.[7]

1.2 Health care system

The Latvian health care system, which is in place since Latvia declared itself independent from the Soviet Union in 1991, is still in a period of change. Due to insufficient medical care structures Latvia remains bottom of the new member states of the

---

1 Population Division of the Department of Economic and Social Affairs of the United Nations Secretariat, World Population Prospects: The 2002 Revision Population Database: http://esa.un.org/unpp (medium variant).

2 ibid.

3 ibid.

4 ibid.

5 ibid.

6 ibid.

7 David Clark/ Michael Wright: Transitions in End of Life Care. Hospice and related Developments in Eastern Europe and Central Asia. Buckingham, Philadelphia 2003, p. 70.

European Union. Patients themselves have to pay for almost any costs occurring for medication and for all dentist treatments. The total health care expenditure is only 4.4 percent in proportion of the GDP, which means only 100 €annually per citizen. The health care system is funded through tax incomes. 21 percent of all occurring health care costs are covered by additional payments. In 1998 the *State Compulsory Health Insurance Agency* was created. The agency is assigned to the *Ministry of Welfare*. A total of eight *Regional Sickness Funds* exist. Only 16 percent of the Latvians aged 18 - 74 years have health insurance although officially all Latvians are entitled to receive basic medical care.[8] This basis care is very limited as patients have to make – informal – payments themselves.

2. Hospice and palliative care in Latvia

2.1 History

- In contrast to other countries palliative care in Latvia is not result of a civil movement. It developed from initiatives by physicians, most of all oncologists and internal specialists.
- In 1995 Christel Pakarinen, of Karuna, Finland, met with the Latvian Minister of Health and some local doctors interested in starting palliative care.[9]
- In 1998 palliative care was included as a topic in the 2nd Baltic Congress of Oncology and Radiology.
- In 2002 palliative care sessions were part of third Baltic Congress on Oncology.
- In the same year, Vilnis Sosars published a brochure on the history of palliative care in Latvia.[10] Sosars heads the country's only adult palliative care inpatient unit which opened in Riga back in 1997. In addition, he leads the national palliative care organisation which has developed quality standards for the field of oncology, education and training programmes, and criteria for certifications in palliative care. The organisation also initiated lectures for general practitioners, nurses and social workers.[11]

2.2 Hospice and palliative care services

So far there is only one adult inpatient palliative care unit in Latvia. Besides one paediatric palliative care unit operates within the University Clinic of Riga and three adult day care centres exist in the cities of Riga, Liepaja and Aizkraukle. There are

8 cp. Official AOK-Website: http://www.aok-bv.de/politik/agenda/euerweiterung/index_01461.html

9 cp. David Clark/ Michael Wright: Transitions in End of Life Care. Hospice and related Developments in Eastern Europe and Central Asia. Buckingham, Philadelphia 2003, p. 71.

10 Dr. Vilnis Sosars: Paliativas Aprupes (Hospisu) Vesture. Riga 2002.

11 Interview with Dr. Vilnis Sosars, 18 February 2004, in Riga. Cp. also David Clark/ Michael Wright: Transitions in End of Life Care. Hospice and related Developments in Eastern Europe and Central Asia. Buckingham, Philadelphia 2003, p. 71.

no official statistics available that give information on the number of palliative care services in Latvia. [12]

As in the two other Baltic countries, small hospitals, in particular those in rural areas, struggle financially. They also suffer from losing doctors who go abroad because of better salaries there. There are plans to turn those hospitals into care homes with small palliative care units. The meagre equipped hospitals have serious financial problems and face the threat of closure.

Such plans exist for Mazsalaca where within a short time a small unit of five beds is set to open. Day care centres are also set to be developed to improve outpatient care provision. [13] Most of meagre equipped hospitals are still from the times of the Soviet occupation.

By this, the government hopes to reduce costs. Politicians argue that those hospitals are no real hospitals but more like houses with beds and therefore should not be paid like hospitals. [14]

Palliative care experts though state that good palliative care is by no means cheaper than common care provided in hospitals or care homes. They call for the implementation of a law regulating palliative care which in their opinion would lead to a more realistic funding system.

However the lack of support from politicians and financial problems in the health care system prevent the development of palliative structures.

Most people in Latvia die at home. However the care by family members is not unproblematic. The living conditions are poor, often a whole family of adults and children have to live in one room or several families have to live together in one house. As a result, ill people have no privacy. Furthermore the housing prices in urban areas are very high. But the situation in rural regions does'nt differ much. Here people often still live in concrete-tower blocks established at the time of the Soviet occupation. An expert from Riga describes the situation:

> The people here have not got the opportunity to choose the place where they die. The care of dying people in institutions is completely insufficient and most people cannot financially afford palliative care. The Families have no space. Not only this, they often feel over stretched with the care. [15]

2.3 Legal regulations and funding

There is no law on palliative care in Latvia. A working group, composed of experts (amongst others Anda Jansone and Vilnis Sosars) and representatives of the Ministry of Health, is currently working on legislation that would entitle every Latvian citizen

[12] Because of this, the data compiled by David Clark/ Michael Wright in 2002, could not be updated by us. Cp. also David Clark/ Michael Wright: Transitions in End of Life Care. Hospice and related Developments in Eastern Europe and Central Asia. Buckingham, Philadelphia 2003, p. 71.

[13] E-mail from Dr. Vilnis Sosars, 14 May 2003.

[14] Interview with Dr. Arkady S. Gandz, 17 February 2004, in Riga.

[15] Interview with Dr. Sergejs Kuznecovs, 17 February 2004, in Riga.

the right to palliative care treatment. These plans are often foiled by the numerous change of government in the country.

Paediatric palliative care is free of charge in Latvia. Adult patients have to make additional payments because the public funds provided do not cover all costs. Patients receiving care at the cancer centre in Riga are asked to pay 10 Lats per day (approx. 15 €). As the average pension is only 60 Lats, most people cannot afford palliative care treatment.

2.4 Organisations

The national Palliative Care Organisation is lead by Vilnis Sosars. The *EAPC East*, which belongs to the *European Association of Palliative Care (EAPC)*, is of great importance for the exchange of information between experts. The organisation is represented on the Internet, releases newsletter on a regular basis and arranges congresses. [16]

2.5 Education and training of professional staff

At the moment there are virtually no palliative care education and training opportunities in Latvia. Some of the experts attended palliative courses in Poland and the USA. Vilnis Sosars gives lectures in palliative care but there are no certifications handed out.

2.6 Volunteers

Similar to the two other Baltic countries, voluntary commitment is hardly existent in Latvia. One expert from Riga sees the Soviet occupation as one reason for the lack of voluntary support: "Voluntary work is regarded rather negative as in the past people were often forced to do voluntary tasks." [17] Although palliative care teams consist of volunteers, they are mainly carried by doctors and nurses.

2.7 Examples

University Paediatric-Clinic in Riga

The University Paediatric-Clinic in Riga is 104 years old. It was the first paediatric clinic, and with 24 units the biggest paediatric hospital in Latvia. With the exception of tuberculosis and cardiac surgery almost all illnesses are treated. A otorhinolaryngology department, a surgical ward, a unit for skin- and eye diseases, and palliative care provision The palliative care team was set up in 1998 on the initiative of the doctor Anda Jansone and her colleagues. In the same year the *Children's Palliative Care Society* was founded. It is involved with the development of *Children's Palliative Care* in Latvia. This is imperative as Anda Jansone's team is the only paediatric institution offering palliative care in the three Baltic countries.

---

16 More information on the Internet: http://www.eapceast.org

17 Interview with Dr. Arkady S. Gandz, 17 February 2004, in Riga.

The *American International Health Alliance* (AIHA) in St. Louis funded the work of the palliative care teams in its early stages. Many of the experts in Riga were trained in St. Louis. The team, which meets twice a week, consists of two doctors, three nurses and one social worker who work part-time. Besides a theologian, a secretary and 14 - 15 volunteers are part of the team as well. Most of the volunteers are student, for example from the Christian academy, or elderly women. They talk and read out to the children, and play with them. The social worker coordinates and supervises the volunteers. The receive instructions at the "volunteer centre" – a NGO in Riga –, which offers training courses for volunteers. [18] The education programme concentrates more on psychological than on medical issues.

In addition, two psychologists care for a total of 600 children in the hospital. Approximately 10 - 15 children per month, most of them cancer patients, are cared for by the palliative team in the inpatient unit. In February 2004, 25 children were looked after in their homes. The average length of stay or care is six months. If possible, the children are admitted home for the last days of their lives. The children staying at the hospital come from as far as 200 km and are normally not older than 18 years. Most of the children have been staying in the hospital already before they were admitted to the palliative care unit. [19] For all patients under 18 years of age, all medical treatments are free of charge in Latvia. Paediatric palliative care is financed completely by the national health fund.

Parents have the opportunity to spend nights in the hospital. When children die, a lot of parents keep in touch with the palliative care team and the hospitals psychologists. The children are remembered in regular gatherings. Even a year after the death of their own child some parents attend those get-togethers.

Information centre for cancer patients in Riga

The *Public Health Research Foundation* in Riga actually is a helpline for cancer prevention. However only five percent of the clients come to the centre for such advice. In fact, 90 percent of the patients are in need of palliative care already. The little office of Sergejs Kuznecovs, the leader of the information centre, is situated in an old backyard. Patients, who have already had cancer treatment, and those in need of palliative care who cannot afford treatment at the cancer centre, sit in the scanty equipped waiting room. Many of them are not going to the cancer centre because they know they are in the terminal stages of their illness and to go there is regarded as the last step with no hope remaining, as several patients say. Instead they go to hospitals with a palliative care service. General practitioners often cannot help the patient as they have no knowledge and skills in palliative care.

---

18 The courses held at the *Centre of Volunteers* do not exclusively focus on palliative care but also on other relevant subjects for volunteers working in hospitals or nursing homes.

19 Palliative care and hospice care are differentiated in the paediatric hospital: Palliative care patients still receive irradiation and chemotherapy whereas hospice patients "only" have their symptoms and pain controlled.

Clients call Dr. Kuznecovs' centre the "office of last hope". This description was coined by a journalists article on the centre. The terminally ill receive psychological support, acupuncture and aroma therapy. Teas and mushrooms are also given to the patients. Mushrooms are either collected in the forests, or can be purchased in pharmacies as capsules or infusions. According to Dr. Kuznecovs it raises patient's hopes for a longer life:

It is no cancer treatment but the mushrooms give them hope and a loss of hope is the main cause of death. Sometimes, I say to the patients: Wait until August when the mushrooms grow – they will help you. Many people live longer because they are waiting for the mushrooms. [20] Amongst the Russian population in Latvia, paraffin is famous as a remedy against cancer.

Kuznecovs patients receive medical education: "If people are informed thoroughly, it facilitates their dying process." [21]

The information centre is unique in Riga. On average, 200 patients are advised every month. The two volunteers – Kuznecovs' children – visit the patients at home. The patients are often very poor. The gap between the rich and the poor is huge. Basic primary health care is available for all patients. Who wants to have better treatment has to make additional payments. Wealthy Latvians go abroad to receive good medical or palliative care. [22] Kuznecovs tells the story of a terminally ill patient. The treatment given was not successful. After the women's death, the husband was ruined financially. Therapy and transport costs were extremely high: "My life is over. I had to sell my house and my car. I will have to live with my son in Riga." [23] Kuznecovs:

Many people today are disappointed: at the time of Soviet occupation, it didn't cost anything to see a doctor. No one has to pay for everything. There is something missing – not only money. The health system is badly organised. Many patients receive a diagnosis when its already too late for treatment.

The *Public Health Research Foundation* is a Non-Governmental organisation that sells predominantly special nutrition for cancer patients. Local pharmacies donate this special food regularly. The food is then sold to patients coming to the information centre. Sometimes patients relatives donate money as well.

Palliative care at the cancer centre in Riga

Since 1997 Vilnis Sosars leads the multidisciplinary team at the cancer centre in Riga providing palliative care for 25 beds. There are also rooms available where relatives can stay overnight. Approximately 50 percent of all cancer patients are in a advanced stage of their illness and are in need of palliative care. 700 patients are cared for by the palliative care team per year. The average length of stay is 9 to 10 days. There is

20 Interview with Dr. Sergejs Kuznecovs, 17 February 2004, in Riga.
21 ibid.
22 ibid.
23 ibid.

a limit of 21 days for patients stay in the inpatient unit. In case of longer stays the hospital has to decide whether it will be able to cover the costs.

The outpatient service is open three days a week for patients with cancer or other illnesses, such as diabetes or neurological diseases, causing pain that need to be dealt with. Patients and relatives can also seek advise in the centre. The multidisciplinary team includes four doctors (two full-time), nurses, social worker, one psychologist, a chaplain and a few number of volunteers.[24]

Palliative care at the Bikur Holim hospital in Riga

In 1995 a rehabilitation department for chronically ill patients was set up at the Bikur Holim hospital in Riga. The reason for this was that the state only covers treatments costs for 2.9 days in normal hospital departments. Patients can stay seven to ten days in the unit. The initiative developed from a cooperation with the AIHA, St. Louis (USA). Within the department, 25 beds are provided for palliative care patients. 60 - 70 percent of the patients are suffering from cancer. Besides pain treatment and psychological support, the patients get food free of charge. This should not be underestimated as most of the patients are very poor. Bikur Holim is located in a Russian quarter in Riga. In former times a lot of Jews and Sinti and Romanies were living here.

15 percent of the occurring costs must be covered by the patients. The hospital can charge patients up to a limit of 25 Lats per day. In case of the patients death, the state pays a fee of 120 Lats to the bereaved to allow the families to pay for the funeral without getting in financial trouble. The hospital is provided with a yearly budget by the state and has to cover all costs within this limit. The funds provided can be used for a total number of approximately 100 patients per month. In case 150 patients have to be cared for, the state still only pays for 100 patients. In contrast, if only 50 patients receive treatment, funds are given to the hospital for this number of patients only.

The people living in the area where the hospital is situated are very poor. For many people palliative care is not affordable. Poverty in general is increasing in the Latvian population, whereas at the same time five to seven percent of the population are very rich, as Dr. Gandz reports. The "middle class" is small, the majority of the population very poor. In the times of the Soviet Union a lot of products were imported at cheap rates from Russia. This is no longer possible which makes it very difficult for Latvia as the country owns no resources and practically no industries.

The palliative care team of the hospital was educated and trained in the USA. There are only a few volunteers working. "Hardly anybody wants to do this work", says Arkady Gandz, the leading doctor of the unit. Most patients spent the last days of their lives in their own homes where they are cared for by the home care team. Palliative care at the patients home is relatively new in Latvia.[25]

[24] Interview with Dr. Vilnis Sosars, 18 February 2004, in Riga.

[25] Interview with Dr. Arkady S. Gandz, 17 February 2004, in Riga.

The Cancer Centre in Riga

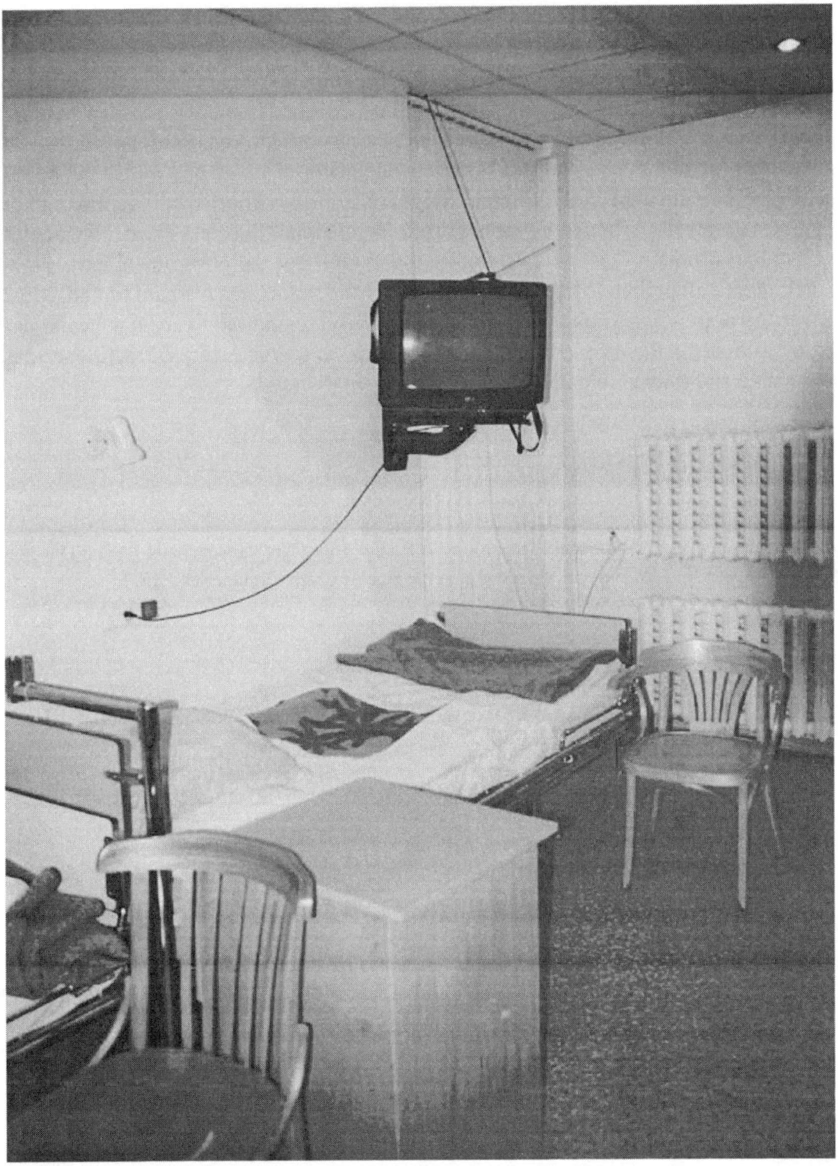

Room in the Cancer Centre, Riga

3. Summary

Palliative care is not wide-spread in Latvia. Nevertheless experts think that palliative care is making progress. One one hand, a atmosphere of departure is sensible but many experts remain doubtful. The prospects and targets differ: Anda Jansone calls for the extension of home care and thinks the development of home and outpatient care is cheaper than inpatient care. Whereas Sergejs Kuznecovs hopes that independent hospices will develop, funded by money from the National Sickness Fund. Nonetheless Kuznecovs remains sceptical as neither the church nor the government have shown real interest in palliative care. Private sponsors and volunteers are hard to find. Moreover the population knows little about palliative care and only very few health care professionals in the hospitals and nursing homes, as well as General Practitioners, are educated and trained in palliative care.

Sources and literature

Clark, David/ Wright, Michael: Transitions in End of Life Care. Hospice and related Developments in Eastern Europe and Central Asia. Buckingham, Philadelphia 2003.

Internet sources

Official Website AOK-Bundesverband: http://www.aok-bv.de/politik/agenda/euerweiterung/index_01461.html

Population Division of the Department of Economic and Social Affairs of the United Nations Secretariat, World Population Prospects: The 2002 Revision Population Database: http://esa.un.org/unpp (medium variant)

List of interviews (in chronological order)

- Dr. Anda Jansone Leader hospice teams *Paediatric Hospital, Riga* Riga, 16 February 2004
- Dr. Arkady S. Gandz Head of the department of rehabilitation *Bikur Holim Hospital* Riga, 17 February 2004
- Dr. Sergejs Kuznecovs Head of the*Public Health Research Foundation Information Centre for Cancer Patients* Riga, 17 February 2004
- Dr. Vilnis Sosars Head of the palliative care unit *Cancer centre,* Riga, 18 February 2004

Lithuania

Michaela Fink

1. General conditions

1.1 Demographics

- In 2000, the Lithuanian population totalled 3,50 million. According to UN-predictions, it is expected to be only approximately 2,53 million inhabitants, by 2050.[1]
- Since the early to mid 1950s the average life expectancy of 64.8 has risen to 72.7 years of age by 2000. By 2050 another rise is expected bring the average life expectancy at birth to 79.7.[2]
- The median age is will rise from 36.0 years in 2000 to 44.4 by 2050.[3]
- In 1950, people 65 years or older in Lithuania constituted 9.4% of the population. In 2000, it was already 14.0% and is projected to grow to 24.9% by 2050.[4]
- Similarly, people aged 80 years or older constituted 1.5% of the population in 1950. That percentage grew slightly in 2000 to 2.4 and is estimated to grow to 8.5 by 2050.[5]
- The annual mortality rate is expected to rise from 11,6 per 1000 inhabitants between 2000 - 2005 to 14,8 per 1000 inhabitants by 2045 - 2050.[6]
- The main causes of death are cardiovascular diseases, cancer and external causes.[7]
- 48 percent of the population dies at home, 52 percent in institutions.[8]

---

1 Population Division of the Department of Economic and Social Affairs of the United Nations Secretariat, World Population Prospects: The 2002 Revision Population Database: http://esa.un.org/unpp (medium variant).

2 ibid.

3 ibid.

4 ibid.

5 ibid.

6 ibid.

7 Department of Statistics to the Government of the Republic of Lithuania (Statistics Lithuania): http://www.std.lt/web/main.php?parent=864

8 Email from Jovita Demskyte, 03 May 2003.

1.2 Health care system

Lithuania's health care system is financed to 50 percent through tax revenues. The Health Insurance Law was approved in 1996 in Lithuania. It foresees a compulsory health insurance for all permanent residents in Lithuania, independently of their citizenship. This compulsory health insurance is carried out by one state institution – the State Patients' Fund (SPF). In 2003 the SPF spent 158,8 Euro on average per one insured person. Visits to the doctor, treatment at the hospital (including medicines) and rehabilitation are completely compensated from the Compulsory Health Insurance Fund. Those who are not insured may apply only for a necessary medical aid. Such persons pay for other services under the prices set by the Ministry of Health. An additional private health insurance is foreseen in the Health Insurance Law, however it is still not popular in Lithuania and is used by a small part of the population with high income.[9] Funds used by the health sector in Lithuania represented 5.75 per cent of the GDP in 2002.[10]

2. Hospice and palliative care in Lithuania

2.1 History

- 1993 the *Charity* founded the *Terminal Care Hospital* in Kaunas. In the same year Norwegian experts held a palliative care course at the *Kaunas University of Medicine*, which became the starting point of future activities.
- In the Nineties many so called *Supportive Treatment* and *Nursing Hospitals* developed. Some of those institutions provide palliative care today.
- On the initiative of the *Lithuania Palliative Medicine Association* and the *Lithuanian Pain Society* courses on palliative care were established and important English literature on the topic was translated into Lithuanian. The Journal on Pain Therapy (*Skausmo Medicina)*, edited by the *Lithuania Palliative Medicine Association*, focuses not just on palliative medicine but also on various other aspects of palliative care.
- A pain clinic opened in 1994 in the department of anaesthesiology of the University Hospital of Vilnius.
- A Lithuanian-Polish symposium of palliative care was organised by Prof. Jacek Luczak (Poznan, Polen) and Dr. Jane Baubliene (Vilnius, Lithuania) in 1996. It was attended by over 200 participants.
- In 1998 the *Poznan Declaration* was made during the 9th Palliative Medicine Advanced Course by the participants from nine Eastern European countries, with Lithuania one of them. The declaration included regional analysis of palliative care issues, stated goals to achieve in the palliative care field (national policy, educa-

9 http://www.sam.lt/en/sam/HP/

10 AOK-Bundesverband: http://www.aok-bv.de/politik/agenda/euerweiterung/index{_}01461.html

tion, drug availability, multidisciplinary teams, public awareness) and gave some recommendations of how to do that. [11]

- Inspired by the *Poznan Declaration* the *European Palliative Care Task Force (ECEPT)* was created in 1999. The international association was meant to group palliative care professionals from Eastern and Central Europe, the people who take leading part in the field of caring for the terminally ill. ECEPT is based in Poznan, Poland. [12]
- In 1999, with the support of the *Poznan Declaration,* the *Eastern and Central* (ECEPT), with its Headquarters in Poznan (Poland), was established.
- In 2001, Dr Arunas Sciupokas of the *Kaunus University of Medicine* was awarded with an *Open Society Institute* grant for a project on the development of national policies for palliative care in the three Baltic countries of Lithuania, Latvia and Estonia. [13]
- In 2002 Dr Raimonde Ulianskiene, working with nursing colleagues from England, started a palliative care education and strategy development programme within *Panevezys County Governor's Administration,* with a primary objective to educate in palliative care 50 percent of family doctors and 80 percent of relevant specialists. [14]

2.2 Hospice and palliative care services

The *Kaunas Terminal Care Hospital* is one of the very few hospitals in Lithuania with palliative care beds. At the same time it was the first of its kind in the Baltic countries and also one of the first nursing homes, know as *Nursing Hospitals* in Lithuania. Today there are 66 *Nursing Hospitals*, who most of all provide care for elderly people with multiple clinical pictures and functional troubles. There is no paediatric palliative care on offer so far.

About half of the dying patients receives care in hospitals, primarily in *Support Treatment* and *Nursing Hospitals*. The other half of the patients are cared for at home by general practitioners or by their families.

There are five home care services providing palliative care. Officially they are not regarded as palliative care services as there is no national policy regulating palliative care to date. [15]

2.3 Legal regulations and funding

As mentioned above there is no national policy regulating palliative care up to now. The government shows little interest in the topic. Presumably because a national policy would be linked with a special funding system. According to experts the costs for

---

[11] Eastern and Central Europe Palliative Task Force: http://free.med.pl/ecept/en_index.html

[12] ibid.

[13] cp. David Clark/Michael Wright in: Transitions in End of Life Care. Hospice and related Developments in Eastern Europe and Central Asia. Buckingham, Philadelphia 2003, p. 77.

[14] cp. ibid.

[15] Interview with Prof Arvydas Seskevicius, 23 February 2004, in Kaunas.

palliative care are much higher than for "normal care" which seems to act as a deterrent for health care planers. A daily rate is provided to services that provide palliative care in the so called *Nursing Hospitals*. The state covers the costs for four month of treatment for every patient per year. After that maximum period of time patients are either admitted home or have to pay for occurring costs themselves: The total costs for month are approximately 1200 Litas (342,9 €). As they monthly income is between 50 and 80 €most people cannot afford to stay in a hospice.

The daily rate paid by for care in *Nursing Hospitals* paid by the insurance companies is 40 Litas (11,5 €) per patient. This however does not cover the costs incurred by palliative care. According to Arvydas Seskevicius, the head of the *Lithuania Palliative Medicine Association*, the daily costs for palliative care is about 80 Litas (23 €). The nursing homes and hospitals are forced to balance out those deficits. [16]

2.4 Organisations

In 1995 the *Lithuania Palliative Medicine Association* was founded. Since 2003 the association is headed by Prof.Arvydas Sescevicius, Leader of nursing education at the *Kaunas University of Medicine*. Most of the members are doctors (oncologists and anaesthesiologists) but also nurses and social workers. Once or twice a year the organisations stages national conferences.

The *Lithuanian Pain Society* has existed since 1998. It is led by Dr. Arunas Scipokas. The two associations work closely together. [17]

2.5 Education and training of professional staff

There are neither consultants in palliative medicine nor nursing staff with the opportunity to obtain certificate education and training programmes in Lithuania. Pain management is a small element of the medical course but palliative care as a subject is not taught at most universities. One exception is the *Nursing Department* at *Kaunas University of Medicine* where a palliative care education programme, led by Arvydas Seskevicius, has offered courses on a regular basis for the students since 2000. Seskevicius also gives courses at the *Red Cross Supportive Treatment and Nursing Hospital* in Kaunas. The courses focus on palliative care, geriatric care, cancer care, the social problems of terminally ill patients, communication, rehabilitation, bioethics and nutrition. Furthermore Seskevicius offers seminars on palliative care for general practitioners. Palliative care courses are also provided at the *University Hospital* in Vilnius.

---

[16] Email from Prof Arvydas Seskevicius, 25 September 2004.

[17] Interview with Prof Arvydas Seskevicius, 23 February 2004, in Kaunas.

2.6 Volunteers

Palliative Care is first and foremost a matter of health care professionals. Volunteers are few and far between also because there is no broader palliative care provision structure in place.

2.7 Examples

Terminal Care Hospital in Kaunas

The *Kaunas Terminal Care Hospital* was founded by the *Charity* in 1993. It provided care in nine beds for seriously ill and very poor patients. Since 1995 there is also a home care service giving palliative care. Student apprentices of the *Kaunas University of Medicine* work in both inpatient and home care.

The Terminal Care Hospital, Kaunas

In 2003, a total of 45 patients were cared for in the inpatient sector. Ten of those were terminally ill. Cancer patients and people suffering from neurological diseases are the main patient groups receiving care but also poor and derelicts with incurable diseases. Spiritual care in the last few days of life is of paramount importance for the caring team. The multidisciplinary team consists of 18 nurses, 1,5 doctors, 4 back

Floor in the TCH

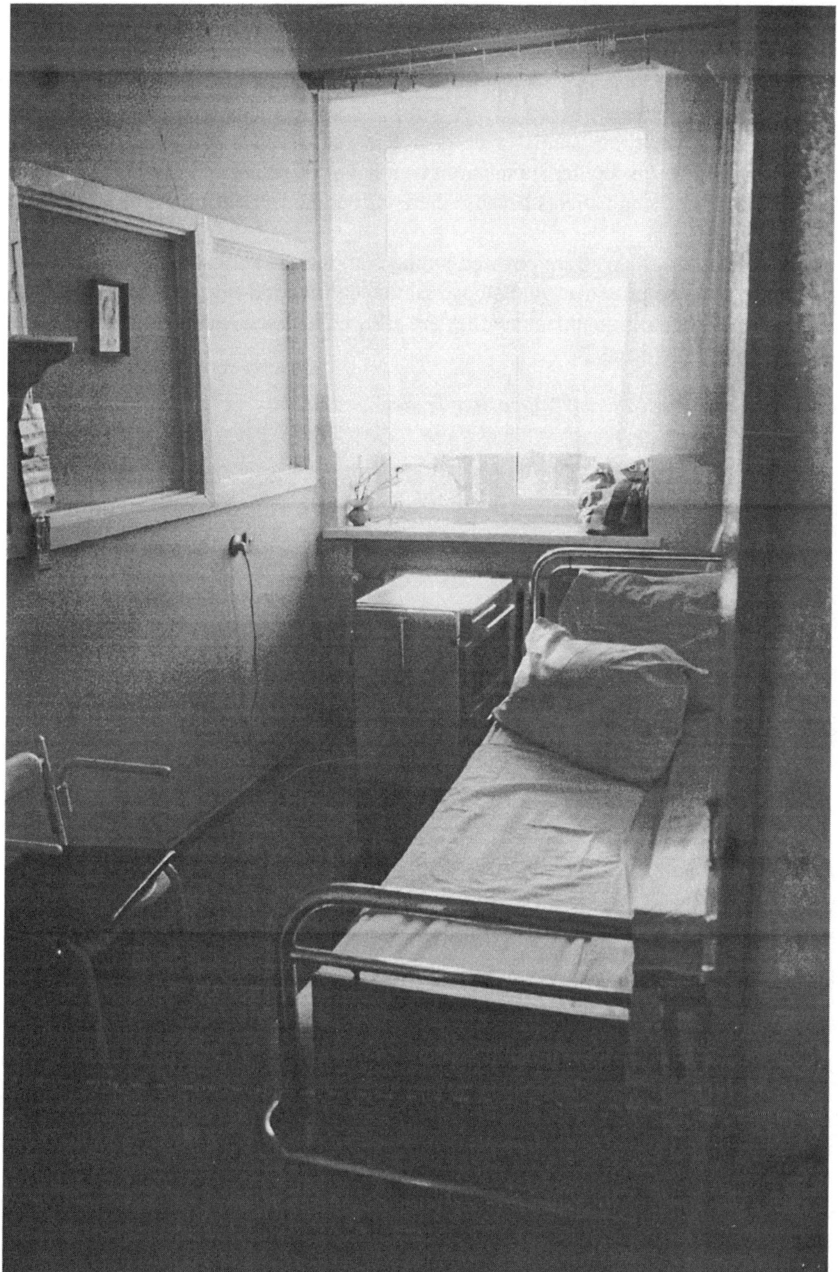

Room in the TCH

staff (assistant nurses and so called "social helpers") and some volunteers. "In the past we've had 44 volunteers", says Dr. Poniškaitienė, the head physician. "Today there are only a few because the economical situation is difficult for a large part of the population in Lithuania."

The rooms are either single or double. The guestroom is made into a four-bed room in case that all regular rooms are occupied with patients already. There is no separate unit for dying patients because there is no national policy existing legislating palliative care.

50 percent of all costs are covered by the National Sickness Funds, the other 50 percent have to be provided by the hospital through fundraising. Patients are not required to pay for their treatment but they are allowed to donate money if they have the financial means to do so. [18]

Palliative care at Red Cross Supportive Treatment and Nursing Hospital in Kaunas

Kitchen at the Red Cross Supportive Treatment and Nursing Hospital, Kaunas

The *Red Cross Supportive Treatment and Nursing Hospital* in Kaunas was originally set up by the *Red Cross* as a clinic for tuberculosis patients in 1993. In 2000 it was transformed into a *Supportive Treatment and Nursing Hospital*. Today ten percent of 140 beds are allocated to patients in the terminal stage of their illness. The team includes 29 nurses, four doctors, two social worker, three physiotherapists, 29 back staff

[18] Interview with Dr Inesa Marja Poniškaitienė and Dr Rita Kabašinskienė, 23 February 2004, in Kaunas.

and one priest (80 percent of the Lithuanian population are Catholic). There are no volunteers part of the team.

With the daily rate of 11.5 € per patient, for a maximum time of four months, provided by the Sickness Fund, the hospital has to pay for medication, food, power and water supply and personnel costs. [19]

3. Summary

As in the two other Baltic countries, a lack of state commitment and financial difficulties, slow down the development of broader palliative care structures. Experts try to encourage politicians to intensify their efforts. The introduction of a national policy on palliative care and with that a more reliable funding are seen as the primary targets by experts working in the field. In view of the high number of Lithuanian people dying in institutions, such as hospitals and nursing homes, the development of more home care and outpatient services are much-needed.

As in Estonia and Latvia experts in Lithuania have great interest in exchanging information's with colleagues from other countries. Cooperation with services from abroad are intended and with that, the hope to get financial support.

Sources and literature

Clark, David/ Wright, Michael: Transitions in End of Life Care. Hospice and related Developments in Eastern Europe and Central Asia. Buckingham, Philadelphia 2003.

Marciulioniene: The first hospice in Lithuania. In: Hospice Bulletin. Hospice Information Service. St. Christopher's Hospice. 3 (1) April 1996, p. 12.

Email from Jovita Demskyte, Nursing Department, Kaunas University of Medicine, 03 May 2003.

Email from Prof. Arvydas Seskevicius, *Nursing Department, Kaunas University of Medicine*, 25 September 2004.

Internet sources

AOK-Bundesverband: http://www.aok-bv.de/politik/agenda/euerweiterung/index_01461.html

Eastern and Central Europe Palliative Task Force: http://free.med.pl/ecept/en_index.html

Population Division of the Department of Economic and Social Affairs of the United Nations Secretariat, World Population Prospects: The 2002 Revision Population Database: http://esa.un.org/unpp

---

19 Interview with Prof Arvydas Seskevicius and Dr S. Janceviciene, 23 February 2004, in Kaunas.

List of interviews (in chronological order)

- Prof Arvydas Seskevicius (Head Physician) Lithuanian Palliative Medicine Association *Nursing Care Department, Kaunas University of Medicine* Kaunas, 22 February 2004
- Dr Inesa Marja Poniškaitienė (*Head Physician*), Dr Rita Kabašinskienė *Kaunas Terminal Care Hospital* Kaunas, 23 February 2004
- Dr S. Janceviciene (Director) *Red Cross Supportive Treatment and Nursing Hospital,* Kaunas, 23 February 2004

Netherlands

Felix Schumann

1. General conditions

1.1 Demographics

- In 2004, the Netherlands had a total population of 16.2 million; 1.3 million more than in 1990.[1] According to predictions though, the rise in population will drop from 0.35 percent to 0.18 percent per decade.[2]
- The average life expectancy was 78.35 years in 2002. By 2020 another rise is expected bringing the average age to 79.55 years.[3]
- The demographic change will also be evident in the higher number of people aged 65 years or older: In 2005, people 65 years or older will constitute 14.1 percent of the population, in 2025 it will already be 21,2 percent.[4]
- Similarly, the proportion of people aged 80 years or older is constantly rising and will make up 3.6 percent of the Dutch population in 2005. By 2020 a rise to 4.4 percent is expected.[5]
- The older-person dependency ratio; the number of people aged 15 to 64 years per older person over the age of 65, was 63.0 percent of the total population in 1950. In contrast to several other European countries, the support ratio increased to 67.9 percent. However it is expected to drop massively to 59.5 percent by 2050.[6]
- In 2000 more than 140,000 people died in the Netherlands. Cancer is the most common non-acute cause of death – almost 40,000 Dutch people died from cancer in 2000.[7] Of the approximately 40,000 people who die of cancer, 65 percent die at

1 Statistics Netherlands: http://www.cbs.nl
2 Population Division of the Department of Economic and Social Affairs of the United Nations Secretariat, World Population Prospects: The 2002 Revision Population Database: http://esa.un.org/unpp (medium variant).
3 ibid.
4 ibid.
5 ibid.
6 ibid.
7 Statistics Netherlands. Vademecum gezondheidsstatistiek. Voorburg/Heerlen. 2000. Cited in: Ministry of Health, Welfare and Sport in the Netherlands: Palliative care for terminally ill patients in the Netherlands. Dutch Government Policy. The Hague 2003, p. 5.

home, over 25 percent occur in hospitals, around 6 percent die in nursing or care homes. The number dying in an independent professionally staffed hospice or a volunteer hospice ("hospice house") is less than 1 percent.[8]

1.2 Health care system

In the Netherlands, three parallel areas of insurance coexist: the area is a national health insurance scheme for exceptional medical expenses; the second area consists of different regulatory regimes – one for compulsory health insurance through sickness funds for those under a certain income, and another for private health insurance, mostly voluntary; and the third area is voluntary supplementary health insurance. These different areas and the systems that constitute them are steered and supervised by the Dutch Ministry of Health, Welfare and Sports and have (at least) partly different relationships to the insured on the one side and the providers on the other side. These three areas characterise the organisational structure of the Dutch health care system.[9]

One of the main objectives is to guarantee access to a system of health care facilities and services of high quality. To foster this, the Dutch health ministry has established the social health insurance schemes under the *Exceptional Medical Expenses Act (Algemene Wet Bijzondere Ziektekosten, AWBZ)* and the *Sickness Fund Act (ZFW).*[10] But in 2005 a new system will be introduced with one basic insurance for all people and a voluntary supplementary health insurance.

The Exceptional Medical Expenses Act (*AWBZ*) came into force on 14 December 1967, with phased implementation of its content beginning on 1 January 1968. With the introduction of the *Health Insurance Bill* in 1962 (which later became the Sickness Fund Act), the then Minister of Health also launched the idea of an insurance scheme covering the whole population for serious medical risks. This cover included expenses that anyone faced through serious illness or long-term disability – notably mental illness requiring prolonged nursing and care, and congenital physical or mental handicap – expenses that virtually no one is in a position to bear without help from the state or elsewhere.[11] The income-dependant premium is collected via taxes. The home care, nursing, care in nursing homes and homes for the elderly and care of the handicapped fall under this Act. For those with an income below a certain threshold, the income threshold, insurance is compulsory via the *National Health Insurance Act*, or *ZFW*.[12]

Since April 2001, the *Health Care Insurance Board (CVZ)* has been made up of nine independent members appointed by the health minister. Previously, the Board

---

8 A.L. Francke/ D.L. Willems: Palliatieve zorg vandaag en morgen. Feiten, opvattingen en scenario's. Maarssen: Elsevier gezondheidszorg, 2000. Cited in: Ministry of Health, Welfare and Sport in the Netherlands: Palliative care for terminally ill patients in the Netherlands. Dutch Government Policy. The Hague 2003, p. 5.

9 http://www.euro.who.int/Document/E84949.pdf

10 ibid., p. 14.

11 ibid., p. 9.

12 National Information Centre for Palliative Care: http://www.palliatief.nl/nationaal/

consisted of the major health care interests in the Netherlands, including employers, trade unions, health insurers, physicians, consumer groups and the government. The main responsibilities of the Board are to manage the implementation of the Exceptional Medical Expenses Act (*AWBZ*) and the *Sickness Fund Act (ZFW)*, finance the executive bodies (i.e. sickness funds) and manage the collective resources provided by these laws.

2. Hospices and palliative care in the Netherlands

2.1 History

In 1975 the nursing home ‚Antonius-IJsselmonde' in Rotterdam, was the first institution in the Netherlands to work on the theme palliative care and to improve special care for the dying. [13] In hindsight the time after 1975 is regarded as the period of reversal. After 1975, death and dying were decreasingly considered a taboo a period and society started to acknowledge its duty to care for terminally ill people. [14] After 1985 initiatives were developed to stimulate home care services in cooperation with ‚Antonius-IJsselmonde'. In 1993 the first palliative care unit in a Dutch nursing home opened in the same institution. [15] This unit demanded a new approach to end-of-life care through adequate pain and symptom control, communication between care workers and patient and meeting the patient's needs. [16]

The first hospices were established later than in other neighbouring countries such as Great Britain, Germany and Belgium. In 1991 *Johannes Hospice* in Vleuten was founded and in 1992 *Hospice Kuria* in Amsterdam started its work. In establishing the first hospices, people also wanted to make a concrete statement in the euthanasia discussion as a counterbalance to the euthanasia movement. [17] In 1996 the *Netwerk Palliatieve Zorg voor Terminale Patiënten Nederland NPTN* (Dutch Network of Palliative Care for Terminally Ill Patients) was set up to encourage and develop Dutch palliative care services. [18]

Palliative care was recognised as a political issue in 1996 when the Ministry of Health issued a policy statement declaring the need to further develop palliative care in the Netherlands. One of the reasons for this development were suggestions made

13 Interview with Frans Baar, 10 March 2004, in Rotterdam.

14 Rien Janssens/ Henk ten Have: Palliative care in the Netherlands. In: Palliative Care in Europe. Edited by Henk ten Have u. Rien Janssens. Amsterdam 2001, p. 20.

15 ibid., p. 20.

16 Baar, Frans/ van der Kloot Meijburg, Hermann: The role of the physician in nursing home care in The Netherlands. In: Clark, David/ Hockley, Jo: Palliative Care for Older People in Care Homes. Buckingham 2002, p. 5.

17 National Information Centre for Palliative Care: http://www.palliatief.nl/nationaal/

18 ibid.

"by members of Parliament that a further proliferation of hospices was likely to lead to a reduction of the number of euthanasia cases" [19].

The following questions dominated the political debate from 1996 onwards: [20]

- Who should offer palliative care services?
- Should there be palliative care experts among the professionals or should palliative care be integrated into existing health care structures?

Politics decided in 2000 to respond to the second question with a so-called "general approach": all professionals, such as doctors and nurses, should be educated to deliver palliative care when a patient needs it. [21] Therewith the general approach allows the dying patient to remain in their familiar surroundings. This is in line with the needs and wishes of the majority of terminally ill patients in the Netherlands as recent research indicates. [22]

The programmes that were initiated by the Ministry of Health in 1997 had and still have a major impact on the development of palliative care in the Netherlands. In the following the main points are listed:

- the *ZonMw Palliative Care Programme* (1997 - 2002)
- the setup of 6 *COPZs* (1998 - 2003)
- the integration of hospice services into the public health care system through the *PIH-recommendations* (since 1999)
- the integration of *COPZs* into *Integrale Kankercentra* (since 2003)
- the centre *AGORA* (since 2003)

Dutch research on palliative care was first and foremost stimulated by the *ZonMw Palliative Care Programme* [23]. *ZonMw* has allocated grants to a number of different projects that aim to improve palliative care specific target groups, including children, ethnic minorities and patients with amyotrophic lateral sclerosis. It also gives money to projects that intend to improve palliative care in care homes and projects undertaken by the *National Association of Terminal Care Volunteers Trust (VTZ)* to strengthen the role of volunteers. [24]

In 1997 the Ministry of Health, Welfare and Sport decided that six *COPZs* [25] *(Centres for the Development of Palliative Care)* should be set up to develop and guide palliative care in the Netherlands. The six centres were assigned to initiate projects in two main areas – ‚structural change and care coordination in the palliative care sector' and ‚knowledge development and expertise enhancement in the palliative care

19 Rien Janssens/ Henk ten Have: Palliative care in the Netherlands. In: Palliative Care in Europe. Edited by Henk ten Have u. Rien Janssens. Amsterdam 2001, p. 20.

20 ibid., p. 34.

21 ibid.

22 M. Klinkenberg: De laatste levensfase van ouderen. Gezondheid en welzijn van ouderen in de laatste drie maanden van hun leeven. Free University Amsterdam, Social Medicine Department EMGO/LASA, 2001. Cited in: Ministry of Health, Welfare and Sport in the Netherlands: Palliative care for terminally ill patients in the Netherlands. Dutch Government Policy. The Hague 2003, p. 6.

23 cp. ibid., p. 16 et seq.

24 cp. ibid.

25 cp. ibid., p. 17 et seqq.

sector'.[26] The *COPZs* officially started operating in 1998 in six cities: Amsterdam, Groningen, Maastricht, Nijmegen, Rotterdam and Utrecht. In the following years the *COPZs'* worked on the development of education programmes, research projects and consultation teams. In mid- 2002 there were ten regional consultation teams that were being directed by the *COPZs'*. Around 70 percent of the team members are nurses, the others include general medical specialists, GP's, psychologists with specific palliative care education and social workers. In 2000 the *COPZ Evaluation Committee* concluded that, in principle, the *COPZs'* regional consulting teams were accessible to care workers providing care for 43 percent of the Dutch population.[27] In another report, recommendations were made to let the *Integrale Kankercentra IKC* (*Comprehensive Cancer Centres CCC*) take over tasks from the *COPZs'* in medium term.

In 1999 the Ministry of Health, Welfare and Sport set up the *Hospice Care Integration Project Group (PIH)* to work on *PIH-recommendations* for the various palliative care services[28]. The main task of the *PIH* was to integrate the different types of services (professionally staffed hospices, volunteer-run hospices and hospice units)into regular health care. In addition, the *PIH* established ten palliative care pilot-networks to evaluate the cooperation between the different palliative care institutions (hospice facilities, hospitals, nursing homes, care homes and home care services). The evaluation of the network suggests that the cooperation between the providers of palliative is improving. It shows that the flexibility and availability of care improves if people cooperate with each other in accordance with the network model. Consequently the better collaboration between the different services improves the probability to meet the patients wishes and needs more adequately.

In 2002 the Dutch Ministry of Health, Welfare and Sport decided to integrate the *COPZs'* into the *IKC* (*CCC*).[29] The nine *IKC* are regional organisations that advise, support, and train care providers (medical specialists, general practitioners, nursing home directors, nurses and others) in regard to diagnosing, treating, counselling and caring for cancer patients.

The palliative care departments in the *IKC's* took over the tasks of supporting consultation teams, networks and care providers from the *COPZs'*.

In order to support the exchange and coordination between palliative care services, the national support point *AGORA* was established by the National Ministry of Health, Welfare and Sport in 2003.[30] *AGORA* is intended to support providers of palliative care. The national centre should act as a kind of marketplace[31] where carers can learn

26 cp. ibid., p. 17.

27 cp. ibid., p. 18.

28 cp. ibid., p. 19 et seqq.

29 cp. ibid., p. 24 et seqq.

30 cp. ibid., p. 25 et seq. Cp. National Information Centre for Palliative Care: http://www.palliatief.nl/nationaal/ The National Information Centre runs a very good website containing the important aspects of palliative care in the Netherlands as well as a extensive forum staff members. The various networks in the Netherlands can be find via a digital map.

31 In ancient Greek Agora means market place.

more about the important trends and initiatives relating to palliative care. *AGORA* targets to:

- bring about more interaction between care providers concerning care innovations, expertise enhancement, quality projects etc. at a national level, which in turn should result in:
- b. more coordination between care providers in regard to palliative care initiatives;
- c. more information sharing with foreign organisations and care providers about palliative care in the Netherlands and elsewhere. [32]

These aims are carried out through different activities such as organised national meetings about subjects such as network development and expertise enhancement, and maintaining a website with information about palliative care.

Alone in 1998, the Dutch National Ministry of Health, Welfare and Sport spent 15 million €on the development of palliative care services and their integration into regular health care. [33] This may illustrate the significance of the development of palliative care in the Netherlands over the past few years. The specialised palliative care facilities have shown an impressive growth of 365 percent between 1997 and 2003. [34]

2.2 Hospice and palliative care services

Between 1997 and 1999, six percent of the Dutch population provided informal care to terminally ill people. [35] Since 1997 home care organisations have been supplying ‚support for informal carers'. [36] They give psychosocial counselling, advice, instruction and information for informal carers. In case care provided by relatives, friends and home care services does not cover the needs of the patient, an inpatient stay is then considered as an alternative option. There are a variety of palliative care services that come into consideration for this purpose.

In March 2004 there were approximately 590 palliative care beds in the Netherlands. Estimation is difficult because criteria for palliative care beds differ throughout the country. [37] According to a report by the Dutch Ministry of Health, Welfare and Sport palliative care is provided by different types of services: [38]

1. General Practitioners
2. Home care services
3. Nursing homes

---

32 Ministry of Health, Welfare and Sport in the Netherlands: Palliative care for terminally ill patients in the Netherlands. Dutch Government Policy. The Hague 2003, p. 26.

33 Ria de Korte-Verhoef: Developments in palliative care services in the Netherlands. In: European Journal of Palliative Care, 2004; 11 (1), p. 34.

34 ibid., p. 36.

35 The National Public Health Compass: http://www.rivm.nl/vtv/data/site_kompas/index.htm Cited in: Ministry of Health, Welfare and Sport in the Netherlands: Palliative care for terminally ill patients in the Netherlands. Dutch Government Policy. The Hague 2003, p. 12.

36 ibid., p. 8 ; p. 12 et seq.

37 Interview with Dr. André Rhebergen, 09 March 2004, in Amsterdam.

38 Ministry of Health, Welfare and Sport in the Netherlands: Palliative care for terminally ill patients in the Netherlands. Dutch Government Policy. The Hague 2003, p. 7.

4. Care homes
5. Independent professionally staffed adult and children's hospices
6. Volunteer-run hospices ("hospice houses")
7. Hospitals
8. Volunteer Organisations

The different services will now be described in detail:

1. General practitioners (GP's)

Altogether there are 7,800 practising GP's in the Netherlands for a population of over 16 million. The GP's are usually the main provider for people who receive palliative care at home. In principle every citizen in the Netherlands has his own GP who can be consulted without the need of referral.[39] The palliative care offered by the GP's related largely to managing pain and other symptoms and problems. Of the essential elements in the context of palliative care, the emotional support of patients and their families is provided by GP's.[40] Research has revealed that a Dutch GP has contact a total of 26 times with a cancer patient in the palliative care phase.[41] The care of terminally ill patients requires approximately 45 minutes per working week from the GP. However the total amount of time that a GP devoted to palliative care will be greater than this.[42] Many GP's only deal with a few number of terminally ill patients per year. Due to the lack of experiences in the care for the dying, additional training and education opportunities have been created for GP's to enable them to acquire skills in the area of palliative care. For example, the *Dutch Association of General Practitioners* set up a course on palliative care for GP's with an advisory role. The six Centres for the development of Palliative Care have created specialist multidisciplinary consulting teams such as described in 2.1.

2. Home care services

In the Netherlands, there are approximately 120 official, professional home care organisations who provide home care – together with the GP's – for more than 360,000 patients annually.[43] Since 2002, terminally ill patients can receive 24-hour care provided by registered nurses, other carers and home assistants. Volunteers supply any additional help when needed.[44]

[39] NIVEL – Dutch Centre for Primary Health Care. Cited in: ibid., p. 8.
[40] ibid., p. 8.
[41] M. van den Muijsenbergh: Palliatieve Zorg door de huisarts. Ervaringen van huisartsen, patienten en naasten. Dissertation. Leiden: Leiden University, 2001. Cited in: ibid., p. 8.
[42] ibid., p. 8.
[43] Ria de Korte-Verhoef: Developments in palliative care services in the Netherlands. In: European Journal of Palliative Care, 2004; 11 (1), p. 34.
[44] ibid., p. 34.

3. Nursing homes

Currently there are approximately 330 nursing homes in the Netherlands, with around 57,600 beds.[45] The main important target group of the nursing homes is made up of elderly people with somatic or psycho-geriatric problems who need help in the late stages of their illness. The basic task of the nursing home includes reactivation and rehabilitation, care for patients with chronic or protracted illnesses and special forms of care (for example brain damage patients or coma patients).[46] Nursing home doctors, specialising in geriatrics, work alongside a multidisciplinary team with nurses, social workers, psychologists, chaplains, paramedics and occupational therapists.[47] Nowadays, nursing home care is often characterised by professionals as multi- and interdisciplinary, multi-dimensional and multi-methodical (3M-model). This model has been developed as a result of experiences with the care of chronically ill and dying patients.[48]

In December 2003 there were 43 units which gave brief care to non-resident terminally ill patients.[49] These unit's purpose is to enable the patient to remain in suitable surroundings who at the same time fit the needs of the patient and their families. They are usually located in the nursing home or buildings that are closely situated in a nearby facility. Admissions to these units is often limited to between four and six weeks.

4. Care homes

There are around 1365 care homes in the Netherlands, with a capacity of approximately 112,400 beds.[50] The residents usually have a single room, or a double room in the case of married couples. In many cases care homes offer external services to elderly people living at home. The average waiting time for a place is 66 weeks. For this reason, a place in a care home is not beneficial for palliative care patients. However, there is also a short stay option with a total of 27,530 places available to patients with palliative care needs. The maximum stay for palliative care patients is 12 weeks.[51]

In December 2003 there were 32 separate palliative care units in homes for the elderly with a capacity of 69 beds. The number of beds ranges from one to seven.[52] Care

---

45 The National Public Health Compass: http://www.rivm.nl/vtv/data/site_kompas/index.htm zit. n. Ministry of Health, Welfare and Sport in the Netherlands: Palliative care for terminally ill patients in the Netherlands. Dutch Government Policy. The Hague 200, p. 9.

46 ibid., p. 3.

47 Ria de Korte-Verhoef: Developments in palliative care services in the Netherlands. In: European Journal of Palliative Care, 2004; 11 (1), p. 35.

48 ibid., p. 6 et seq.

49 ibid., p. 36.

50 The National Public Health Compass: http://www.rivm.nl/vtv/data/site_kompas/index.htm zit. n. Ministry of Health, Welfare and Sport in the Netherlands: Palliative care for terminally ill patients in the Netherlands. Dutch Government Policy. The Hague 2003, p. 10.

51 Ria de Korte-Verhoef: Developments in palliative care services in the Netherlands. In: European Journal of Palliative Care, 2004; 11 (1), p. 35.

52 ibid., p. 36.

is provided by nurses or professional carers who are supported by pastoral workers as well as volunteers. The GP has the final responsibility for all medical decisions. Similar to hospice units and in nursing homes, the length of stay in care homes is between four to six weeks.[53]

5. Independent professionally staffed adult and children's hospices

As has been shown in the preceding sections, there are many options in the Netherlands for outpatient palliative care as well as inpatient care traditionally offered by nursing and care homes. This is why the number of Dutch citizens that die in an independent hospice is still relatively low with less than one percent.[54] In December 2003 there are 23 independent hospices providing care for a total of 134 beds. The number of beds per hospice ranges from three to ten beds.[55] Nurses make up the core team in an independent hospice. The medical responsibility is borne by the patient's own GP or in other cases by a hospice doctor or medical specialised associated with the hospice.[56] Further support is provided by volunteers psychologists, occupational therapists and other professionals. Almost all hospices have a confessional background.

Children's hospices are similar to the independent hospices. In these facilities children up to the age of 18 years are cared for. It is common to admit children to the hospice for a limited period of time to give parents a temporary break. In December 2003 there were five children's hospices in the Netherlands.[57]

6. Volunteer-run hospices ("hospice houses" or "almost-at-home-houses")

The so called "hospice houses" or "almost-at-home-houses" (in Dutch "hospicehuis" or "bijna-thuis-huis") have little in common with other in-patient services. They are run by volunteers and are often situated in private houses in common neighbourhoods. The number of beds in those houses, which offer basic care to the patients, ranges from one to six. They are run by trained volunteers supported by GP's and professional home care nurses who provide professional care.[58] The volunteers work together as closely as possible with relatives and friends of the patient in order to offer daily care to the patient.[59] It is common that the patient's own GP is responsible for providing

53 Ministry of Health, Welfare and Sport in the Netherlands: Palliative care for terminally ill patients in the Netherlands. Dutch Government Policy. The Hague 2003, p. 10.

54 A.L. Francke/ D.L. Willems: Palliatieve zorg vandaag en morgen. Feiten, opvattingen en scenario's. Maarssen: Elsevier gezondheidszorg, 2000. Cited in: Ministry of Health, Welfare and Sport in the Netherlands: Palliative care for terminally ill patients in the Netherlands. Dutch Government Policy. The Hague 2003, p. 10.

55 Ria de Korte-Verhoef: Developments in palliative care services in the Netherlands. In: European Journal of Palliative Care, 2004; 11 (1), p. 35 et seq.

56 Ministry of Health, Welfare and Sport in the Netherlands: Palliative care for terminally ill patients in the Netherlands. Dutch Government Policy. The Hague 2003, p. 11.

57 Ria de Korte-Verhoef: Developments in palliative care services in the Netherlands. In: European Journal of Palliative Care, 2004; 11 (1), p. 36.

58 ibid., p. 35.

59 Ministry of Health, Welfare and Sport in the Netherlands: Palliative care for terminally ill patients in the Netherlands. Dutch Government Policy. The Hague 2003, p. 11.

the medical care. "Hospice houses" are best suited for those patients who rather need psycho-social care than medical support.[60] The stay in an "almost-at-home-house" is free. In most of those houses a small financial contribution is requested, if possible. In most cases it is done to comfort the family involved, so that they don't feel obligated in any way.[61] In December 2003 there were 29 volunteers-run hospices in the Netherlands.[62]

7. Hospitals

In 2003, three of the total 137 hospitals in the Netherlands had a hospice unit. The number of beds varies from three to seven beds in those units.[63] Patients usually stay in the hospitals for a short period of time to receive palliative medication and acute medical treatment. In case of successful symptom control patients are either allowed to return home, into a hospice or a "hospice house". Although most experts in the Netherlands think that hospitals are not the ideal setting for palliative care, 31 percent of the patients with a non-acute cause of death die in hospitals each year.[64]

8. Volunteer Organisations[65]

The voluntary organisations *VTZ* und *VHN* are the most important umbrella organisations for the support and coordination of voluntary work. Volunteers in the Netherlands work in home care, hospices, hospice houses, in palliative care units in nursing and care homes as well as in hospitals.

The work done by regional networks and consulting teams is highly important for the provisions for palliative care. In 2001, the *PIH* recommended the development of regional networks. Since 2002 all services (home care, nursing and care homes, hospices) in the palliative care sector work together in integrative networks. Insurances pay for palliative care only if the institution is part of a regional/local network. In 2004, there were about 60 networks in the Netherlands.[66] For example, there were 9 networks in the region Amsterdam/North-West Netherlands.

In 2002 there were a total of 20 consulting teams in the Netherlands. A first evaluation report was published in 2001 - 2002. The report revealed there were 2357 consultations and on average there were 0.25 consultations per 1000 members of the population. Most consultations were carried out over the telephone. In 19 percent of the

---

60 ibid., p. 11.

61 Interview with Jan Ruyten, 04 March 2004, in Woerden.

62 Ria de Korte-Verhoef: Developments in palliative care services in the Netherlands. In: European Journal of Palliative Care, 2004; 11 (1), p. 36.

63 ibid., p. 36. Ministry of Health, Welfare and Sport in the Netherlands: Palliative care for terminally ill patients in the Netherlands. Dutch Government Policy. The Hague 2003, p. 12.

64 Ria de Korte-Verhoef: Developments in palliative care services in the Netherlands. In: European Journal of Palliative Care, 2004; 11 (1), p. 35.

65 cp. Ministry of Health, Welfare and Sport in the Netherlands: Palliative care for terminally ill patients in the Netherlands. Dutch Government Policy. The Hague 2003, p. 12.

66 Interview with Dr. Wim Jansen, 09 March 2004, in Amsterdam.

cases the patient was visited.[67] Although, nurses were often the first members from the teams in contact with the person seeking advice, virtually all cases were considered in multi-disciplinary discussions. The questions were primarily related to pain and other somatic complaints, pharmacological subjects, psychological problems or the organisation of care.[68]

2.3 Legal regulations and funding

In the Netherlands palliative care is part of regular health care.[69] In the Dutch health care system the *AWBZ* is important for the funding of palliative care (see 1.2).[70] Everyone living in the Netherlands contributes to the *AWBZ*. In addition, the state subsidises the *AWBZ*.

The *AWBZ* insures those severe medical risks which are not covered by compulsory or private health insurance. This includes all kinds of care and nursing in/by *AWBZ* institutions (including day care) and certain forms of care at home.[71] Since 1998 there are opportunities to take leave for people with job obligations who want to care for a family member who is terminally ill. A scheme for such carers exists in the *Financing Career Break Act* (*Wet Financiering Loopbaanonderbreking*). Through this act people can take temporary leave for a minimum of one month and a maximum of six months in order to give volunteer care either at home or in palliative care institutions. During this period the person on leave receives financial support from the state. In 2002 this was a maximum of 490,54 €gross per month. Very few people take advantage of the scheme because it has been given very little publicity. The limited financial contribution is probably an obstacle for potential carers. There is no statutory right to this leave as the employer must give agree to the proposal.[72]

The following section gives information about the funding of the different types of services (as introduced in 2.2):

1. *General Practitioners*
   The service provided is covered by the patient's private insurance or the health insurance fund insurance.[73]

---

67 cp. COPZ Evaluation Committee. 2001 Annual Report. Utrecht: COPZ Evaluation Committee, 29 March. 2002. Cited in: Ministry of Health, Welfare and Sport in the Netherlands: Palliative care for terminally ill patients in the Netherlands. Dutch Government Policy. The Hague 2003, p. 18.

68 cp. COPZ Evaluation Committee. 2001 Annual Report. Utrecht: COPZ Evaluation Committee, 29 March. 2002. Cited in: Ministry of Health, Welfare and Sport in the Netherlands: Palliative care for terminally ill patients in the Netherlands. Dutch Government Policy. The Hague 2003, p. 18 et seq.

69 Ministry of Health, Welfare and Sport in the Netherlands: Palliative care for terminally ill patients in the Netherlands. Dutch Government Policy. The Hague 2003, p. 6 et seq.

70 German Federal Ministry for health and Social Security: Europe's Social-Compass. A comparison of Social Security in Europe. Bonn 2003, p. 42.

71 Communication Department of the Ministry of Social Affairs and Employment and Public Relations Department of the Ministry of Health, Welfare and Culture: A short survey of social security in the Netherlands. Half-yearly summary January 2004. The Hague 2003, p. 10.

72 cp. National Information Centre for Palliative Care: http://www.palliatief.nl/nationaal/

73 Ministry of Health, Welfare and Sport in the Netherlands: Palliative care for terminally ill patients in the Netherlands. Dutch Government Policy. The Hague 2003, p. 8.

2. *Home care services*
   The national insurance *AWBZ* pays for care provided by home care organisations. Sometimes the patient contributes a small amount as well. [74]
3. *Nursing homes*
   The *AWBZ* finances the large part of costs that occur in nursing homes. [75]
4. *Care homes*
   The same way of financing applies for the treatment in palliative care units in care homes. [76]
5. *Independent professionally staffed adult and children's hospices*
   Most services provided in hospices are paid by the *AWBZ*. Nevertheless, Dutch hospices still rely on donations, sponsorship and grants. [77]
6. *Volunteer-run hospices ("hospice houses")*
   The funding of hospice houses differs. Most hospices depend on donations and grants as well as small contributions made by the patients. The existing financial support provided by the *AWBZ* differs greatly throughout the various regions [78]
7. *Hospitals*
   Most of the costs that occur in hospitals are paid by the patient's private or health insurance fund insurance. [79]
8. *Volunteer Organisations*
   The coordination, transport, training and supervision of volunteers is covered by a wide range of sponsors, donations and gifts. The coordination of voluntary work is also financed by the Dutch Ministry of Health, Welfare and Sport. [80]

In the following information gathered in 2.2 and 2.3 is summarised in the table 1:

---

74 M. Ijzerman/ C.M. Scholten: Wachtlijsten in den thuiszorg. Tweede meting van de quick scan onder toegelaten instellingen. in: Research en Beleid, Leiden 1999. Cited in: Ministry of Health, Welfare and Sport in the Netherlands: Palliative care for terminally ill patients in the Netherlands. Dutch Government Policy. The Hague 2003, p. 8.

75 ibid., p. 9.

76 ibid., p. 10.

77 ibid., p. 11.

78 Personal correspondence with Jan Ruyten, 15 September 2004.

79 Ministry of Health, Welfare and Sport in the Netherlands: Palliative care for terminally ill patients in the Netherlands. Dutch Government Policy. The Hague 2003, p. 7.

80 ibid., p. 12.

Providers of palliative care	**Total number**	**Main sources of finance**
General Practitioners	approx. 7800	Patient's private or health insurance fund insurance
Home care organisations	approx. 120	*AWBZ* and small patient personal contribution
Nursing homes	approx. 330 with 43 of those with a palliative care unit	*AWBZ* and small patient personal contribution; incidental donations, sponsorship and grants etc. (in the case of hospice unit)
Care homes	approx. 1360 with 32 of those with a palliative care unit	*AWBZ* and small patient personal contribution; incidental donations, sponsorship and grants etc. (in the case of hospice unit)
Independent professionally staffed adult hospices	23	private or health insurance fund insurance, *AWBZ*; donations, sponsorship and grants; often patients contribution towards cost of maintenance and accommodation
Children's hospices	5	
Hospice houses	29	
Hospitals	approx. 137 with 3 of those with a palliative care unit	private insurance or health insurance fund insurance; incidental donations, sponsorship and grants etc. (in the case of hospice unit)
Volunteer Organisations	approx. 170	government grant (for coordination of volunteers); incidental donations, sponsorship and grants etc.

Table 1: Providers of palliative care in the Netherlands and their most important sources of finance (December 2003) [81]

[81] ibid., 7. Ria de Korte-Verhoef: Developments in palliative care services in the Netherlands. In: European Journal of Palliative Care, 2004; 11 (1), p. 34 - 37. Table modified by Felix Schumann.

2.4 Organisations[82]

Netwerk Palliatieve Zorg voor Terminale Patiënten Nederland (NPTN)

The Netherland's Palliative Care Network for Terminally Ill Patients (NPTN) with the *National Support Group for Palliative Terminal Care Association* is a national organisation of more than 120 affiliated organisations/individuals, working together to contribute to the further development of palliative care in the Netherlands. The *NPTN* is the main contact point for members of the government.

AGORA

Agora operates as the *National Information Centre for Palliative Care.* It is an independent information point for organisations that concentrate on palliative care.

Arcares

*Arcares*is the Umbrella organization for nursing homes and homes for the elderly. It functions as the platform for palliative terminal care in nursing homes.

Landelijke Vereniging voor Thuiszorg (LVT)

The *LVT* is thesector organisation of institutions for family care, 'cross-work', maternity care and graft administration in The Netherlands.

Vrijwilligers Terminale Zorg (VTZ)

The *VTZ* is the national foundation for voluntary palliative terminal care, an association of about 175 affiliated voluntary organisations in the Netherlands. The 4000 volunteers provide support to those in their final stages of life, their families and friends, both at home as and in almost-at-home houses and hospices.

Vrijwilligers Hospicezorg Nederland (VHN)

Netherlands Association of Volunteers Hospice Care (*VHN*) is the second umbrella organisation that coordinates and supports volunteers. The organisations *VHN* and *VTZ* will be united on the 1st of January 2005. The new association, with more that 200 members (organisations), will carry the name VPTZ (*Vrijwilligers Palliatieve Terminale Zorg*).[83]

2.5 Education and training of professional staff

In many curricula of basic training of doctors and nurses palliative care is already integrated. The plan is to implement palliative care in all areas. Special training in palliative care exist nation-wide but differ concerning the content very much throughout the regions. It is the intention to make certified training courses.[84]

---

82 cp. National Information Centre for Palliative Care: http://www.palliatief.nl/nationaal/

83 Interview with Jan Ruyten, 04 March 2004, in Woerden.

84 Interview with Ria de Korte-Verhoef, 05 March 2004, in Utrecht.

The VU University medical centre in Amsterdam introduced palliative care in the medical curriculum in 2003. The 9 Integrale Kankercentra (Comprehensive Cancer Centres) support and facilitate the development of the networks for example offering palliative care training for Doctors, nurses and other caretakers. [85]

One example for regional distinctions is the training programme that is offered by *Hospice Kuria* in Amsterdam: For many years, a three-day-course in pain management for nurses has been offered in cooperation with the department of anaesthesiology at *VU University medical centre. Hospice Kuria* and the department of anaesthesiology of VU University medical centre provides a nurse training in pain management in palliative care with about 80 participants from all over the country on an annual basis. The same training is also provided for GP's and nursing home doctors. *Kuria* has also own programmes for volunteer training. [86]

The introduction of a consultant in palliative medicine is not expected in the Netherlands and would be rather counterproductive to the general approach laid out in 1998. According to this approach all kinds of professionals should be qualified in the care of the terminally ill and dying patients.

2.6 Volunteers

Dutch volunteers offer their help in various areas in the field of terminal palliative care. Above all they give psychosocial support to the dying and practical help to the relatives. The volunteer support is very important; estimates indicate that more than 75 per cent of the care given to the chronically ill in the home environment is provided by volunteer carers. [87] Beside their work in the patient's home volunteers are actively involved in hospices, hospice houses and palliative care units in care homes, nursing homes and hospitals. The almost-at-home-houses have a special role in the Dutch palliative care field because volunteers have a leading function and are supported by professionals. The other palliative care institutions work in the opposite way. [88] As has been mentioned before, the costs of coordination, transport, training and supervision are covered by sponsors, donations and gifts. The coordination of voluntary work is also financed by the Dutch Ministry of Health, Welfare and Sport.

The organisations *VHN* and *VTZ* will be united on the 1st of January 2005. The *VTZ* runs a central office and a website from where people can access the 180 different local volunteer groups. The local groups that are organized in *VTZ* form a network that covers around 90 percent of Dutch communities. *VTZ* and *VHN* have between 6000 and 6500 volunteers. They are mostly women between 35 and 70 whose interest in palliative care grew through personal experience with dying relatives. [89]

85 Interview with Dr. Wim Jansen, 09 March 2004, in Amsterdam.

86 ibid.

87 National Information Centre for Palliative Care: http://www.palliatief.nl/nationaal/

88 Interview with Jan Ruyten, Boi Jongejan and Ingrid H. Versteeg, 04 March 2004, in Woerden.

89 ibid.

Both organizations *VHN* and *VTZ* have introduced quality criteria. Training often starts in the almost-at-home-houses as a basis, which consists of 8 three-hours training sessions. There is a nation-wide training concept which is organized by *VTZ* and *VHN*.[90] The training is paid for by the organisations and not by the volunteers. Volunteers are insured during their hospice work by a common liability insurance procured for all regional groups.[91]

The Dutch hospice houses offer a special type of service that exists nowhere else in Europe. They are small institutions, run by volunteers and located in the neighbourhood, that provide basic care for patients who are no longer able to remain in their own homes. The hospice houses represent the Dutch hospice movement that operates in local neighbourhoods. The function of Dutch hospice houses can be summed up by a statement by a staff member who said: "We have institutionalised death. Now we must de-institutionalise it." As the hospice houses operate as neighbourly initiatives, they mainly rely on donations and contributions. For example, the local cheese salesmen delivers for free as does the gardener in the neighbourhood.

2.7 Examples

A profile of the national palliative care provision structure is presented below and examples are given in the form of detailed descriptions of a specific palliative care network and one hospice.

The diagram below illustrates the structure of the Dutch palliative care provision. The integration of palliative care into the national health care is reproduced in four levels. It starts at the top with a national administration and ends at the bottom at the level of a local hospice.

The nine national cancer centres on top precede the lower level institutions. The cancer centre in Amsterdam (Region North-West Netherlands) represents one of the centres. In this region nine palliative care networks are active and integrated in the cancer centre. One level below, the *Network Palliative Care in Amsterdam* is one example of those nine networks just mentioned. It contains eleven palliative care services that provide inpatient and outpatient care for dying patients as well as the consulting team "*Helpdesk Amsterdam*", which operates as the contact point for doctors and nurses. One the lowest level, *Hospice Kuria* in Amsterdam represents a local institution.

[90] ibid.

[91] ibid.

***9 Integrale Kankercentra* (national cancer centres), Supporting and advice function including specialised consulting teams:**

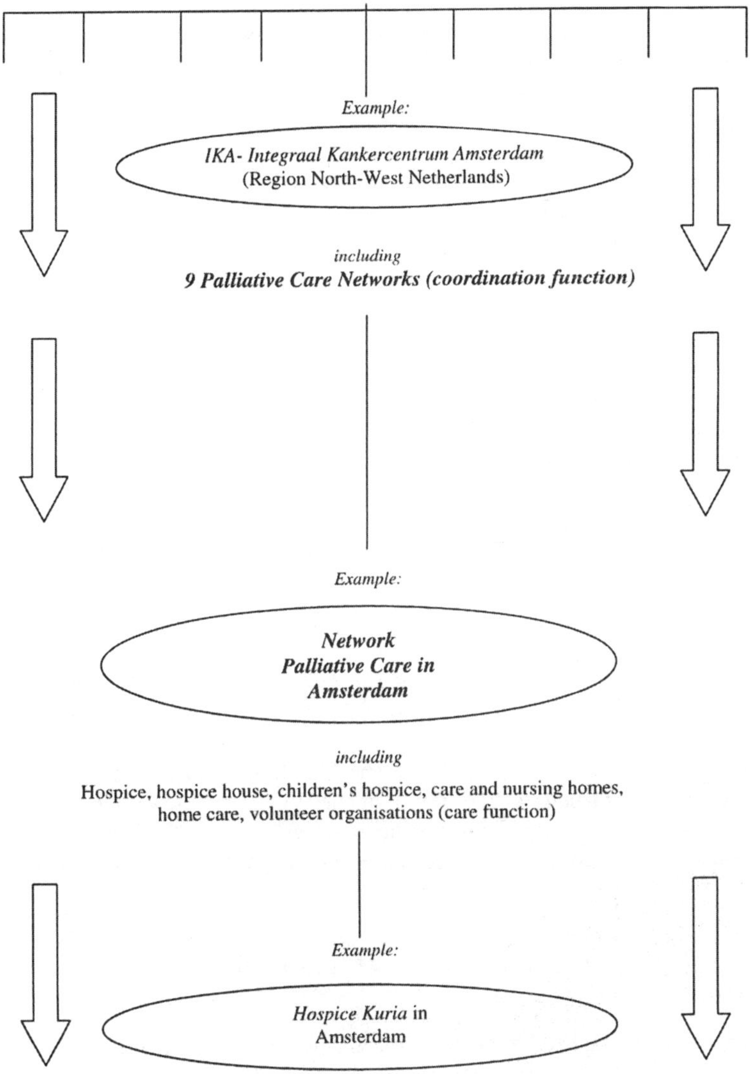

Diagram 1: A profile of the national palliative care provision structure in the Netherlands (2004) [92]

The diagram shows the top-down structure of the Dutch palliative care provision. It has to be recognised that services like *Hospice Kuria* have existed for many years before palliative care was integrated into the public health care system.

Example of a Network: Network Palliative Care in Amsterdam

As a representative for approx. 60 palliative care networks, the *Network Palliative Care in Amsterdam* is presented here. It was founded in 2001 and contains all services which provide palliative care in Amsterdam: [93]

- *Hospice house Veerhuis* (4 Beds)
- *Hospice Kuria* (10 Beds)
- *Children's hospice Het Lindenhofje* (12 Beds)
- Nursing home *De Buitenhof* (6 Beds)
- Nursing home *Douwes Dekkerhuis* (4 Beds)
- Nursing home *Leo Polakhuis* (5 Beds)
- Nursing home *Sint Jacob* (4 Beds)
- Nursing home *De Die* (2 Beds)
- Nursing home *Slotervaart* (4 Beds)

In addition the following services are also part of the network:

- Consultation team *'Helpdesk Amsterdam'*
- Home care service Amsterdam
- Volunteer-organisation *Markant*

The network employs two coordinators whose wages are paid by insurance companies. In 2004 the Association of Comprehensive Cancer Centres (ACCC) imposed quality criteria for networks.

Example for a regional institution: Hospice Kuria, Amsterdam

Valeriusplein is located in the South of Amsterdam surrounded by parks and large houses. Hospice Kuria is situated in one of those houses since it was founded as the second Dutch hospice back in 1992.

The ten single rooms are placed in two halls. In front of the hospice leader's office door is a photo of Queen Beatrix. In the Nineties she visited the very few hospices to support the palliative care movement in the country. Corry van Tol-Verhagen, Director of the hospice and the associated foundation *Kuria* speaks of the beginnings of their work:

> When we started, the British hospice served as a role model for us. Since then, we have become experts ourselves and became partners for hospices abroad to share information and to learn from each other. [94]

12 years ago the hospice started their work against existing problems:

---

92 Diagram: Felix Schumann

93 cp. *Network Palliative Care in Amsterdam*: http://www.palliatief.nl/amsterdam/

94 Interview with Corry van Tol-Verhagen and Jaap Gootjes, 09 March 2004 in Amsterdam.

Hospice Kuria, Amsterdam, Courtesy of Hospice Kuria

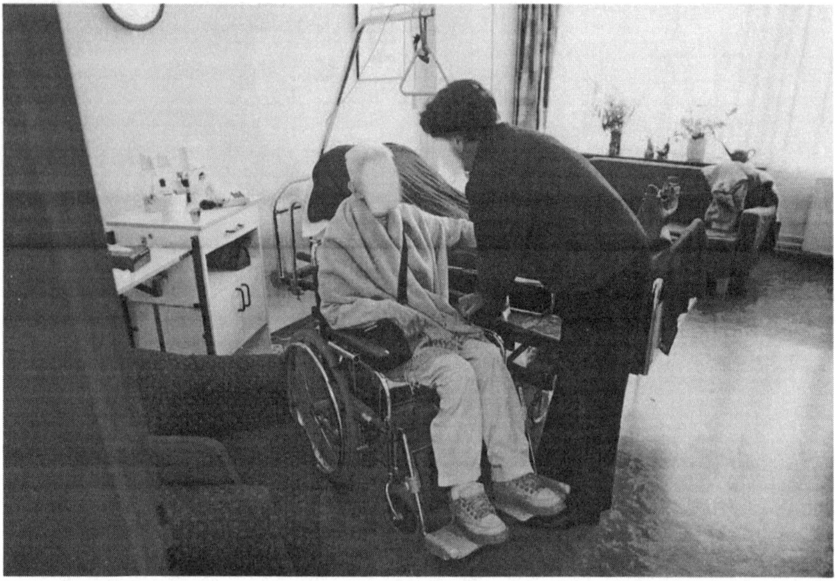

Hospice Kuria, Amsterdam, Courtesy of Hospice Kuria

"In the Netherlands there was a huge discussion about good laws for euthanasia, but only few for the development of knowledge for End-of-life care. That was our mission" [95], says Jaap Gootjes, the *Manager of Nursing* at the hospice. The lack of knowledge concerned professionals and society as a whole. *Hospice Kuria* took the challenge to improve care for the dying to give an answer to the euthanasia discussion.

The early days of the hospice were also affected by the help for patients with HIV/AIDS who were forced to live in great social isolation at the time. Although they expressed the desire to die at home, most of them died in hospitals. Corry van Tol-Verhagen: "In the beginning, 70 percent of our patients where HIV/AIDS -patients. They were one of the reasons why we started a hospice." [96]

Today, the hospice has 5 percent AIDS patients, the outweighing number of the patients are cancer patients (90 percent). The average age is 61 - 62. 60 percent of the patients are admitted from hospitals, 40 percent of patients come from their homes. The average duration in the hospice is 22 - 23 days. The *‚Bewohners'* (*guests*), as they are called by staff members, are insured and in addition have to pay 7.50 €per day. [97]

The core team consists of 22 nurses, one social worker, a doctor and 200 volunteers. If necessary, medical and nursing experts can be called on as well as pastoral staff. For many years the hospice offers courses in pain management to nurses and doc-

95 ibid.
96 ibid.
97 ibid.

tors from the whole country. Normally members of the team, no matter if they work as professionals or volunteers, undergo training inside *Hospice Kuria* before they start their work. It is also common to offer "on-the-job-training" and to allow professional nurses from other institutions to gain some hands-on-experience in palliative care. Volunteers who work for the hospice do not have to pay for their training. The *Kuria foundation* has set the following goals: the financial support of care in the hospice, the assistance in home care through volunteers and the improvement in expertise of nursing staff, doctors and volunteers through education carried out by *Kuria*.

2.8 Euthanasia

Euthanasia has been a widely disputed issue among the Dutch public for some time. At the same time the international debate has influenced the political and social discussion in the country. Two sides dominate the debate: One party asserts that requests of euthanasia are virtually never forthcoming if high quality palliative care is being provided. On the other hand there are people arguing that even the best palliative care cannot always prevent a request for euthanasia. [98] A common attitude shown by experts in the Netherlands is their expressed belief that the new euthanasia legislation has been incorporated for the good of the patient. However euthanasia is regarded as makeshift when all other options have been exhausted and the patient expresses his desire to receive help.

In the Netherlands euthanasia is taken to mean termination of life by a doctor at the request of a patient. This also includes doctor-assisted-suicide. Euthanasia is not taken to mean abandoning treatment if (further) treatment is pointless. In such cases it is part and parcel of normal medical practice that the doctor abandons treatment and lets nature take its course. The same applies to administrating large doses of opiates for pain relief and whereby a side effect is that death occurs more quickly. [99]

Nevertheless there are cases when euthanasia is carried out without the request of a patient:

There are about 900 cases of euthanasia without explicit request annually, for example concerning dementia patients. Those cases happen without the explicit request of the patient and therefore don't belong to legal euthanasia practice. [100]

In the past decades Dutch legislature was in favour of the regulation and transparency of euthanasia. On 10 April 2001, the Dutch parliament passed a new Act on euthanasia, the *Termination of Life on Request and Assisted Suicide* (Review Procedures) Act

---

98 cp. Ministry of Health, Welfare and Sport in the Netherlands: Palliative care for terminally ill patients in the Netherlands. Dutch Government Policy. The Hague 2003, p. 28.

99 Ministry of Health, Welfare and Sport in the Netherlands: Palliative care for terminally ill patients in the Netherlands. Dutch Government Policy. The Hague 2003, p. 28.

100 Interview with Prof. Dr. Henk Jochemsen, 01 March 2004, in Amsterdam.

which came into effect on 1 April 2002. [101] The care criteria for doctors are as follows. The doctors must:

a) be satisfied that the patient's request is voluntary and well-considered. *Note*: This means that the request must not be made owing to pressure from or influence by other people or as the result of a mental disorder. The patient must fully understand the nature of his condition, his prospects and the types of treatment available. He must also have repeatedly expressed the wish to die;
b) be satisfied that the patient's suffering is unbearable, and that there is no prospect of improvement;
c) inform the patient about his situation and further prognosis;
d) discuss the situation with the patient and come to the conclusion that there is no reasonable alternative;
e) consult at least one other physician with no connection to the case, who must then see the patient and state in writing that the attending physician has satisfied the due care criteria listed in a. to d. above; and f. exercise due medical care and attention in terminating the patient's
f) life or assisting in his suicide. *Note*: The doctor must perform euthanasia himself. He may not have someone else do it. In cases of assisted suicide, the doctor must remain with or near the patient until death occurs. [102]

Doctors who do not fulfil or may have not fulfilled the criteria of the euthanasia may be prosecuted. Doctors have to report their actions to the regional committees. The *Regional Euthanasia Review Committee* reviews the medical actions of the doctor. Each of the five review committees has three independent members – lawyer/chair, a doctor and ethicist. If a review committee comes to the conclusion that the doctor exercised reasonable care, the committee notifies the doctor of this. No further notification is then sent to the Public Prosecution Service. [103] In the Netherlands doctors are under no obligation to perform euthanasia. Likewise the patient has no legal right to euthanasia. [104]

For some years the number of reported cases of euthanasia decreases:

- 2001 there were 2054 reported cases (of which 1819 were cases of euthanasia, 191 cases of assisted suicide und 44 cases of a combination of the two) [105]
- 2002 a number of 1882 cases were reported (1672 cases of euthanasia, 184 assisted suicide and 26 a combination of the two) [106]

---

[101] Ministry of Health, Welfare and Sport and the Ministry of Justice in the Netherlands: Euthanasia. The Netherland's new rules. Den Haag 2002, p. 1.

[102] ibid., p. 5 et seq.

[103] Ministry of Health, Welfare and Sport in the Netherlands: Palliative care for terminally ill patients in the Netherlands. Dutch Government Policy. The Hague 2003, p. 29.

[104] Ministry of Health, Welfare and Sport and the Ministry of Justice in the Netherlands: Euthanasia. The Netherland's new rules. Den Haag 2002, p. 4.

[105] Regionale toetsingscommissies euthanasie (Ed.): Jaarverslag 2001. Arnhem 2002, p. 11.

[106] Regionale toetsingscommissies euthanasie (Ed.): Jaarverslag 2002. Arnhem 2003, p. 12.

– 2003 there were 1815 reported cases (of which 1626 were euthanasia, 148 assisted suicide and 41 a combination) [107]

The following questions arise: Are all actual cases of euthanasia (requested by the patient) reported or is the number much higher in reality? Experts estimate that only 50 percent of the actual cases of euthanasia are reported.

In case the observed trend of fewer cases of euthanasia is real, what are the reasons for the decrease? Amongst other things there are two approaches to explain the phenomenon: The first indicates that cases of terminal sedation have increased over the past few years and with it, the possible side effect that (terminal) sedation can hasten the patient's death. However terminal sedation is not classified as euthanasia and does not have to reported to the committees. The second, more optimistic approach, argues that the recent decline of euthanasia cases is due to the growing and improving palliative care structured in the Netherlands. More doctors are now aware of palliative care and its possibilities for the better of the patient.

Dutch hospices, often rooted in Christian communities, are opponents to euthanasia. They stress that the options of palliative care outweigh the request for euthanasia. [108] At a global level there are many disagreements on the acceptability of euthanasia. [109] However there seems to be a consensus among experts "that a further development of palliative care can diminish the number of euthanasia cases" [110]. Nursing home doctors say that euthanasia is inadequate for dementia patients because "We simply don't know what the patients want" and "If euthanasia is provided, the patient has to ask for it!" [111]

The practice of euthanasia is unusual in Dutch hospices. The same applies for palliative care units in care and nursing homes. The demand for euthanasia is lower than one might expect:

At the *Hospice Kuria*, Amsterdam, within ten years work, only three out of 700 patients requested euthanasia. [112] In case a patient asks for euthanasia, hospice staff members may bring the patient to another place where a doctor is willing to give euthanasia, for instance at the patients home or in hospital.

The criticism on the legalisation of euthanasia from abroad turned out to be an incentive for the establishment of palliative care. By integrating palliative care into the public health care system the state showed its responsibility for a proper care for the terminally ill.

Regardless of the introduction of the euthanasia act, questions remain if the act itself resolves all problems involved when doctors play an active role in the death process of a patient. Even though the new legislation and its translation into practice

---

107 Regionale toetsingscommissies euthanasie (Ed.): Jaarverslag 2003. Arnhem 2004, p. 11.

108 Interview with Ria de Korte-Verhoef, 05 March 2004, in Utrecht.

109 Rien Janssens/ Henk ten Have: Palliative care in the Netherlands. In: Palliative Care in Europe. Edited by Henk ten Have u. Rien Janssens. Amsterdam 2001, p. 13.

110 ibid., p. 16.

111 Interview with Ria de Korte-Verhoef, 05 March 2004, in Utrecht.

112 Interview with Dr. Wim Jansen, 09 March 2004, in Amsterdam.

is said to be the result of a more open and liberal discussion, certainly not all cases in which doctors are actively involved fall under the euthanasia act. One cannot assume that all such cases are reported to a committee. In the Netherlands, there is a lack of transparency of "indirect euthanasia" and "euthanasia without request". In the end, it is estimated that only 30 percent of the cases when the physician has the explicit intention to hasten death are reported to the euthanasia committees (which is not to say that all those cases are full blown euthanasia cases).[113]

It has to be investigated carefully if terminal sedation is becoming a substitute for euthanasia.

The cases of correct terminal sedation do not belong to the legal practice of euthanasia, but in practice the intention of the doctor to hasten death and the effect of his treatment can be just the same as in euthanasia cases. Then the distinction between terminal sedation and euthanasia becomes confused.[114] However it should not be overlooked that most people in the Netherlands are satisfied with the euthanasia act.[115] Among its own citizens the reception of the euthanasia act has always been good in the Netherlands. For most Dutch people euthanasia still is an option that stands for the patients independence and self-control at the end of life in case distress becomes unbearable.

3. Summary

"Palliative Care is basic care!"[116] With very few exceptions this approach – palliative care is basic care – has been implemented on a nation-wide basis. The provision with palliative care is put into practice almost all over the country. At the same time palliative care is not regarded as a special discipline carried out by some experts. In contrast, a general approach has been followed in the Netherlands since 1998. As part of this concept, doctors and nurses are asked to acquire basic skills in palliative care. Some experts say that the attention towards palliative care led to some positive developments in the country. The stimulation of structures in research and networking through the COPZ's has worked out well but should have been prolonged.[117] There has been a remarkable growth in palliative care institutions between 1997 and 2003. Nonetheless, the quality of care provided differs between the institutions. Probably some palliative care units have been built without adequate patient-oriented training and qualification of carers.[118]

The hospice movement in the Netherlands is rather small. The two big volunteer organisations

---

[113] Interview with Prof. Dr. Henk Jochemsen, 01 March 2004, in Amsterdam.
[114] ibid.
[115] Interview with Ria de Korte-Verhoef, 05 March 2004, in Utrecht.
[116] ibid.
[117] Interview with Dr. André Rhebergen, 09 March 2004, in Amsterdam.
[118] ibid.

VHN und *VTZ* represent this civil movement. Today palliative care in the Netherlands is predominantly the result of a top-down approach, a highly political and administrative issue.

In how far there is a interdependence between euthanasia and palliative care remains a unresolved question, not only in the Netherlands but also internationally: Is the commitment for palliative care shown by the Dutch government the oblique reaction to the criticism on the euthanasia act from abroad? Is there no need for a euthanasia act if a good provision with palliative care is provided?

In future quality specification – developed by the cancer centres – have to be met by networks and consulting teams. Three *Centres of Excellence in Palliative Care* are developed in academic medical centres in Amsterdam, Nijmegen und Rotterdam. One of the main objectives is to link the departments involved, to install a palliative care programme in medical curricula and to integrate research, care and education in palliative care. [119] These institutions are one of the reasons why Dutch experts are optimistic about the future development of palliative care in their country.

Sources and literature

Barthold, Stefanie: Das Gesundheitssystem der Niederlande – Ein Vorbild für Deutschland? Unpublished paper, Europa-Universität Viadrina. Frankfurt/Oder 2004.

Communication Department of the Ministry of Social Affairs and Employment and The Public Relations Department of the Ministry of Health, Welfare and Culture: A short survey of social security in the Netherlands. Half-yearly summary January 2004. The Hague 2004.

COPZ Evaluation Committee. 2001 Annual Report. Utrecht: COPZ Evaluation Committee, 29 March 2002.

Have, Henk ten/ Janssens, Rien (Ed.): Palliative Care in Europe. Amsterdam 2001.

Korte-Verhoef, Ria de: Developments in palliative care services in the Netherlands. In: European Journal of Palliative Care, 2004; 11 (1).

Ministry of Health, Welfare and Sport in the Netherlands: Palliative care for terminally ill patients in the Netherlands. Dutch Government Policy. The Hague 2003.

Ministry of Health, Welfare and Sport and the Ministry of Justice in the Netherlands: Euthanasia. The Netherland's new rules. Den Haag 2002.

Regionale toetsingscommissies euthanasie (Ed.): Jaarverslag 2001. Arnhem 2002.

Regionale toetsingscommissies euthanasie (Ed.): Jaarverslag 2002. Arnhem 2003.

Regionale toetsingscommissies euthanasie (Ed.): Jaarverslag 2003. Arnhem 2004.

Internet sources

Dutch Foreign Ministry: http://www.minbuza.nl/

National Information Centre for Palliative Care: http://www.palliatief.nl/nationaal/

[119] Interview with Dr. Wim Jansen, 09 March 2004, in Amsterdam.

The National Public Health Compass: http://www.rivm.nl/vtv/data/site_kompas/index.htm
Population Division of the Department of Economic and Social Affairs of the United Nations Secretariat, World Population Prospects: The 2002 Revision Population Database: http://esa.un.org/unpp
Statistics Netherlands: http://www.cbs.nl

List of interviews (in chronological order)

- Prof. Dr. Henk Jochemsen, Director of the *Lindeboom Institute for Medical Ethics* and *Lindeboom Chair for Medical Ethics* in Amsterdam. Amsterdam, 01 March 2004
- Drs. Cilia Galesloot, Leader of palliative care section (Sector palliatieve zorg) at *Integraal Kankercentrum Oost* Nijmegen, 03 March 2004
- Jan Ruyten, Vice president *VHN*, Drs. Boi Jongejan, Director at *Integraal Kankercentrum West* and Quality Assurance Representative of the *VHN*, Ingrid H. Versteeg, Coordinator of Education at *VHN* Woerden, 04 March 2004
- Drs. Ria de Korte-Verhoef, Secretary at the *Review Committee for Centres for development of Palliative Care (COPZs)* Utrecht, 05 March 2004
- Corry van Tol-Verhagen, Director at *Hospice Kuria* and *Foundation Kuria*, Jaap Gootjes, Care manager at *Hospice Kuria*, coordinator *Network Palliative Care in Amsterdam*, 09 March 2004
- Drs. André Rhebergen, Director National Information Centre for Palliative Care *AGORA*, Amsterdam, 09 March 2004
- Drs. Wim Jansen, Coordinator *Network Palliative Care in Amsterdam*, coordinator National Information Centre for Palliative Care, *AGORA*, Board member *Helpdesk Amsterdam*, Editor of the *Dutch Journal of Palliative Care* Amsterdam, 09 March 2004
- Drs. Frans Baar, Director at the nursing home *Antonius-IJsselmonde*, Rotterdam, 10 March 2004
- Drs. Marlies van de Watering, Doctor at *Hospice Bardo* Hoofddorp, 10 March 2004

Norway

Felix Schumann

1. General conditions

1.1 Demographics

- In 2004, the total population of Norway was 4,5 million. The annual growth is 0.57 percent.[1] According to predictions, the population will drop to 5.4 million inhabitants by 2050.[2] Similar to other European countries, Norway is experiencing a period of low birth rates, which nevertheless are higher than in other Scandinavian countries.[3]
- The average life expectancy of 79.3 is expected to grow to 84.9 years of age by 2050, whereas the median age will rise significantly from 37.0 years in 2000 to 43.8 by 2050.[4]
- In 1950, people 65 years or older in Norway represented 9.7% of the population. In 2000, it was already 15.3% and is projected to grow to 24.3% by 2050.[5]
- People aged 80 years or older constituted only 1.7% of the population in 1950. That percentage grew in 2000 to 4.4 and is estimated to grow to 9.5 by 2050.[6]
- In contrast, the number of people aged 15 to 59 years per older person over the age of 60, was 60.5% of the total population in 2000 and is expected to drop to 53.7% by 2050.[7]
- In 2000, more than 44.000 people died in Norway.[8] The most frequent death causes were cancer (10.400) and cardiovascular diseases (18.191). Approximately 15 percent of the patients died at home, 40 percent in hospitals and 40 percent in nursing

1 Norway. Embassy and Consulate General. The official site in the UK http://www.norway.org.uk/

2 Population Division of the Department of Economic and Social Affairs of the United Nations Secretariat, *World Population Prospects: The 2004 Revision* and *World Urbanization Prospects: The 2003 Revision*. Official Homepage of the United Nations: http://esa.un.org/unpp

3 Norway. Embassy and Consulate General. The official site in the UK http://www.norway.org.uk/; European Observatory on Health Carc Systems: Health Care Systems in Transition. Copenhagen 2000, p. 12.

4 ibid.

5 ibid.

6 ibid.

7 ibid.

8 Statistics Norway: http://www.ssb.no

homes.[9] 55 percent of the cancer patients died in a hospital, 31 percent in nursing homes and 11 percent at home.[10] On the contrary, 66 percent of the cancer patients expressed the wish to spend the last days at home.

1.2 Health care system

Norway is a welfare state and one of the richest countries in the world. "The most important feature of the Norwegian health care system is the predominance of tax-financed public provision. The whole resident population of Norway is covered for needs and the financial burden of using health care services. As there is no premium-based financing, there is only a small connection (limited to out-of-pocket payments) between individual health risks and costs. Thus, the health care system is financed through taxation and out-of-pocket payments."[11]

The health care system is organised on the three tiers: state, counties and municipalities. The state has the responsibility for a few very specialized hospitals, for university education and research, for health and other registries, and for institutions like the National Institute of Public Health, the National Board of Health and the Ministry of Health. Amongst other areas, the 19 counties are responsible for hospitals and specialized outpatient care, whereas the 435 municipalities cover the domain of primary health care and of the elderly.[12] In 1974 the country was divided into five health regions, each with a regional teaching hospital. To facilitate planning and cooperation, regional health committees were established in each region.[13]

All residents of Norway or people working in the country are insured under the *National Insurance Scheme (NIS)*. "Persons insured under the *NIS* are entitled to the following benefits: elderly, survivors and disability, basic care in case of disablement, rehabilitation, occupational injury, single parents, monetary reimbursement in case of sickness, maternity, adoption and unemployment, health care, and funeral expenses. Disability benefits comprise of basic benefits, care benefits and disability pensions.[14]" The NIS is financed by contributions from employees, the self-employed and other members, employers' contributions and state funding.[15] Health insurance contributions are based on a certain percentage of gross income, employees pay 7.8 percent, self-employed up to a maximum of 10.7 percent. The employer's contribution is14.1 percent. Taxes are charged by the 19 counties and 435 municipalities.[16]

---

9 Interview with Dr Dagny Faksvåg Haugen, 25 March 2004, in Bergen.

10 ibid.

11 Norway. Embassy and Consulate General. The official site in the UK: http://www.norway.org.uk/

12 European Observatory on Health Care Systems: Health Care Systems in Transition. Copenhagen 2000, p. 7.

13 ibid., p. 12.

14 ibid., p. 21et seq.

15 ibid.

16 Julia Bathelt: Das norwegische Gesundheitssystem. Öffentliche und steuerfinanzierte Versorgung mit hoher Eigenbeteiligung der Patienten – Folge 4 der Reihe "EU-Gesundheitssysteme" der Ärztekammer Nordrhein. 2003. Published at: http://www.aekno.de/htmljava/i/themenmeldung.asp?id=403\&jahr=2003

At the end of 1999 approximately 1.1 million people were mainly relying on social insurance, including 900.000 pensioners. In the same year, social insurances made 13.6 percent of the total GDP, that is 34.3 percent of the national budget. [17]

The number of hospitals beds per capita is only half as high as in most European countries but at the same time there are twice as many beds in nursing homes. The number of nursing staff per patient in hospitals and nursing homes is also twice as high compared to other Neighbouring countries. Nevertheless health care expenditures are not higher than in most other countries. [18]

The public awareness of social justice is characteristic for Norway. The national debate on the key aspects of the health care system show that the care for chronically, psychic and seriously ill, and dying patients, are top priorities. [19]

2. Hospice and palliative care in Norway

2.1 History

As in many other countries, the development of palliative medicine in Norway was influenced by the "hospice care philosophy", which developed in the UK from the mid sixties. [20]

The hospice movement in Norway was introduced by the Franciscans in Oslo. The home care programme *Fransiskushjelpen* started in 1977 and is still operating today. [21] It offers hospice care for the dying at home and bereavement support for the bereaved.

In Norway, the development of consulting groups for non-specialised palliative care was established already in the early eighties of the last century. These groups were found in hospitals and are regarded to be the start of palliative care in Norway. However, these groups worked as consultants without direct patient contact. Interdisciplinary pain groups were developed at the same time, and in some hospitals (Bergen), these groups were considered as being highly influenced by the hospice philosophy. [22] In 1984 an a initiative was created on the topic care for "the seriously ill and dying". This had an important impact on the interest of healthcare personnel in the care for the dying. [23]

The first multidisciplinary pain clinic, with a palliative care support team, was opened at the *University Hospital of Bergen* in 1983. Their main task was the treatment

---

17 Norway. Embassy and Consulate General. The official site in the UK: http://www.norway.org.uk/

18 Personal correspondence with Dr Bettina Sandgathe Husebø.

19 ibid.

20 Stein Kaasa: Development of palliative medicine in Norway and the other Scandinavian countries. Lecture at the DGP-congress, 28.09.2000. Stuttgart 2000.

21 Nils Mageroy: Palliative Care in Norway. Document published at: http://www.hospicecare.com/Newsletters/march2000/page3.html

22 Stein Kaasa: Development of palliative medicine in Norway and the other Scandinavian countries. Lecture at the DGP-congress, 28.09.2000. Stuttgart 2000.

23 Nils Mageroy: Palliative Care in Norway. Document published at: http://www.hospicecare.com/Newsletters/march2000/page3.ht

of chronic pain and to provide palliative care for seriously ill and the dying in the hospital as well as in their homes. For the first five years the funding of the hospital was ensured by the Norwegian Cancer Society.

The clinic, as the early days of pain therapy and palliative care in Norway, are particularly associated with Stein Husebø, who was one of the first physicians in the country, who supported and campaigned for the needs of the dying.

Since 1985, a three-day seminar for medical students is held at *University Hospital of Bergen* Palliative medicine is one of the main subjects. [24]

In 1988 the first Scandinavian Congress for Palliative Care with more than 1.100 participants was staged in Bergen, followed by a series of conferences in the Scandinavian countries. [25]

The first multidisciplinary palliative care department was founded in Trondheim in 1991/1992, followed by the introduction of the first *Norwegian Chair for Palliative Medicine* in Trondheim a year later. [26] In 1994 *Hospice Lovisenberg* opened in Oslo.

The past ten year have brought great changes for palliative care in conjunction with the involvement of Norwegian politics. A first report by the Norwegian government on palliative care was released in 1984, followed by a second report in 1999.

The first report recommended the following steps: [27]

- Establishment of a *Chair for Palliative Medicine* linked to a hospital
- Integration of Palliative Care into the public health care system
- Stimulation of voluntary commitment

The second set the following goals: [28]

- At the community level, palliative care must be available for all patients
- Beds for palliative care must be situated in the nursing homes
- Palliative medicine units must be established at community hospitals, including a consulting team
- Departments of palliative medicine must be established at all university hospitals, including chairs in palliative medicine and a research program

To realise the reports recommendations, as part of the *Norwegian National Cancer Plan* (1999 - 2003), five regional centres of excellence for palliative care were established, one in each of Norway's five health care regions.

The tasks of the five centres are: research, coordination, support and development of palliative care services. The centre follows a multidisciplinary approach and supports the local palliative care services. [29]

---

24 Personal correspondence with Dr Bettina Sandgathe Husebø.

25 ibid.

26 Interview with Prof Stein Kaasa, 23 March 2004, in Trondheim.

27 ibid. The first report was published as document NOU 1984, p. 30.

28 Stein Kaasa: Development of palliative medicine in Norway and the other Scandinavian countries. Lecture at the DGP-congress, 28.09.2000. Stuttgart 2000. The second report was published as document NOU 1999, p. 2.

29 Regional Centre of Excellence for Palliative Care, Western Norway, Haukeland University Hospital, Bergen, Norway: Presentation of the Network Model for the Regional Centre of Excellence for Palliative Care, Western Norway. Unpublished document.

In addition it was decided to set up palliative care units at the Norwegian University hospitals in Trondheim, Bergen, Oslo and Tromsø. Against the background of the current high public awareness for palliative care [30], further developments can be expected in the near future.

2.2 Hospice and palliative care services

The provision of palliative care in Norway is structured as follows: *Centres of Excellence for Palliative Care* have been set up in the five *Health Regions* of the country. The *Centres of Excellence* are situated in hospitals and thus operating at a county level. They run research and training centres, and coordinate a network of professionals in the region. The staff members work in hospitals, nursing homes and in primary health care. From an administrative point of view, they work at both municipality level (nursing homes and primary health care) and at county level (hospital). Thus palliative care is being provided in most regions and on the different levels of the health care systems. In 2004, there are around 190 palliative care beds, 60 of those in hospitals, and 130 in nursing homes. [31] Today there are two Norwegian hospices, located in Bergen and Oslo. In general it is expected that the number of hospice and palliative care services in nursing homes and hospitals will increase. To deliver insight into the practice of palliative care services in Norway, the *Centre of Excellence for Palliative Care* in the region of Western Norway will be pictured in the following.

The *Health Region* Western Norway has its centre in Bergen and covers 0,9 million people. Approximately 2100 cancer patients die each year in this region. The *Centre of Excellence for Palliative Care* exists since 2001. It consists of a training and research unit at the *University Hospital of Bergen*, which is linked with a multidisciplinary network in the *Health Region* close to Bergen. This network includes five physicians, nine nurses, two physiotherapists, one chaplain and one social worker. [32] Staff members have been working in palliative care services in hospitals or in the primary health care sector before they start their work in the centre. For each staff member one day of the week is reserved for research, teaching, consultation services or development work for palliative care in the region.

So far three nursing homes in the region, and one 5-bedded unit in the local hospital (*Sunniva Hospice* at *HaraldsplassDiakonie-hospital)* in Bergen, belong to the network. In 2003 it was decided to establish palliative care units in all four major hospitals in the region. [33]

---

30 Interview with Dr Dagny Faksvåg Haugen, 25 March 2004, in Bergen.

31 Personal correspondence with Dr. Dagny Faksvåg Haugen.

32 Regional Centre of Excellence for Palliative Care, Western Norway, Haukeland University Hospital, Bergen, Norway: Presentation of the Network Model for the Regional Centre of Excellence for Palliative Care, Western Norway. Unpublished document.

33 Interview with Dr Dagny Faksvåg Haugen, 25 March 2004, in Bergen.

The members of the network:[34]

- give advice to health care professionals, in hospitals, nursing homes, and primary care
- arrange courses and other teaching sessions
- prepare guidelines and information material
- aid local hospitals and communities in planning and establishing palliative care services: multidisciplinary pain teams, palliative care teams, palliative beds or units
- work to establish better routines for patient referral and communication between hospitals and primary care
- work in cooperation with hospitals, primary care professionals, educational institutions, the *Norwegian Cancer Society*, and other non-profit organisations

The centre carries out a number of research projects. Amongst other aspects, they focus on medication, physiotherapy, symptom assessment and initiate comparative studies involving different regions. The organisational structure of the centres allows for access to hospitals and primary health care services in the region.

The four other *Centres of Excellence for Palliative Care* are located in Trondheim (*Health Region* Central Norway), Oslo (*Health Regions* Eastern and Southern Norway) and Tromsø (*Health Region* Northern Norway).

The Norwegian Society for Palliative Medicine (*Norsk forening for palliativ medisin)* was called on by a committee of the *Norwegian Medical Association* to develop a standard for palliative care. The aims were to ensure an adequate organisation of the services, as well as to ensure the necessary quality of the clinical work in palliative care by defining minimum requirements for the medical contents and competence.[35] The standard for palliative care is based on the recommendations of two national reports, *Norwegian Cancer Plan* from 1997 and *Plan for the Care of Incurably Ill and Dying Patients* from 1999 (NOU 1999: 2). It includes the following points and areas:[36]

- definitions of palliative care
- basic palliative care is described
- organisation of palliative care services on all levels:
  - five regional university hospitals are all to have a regional palliative care centre, consisting of a clinical palliative medicine unit and a regional centre of excellence for palliative care
  - Other hospitals shall have a palliative care centre with a multidisciplinary team and, in most cases, a palliative care inpatient unit
  - The family doctor is responsible for the patient in the home
  - Patients in home care need access to palliative care units in nursing homes.

---

34 Regional Centre of Excellence for Palliative Care, Western Norway, Haukeland University Hospital, Bergen, Norway: Presentation of the Network Model for the Regional Centre of Excellence for Palliative Care, Western Norway. Unpublished document.

35 Dr. Dagny Faksvåg Haugen/ Task force group of the Norwegian Association for Palliative Medicine: Norwegian Standard for Palliative Care. Unpublished document. 2004.

36 ibid.

- Cooperation between the different levels of the health care system, network of palliative care or cancer nurses in hospitals and in primary care
- chapters on education/competence and research
- Quality indicators to monitor the effects of the recommendations given.

The introduction of the Norwegian Standard for Palliative Care is expected in autumn 2004.

2.3 Legal regulations and funding

Palliative Care is part of the public health care system and thus to a great extent covered by the Norwegian Social Insurance Fund *NIS*. The institutions, where palliative care is practised – hospitals (1)and services of the primary sector (2) – are funded within the public health care system. [37]

1. As mentioned before, hospitals operate at a county level. Treatment is free of charge. [38]
2. Institutions of the medical primary care are funded by the Norwegian municipalities. In the palliative care sector these include: [39]
   a) General practitioners: A co-payment of 15 €per home visit by the doctor is required by the patient. For medication the co-payment share is 36 percent, but no more than 30 €. Drugs, that are used for the treatment of chronically ill, for children, for cancer patients and in palliative medicine, are completely covered by the social insurance. In general, the rule applies, that all medical treatments exceeding a co-payment of 200 €, are free of charge. [40]
   b) Home care nursing services: Approximately half of the occurring costs in medical primary care are covered by local taxes, around 15 percent through cost sharing amounts, and 35 percent through state subsidies. Most of the municipalities (80%) now provide services 24 hours a day. [41] For home care service, patients pay a low co-payment depending on their income.
   c) Nursing homes: The financing of nursing homes happens in a similar way to the funding of home care. If someone stays in a nursing home for only a short time, he or she has to pay about 20 €per day. In case of a longer stay, 75 percent of the pension is retained. The personal property remains untouched. [42]

---

37 Interview with Dr Dagny Faksvåg Haugen, 25 March 2004, in Bergen.

38 Julia Bathelt: Das norwegische Gesundheitssystem. Öffentliche und steuerfinanzierte Versorgung mit hoher Eigenbeteiligung der Patienten – Folge 4 der Reihe "EU-Gesundheitssysteme" der Ärztekammer Nordrhein. 2003. Published at: http://www.aekno.de/htmljava/i/themenmeldung.asp?id=403\&jahr=2003

39 ibid.

40 ibid.

41 European Observatory on Health Care Systems: Health Care Systems in Transition. Copenhagen 2000, p. 55.

42 Personal correspondence with Dr Bettina Sandgathe Husebø.

2.4 Organisations

Council for Care in the final stages of life

On an initiative by Stein Husebø and others, the *Norwegian Cancer Society* set up a *Council for Care in the final stages of life* in 1984. Since then the council organises annual nationwide conferences on palliative care, attracting more than 500 participants in average. The *Norwegian Cancer Society* supports the council with about 100.000 €each year.

In the beginning, the journal OMSORG appeared as an information brochure of the council. Now it is issued four times a year as the *Scandinavian Journal for Palliative Care.* More than 4.000 subscribers underline the major impact of the journal on the development of palliative care in Scandinavia. In 2000, the council was replaced by the Norwegian Umbrella organisation *Norsk Palliativ Forening.* [43]

Norsk Palliativ Forening

Since 2000, the Norwegian Umbrella organisation *Norsk Palliativ Forening* represents the interests of all professionals, and the various professions involved in palliative care.

Norsk forening for palliativ medisin (NFPM)

The *Norwegian Association for Palliative Medicine* is part of the umbrella organisation. It is responsible for the *Norwegian Standard for Palliative Care* (see 2.2) and one of the organisers of the *Nordic Specialist Course in Palliative Medicine* (see 2.5).

2.5 Education and training of professionals

On a regular basis the five *Centres of Excellence for Palliative Care* offer advanced training courses in hospitals, nursing homes, universities and other institutions. For example, the centre in Bergen hosted 260 different courses in 2003, with 6500 participants with medical or nursing background. [44] Pain therapy, symptom control, communication and spiritual care are among the topics dealt with in the courses.

Norwegian General Practitioners are expected to take part in a 7 day course in pain therapy and palliative medicine every five years. [45] However medical curricula vary from university to university. Every semester courses in palliative care are held at the palliative centre in Trondheim, which is linked with *St. Olav University Hospital.* Students often write seminar papers on palliative care topics [46] The same palliative centre offers so called tele-medical teaching units. Members of local nursing homes

---

43 ibid.

44 Interview with Dr Dagny Faksvåg Haugen, 25 March 2004, in Bergen.

45 Hans-Peter Bischof/ Katharina Heimerl/ Andreas Heller (Eds.): "Für alle, die es brauchen". Integrierte Palliative Versorgung – das Vorarlberger Modell. Freiburg im Breisgau 2002, p. 131.

46 Interview with Prof Stein Kaasa, 23 March 2004, in Trondheim.

and hospitals can access the sessions via video stream. In total, a number of 15 - 20 courses are given annually, which address physicians and nurses.[47]

There is one peculiarity in the medical education that needs to be pointed out:[48]

The *Nordic Specialist Course* is a joint venture between the associations for palliative medicine in the Nordic countries (Denmark, Finland, Iceland, Norway, Sweden). Facing the situation that new palliative care units and programmes might be established without the appropriate medical staffing, the course is a response to the urgent need to educate doctors in the Nordic countries in palliative medicine at a specialist level. It is a theoretical specialist training course in 6 modules over 2 years. The first course was staged in 2003 - 2004 with 29 participants, six of those from Norway. The course is set to elevate the competence in palliative medicine amongst the Nordic countries, and is regarded as a milestone towards the establishment of palliative medicine as a medical specialty in the Nordic countries.[49] The authorities of the Nordic course group decided to use the British Curriculum in Palliative Medicine, level C, as the basis for the course content. Attention has also been paid to the EAPC Curriculum and the Swedish Curriculum.

The *Norsk forening for palliativ medisin,* on of the organisers of the *Nordic Specialist Course*, provides regular courses in palliative medicine for physicians.

2.6 Volunteers

Volunteers work in different palliative care institutions: hospitals, nursing homes and in home care services.[50] There are currently no statistics providing an insight into the number of volunteers working in palliative care nationwide. With the exception of the *Red Cross*, there is generally no common tradition of voluntary work in Norway.[51] However in the region of Bergen a number of around 200 volunteers support palliative care services.[52] At the *Sunniva Hospice* in Bergen, about 30 volunteers commit their free time,[53] whereas in *Røde Kors Sykehjem Bergen* more than 80 volunteers are active.[54]

---

47 ibid.

48 Nordic Specialist Course in Palliative Medicine 2005 - 2006. General information. Course content. Ap plication procedure. Unpublished document.

49 Interview with Dr Dagny Faksvåg Haugen, 25 March 2004, in Bergen.

50 ibid.

51 Personal correspondence with Dr Bettina Sandgathe Husebø.

52 Interview with Dr Dagny Faksvåg Haugen, 25 March 2004, in Bergen.

53 Personal correspondence with Dr. Dagny Faksvåg Haugen.

54 Personal correspondence with Dr Bettina Sandgathe Husebø.

2.7 Examples

Palliative Centre at Trondheim St. Olav University Hospital

The palliative centre in Trondheim is one of the most comprehensive ones of its kind in Scandinavia.[55] It is situated inside *St. Olav University Hospital* and incorporates research, education and clinical practice. The *Centre of Excellence for Palliative Care* of the *Health Region* Central Norway is also located in the hospital. Authorities of *Health Region* Central Norway have set the target to establish around 15 palliative care units in nursing homes.[56]

The palliative care unit contains 12 beds, 95 percent of the patients are suffering from cancer. In.2003, 307 patients have been cared for on the unit. That year about 100 people died on the unit. The average length of stay is between 11 an 12 days.[57]

In addition, consulting services are provided for other units within the hospital, 12 palliative care beds in a nursing home in Trondheim and patients are also cared for at home.

The multidisciplinary team consists of five physicians, 30 nurses, one physiotherapist, one chaplain, a social worker and a dietician.

On a regular scale the centre offers advanced training for medical and nursing staff and runs an extensive research programme.

Red Cross nursing home in Bergen (Bergen Røde Kors Sykehjem)

Bergen Røde Kors Sykehjem is the biggest private nursing home in Norway. The building is situated alongside one of the numerous, winding streets, which lead from the picturesque city centre into the mountainous parts of Bergen. The nursing homes provides space for 208 beds where people with complex diseases are cared for. The institution contains nine departments of which seven are long-term care units. Every department has about 17 - 27 patients. Two units are designed for the needs of people suffering from dementia.[58] A short term unit for 22 rehabilitation patients and a day care centre for 45 people complete the broad services on offer.

The nursing home is a private institution which receives financial support from the municipality of Bergen. 230 posts are shared by 450 staff members. The multidisciplinary team includes nurses, physicians, physiotherapists, occupational therapists, chaplains, psychologists, musical therapists and more than 80 volunteers. The average age of patients on the seven long term care units is 88 years. On average these patients have six to seven acute diagnoses.

Under the guidance of the *physician SteinHusebø*the*National Project Palliative Care for the Elderly was started at the Red Cross* nursing home in Bergen back in 1998. The basic idea of the project was to provide palliative care for all seriously ill

---

55 Interview with Prof Stein Kaasa, 23 March 2004, in Trondheim.

56 ibid.

57 ibid.

58 Homepage Røde Kors Sykehjem: http://www.hospice.no/index.de.shtml

and dying patients, regardless of their age, diagnosis or where they live and not just for younger, seriously ill cancer patients. The project was funded by the *Norwegian Health Ministry* and the*Norwegian Red Cross*. It was limited to five years (1998-2003) and is continued locally and internationally as a European project. [59]

As the first nursing home in Norway *Bergen Røde Kors Sykehjem* opened a palliative department in June 2000 providing care for 8 beds. This initiated a debate on palliative care for elderly and people in need of high-maintenance care in Norway. About 130 patients are cared for each year. 98 percent of the patients are cancer patients and 75 percent are admitted directly from hospitals. The average length of stay is 19 days. The department is set to be expanded by a six-bedded long-term hospice unit to provide care for people who cannot go home. The aim is to ensure that all patients are treated in line with the hospice philosophy. Every year approximately 150 patients die in the nursing home, which means about 3 - 4 dying patients each. For more than 95 percent of the patients will eventually die in the nursing home. [60]

The focus on palliative care is speciality of the nursing home. So far the hospice philosophy and palliative care were mainly aimed at seriously ill cancer patients and their relatives. Against the background of experiences made by staff members in the nursing home that older dying patients are often overlooked, whereas in contrast dying cancer patients receive more nursing and medical care, *Røde Kors Sykehjem Bergen* pushes for more social and medical equity in order to ensure all patient groups in need of palliative care are considered. Speaking on the importance of cancer patients and the elderly in palliative care, Dame Cicely Saunders noted at a conference in Bergen in 1999: "I deliberately addressed the provision of tumour patients. I knew that I wouldn't be able to solve the misery of our old elderly citizens. That problem was to big for me." [61]

To work in a nursing home as a physician is less prestigious than in hospitals. Doctors working there earn less than in their colleagues in hospitals. In many areas in Norway nursing homes take over tasks of hospitals despite being restricted in their resources regarding staff and special training. [62] Since 2003 the interests of Care Home Medicine in the research department of the university of Bergen have been financially supported by the *Kavli* Research Centre for Dementia and a government grant. [63]

Currently four German doctors and one Norwegian physician are employed at *Røde Kors Sykehjem*. This is due to the fact that vacant posts are advertised in Norway and Germany. German physicians regard the work in Norway as very attractive and are familiar with it through numerous training courses and lectures given by Stein and Bettina Husebø in Germany. Bettina Sandgathe Husebø reports:

---

[59] Project: *Würde im Alter* at the IFF (Faculty for Interdisciplinary Further Education and Research) at the University of Klagenfurt, Austria, with connections to the Red Cross Care Home in Bergen.

[60] Homepage Røde Kors Sykehjem: http://www.hospice.no/index.de.shtml

[61] Bettina Sandgathe Husebø: Palliativmedizin in der Geriatrie. Lecture Symposium "Palliativmedizin – Verknüpfung von Körper und Geist", 26.-27. September 2003, in Bonn.

[62] ibid.

[63] Personal correspondence with Dr Bettina Sandgathe Husebø.

I'm working together with about the thirteenth German doctor in the past seven years, they are all very much interested in questions concerning palliative care and geriatrics – the link between the two is very exciting! At the same time the chance to combine research with clinical practice provides an incentive .[64]

The multi-professional, interdisciplinary team tries to deal with complex problems of patients in the best possible way. To ensure this, the multidisciplinary approach is strictly followed by the nursing home and being transformed into the daily work for some years now. For 15 years there have been great changes in the house, new care methods have been established, structures for patients and staff members were opened up and a constant multidisciplinary development took place. The focus is laid on the individuality of patients and on the competence and satisfaction of staff members. Bettina Sandgathe Husebø:

We have great influence on the life of the patient. We should not believe that we can provide *the* "good"death or *the* hospice death. The way someone lives, someone dies – the life quality and quality of death are very individual. We want to offer the patients and their relatives a comfortable place where competent pain therapy, symptom control and teamwork allow for good moments. Above all we must not forget those who have to provide this work: the staff. Competence, motivation and creativity have to developed anew every day. This requires strength.[65]

The old building of the *Red Cross* nursing home needs to be refurbished and is not on the same high level with the patient-orientated and generous architecture of the new nursing home that was recently established. The move into the nearby purpose built building is expected in 2004.

Hospice Lovisenberg in Oslo

Hospice Lovisenberg was set up in 1994 and is part of the *Diaconal Hospital Lovisenberg*, located in a quiet living area in Oslo. The hospital marks a historical milestone in the Norwegian care culture. Nurse Cathinka Guldberg, Norway's first professional nurse, founded the *Diaconal Hospital* in 1883. In turn she had been trained at *Kaiserswerther Diakonie* in Düsseldorf, founded by Theodor ad Friederike Fliedner in 1836. *Hospice Lovisenberg* appears to be a very friendly, homelike place that is placed in two buildings linked with one another.

The interdisciplinary team includes physicians, nurses, physiotherapists, a occupational therapist, a dietician, a music therapist and a chaplain. At the moment, two volunteers are working in the hospice.

Although the hospice and the *Diaconal Hospital* are privately run, the salaries are paid by the public health care system. The funding system of inpatient units, which also applies for hospices, is often not for the advantage of hospices and their patients: The more patients are admitted, the more money is distributed. This also means, the longer a patient stays in the hospice, the less money is paid. Therefore the regulation

64 Personal correspondence with Dr Bettina Sandgathe Husebø.
65 ibid.

applies that most patients, who are in a stable condition after the standard warranted 14-day stay, are released, either home or into a nursing home. In case the condition of the patient has either worsened or not improved, the patients remains in the hospice. The funding by the public health care system puts the patients under some considerable pressure. They may have to leave the hospice even though they do not want to. Thus the hospice management are forced into a ethical dilemma, which is intensified by long waiting lists for hospice beds.

From the point of view of staff members it would be desirable that patients can remain in the hospice without a time limit. [66] The average length of stay in the hospice is currently 15 days. [67]

> In general it would have been easier for us to call as a palliative care unit. Then we would have fitted into the pattern made up my politicians [...] Perhaps we should re-named ourselves but coming back to 'What's in a name': The name "hospice" is very important for us. [68]

The inpatient hospice has 12 beds. In 2001 a total number of 459 patients were admitted into the hospice. 161 of those patients died in the hospice. The day care clinic at *Hospice Lovisenberg* cared for 156 patients in the same year. In total there were 2321 visits. The day care clinic is funded separately to the inpatient hospice as money is provided for every single visit of patients. In average 12 to 15 patients come to the day care clinic each day. Most patients come from Oslo. [69]

Bereavement support is provided for relatives: two times a month, in total a maximum six times relatives are invited to the hospice where they can share experiences with others who have lost a family member or a friend. They can talk about their loss and also meet staff members of the hospice team.

The hospice regularly offers advanced training for nursing staff and physiotherapists. In the summer of 2004 *Hospice Lovisenberg* opened a "satellite hospice" in the city of Hamar, two hours north from Oslo. The hospice there is a day care clinic with 10 staff members. Beyond that there is a cooperation with the home care service *Fransiskushjelpen* as well as the palliative care unit and the*Centre of Excellence for Palliative Care* (*Health Region* Eastern Norway) at the close-by *Ullevål Hospital* in Oslo.

The popularity of the hospice has risen among the population, every month articles about the hospice can be found in Oslo newspapers. According to hospice staff, young people are also showing a rising interest to reflect on topics as dying and death, palliative care and hospice. [70]

---

66 Interview with Lisa Scheibert, Unui Vidvei and Dr Wlodek Sypula, 22 March 2004, in Oslo.

67 Interview with Sølvi Jørgensen, 22 March 2004, in Oslo.

68 ibid. The lecture ,What's in a name?' by Dame Cicely Saunders (Palliative Medicine 1987: p. 1; p. 57 - 61) deals with the specific meaning of the term hospice for the content and alignment of hospice work, the apparent modern heir of the Christian-Medieval hospices.

69 Interview with Lisa Scheibert, Unui Vidvei and Dr Wlodek Sypula, 22 March 2004, in Oslo.

70 ibid.

The Hospice Lovisenberg, Oslo

Dinner-room in the Hospice Lovisenberg

3. Summary

Palliative Care in Norway is found in different settings: in nursing homes, hospitals, home care and in two hospices. The funding of services is mainly provided by the public health care system. The main aim is to offer palliative care services all over the country. By the establishment of *Centres of Excellence for Palliative Care* at the

Room for family members in the Hospice Lovisenberg

University Hospitals in Oslo, Trondheim, Bergen and Tromsø Norway has made major steps to achieve this target. The five centres feature public support for palliative care services, regional network and a combined research and training centre. Their aim is also to achieve the provision with palliative care on a nationwide scale. Similar extensive programmes (network, research and training) are only to be found in the Netherlands. The broad education and training schemes are important building blocks for the access of palliative care in the whole health care system. One outcome of the education is that nursing staff in the whole of Norway are prepared to deal with death and dying of patients, and therefore are able to offer adequate support.

Schemes are developed by political authorities, that aim to establish palliative care primarily in nursing homes (on a municipality level) and in hospitals (on a county level). Experiences so far signal that nursing homes are appropriate places for end of life care. Further inpatient hospices, as*Hospice Lovisenberg*, will probably not develop but new services in existing hospice and palliative care settings. [71] A characteristic of palliative care in Norway is the focus on all patients, independent from their diagnosis, and on the elderly. Research projects and various publications have attracted interest by the media and imitated a public debate on elderly and sick citizens.

The *Nordic Specialist Course in Palliative Medicine* is an extraordinary joint venture between five countries and illustrates the ambition to establish palliative medicine as a medical speciality. Not only the cooperation of all Scandinavian countries but also the combination in form and content of British, Swedish and European curricula, is an example for a ongoing growing international network in palliative care.

Both the *Centres of Excellence for Palliative Care* and the*Norwegian Standard for Palliative Care* use the existing structure of the health care system to implement palliative into the public health care system. The *Norwegian Standard for Palliative Care* goes even further than previous guidelines and recommendations for palliative care on both international and national level. [72] It defines quality level and demands on quality for palliative care in Norway and gives detailed information on the development of palliative care services. The realisation of those standards in Norway seem to be possible as the population is comparatively low and the number of experts clear and therefore suitable for close cooperation. [73] It remains to be seen whether the introduction of palliative care standards will benefit the organisation and quality of palliative care. Last but not least the coordination of palliative care services, involving patient transfer between hospitals, home care and nursing homes, poses a big challenge. [74] Because of this, since 2004 public support was made available to facilitate communication and cooperation between municipal and state services. [75]

---

71 Interview with Sølvi Jørgensen, 22 March 2004, in Oslo; Interview with Prof Stein Kaasa, 23 March 2004, in Trondheim.

72 Interview with Dr Dagny Faksvåg Haugen, 25 March 2004, in Bergen.

73 ibid.

74 ibid.

75 Personal correspondence with Dr Bettina Sandgathe Husebø.

Sources and literature

Bischof, Hans-Peter/ Heimerl, Katharina/ Heller, Andreas (Hg.): "Für alle, die es brauchen". Integrierte Palliative Versorgung – das Vorarlberger Modell. Freiburg im Breisgau 2002.

European Observatory on Health Care Systems: Health Care Systems in Transition. Copenhagen 2000.

Faksvåg Haugen, Dagny/ Task force group of the Norwegian Association for Palliative Medicine: Norwegian Standard for Palliative Care. Unpublished Document. 2004.

Husebø, Bettina Sandgathe/ Husebø, Stein: Palliative care – also in geriatrics? Schmerz 2001; 15: p. 350 - 6.

Husebø, Bettina Sandgathe/ Husebø, Stein: De siste dager og timer. Medlex Norsk Helseinformasjon, p. 17 - 20. Oslo 2001.

Husebø, Bettina Sandgathe: Palliativmedizin in der Geriatrie. Vortrag auf dem Symposium "Palliativmedizin – Verknüpfung von Körper und Geist" from 26.-27.09.2003 in Bonn.

Husebø, Bettina Sandgathe/ Husebø, Stein/ Hysing-Dahl, Britt: Old and given up for dying? Palliative care in nursing homes. Illness, Loss and Crisis 2004; 1: p. 75 - 89.

Nordic Specialist Course in Palliative Medicine 2005 - 2006. General information. Course content. Application procedure. Unpublished document.

Regional Centre of Excellence for Palliative Care, Western Norway, Haukeland University Hospital, Bergen, Norway: Presentation of the Network Model for the Regional Centre of Excellence for Palliative Care, Western Norway. Unpublished document.

Internet sources

Bathelt, Julia: Das norwegische Gesundheitssystem. Öffentliche und steuerfinanzierte Versorgung mit hoher Eigenbeteiligung der Patienten – Folge 4 der Reihe "EU-Gesundheitssysteme" der Ärztekammer Nordrhein. 2003. Published at: http://www.aekno.de/htmljava/i/themenmeldung.asp?id=403&jahr=2003

Homepage Bergen Røde Kors Sykehjem: http://www.hospice.no/index.de.shtml

Kaasa, Stein: Development of palliative medicine in Norway and the other Scandinavian countries. Presentation at the DPG-Congress on 28.09.2000. Published at: http://www.thieme.de/abstracts/palliativmedizin/abstracts2000/daten/p1_3.html

Kaasa, Stein: A systematic approach to palliative care in a hospital and community setting: An interview with Stein Kaasa. In: Innovations in End-of-Life Care, 2001; 3 (4). Published at: http://www.edc.org/lastacts

Nils Mageroy: Palliative Care in Norway. Document published at: http://www.hospicecare.com/Newsletters/march2000/page3.ht

Norway. Embassy and Consulate General. The official site in the UK: http://www.norway.org.uk/

Population Division of the Department of Economic and Social Affairs of the United Nations Secretariat, World Population Prospects: The 2002 Revision Population Database: http://esa.un.org/unpp

Statistics Norway: http://www.ssb.no

List of interviews (in chronological order)

- Sølvi Jørgensen, Head, *Hospice Lovisenberg* in Oslo, 22 March 2004
- Lisa Scheibert, Nurse, *Hospice Lovisenberg* in Oslo, Unui Vidvei, Physiotherapist, *Hospice Lovisenberg* in Oslo and Dr Wlodek Sypula, Physician, *Hospice Lovisenberg* in Oslo, 22 March 2004
- Prof. Dr. Stein Kaasa, Professor for Palliative Medicine and Head of the Palliative Centre at *St. Olav University Hospital* in Trondheim, Head of the *Centre of Excellence for Palliative Care* in Trondheim (*Health Region* Central Norway), Head of the *European Association for Palliative Care* (EAPC), Trondheim, 23 March 2004
- Bente Kristiansen, Head nurse, Palliative care unit at Palliative Centre at *St. Olav University Hospital* in Trondheim, 23 March 2004
- Dr. Dagny Faksvåg Haugen, Head, *Centre of Excellence for Palliative Care* in Bergen (*Health Region* West Norway), Head of *Norsk forening for palliativ medisin*, Bergen, 25 March 2004
- Dr. Bettina Sandgathe Husebø, Head Physician, *Bergen Røde Kors Sykehjem,* Collaborator at the *Centre of Excellence for Palliative Care* in Bergen (*Health Region* West Norway), 26 March 2004

Poland [1]

Reimer Gronemeyer

1. General conditions

1.1 Demographics

- In 2000, the population of Poland totalled 38.6 million. According to predictions, the population will drop to 31.9 million inhabitants by 2050. [2]
- In the same time the average life expectancy of 74.3 is expected to grow to 80.5 years of age by 2050, whereas the median age will rise from 35.2 years in 2000 to 50.8 by 2050. [3]
- 1950, people 65 years or older in Poland constituted 5.2% of the population. In 2000, it was already 12.1% and is projected to grow to remarkable 29.8% by 2050. [4]
- Similarly, people aged 80 years or older constituted 0.7% of the population in 1950. That percentage grew in 2000 to 2.0 and is estimated to grow to 8.1 by 2050. [5]
- The number of people aged 15 to 59 years per older person over the age of 60, was 64.2% of the total population in 2000 and is expected to drop to 48.9% by 2050. [6]
- The annual mortality rate is expected to rise from 9.7 per 1000 inhabitants between 2000 - 2005 to 15.3 per 1000 inhabitants by 2045 - 2050. [7]
- 82.600 of the 385.000 people dying each year in Poland die of cancer patients. [8] In 2001 there were 223.7 cases of cancer per 100.000 inhabitants. On the whole there are about 435.000 cancer patients per year in Poland. The number of cancer infections continues to rise in Poland (in 1996 there were 110.000, in 2002 already 125.000.) The number of cancer patients suffering from pains amounts to 150.000

---

1 Translated by Larissa Budde.

2 Population Division of the Department of Economic and Social Affairs of the United Nations Secretariat, *World Population Prospects: The 2004 Revision* and *World Urbanization Prospects: The 2003 Revision*. Official Homepage of the United Nations: http://esa.un.org/unpp

3 ibid.

4 ibid.

5 ibid.

6 ibid

7 ibid.

8 Michael Wright/David Clark: The development of palliative care in Poznan, Poland, in: European Journal of Palliative Care. 2003/10, p. 26 - 29.

people in Poland.[9] Annually about 600 children in Poland die of cancer, 77 percent in hospitals.[10]

- More than 55 percent of the cancer patients in 2002 died in hospitals, 12 died in hospices, 30 percent died at home, cared for by hospice services and palliative care institutions.

1.2 Health Care System

The health insurance in Poland suffered a series of changes in the last few years which makes it impossible to say anything specific about it. Following the replacement of socialistic planned economy, a number of health insurance companies developed in Poland, but these were been abolished once again when a communistic party entered government. A national health fund (*Narodowy Fundusz Zdrowia*) was established – financed by compulsory contributions from wages and income – which guarantees treatment free of charges to all Polish citizens. There are long waiting lists, so in practice the desired treatment often can be received only by private additional payments. Expectations are that, sooner or later, private health insurances will be allowed once more.[11]

2. Hospice and palliative care in Poland

2.1 History[12]

In Poland both theory and practice of hospice services have been copied from English examples. Compared to other socialistic countries the hospice movement in Poland started early. In 1976 the initiative of Halina Bortnowska, editor of a Polish catholic weekly newspaper, developed into a ward for dying people in a hospital in Kraków. In 1978 Dame Cicely Saunders visited Kraków and supported the initiative. In 1980 a group calling itself "*Gesellschaft der Freunde der Kranken-Hospiz*", ("Society of the friends of hospices"), arose from the Solidarność movement. This organization continued the work by developing further hospice services (*Towarzystwo Przyjaciól Chorych Hospicjum*). The national-socialistic government did not welcome such institutions. The memory of that is still evident today: the *Lazarus-Hospice*, which arose from this initiative, is located in direct neighbourhood to a church dedicated to Fatima, which itself was built despite the bitter opposition of the government in Nowa Huta. The government wished to keep Nowa Huta a "church-free" place beside the old

---

[9] Interview with Anna Szczerbak, 11 August 2004, in Poznan. Cp. also http://www.oncology.am. poznan. pl/ecept

[10] http://www.hospicjum.waw.pl

[11] Interview with Michał Sobolewski, 13 August 2004, in Warszawa, also with Jolanta Stokłasa on 16 August 2004 in Kraków. Information on earlier development provides David Clark (http://eolc-observatory.net/global_analysis/poland_health_care.htm).

[12] comp. David Clark/Wright, Michael: Transitions in End of Life Care, Hospice and related developments in Eastern Europa and Central Asia. Buckingham 2003, p. 215 - 231.

Kraków.[13] The construction of the futuristically looking concrete church demanded casualties among the workers, who stood up in favour of building the church. Despite the governmental opposition in 1982 a day care unit was established, which was originally carried by volunteer workers alone. An information centre could be established in 1993, and in 1998 the *Lazarus-Hospiz* for the first time received patients on an inpatient basis.[14] For the current work of the Kraków Hospice see 2.7.

Before the unification of West and East Germany hospices and hospice services were founded in other regions of Poland as well. In 1984 a chaplain established an outpatient hospice service in Gdańsk, (*Hospicjum Pallotinum*). In 1987 a hospice service was founded in Poznań – consecutively in a number of other cities hospice services arose as well. Most of these services were kept up in an honorary capacity and run by doctors, nurses and volunteers. To visit the patient at home the private car – if there was one – was used. In Poland therefore palliative care started out as a religious and humanitarian civil movement. In the course of that Poznań developed into the Polish centre of palliative care – especially by the initiatives of Jacek Łuczak – and connects governmental and non-governmental organizations. Already in the early stages both an inpatient and a day care hospice were established there. The *Hospice Palium* turned into an important national and international location for the training in palliative care, yet training courses take place in Bydgoszcz, Gdansk, Katowice, Posnan and Warszawa as well.

Though during the 80s hospice services grew out of religious and civil engagement towards the end of the 80s the Polish Health Ministry started to support palliative care as well. Palliative care units, which were supposed to follow the example of the hospice services and be run by multi-disciplinary teams, were founded in Poznań (*Karol Marcinkowki University of Medical Sciences*) and in other regions. A simultaneous development of state-run palliative care units, pain therapy clinics etc. on the one hand and the development of non-governmental hospice services on the other hand followed: in 1992 the first independent hospice was founded in Elblag and at the same time a palliative care Unit was established in Bydgoszcz. The swift successive institution of hospices in Białystok, Toruń, Mysłowice and Łomza shows that civil and ecclesiastical engagement increased after the unification (in several cases former nursing schools were turned into hospices). At the same time the number of state-run palliative care units increased.

In 1991 the Health Ministry developed a provisional programme to define palliative care as a part of the national health policy. In 1993 the government supported

---

[13] Jerzy Drażkiewicz describes the development from the church-influenced phase to the Solidarność Phase up to the stage of the independent worldly community. Jerzy Drażkiewicz: W stronę człowieka umierajacego. O ruchu hospicjów w Polsce), University of Warszawa, Faculty for Sociology, Warszawa 1989.

[14] Interview with Jolanta Stokłosa, 16 August 2004 in Kraków, see also the annual report 2003 of the "Gesellschaft der Freunde der Kranken", Hospicjum św Łazara, Kraków. cp. also Janina Jujawska Tenner: The Beginnings of Hospice Care Under Communist Regime: The Cracow Experience. In: C. Saunders/R. Kastenbaum (Ed.): Hospice Care on the International Scene. New York 1997, p. 158 - 166.

palliative care in Poland for the first time with about 16 million Euros. The money was distributed among all provinces (Wojwodschaften). More than 80 such governmental palliative care services already existed in 1993.

The *National Council for Palliative Care/Hospice Care* was also founded in 1993, with Jacek Łuczak serving as its first director. In the year 2003 the council was dissolved to form a national council of experts and a number of national expert committees which are currently active. [15]

At present the palliative care in Poland is being developed with respect to the definitions issued by the *World Health Organization*. Guidelines on palliative care were created by the Ministry of Health by a team of 7 experts in palliative medicine. It follows the guidelines of the *World Health Organisation* of 2002. It is stated:

- that dying is to be regarded a natural process;
- that death is neither induced nor artificially delayed;
- that pains is eased;
- that patients and families receive psychological, spiritual and social support;
- that the values of patient and family are respected;
- that 24-hour care is guaranteed 7 days a week;
- that the care by multi-disciplinary teams is offered;
- that at least a part of the medical personnel is specialized in palliative care;
- that palliative care is free of charge for patient and family;
- that palliative care is rendered without regard to gender, race, age, nationality or religion.

These rules are widely accepted by governmental as well as private organizations. Nevertheless, it must be remembered to retain a clear distinction between state-run and non-governmental palliative services in Poland. Due to poor financial support the governmental units often tend to reduce their services to pain treatment; they are organized in palliative-medical hospital wards, in palliative outpatient units and home care services. The Health Ministry also recognises the need to guarantee an acceptable life-quality to dying people not only as regards medical concerns but also regarding psychological and spiritual aspects. Nevertheless a differentiated palliative support will be hard to find in the non-governmental sector, which in itself is strongly influenced by ecclesiastical orientations.

2.2 Hospice and palliative care services

Poland today has all customary services that have been developed for palliative care:

- inpatient hospices and palliative-medical units
- outpatient palliative-medical and home care services
- palliative-medical and palliative day care facilities
- palliative-medical and outpatient hospital services for pain therapy

---

[15] Quoted according to: Ministry of Health: The program of developing Palliative/Hospice Care in Poland, Warszawa 1998 and information by Krystyna de Walden-Gałusko.

- Lymphoedema clinics
- Support groups of nurses and doctors in hospitals
- Support groups of volunteers for poor patients

Including governmental and non-governmental institutions Poland currently has about 270 palliative care services. The number of beds in 110 inpatient facilities amounts to 1268. This includes purely palliative-medical institutions, which only provide pain therapy but no qualified palliative care. The Health Ministry therefore counts 803 proper beds for palliative care. There are 155 outpatient palliative care services (95 non-governmental, 60 state-run), 126 outpatient palliative-medical services and clinics for pain treatment (52 non-governmental, 74 state-run, 9 Lymphoedema-clinics, 12 day care units, 7 outpatient children hospices. [16]

A marked increase can be observed:
- In 1991 there were 83 institutions for palliative care in Poland;
- In 1992 there were 190;
- In 2001 there were 260 and
- in 2002 there were 270 institutions. [17]

The numbers are still changing since a number of smaller hospitals in Poland have been turned into hospices or are in the process of becoming hospices.

This does not yet meet the standards demanded by the WHO. The WHO suggests fifty hospice- or palliative-medical beds per million inhabitants. As Poland currently provides 803 such beds there is – if the suggestions of the WHO should be met – still a shortage of about 1200 beds. Also, according to reports in the Health Ministry, there are still too few doctors and nurses trained in palliative care. The offers of hospice- and palliative care are markedly concentrated in the cities, whereas in the country the opportunities for sick people are scarce. Especially in the province of Ślaskie – Katowice – the activities of non-governmental hospices and hospice services are markedly intense in the industrialized parts of the country.

It is mainly the non-governmental organizations that provide palliative care in Poland. The *National Forum on Hospice Movement* in Kraków lists the following numbers: [18]

In 2004 108 non-governmental hospices and hospice services offer spiritual and medical support for dying people in Poland. The greater part of these people suffers from cancer and have entered the final stage of their lives. The hospices and hospice services support the family as well – a kind of help which continues after the death of the patient. In Poland the following organizations are active:
- 63 organizations of laymen
- 45 church groups (17 of which are run by the Caritas).

These organizations offer:

[16] Interview with Michał Sobolewski, 13 August 2004, in Warszawa. Interview with Anna Szczerbak, 11 August 2004, in Poznań, comp. also http://www.hospiceinformation.info. The annual statistic book for Poland of the year 2003 gives different numbers – for example, for 2002 only 41 hospices are listed.

[17] Interview with Michał Sobolewski, 13 August 2004, in Warszawa.

[18] Reports handed over by Jolanta Stokłosa during the interview on 13 August 2004 in Kraków.

- 94 outpatient hospice services
- 31 inpatient hospices
- 12 day care units.

The foundation of an outpatient children hospice in Warszawa in 1994 must be mentioned, which was followed by similar institutions in Poznan, Lublin, Lódz and Myslowice.

Non-national hospices and Hospice-services in Poland

2.3 Legal regulations and funding

§ 19.5 of an act concerning the health care (issued on October 14th 1991) ensures the rights and the dignity of dying patients. In the same year a provisional act concerning the establishment of palliative care in Poland was released, which brought about the grant of financial support for palliative care in 1993. The Polish law on nursing has been restructured recently, so that churches, charity organisations and private institutions are allowed to open advice centres, hospitals and hospices. Institutions may form treaties with the health insurance companies, i.e. the *National Health Fund (Nationalen Gesundheits-Fonds)* to receive financial support. While a medical expert has to be the manager of such an institution the foundation may be initiated by laymen as well. 2003 saw the release of a new act on health care, § 39,1 of which demands the insurance of palliative care and sets down that the *National Health Fund* generally bears 60% of the costs for palliative care in non-governmental institutions. The remaining costs have to be raised by the institutions themselves. About sixty percent of the non-governmental institutions possess such treaties. According to the carriers there is a regional aberration of the refund for costs of 40 to 60%. The *Lazarus-Hospice* in Kraków (comp. 2.8) released the following figures:

- the governmental subsidy for the advice centres amounts to 27 Zloty per patient (about 7 €);
- home care by hospices is supported with 20 to 38 Zloty per day (this corresponds to 5 to 10 €);
- the subsidy for inpatient treatment amounts to 150 Zloty (this corresponds to 35 €).
- The actual cost for inpatient accommodation amounts to 250 Zloty (about 62 €).

According to press releases the *National Health Fund* intends to restrict the duration of palliative support to 90 days.[19] The Health Ministry spend

- 94 922 000 Zloty for palliative care in 1999ausgegeben (about 24 million €)
- 451 883 000Zloty in 2003 (about 113 million €)
- 473.679 000 Zloty in 2004 (about 114 million €).

In comparison: Whereas in Germany the cost of an inpatient stay in a hospice amounts to 260 €, in Poland it is 35 €. Home visits by a doctor cost 8 €, whereas in Great Britain 80 pounds have to be paid (approx. 115 €).

The non-governmental carriers try hard to raise their budget with the help of several fund-raising-activities and appeals for donations. For example the "*First Walk for Hospice*" was organised, as well as the sale of flowers on the street and collections of donations in supermarkets etc.

2.4 Organisations

ECEPT
Eastern and Central Europe Palliative Care Task Force
c/o Palium Hospice
Os.Rusa 25
61 - 245 Poznań

[19] Głos Pomorza on 29 September 2003.

Towarzystwo Przyjaciol Chorych Hospicjum
National Forum of the Polish Hospice movement Św. Łazarza Ul. Fatimska
17, 31 - 831 Kraków founded in 1981

The Polish government, especially the health Ministry, consults mainly the *Polish Society for Palliative Medicine*, led by their president Prof. Dr. Krystyna de Walden-Gałuszko, on matters concerning palliative care,

Polskie Towarzystwo Medycyny Paliatywnej, (Polish Society for Palliative Medicine)
founded in 2001
08 - 094 Bydgoszcz,
Roentgena 5

Polskie Towarzystwo Psychoonkologiczne (Polish Society for Psycho-Onkology)
founded in 1993
80 - 211 Gdańsk,
Dębinki 2

2.5 Education and training of professional staff

According to the Health Ministry in Warszawa eleven medical academies in Poland offer palliative-medical courses. Currently 70 doctors in Poland have received special training in palliative care, in 2004 a further 20 will finish their training.

The specialist courses on palliative medicine are organised in Bydgoszcz, Gdańsk, Katowice, Kraków, Poznań, Warszawa, Wrocław. The Palliative Care Resource and Training Centre in Poznań (managed by Professor Jacek Łukzak) offers courses for medical personnel – including participants from other East-European countries – with theoretical and practical orientation. The courses include: visits to palliative-medical patients, a lymphoedema-clinic, a clinic for pain treatment, a day care hospice etc. The courses are arranged in cooperation with the medical faculty of the *Karol Marcinkowski Universität* in Poznan, the *Polish Association of Palliative Care*, the *Eastern and Central European Task Force (ECEPT)*, which in turn is supported by the *OSI (Open Society Institute*, New York). The future financial support of these trainings remains insecure nevertheless.

The childrens hospice in Warszawa (see 2.7) arranges national and international classes on paediatric palliative care aimed at paediatricians and paediatric nurses specialized into cancer disease, as well as for employees of hospices and hospice services. Up to now 875 people have taken part in these courses, and hospice services for children have been founded in 36 regions of Poland. Additionally, the centre offers courses on paediatric palliative care with a duration of four weeks.

The *"Regionalny Zespól Opieki Paliatywnej – Dom Sue Ryder"* in Bydgoszcz hosts "Palliative Care Regional Education Programs". Krakow offers the best conditions in the training of volunteers, Gdansk is at the top regarding the training in psychological support for the families and medical employees. Gdańsk Medical University, together with the *Polish Association for Psycho-oncology*, organises courses twice a year ("Psychological care for terminally ill cancer patients and their families") for participants from all Polish hospices:

2.6 Volunteers

According to empirical research concerning volunteers in Polish hospices and hospice services M. Górecki states that 85 percent of the volunteers are women, of an average age of 51, mostly without familial duties. The greater part possesses higher education, and many are working – or have worked – in the medical sector. They are mostly "born volunteers" with a pronounced altruistic motivation, says Górecki. Still, nine out of ten find themselves faced with serious problems in supporting dying people. Many deplore the lack of coordination and necessary medicines, and complain of helplessness in the face of the suffering of the dying and the desperation of their families. Working in the hospice generates three main effects

- A reduction of the personal fear of death,
- A change in the value system with approaching death (material aspects lose impact),
- An increased tolerance of the convictions and behaviour of other people. [20]

Almost all non-governmental hospices and hospice services receive support from volunteers. The forum of the North Polish hospice movement states the overall number of volunteers of 2500. In 45 Polish non-governmental hospices and hospice services the care is completely handled by volunteers. [21]

Most hospices organise preparation-courses for the volunteer helpers. When no courses are available new honoraries first work with experienced volunteers.

In Poland the general conditions for the work of volunteers in charitable organizations are laid down in an act from April 2nd 2003. According to this volunteers are expected to present a certificate of hepatitis B vaccination, they do not receive wages and the hospice should provide their insurance. In governmental institutions voluntary work is not permitted for reasons of insurance. In Koszalin volunteers in hospice services receive a passport allowing them a discount on public transportation.

2.7 Examples

The institutions introduced in the following paragraph are characteristic of the current situation in Poland: On the one hand a hospice in Kraków mainly founded by a non-governmental initiative, on the other hand a palliative care Unit in Poznań, which is a mostly state-run institution. Furthermore, the struggles for survival of a small fringe hospice (Koszalin) are described, as well as an outpatient hospice service in Poznań,

[20] M. Górecki: Hospicjum w służbie umierajacym, w: T. Pilch, J. Lepalczyk (red.): Pedagogika społeczna Wyd. Akademickie "Zak", 2000.

[21] "Hospicja w Polsce", report, handed over by Jolanta Stokłasa on 13 August 2004 in Kraków.

an inpatient Caritas-hospice in Warschau and an outpatient children hospice, located in Warszawa as well.

Towarzystwo Przyjaciól Chorych Hospicjum/Lazarus-Hospice, Kraków[22]

("Society of the friends of hospices", *Lazarus-Hospice)*

The extensive pre-history of the *Lazarus-Hospice* in Kraków plays an important role for palliative care in Poland (see 2.1). Today the hospice's work consists of:

- Outpatient hospice services. In 2003 839 patients were treated on outpatient basis. An average of 148 patients was cared for simultaneously, usually for a duration of 44 days. The outpatient hospice service is carried by six part-time working doctors (which sums up to 3.5 full-time doctors). 7.5 jobs for nurses are offered and 32 volunteers work there.
- An inpatient hospice consisting of 30 beds, distributed amongst three departments. The rooms have three beds each, which can be moved to the terrace or into the garden. Relatives can stay at the hospice. In 2003 332 patients were cared for. The average duration of stay is 31 days. The hospice employs three part-time doctors (sums up to 2.5 full-time jobs), 25 nurses, one psychologist, on specialist for rehabilitation, 48 volunteers. Conditions on working for the inpatient hospice are: the social situation of the patients is difficult (for example people living on their own); home care is not possible – the patient is admitted for an unlimited duration; the symptoms of the illness are hard to control, or the family is unable to care for the patient on its own due to sickness or poverty. In this case the patient is admitted for limited duration.
- Day care
- Palliative-medical advice
- Support during mourning

The hospice of the *"Gesellschaft der Freunde der Kranken"* ("Society of the friends of hospices"), has 6500 members over the whole country as this hospice is one of the oldest in Poland and is connected with the history of resistance against the national-socialistic government before the re-unification. This completely honorary service is still carried by 120 *volunteers*, 30 of these performing administration and cleaning work while the remaining volunteers care for the patients. More than 400 volunteers additionally help with fund-raising-activities on a regular basis.

Patients with a life-expectancy of less than half a year are admitted, though recently more young and middle aged patients are turning up. Generally hospitals refer the patients to the hospice, often without the doctors informing the patients they are being admitted to a hospice and instead suggesting to them they are going on a course of treatment. Since the hospice's management on the other hand wishes the patients to be informed, a psychologist visits the hospital and talks to the patients. After that, a talk with the hospice's doctor is arranged, who gives information on the patient's illness: "We explain all that he wants to know" – several patients do not wish to address

22 Interview with Jolanta Stokłasa, 13 August 2004, in Kraków.

Lazarus-Hospice, Kraków

their illness, and that is respected as well. In the hospice a commission decides on the patient's admission. On occasion patients whose relatives want to go on holiday for two weeks or otherwise need a temporally restricted relief are admitted as well. The financial situation of the patients is irrelevant, and even patients not financed by the *National Health Fund* (as they do not have an insurance) are admitted. Occasional requests for euthanasia arise, though this desire generally abates with adequate pain therapy. The hospice rejects all forms of euthanasia. Though a priest visits the institution on a daily basis the patients do not have to be Catholics to be admitted. The patients die in their own rooms, though sometimes a partition is raised towards the end. Experience proves that it is a relief for the patients to see another patient die peacefully. In some cases the patients wish to die at home – this wish is always granted when possible. 20 out of 100 patients voice this desire. The relatives have the opportunity to sleep overnight in the hospice and may visit around the clock.

Hospice Palium, Poznań[23]

One example for a rather palliative-medically oriented initiative is *Hospice Palium* in Poznań, working closely with governmental units. This version is closely linked

[23] Interview with Aleksandra Kotlińska-Lemieszek and Anna Szczerbak, 11. August 2004, in Poznań.

with the name of Jacek Łukcak. Łukcak, a medical professor, founded one of the first palliative care units in 1989 as part of the oncology ward of a hospital. Up to then palliative care lay almost exclusively in the hands of Catholic hospice initiatives. Today the *Hospiz Palium* offers a large building provided by the government. This former part of a hospital located nearby has been renovated with the help of donations. The hospice offers several services:

- The inpatient hospice has 15 beds, and at the end of 2004 a further 9 beds will be added. The *National Health Fund* supports the hospice *Palium* with 145 Zloty (about 36 €) per day and patient. The duration of stay amounts to 5 - 7 days. Some patients are released to their homes after successful pain therapy. Other patients stay up to six months – for example when they do not have any relatives. The patients do not have to pay anything. Two other palliative care units exist in Poznań as well, integrated into hospitals.
- Outpatient hospice services care for about 60 patients. These are usually visited at home four times a week.
- The day care centre admits up to 12 patients per day.

Additional facilities are one lymphodema-clinic and one clinic for the treatment of chronic pain.

One half of the patients suffer from cancer, others from chronic pain, neurological illnesses etc., as well as from chronic pain after cancer therapies. On occasion the hospice also admits children if there is no way to treat them at home. The hospice offers two rooms for relatives. According to the ministerial prescriptions the personnel consists of: one nurse attending to an average of 1.5 beds and two doctors attending to an average of ten beds. For the outpatient sector: one nurse attends to an average of six patients, one doctor attends to an average of thirty patients.

Thirty volunteers work for the inpatient hospice and the day care centre. The volunteers are not permitted to work in the outpatient sector for reasons of insurance. The volunteers are generally either students or pensioners. Additionally, 150 students help with fund-raising-activities for the Palium. It is condition that none of the honorary workers has lost a close relative during the previous year of starting at the hospice. The volunteers meet once a month. An interview with a psychologist precedes the training, which consists of a practical and a theoretical part.

Warszawskie Hospicjum dla Dzieci[24] *(Children Hospice in Warsaw)*

The *Warsaw Children Hospice* was founded in September 1994 and is an outpatient service attending mainly to children whose parents or doctors have decided that no further therapy is possible. The hospice offers professional medical home care and continues to support the whole family after the death of the child. The team consists of specially trained nurses, pain therapists and social workers. This service is available

24 Interview with Tomasz Dangel, 12 August 2004, in Warszawa. Cp. also Friedrichsdorf, Stefan/Brund, Sandra/Zernikow, Boris: Comprehensive care for dying – The Warsaw Hospice for Children. In: European Journal of Palliative Care 2003.

7 days a week and 24 hours a day. It is free of charge, and includes patients aged up to 18 years. The supported patients remain in the hospice service's care even when they exceed that age limit. For example, a child suffering from amyotrophia remained in the hospice for eight and a half years. The average duration of care for cancer patients amounts to 50 days, that of patients with other illnesses may amount to half a year. Since 1994 the Warsaw Children Hospice has cared for 153 children. An average of 22 children are supported simultaneously. In 2004 the personnel consisted of three doctors (two anaesthetic specialists, one paediatrician), eight nurses, three social workers, one psychologist, one priest, one physiotherapist, one PR specialist, one computer expert and one accountant. 20 people work as volunteer helpers. According to Thomasz Dangel methadon is more suited for pain therapy than morphine, but employed less as it is regarded too cheap and therefore commercially uninteresting. It is not possible to treat every kind of pain by medicine. In some cases – without violating the laws of the Catholic Church – terminal sedations are practiced (the children announce clearly that they wish to sleep). The outpatient palliative care explicitly includes the therapy of after-effects of cancer therapies.

Children Hospice service, Warszawa

The hospice is financed by donations and subsidies from the *National Health Fund,* which pays 75 Zloty (about 19 €) per patient, though the real cost amounts to 300 Zloty (72 €) per day. Since the topic of terminally sick children receives great resonance with possible donators the financing by donations is not that difficult. To improve the financial situation the hospice runs a dental clinic fort the treatment of disabled children ("Our government provides money for dental surgery but not for palliative care"). Above the plain care services the hospice further supports poor families: flats are renovated, medicines and medical material are bought. Before they take over the nursing service a social worker is sent to the family, and if necessary the child is accommodated at the hospital for two weeks while the flat is being renovated (often dwellings in the country do not have running water, much less a bath). The hospice increasingly attends to children of poor families since the hospitals reject those patients in favour of wealthier clients. Of the children dying in Poland 80 percent do so in a hospital. The hospitals often conduct chemo-therapies to the end and sometimes even experiment with different therapies. The children then die of the after-effects of the treatment. According to Dr. Tomasz Dangel children often receive unnecessary respirators, even though they do not want them. Suspicion: employing respirators the hospitals receive higher subsidies from the government.

Dr. Tomasz Dangel, manager of the institution, considers inpatient hospices for children a wrong development. Home care is both better suited and cheaper.

Hospicjum Domowe, Poznań[25]

This outpatient hospice service was founded in 1997 and started out as a solely honorary institution. The present team consists of the medical head Dr. Jakrzewska-Sawińska, a Catholic nun, a psychologist and 60 honoraries. The hospice society has 200 members and employs 20 part-time doctors and 25 part-time nurses.

This hospice takes care of children within a range of about 100 kilometres and also supplies respirators to enable the children to stay at home. Currently the hospice attends to 50 children, 15 of which need a respirator. Krysztof is unable to move anything but his thumb, and his mother carries out his instructions on the computer – he has his own website.[26]

The hospice also takes care of chronically ill patients, especially old people suffering from pain, depression or bed sores. To finance these services by governmental subsidies is problematic as the patients are not necessarily in the final phase. The authorities expect the family doctors to take over the treatment of these persons, but the doctors often lack any experience with such patients and have no time for their treatment. The hospice attends to 400 - 500 sick people each year – 85 percent of these patients are older than 65 years, and 42 percent suffer from pain. Aside from the outpatient services the hospice also runs an outpatient geriatric polyclinic.

---

25 Interview with Anna Jakrzweska-Sawińska, 11 August 2004, in Poznań.

26 http://www.krysztof.republika.pl

Hospicjum Domowe, Poznań

Hospicjum in. sw. M. M. Kolbe (Maximilian-Kolbe-Hospice), Koszalin[27]

The Koszalin hospice is one example of a non-governmental hospice-engagement. It is a very small hospice in an outer region of Poland. Since September 1st 1991 an out-patient hospice service is in existence there. Some time later, this service was moved to the local Caritas building. In 1998 the city's authorities granted 100 000 Zloty to fund the work of the running year. An inpatient hospice is being built in the facilities of the hospital for lung diseases. Five nurses and two doctors attend to the hospice's five beds. Since 1999 the hospice's existence is continually threatened by financial bottlenecks. Charitable concerts are being organised and appeals for donations formulated. In 2000 162 people were admitted to the inpatient hospice, 168 were taken care of at home. There is a lack of volunteers. In 2001 the financial difficulties reached a new peak. The governmental subsidies amount to 100 Zloty (circa 25 €) but the actual cost for the nursing services amounts to 172 Zloty per day (circa 43 €).[28] The medical head and the psychologist have received no wages for a very long time. "Often

[27] Written reports by Elzbieta Piotrowska.

[28] Again, the official figures differ from those reported by the carriers of the institutions themselves. It is out of the question that costs are higher within the cities than in the country or in the smaller cities. This may be one explanation for divergences.

the patients demand more expensive medicines, which of course increases the financial expenses" says the president of the Koszalin hospices society.[29] In February 2004 the Medison-GmbH, owner of the building containing the hospice, demanded a one hundred percent rise in rent. Currently, this poses a definite threat to the hospice's existence.

3. Summary

Hospice services in Poland were organised very early and made up an essential part of the oppositional movements of the reunification. Initially these services were mostly carried by honoraries with close ties to the Catholic church. Palliative care, as part of the health policy, only really started after the reunification. Against the background of this past as former civil movements the present net of available palliative care in Poland is therefore relatively good. The hospice services run by non-governmental institutions continue to be important and often better than governmentally supported palliative-medical services. At present, the non-governmental services appear less as civil movements than as institutionalised non-governmental services, carried mainly by organisations like the Caritas. Probably though, in non-governmental institutions personal attention and humanitarian engagement are more observable.

Sources and Literature

Dangel, Tomasz: The Status of Pediatric Palliative Care in Europe. Journal of Pain and Symptom Management 2002/24, p. 160 - 165.

Dangel, Dangel: The Status of Pediatric Palliative Care. Journal of Pain and Symptom Management 2002/24, 222 - 224.

David Clark/ Wright, Michael: Transitions in End of Life Care, Hospice and related developments in Eastern Europa and Central Asia. Buckingham 2003, p. 215 - 231.

Drażkiewicz, Jerzy: W stronę człowieka umierajacego. O ruchu hospicjów, University of Warszawa, Faculty of Sociology. Warschau 1989.

Friedrichsdorf, Stefan/ Brund, Sandra/Zernikow, Boris: Comprehensive care for dying – The Warsaw Hospice for Children. In: European Journal of Palliative Care 2003.

Górecki, M.: Hospicjum w służbie umierajacym, w: T. Pilch, J. Lepalczyk (red.): Pedagogika społecna Wyd. Akademickie "Zak". 2000.

Health program for Palliative Ministry of Health. Accessibility and effectiveness of palliative care –improvement of under and postgraduate education of palliative care. Gdańsk, 2002.

Łuczak, Jacek/ Kluziak, Maciej: The formation of ECEPT (Eastern and Central Europe Palliative Task Force) a Polish initiative. In: Palliative Medicine 2001/15, p. 259 - 260.

Łuczak, Jacek et al.: Poland Cancer Pain and Palliative Care, in : Journal of Pain and Symptom Management 2002/24, p. 215 - 221.

[29] Krystyna Wierzchowicka, president of the hospice society in Koszalin, taken from the newspaper Głos Pomorza, 03 July 2001.

Łuczak, Jacek/ M. Kluziak: Beacon Sites in Eastern Europe – PC Centre in Poznan – The Future, Vortrag auf dem 8. Kongress European Association for Palliative Care, The Hague April 2003.

Materiały dla Wolontariuszy, edited by Hospicjum Kraków. Kraków 2001.

Ministry of Health: The programme of developing palliative-hospice care in Poland. Warsaw Ministry of Health 1998.

Ministry of Health and Welfare: Standard of medical service provision "Palliative Medicine". Prepared by Jacek Łuczak. Warsaw 1999.

Tenner, Janina Jujawska: The Beginnings of Hospice Care Under Communist Regime: The Cracow Experience. In: International Hospice Care. In: Saunders, Cicely/ Kastenbaum, Robert (Ed.): Hospice Care on the International Scene. New York 1997, p. 158 - 166.

Walden-Gałuszko, Krystyna de: "U kresu", Opieka psychopaliatywna, czyli jak pomóc choremu, rodzinie I personelowi medyczenemu środkami psychologicznymi. Gdańsk 1999.

Walden-Gałuszko, Krystyna de, Majkowicz, Mikołaj: Model oceny jakości opieki paliatywnej realizowanej w warunkach ambulatoryjnych. AMG. Gdańsk 2000.

Walden-Gałuszko, Krystyna de, Majkowicz, Mikołaj: Model oceny jakości opieki paliatywnej realizowanej w warunkach stacjonarnych. AMG. Gdańsk 2001.

Walden-Gałuszko, Krystyna de (ed.): Podstawy medycyny paliatywnej. PZWL, Warszawa 2004 (Handbook for doctor and medical students).

Wright, Michael/ Clark, David: The development of palliative care in Poznan, Poland, in: European Journal of Palliative Care. 2003/ 10 (1), p. 26 - 29.

Warsaw Hospice for Children (Ed.): 2nd European Course on Palliative Care for Children, Textbook, Warsaw 2001.

Warsaw Hospice for Children (Ed.): 3rd European Course on Palliative Care for Children. Textbook Warsaw 2003.

Periodicals

The Hospice Journal, edited by Warszawskie Hospicjum dla Dzieci (appearing quarterly)
Newsletter, edited by ECEPT (Eastern and Central Europe Palliative Task Force), Poznań

Internet sources

Population Division of the Department of Economic and Social Affairs of the United Nations Secretariat, *World Population Prospects: The 2004 Revision* and *World Urbanization Prospects: The 2003 Revision*. Official Homepage of the United Nations: http://esa.un.org/unpp

http://gdzie.pl/hospicjum (list of hospices)

http://www.hospiceinformation.info

http://www.oncology.am.poznan.pl/ecept (current data on palliative care in Poland)

List of interviews (in chronological order)

- Dr. n. med. Anna Jakrzewska-Sawińska (director) Krysztof Jakrzewska-Sawińska *Wielkopolskie Stowarzyszenie Wolontariuszy Opieki Paliatywnej Wiekopolskie Hospicjum dla Dzieci* Hospicjum Domowe, Poznań 11 August 2004
- Aleksandra Kotlińska-Lemieszek, MD Anna Szczerbak, Executive Director *Ecept und Hospice Palium,* Poznań 11 August 2004
- Dr.med. Tomasz Dangel, Director *Warszawskie Hospicjum dla Dzieci,* Warszawa, 12 August 2004
- Michał Sobolewski (Director) Barbara Witkowska Barbara Bitner Anna Jakobinska-Chmielewska Kataryna Skolenska, Theresa Bondarewicz *Ministry of Health,* Warszawa, 13 August 2004
- Krystyna Łakomska (medical head) *Centrum Charytatywne "Res Sacra Miser" Hospicjum stacjonarne,* Warszawa, 13 August 2004
- Dr. Jolanta Stokłasa (head woman) Krystyna Kochan (psycholgist and social worker) Franciszek Kuzmicki (volunteer) *Towarzystwo Przyjacioł Chorych Hospicjum Św. Łazarza,* Kraków, 13 August 2004

Slovakia

Felix Schumann

1. General conditions

1.1 Demographics

- In 2000, Slovakia's population numbered 5.4 million. According to population predictions, this number will drop to 4.6 million inhabitants by 2050.[1] The real birth rate in Slovakia has been decreasing since 1980.[2]
- The average life expectancy of 74.0 is expected to grow to 80.4 years of age by 2050, whereas the median age will rise enormously from 34.1 years in 2000 to 51.8 by 2050.[3]
- In 1950, people 65 years or older in Slovakia constituted 6.7% of the population. In 2000 it was already 11.4% and is projected to grow to 30.5% by 2050.[4]
- Similarly, people aged 80 years or older constituted only 0.9% of the population in 1950. That percentage grew in 2000 to 1.8 and is estimated to grow to 8.2 by 2050.[5]
- The number of persons aged 15 to 59 years per person over the age of 60 was 65.0% of the total population in 2000, and is expected to drop to 48.7% by 2050.[6]
- The annual mortality rate is expected to rise from 9.7 per 1000 inhabitants between 2000 - 2005 to 15.6 per 1000 inhabitants by 2045 - 2050.[7]
- The most frequent causes of death are diseases of the circulatory system, followed by tumours, external causes (injuries, poisonings, homicides, etc.), diseases of the digestive system, and the respiratory system. The five most frequent causes of death accounted for 94% of all deaths in Slovakia in 2000; more than three quarters of

---

1 Population Division of the Department of Economic and Social Affairs of the United Nations Secretariat, *World Population Prospects: The 2004 Revision* and *World Urbanization Prospects: The 2003 Revision*. Official Homepage of the United Nations: http://esa.un.org/unpp

2 World Health Organization Regional Office for Europe: Highlights on Health in Slovakia. Kopenhagen 2001, 17.

3 ibid.

4 ibid.

5 ibid.

6 ibid

7 ibid.

these deaths were due to disturbances of the cardiovascular system and malignant tumours.[8]

1.2 Health care system

All 5.4 million Slovakians are covered by insurance. In 1993 the National Insurance Agency was created, covering social benefits, sick pay and health insurance. A separate health insurance system was developed in 1995[9], with six insurance companies now remaining. In 1999, self-employed persons paid 13.7% of their assessment basis, while employees paid 3.7% of their assessment basis and employers 10% of the sum of all employees' assessment bases.[10] Today the organization of the current health care system is a mixture of decentralized and centralized structures.[11] The Ministry of Health still owns, runs and controls almost all inpatient health care facilities with the authority to appoint and dismiss their directors.[12] Health care in Slovakia is provided on a comparatively high level nationwide.[13] For example, the number of hospital beds per 100 000 population is above the average of the reference countries and the EU average.[14]

2. Hospice and palliative care in Slovakia

2.1 History

The hospice ideas were slowly implemented after the revolution of 1989 in Slovakia. The idea of hospices had been completely new for the general public. The first hospice services in Slovakia were mainly based on the initiative of the physician Dr Kristina Krizanova from Bratislava. There is still a lack of government support for such activities.[15]

In 1995 the first hospital palliative care unit started in Bratislava. The Slovakian hospice movement has existed since 1996 when a number of voluntary organisations confederated. The activities involved with these initiatives range from care for the dying to the organisation of charity events (ie concerts).

---

8 Center for Economic Development (CED): National Human Development Report Slovak Republic 2001 - 2002: http://www.cphr.sk/english/undp2002.htm

9 International Observatory on End of Life Care at Lancaster University: http://www.eolc-observatory.net/

10 AOK-Bundesverband: psg-Serie Beitrittsländer (6): Die slowakischen Krankenkassen werden von Schulden gedrückt: http://www.aok-bv.de/presse/presseservice/psgpolitik/index_02729.html

11 European Observatory on Health Care Systems: Health Care Systems in Transition. Slovakia. Kopenhagen 2000, p. 10.

12 ibid., p. 11.

13 AOK-Bundesverband: psg-Serie Beitrittsländer (6): Die slowakischen Krankenkassen werden von Schulden gedrückt: http://www.aok-bv.de/presse/presseservice/psgpolitik/index_02729.html

14 World Health Organization Regional Office for Europe: Highlights on Health in Slovakia. Kopenhagen 2001, p. 27.

15 PALIUM: Hospic a paliativna starostlivost. Bratislava 2002, p. 15.

In 1997 a day care clinic opened in Martin, providing care in 24 hospice beds. In 2003 a palliative care centre, including a day care unit, palliative care unit and a pain therapy emergency unit were set up in Humenne. In the same year the first Slovakian inpatient hospice was opened in Bardejov.

In order to support hospice services the Slovakian government provided €490.000 from lottery incomes at the end of 2001. 25% of this money was allocated to the expansion of hospice services, 75% to the running costs of those institutions. However it is estimated that the actual required sum is 20 times higher than the funds provided by the government. [16]

2.2 Hospice and palliative care services

In 2003, there were 30 hospice or palliative care initiatives in Slovakia. Some of these initiatives are members of the National Hospice Umbrella Organisation *AHS (Asociacia Hospicovej Starostlivosti Slovenska)*, founded in November 2000, whose head office is located in Trencin. [17]

In 1995 the *Department of Palliative care* was opened within the *National Cancer Institute* in Bratislava. The unit provides care for cancer patients in a total of 19 beds. The average length of stay in 2002 was 12 - 14 days. [18] In the same year 150 people died on the ward.

The palliative care centre in Humenne opened its doors in 2003. The centre consists of a day care and an inpatient palliative care hospital unit as well as a pain therapy emergency department.

The first Slovakian inpatient hospice was set up in 2003 in Bardejov. Home care hospice services exist in the cities Kosice, Nitra, Trencin, Piestany and Bratislava. Inpatient hospices are planned for Nitra, Martin, Spisska Nova Ves, Piestany, Trencin, Kosice, Presov and Bratislava. Once a year, the *International Conference on Hospice and Palliative Care* takes place. The last conference in Trnava on March 26, 2004 drew a lot of international attention.

According to experts – even after the end of the socialist era – health care is still dominated by a paternalistic approach shown by physicians towards the patients. [19] Often the diagnosis is concealed from the patient instead of talking about the seriousness of the illness. In contrast, the interaction between staff and patients in the very few palliative care units is much more open and communicative. However, it is interesting to consider that "80 - 90 percent of all terminally-ill patients in Slovakia demand curative treatment although they are aware it would not have such an effect" [20]. This shows the desperate need for hospice and palliative care.

---

16 ibid., p. 19.

17 ibid., p. 15.

18 Interview with Dr Kristina Krizanova, 06 August 2003, in Bratislava.

19 ibid.

20 Dr Stanislav Fabus, *OZ Hospize Martin* cited as in PALIUM: Hospic a paliativna starostlivost. Bratislava 2002, p. 21.

2.3 Legal regulations and funding

Paragraph 24, act 277/94 of the Slovakian legislation defines hospice care "as a service that offers palliative provision".[21] According to the act, hospice care offers health care provision (inpatient and outpatient) for incurable and dying patients from all age groups:

a. Palliative provision is strongly associated with palliative care at home. It is therefore worthwhile to offer hospice care at the patient's home if possible.

b. Palliative care within existing inpatient services is for several reasons necessary and desirable; for example, it gives relatives the opportunity to have a rest and to rebuild.

c. Inpatient palliative and hospice care should only apply when home and outpatient care is no longer sufficient. The accommodation of patient's relatives in the inpatient settings is always possible.

Hospice and palliative care services are forced to acquire money from other sources as the funding provided by the state is not sufficient. The running costs are covered to a large extent (70 - 90 percent) by health and social insurances. In July 2003, new legislation became effective which for the first time included hospice and palliative care. Unfortunately, the legislators did not consider the fact that hospices and hospital palliative care units treat each other as equal partners who complement one another. However there a huge differences between the daily rates paid for hospital palliative care units and hospices. Whereas the daily rate for hospital palliative care patients is about €24.5 per day, the day's rate for hospice patients. Nevertheless the patients are asked to contribute additional payments – for example, between 3.70 to 14.60 euros per day in Humenne.

On the other hand the Health Ministry proposed to allocate inpatient hospices a comparatively low daily rate – between 7.3 and 21.9 euros. The proposal was rejected by people working in the field as it was regarded well below the actual figure required.[22]

Hospices have to cover the additional costs (10 - 30 percent) through private and alternative sources; for example, through fundraising, sponsoring, subsidies or charity events such as tribute concerts.[23]

2.4 Organisations

The Slovakian Hospice Umbrella Organisation, *AHS*, has existed since 2000. In 2003, 38 individual members and another 10 initiatives were registered members.

---

21 ibid., p. 13.

22 Interview with Dr Peter Krizan, 09 August 2003, in Bratislava. The numbers are up to the end of August 2003.

23 PALIUM: Hospic a paliativna starostlivost. Bratislava 2002, p. 19.

2.5 Education and training of professionals

There are no consultants in palliative medicine nor is there any special training in place for palliative care nursing. This however, could change under the rising pressure by experts and patients. So far pain therapy is a section of neurology and oncology.

Postgraduate advanced training programmes are provided by *Jesenius Faculty of Medicine UK* in cooperation with the hospice group in Martin. Since 1998 a special course is offered for fifth year medical students. At the same time, the *Section for Palliative Care* in the *Slovakian Society on the Study and Cure of Pain (SLS)* in Bratislava has started special training courses in palliative medicine.

Currently the Health Ministry is looking into the possibility to include pain management and palliative medicine as a specialty for physicians, and to integrate it into the curriculum of the *Slovakian Postgraduate Academy of Medicine* in Bratislava.

Asked where Slovakian physicians and nurses receive their education and training in palliative care, the most frequent responses were that professionals go to the Czech Republic or Great Britain, with Canada also mentioned.

2.6 Volunteers

Voluntary work is influenced by the fact it was absent for 40 years in Slovakia. Non-governmental motions retrieved as late as in 1990 [24] but those Volunteers have no official recognition within the health or social care system. [25]

Since 1996 volunteers have been part of hospice work in Slovakia. Above all they give psycho-social support, with the majority of volunteers being university students. The following initiatives are of great importance for voluntary work: *PALIUM* (Bratislava), a group of volunteers working in the *Oncology Department Sv. Alzbety* (Bratislava), the initiative *Hospice of the Holy Bernadette* in Nitra and the hospice group *Matky Bozej* in Piestany.

It is difficult to estimate the number of volunteers working in hospice care but it is likely to be above 100.

The Slovakian initiatives offer training courses for volunteers (in Bratislava, Nitra and Martin). For example, in 1997 the NGO *PALIUM* set up a 10-year plan, which included the aim of education and support for volunteers in hospice care. Since 2002 courses are provided on a regular basis, with interested volunteers taking part in a basis course focusing on medical, psychological, and spiritual dimensions of palliative care. [26]

---

24 Liana Hovancova: Hospice movement in Slovakia. in: Reimer Gronemeyer/ Erich H. Loewy (Eds.) in cooperation with Michael Fink, Marcel Globisch and Felix Schumann: Wohin mit den Sterbenden? Hospize in Europa – Ansätze zu einem Vergleich. Münster 2002.

25 International Observatory on End of Life Care at Lancaster University: http://www.eolc-observatory.net/

26 PALIUM: Hospic a paliativna starostlivost. Bratislava 2002.

2.7 Examples

Palliative Centre in Humenne

The Palliative Centre in Humenne is located in the East of Slovakia. It includes a palliative care unit (15 beds), a pain therapy polyclinic and a day care unit for palliative care patients (15 beds). The palliative centre was opened in July 2003.[27] The multi-disciplinary team of the palliative care unit consists of physicians, nursing staff, physiotherapists and psychologists. The physicians and nurses have taken part in special palliative care training or palliative medicine. Dr Mariana Svatuskova, the Head Doctor of the unit, reports that those received their education in Bratislava at *SLS* or in Czech hospices (Praha, Olomouc and Brno).[28]

Patients who stay in the palliative care unit are asked to contribute additional payments to the €24.5 provided by health and social insurances per day. The amount of the additional payments varies from category to category. The lowest category, a double room with telephone access, costs €3.70 per day. The room is more convenient than in public hospitals, where the patient only contributes €1.20 per day. The second category includes a double room with telephone access, television and physiotherapy every day (with an additional payment of €7.30). A category three room offers the same as category two, but in addition internet access is provided and the room is constantly video controlled by a staff member located in the nursing staff room (for an extra payment of €14.60). All three include a separate toilet and a shower.

The Hospice in Bardejov

The first Slovakian hospice was opened in Bardejov in July 2003. *Hospice in Bardejov* is located in the East of Slovakia and belongs to the *Diocese Kosice*. It has a capacity of 20 beds. An old schoolhouse was transformed into a building where care is provided for dying people. Despite being stretched over three floors, the house exudes a friendly and open atmosphere. The bright yellow facade, and the wooden veranda front and many windows initiate a curiosity about the location.

Dr. Alica Valkyova, founder and Head Doctor of the hospice, talks about the hospice:

> We have eleven employees: one physician, a head nurse, four nurses, a secretary, a caretaker, a cook and two cleaners. As we've just started our work, only seven patients are cared for on the top floor right now. Once the refurbishment has been completed, we will have 20 beds.[29]

Funding for the rebuilding of the house and running costs proves to be difficult as Dr Valkoya says with a smile: "Money was always tight and still is. But we've had the feeling if we didn't start now, the chance might be gone."[30] The main part of the

[27] Interview with Dr Mariana Svatuskova, 08 August 2003, in Humenne.

[28] ibid.

[29] Interview with Dr Alica Valkyova and Lubica Gladisova, 08 August 2003, in Bardejov.

[30] ibid.

funding was provided by the *Diocese Kosice* – the remaining money was acquired through donations.

According to Lubica Gladisova, head nurse of the hospice, most patients come from nearby areas; very few come from as far as Bratislava, which is more than 300 kilometres away. Many patients are suffering from Alzheimer's disease or Dementia, there are also some cases of diabetes and cerebral apoplexy. [31]

As there have been no satisfying legislations on inpatient hospice care, so far the hospice was unable to conclude an agreement with health insurance companies. Furthermore, the current hospice care is financed without any subsidies, thus patients and their relatives have to pay a considerable amount of money themselves. Depending on their socioeconomic status, the additional payments can be as high as €53.60 per day.

The Hospice in Bardejov

3. Summary

The history of hospice and palliative care is only quite brief in Slovakia. All the more impressive is the dedication and persuasion shown by the three inpatient and many ambulant services in order to realise their visions. Through persisting commitment it has succeeded in obtaining money from health insurance funds for inpatient provision, to attract public attention to hospice and palliative care, and to also make a significant contribution to palliative care on the international scene. Without help from the government, in many places in Slovakia efforts are being made to implement patient-

[31] ibid.

orientated hospice concepts and to counter the still existing taboo surrounding death and dying.[32]

At the same time it should not be overlooked that a lack of financial resources is still evident, as donations for hospice work is decreasing and the interest from the Health Ministry is still reserved. Inpatient hospices are planned in Nitra, Trencin, Piestany, Spisska Nova Ves, Kosice und Presov.

A *Goal and Action Plan* by Slovakian experts sets the following targets:

1. Implementation of palliative care into home care provision
2. Implementation of palliative care into existing health care institutions
3. Introduction of national standards for different palliative care settings.[33]

Thanks to the continous commitment by individuals, the chances are good that aims may be realised gradually. It appears that – as in other European countries at present and in the past – enthusiasm for hospice and palliative care will help to eventually overcome the many obstacles that still hamper its development.

Sources and literature

Clark, David/ Wright, Michael: Transitions in End of Life Care: Hospice and Related Developments in Eastern Europe and Central Asia. Buckingham 2002.

Hovancova, Liana: Hospice movement in Slovakia. In: Wohin mit den Sterbenden? Hospize in Europa – Ansätze zu einem Vergleich. Edited by Gronemeyer, Reimer/Loewy, Erich H. in cooperation with Michaela Fink, Marcel Globisch, Felix Schumann. Münster 2002.

PALIUM: Hospic a paliativna starostlivost. Bratislava 2002.

Sadovska, Olga: Department of Palliative Care in Bratislava and the development of the palliative care movement in Slovakia. In: Support Care Cancer. 1997; 5 (6), p. 430 - 434.

Internet sources

AOK-Bundesverband: psg-Serie Beitrittsländer (6): Die slowakischen Krankenkassen werden von Schulden gedrückt: http://www.aok-bv.de/presse/presseservice/psgpolitik/index_02729.html

Center for Economic Development (CED): National Human Development Report Slovak Republic 2001 - 2002: http://www.cphr.sk/english/undp2002.htm

EAPC-East Newsletter Nr. 17/ Dezember 2003. Cited in: International Association for Hospice and Palliative Care: http://www.hospicecare.com/newsletter2004/january04/page6.html

[32] Compare the interviews with Madla Rjabininova, Alena Ferancikova, Vladimir Chlebana, Dr. Monika Gibalova, Olga Vatasoinova und Jiri Stuchly.

[33] EAPC-East Newsletter Nr. 17 – Dezember 2003. Cited in: International Association for Hospice and Palliative Care: http://www.hospicecare.com/newsletter2004/january04/page6.html. The authors are Miriam Cejkova, Monika Gojdova, Patricia Porubcanova und Kristina Krizanova.

European Observatory on Health Care Systems: Health Care Systems in Transition. Slovakia. Kopenhagen 2000: http://www.euro.who.int/document/e69819.pdf

International Observatory on End of Life Care at Lancaster University: http://www.eolc-observatory.net/

Population Division of the Department of Economic and Social Affairs of the United Nations Secretariat, *World Population Prospects: The 2004 Revision* and *World Urbanization Prospects: The 2003 Revision*. Official Homepage of the United Nations: http://esa.un.org/unpp

World Health Organization Regional Office for Europe: Highlights on Health in Slovakia. Kopenhagen 2001: http://www.who.dk/

List of interviews (in chronological order)

- Dr. Kristina Krizanova, Head Doctor, Palliative Care Unit *National Cancer Institute* Bratislava, 06 August 2003
- Madla Rjabininova, Project coordinator, Hospice initiative *Charity Nitra*, 07 August 2003
- Vladimir Chlebana, Head, National Hospice Umbrella Organisation *AHS* Trencin, 07 August 2003
- Alena Ferancikova, Leader, Hospice initiative Piestany, 07 August 2003
- Dr. Monika Gibalova, Director, Home Care Service *Charity Spisska* Spisska Nova Ves, 07 August 2003
- Dr. Mariana Svatuskova, Doctor, Palliative Centre Humenne, 08 August 2003
- Dr. Alica Valkyova, Head of the *Hospice of Mother Theresia* and Lubica Gladisova Head nurse of *Hospice of Mother Theresia* Bardejov, 08 August 2003
- Olga Vatasoinova and Jiri Stuchly, Board of directors, Hospice initiative Kosice, 08 August 2003
- Dr. Krajnakova, Head of nursing home *Kozmu a Damiana* in Presov, 08 August 2003
- Dr. Peter Krizan, Head of the *Merciful Brothers Hospital* in Bratislava, 09 August 2003

Ukraine

Yevgeniya Kononenko

1. General conditions

1.1 Demographics

- In 2000, the population of the Ukraine numbered 49.1 million. It has been predicted that the population will drop drastically to 26.4 million inhabitants by 2050. [1]
- In the same period of time the average life expectancy of 66.1 is expected to increase to 74.7 years of age by 2050, whereas the median age will rise greatly from 37.5 years in 2000 to 51.9 by 2050. [2]
- In 1950, people 65 years or older in the Ukraine constituted for 7.6% of the population. In 2000, this number was already 14.0% and is projected to grow to a remarkable 29.1% by 2050. [3]
- Similarly, people aged 80 years or older constituted for 1.2% of the population in 1950. That percentage grew slightly in 2000 to 2.3 and is estimated to grow to 7.9 by 2050. [4]
- The number of people aged 15 to 59 years per older person over the age of 60, was 61.4% of the total population in 2000 and is expected to drop to 48.1% by 2050. [5]
- The annual mortality rate is expected to rise from 16.3 per 1000 inhabitants between 2000 - 2005 to 19.9 per 1000 inhabitants by 2045 - 2050. [6]
- The main causes of death are cardiovascular diseases (60.3%) and cancer diseases (13.5%). [7] The Ukraine is among the top six countries in the world where HIV/AIDS is spreading fastest. [8]

---

1 Population Division of the Department of Economic and Social Affairs of the United Nations Secretariat, *World Population Prospects: The 2004 Revision* and *World Urbanization Prospects: The 2003 Revision*. Official Homepage of the United Nations: http://esa.un.org/unpp

2 ibid.

3 ibid.

4 ibid.

5 ibid

6 ibid.

7 Звіт про діяльність Всеукраїнського лікарського товариства за 1999 - 2000 роки. Офіційна сторінка Світової Федерації Українських лікарських Товариств [World Federation of Ukrainian Medical Associations]: http://www.sfult.org.ua/news2.html

8 Population Division of the Department of Economic and Social Affairs of the United Nations Sec-

– Approximately 80 percent of all people die at home, the remaining 20 percent spent their last days in institutions.[9] Hospitals keep dying patients only reluctantly as they increase the mortality rate and thus worsen the reputation of the hospitals.[10]

1.2 Health care system

The Ukrainian health care system is experiencing a large crisis. Hospitals are suffering from lack of money, physicians can hardly cover their living expenses from their small salary, most citizens cannot afford to buy much needed pharmaceuticals.[11] The Ukraine and Belo Russia are the only countries of the former Soviet union that, to date, have no health insurance system in place. Nursing health care for the population is, officially, one of the key functions of the state set out in the 1996 Ukrainian Constitution, with Article 49 stating that "the state creates conditions for effective medical services accessible to all citizens".[12] Although the state intends to pay for all treatments costs, in practice a lack of funds means that only a minimum of health care services are accessible for most citizens. As a result, patients have to pay to receive proper health care. Costs for medicines must be covered by the patients themselves. For ten years the parliament has been discussing the introduction of a national insurance system with no resolutions yet to be made. In the meantime, a number of non-governmental organizations (sickness funds, credit unions) as well as various charitable institutions and funds were established as alternatives, with the latter having formed a rather well-developed network of 4805 institutions and funds by 1 January 2001.[13]

The Ukrainian health care system is divided into the following components:

1. Primary health care, outpatient and inpatient care (multidisciplinary hospitals and polyclinics performing specific national functions according to the list approved by the

Cabinet of Ministers of Ukraine).[14] Those are medical institutions provided by the state and accessible for all citizens. Officially the health care services are free. In reality however the public health care budget only covers about one third of the real costs, the rest is paid by the patients themselves. In most cases the medical equipment of public health services and the care standards are very low. This is particularly evident in rural areas where only ten percent of all hospitals feature x-ray equipment for ra-

retariat, *World Population Prospects: The 2002 Revision* and *World Urbanization Prospects: The 2001 Revision*. Official Homepage of the United Nations: http://esa.un.org/unpp (medium variant) Information on HIV/AIDS in the Ukraine is available News Agency Union. News from Ukraine: http://www.unian.net/ukr/news/news-29298.html

9 Interview with Dr. Dzvenislava Chaykivska, 19 January 2004, in Lvov.

10 Interview with Alexey Kalachov, 21 January 2004, in Kiev.

11 Juri Durkot: Gesundheitswesen in der Ukraine – Mit leeren Taschen. In: Wostok 2003:48 (3), p. 78: http://www.indro-online.de/ukrainedt.htm

12 http://www.euro.who.int/Document/E84927.pdf

13 cp. The Medical Association Wuerttemberg supports health reform plans in the Ukraine: http://www.aerztekammer-bw.d/ueberuns/10nw/ukraine.html and http://www.euro.who.int/Document/E84927.pdf

14 http://www.euro.who.int/Document/E84927.pdf

diography, many do not even have telephone or ambulance vehicles.[15] The wages of staff members are below the poverty line. The average monthly wage for doctors is about 45€, nurses average around 35€per month. In addition, the number of medical staff have been slashed by 30 percent. Wages continue to drop. Ukrainian doctors are hardly able to support their families.[16] This also leads to a deterioration of health care services.

2.*Private medical practices.* Private services are expensive and therefore unaffordable for most people. In the meantime there are initiatives similar to private health insurance.

3. *Medical public health care services that offer treatments with costs.* These are health care services funded by the states but patients are liable to pay costs. Part of the revenues go back into the public health budget, others are used to cover staff and pharmaceutical expenses.[17]

2. Hospice und Palliative Care in the Ukraine

2.1 Background

The first hospice services in the Ukraine were founded in 1995. Contradictory statements on the number of current hospice services exist which make it difficult to give reliable information. Almost all inpatient hospices are situated in cities, such as Lvov, Ivano-Frankovsk, Charkov, Lutsk, Cherson and Kiev. There is no documentation available on the history of Ukrainian hospice care. An article on the overview on the recent situation of hospice care in the Ukraine was written by Vladyslav Mykhalskyy, published by the *European Association of Palliative Care.*[18]

2.2 Hospice and palliative care in the Ukraine

Hospice Care in the Ukraine is characterised by two different structures. On the one hand there are public hospices, in most cases called "hospice clinics" (ukr. *лікарня "Хоспіс"*), "departments for intensive care" (ukr. *відділення інтенсивного сестринського догляду*) or "hospice units" (ukr. *хоспісне відділення*). These services regard themselves foremost as medical services with the aim to have the pain and symptoms controlled and treated. Psychosocial aspects play a rather subordinate role. In most cases, the services are units within oncology clinics, some of them are situated in hospitals. Thus they are organised very similarly to common hospital units. Death and dying is still a taboo, patients are often not informed about their diagnosis and prognosis.

---

15 Проблеми фінансування сільської медицини. National Institute for Strategic Studies. Dnipropetrovsk Branch: http://www.db.niss.gov.ua/docs/region/monitor/nov_1-15_ukr.html

16 Mykhalskyy, Vladyslav: Palliative Care in Ukraine. EAPC East: http://www.eapceast.org

17 Interview with Dr. Dzvenislava Chaykivska, 19 January 2004, in Lvov.

18 ibid.

On the other hand there are voluntary hospices run by non-governmental or foreign organisations. The institutions are called "hospice" (ukr. *Хоспіс*), "centre for palliative care" (ukr. *центр паліативної допомоги*) or "hospice units". The voluntary hospices provide social, medical and psychological care for seriously-ill patients.

The distinction between public and voluntary services is not always very clear. *Vale Hospice* in Kiev for example is a private hospice situated in a state clinic funded by both public and private money. There are also hospices that were founded by the state but which are funded through donations.

Hospice units in hospitals or in oncology clinics do not necessarily regard themselves as solely medical services. In how far psychosocial and spiritual care is part of the service depends on the respective teams. In some hospice units patients are allowed to bring along their pets for a short time, they can go for a walk whenever they want or are encouraged to arrange their room to their liking. [19]

2.3 Legal regulations and funding

There is no national policy in the Ukraine regulating the funding or organisation of hospice care. There is also no programme in place coordinating the development of hospice care. [20] In a decree by the Ministry of Health hospices are defined as "prophylactic care services", which provide medical help to incurable patients. According to the decree, hospices are financed by both the state and private donations. [21]

Normally services that have been founded by the state are also run by it although the provided funding does not cover all costs. Hence the staff are underpaid, the facilities cannot be maintained properly and care for patients is insufficient. Mostly the provided funding is hardly enough to cover expenses for pharmaceuticals. [22] Additional money is donated by small companies but on the whole it remains difficult to find sponsors who are willing or able to make contributions on a regular basis. Often the patients have to find ways to provide the necessary funds.

The voluntary hospices receive money from foreign organisations rather than those based in the Ukraine. Alexey Kalachov, Head of the *Vale Hospice* in Kiev, comments on charity funds in the Ukraine: " It is not worth establishing a charity as it brings along more work than money." [23] The support by the state is inadequate. "This makes

---

19 cp. Козирєва, Тетяна: Євген Москвяк: "Тільки Бог знає, як і коли людині піти з життя". Львівський портал. "Ратуша", 30.10.2003 [Webportal der Stadt Lvov]: http://portal.lviv.ua/digest/2003/10/30/113806.html

20 cp. A. Zubov /V. Mykhalskyy: Palliative Care in Ukraine. International Association for Hospice and Palliative Care: http://www.hospicecare.com/regionalnews/reports.htm

21 Наказ від 28.10.2002 про затвердження переліків закладів охорони здоров'я, лікарських, провізорських посад та посад молодших спеціалістів з фармацевтичною освітою у закладах охорони здоров'я. Verkhovna Rada of Ukraine: http://zakon.rada.gov.ua/cgi-bin/laws/main.cgi

22 cp. Jones, Wendy: Palliative Care in Ukraine 2002. EAPC East: http://www.eapceast.org

23 Interview with Alexey Kalachov, 21 January 2004, in Kiev.

us vulnerable", says Dzvenislava Chaykivska, coordinator of the *National Home Care Programme* run by the Charity Lvov. [24]

2.4 Organisations

Lyudmila Andriyishyn heads the *Ukrainian Palliative Care Association.* [25] Amongst the members are surgeons, anaesthesiologist, nurses, social worker, psychologists and volunteers. The experts have both translated (foreign) literature on palliative care into the Ukrainian language and also written a paper on palliative care in the Ukraine, which was distributed to different medical, church and state-run organisations. The organisation represents the Ukraine in the ECEPT and is collaborating with palliative care services from Poland and Hungary. They are also in contact with the British-Russian Hospice Society. [26]

2.5 Education and training of professional staff

Palliative Care is no obligatory part of the medical curriculum in the Ukraine. There are only a very few experts in the field in the country. In 2003 there were seven universities providing education in palliative care. [27] There are hardly any courses for physicians and nurses, who are interested in receiving further training in palliative care. [28] This is also due to the fact that the number of hospices is small at the moment so that the demand for such courses is relatively low. Hospice staff members do usually have no special education or training in palliative care. Staff members become acquainted with palliative care while working in a hospice. [29] Some of the hospice staff have learned from their Polish colleagues, others educate themselves by studying international literature on palliative care. Staff members from *Vale Hospice* are trained by the founder of the service, Elisabeth Glinka, who herself received training at a American hospice. Dzvenislava Chaykivska (*Charity Home Care Programme*) gives courses on first-aid and palliative care for new colleagues. Since 2000 the University of Donetsk offers courses in palliative medicine. [30]

---

24 Interview with Dr. Dzvenislava Chaykivska, 19 January 2004, in Lvov.

25 cp. Open Society Institute – Soros Foundations Network. Project on Death in America. International Directory of professional Palliative Care Associations: http://www.soros.org/initiatives/pdia/focus_areas/a_international_palliative/directory_associations

26 Eastern and Central Europe Palliative Care Taskforce: http://free.med.pl/ecept/en_index.html.cp. International Observatory on End of Life Care: http://eolc-observatory.net/global_analysis/ukraine_associations.htm

27 cp. Vladyslav Mykhalskyy: Palliative Care in der Ukraine. EAPC East: http://www.eapceast.org

28 Interview with Dr. Dzvenislava Chaykivska, 19 January 2004, in Lvov.

29 Interview with Roman Krupnik, 19 January 2004, in Lvov.

30 cp. International Observatory on End of Life Care: http://www.eolc-observatory.net/global_analysis/ukraine_current_services.htm

2.6 Volunteers

There are only a few very number of volunteers working in hospice and palliative care. Hospices, both voluntary and state-run, are foremost founded and dominated by physicians or other professionals such as nurses and social workers. Most of the volunteers are either from a religious background or students (above all from social work).[31] Volunteers do not need to have a special qualification to work in a hospices.

2.7 Examples

In the following examples a voluntary and a state-run hospice service are portrayed.

Hospice at the City Clinic in Lvov

The hospice at the City Clinic in Lvov is situated aside the tenements. The service was founded seven years ago by Boris Bilynskyy, an oncologist at the University of Lvov.[32] The hospice is financed by the state and run by a governmental charity organisation. As the public funds do not cover all expenses, charitable donations have to be acquired. Currently the hospice is supported by the city's brewery.

The hospice is an independent building with 30 beds providing care for cancer patients in the terminal stage of their illness. Normally the patients are referred to the hospice from the oncology clinic. The social or financial situation of the patient is not relevant for admission, homeless people are also cared for in the hospice. The age of the patient is not considered as important. Sometimes even young people from children's homes are admitted to the hospice as no other institution feels responsible for them. The majority of the patients, approximately 70 percent, are pensioners.

The hospice team consists of 18 members, 15 nurses and three internists. Neither psychologists nor volunteers are part of the team. Staff members have no qualification in palliative care. "We educated ourselves, we know the basics, one learns a lot while working in this field", says the doctor Roman Krupnik.

About half of the patients are cared for at home. Officially there is no home care service but there are plans to establish one very soon. At the moment staff members visit the patients in their homes on a voluntary basis to provide them with proper pain treatment. They are supported by the *Home Care Programme* run by the *Charity Lvov*.

Pain therapy is regarded as the main priority for the service but psychosocial aspects are also considered. Once a week a chaplain from the Greek-Orthodox church comes to the hospice and prays with the patients.

The topic death is only discussed on the patients request. Normally the patients remain in the hospice until they die. If patients wish to die at home and adequate care

---

[31] Interview with Dr. Dzvenislava Chaykivska, 19 January 2004, in Lvov.

[32] ср. Козирєва, Тетяна: Євген Москвяк: "Тільки Бог знає, як і коли людині піти з життя". Львівський портал. "Ратуша", 30.10.2003 [Official website of the city of Lvov]: http: //portal.lviv.ua/digest/2003/10/30/113806.html

can be provided, the dying person is allowed home. Patients, who remain in the hospice for several months, can go home for a period of time as well with the opportunity to go be re-admitted if necessary.

The demand for hospice beds is higher than the actual number of places available. At the beginning this was rather different as many people feared to go to the hospice as some people called it the "House of Death". Today the hospice is unable to meet the demands of the 800,000 inhabitants in the city and another 200,000 living in the suburbs. [33]

Stadtklinik Hospiz, Lvov

Vale Hospice in Kiev

With the help of the municipal health administration and a deputy of the Ukrainian Parliament, Elizabeth Glinka, President of VALE Hospice International, founded Ukrainc's first free hospice for cancer patients in April 2001. It was officially opened on September 1, 2001 as a department within the oncology clinic in Kiev. The team is led by the oncologist Alexey Kalachov. There are 14 rooms in the hospice with a total of 15 beds. A total of 30 members of staff are employed, including nurses, assis-

[33] Interview with Roman Krupnik, 19 January 2004, in Lvov.

tants, cleaners, dispatchers, maids and cooks.[34] The hospice covers an area of the city numbering about 305,000 inhabitants. Patients from other districts of the city are also admitted to the hospice if social circumstances require it.

Kalachov reports that it was very difficult to realise projects. There was no support from the government at the beginning. Eventually Elisabeth Glinka was able to convince people of the relevance of hospice care. Plans were made and implemented quickly. The first patients were admitted even before refurbishment was finished.

The patients are from different age groups, most of them are sixty years or older. There are single and double rooms, each bedroom contains four beds.[35]

An integral aspect of the Hospice programme is a Home Care Service, which supports those patients who wish to remain at home with their families. The Home Care Service is regarded as the heart and origin of the hospice.[36] The team provides social and medical support to patient and family. On average 60 patients are cared for at home. Two nurses and a driver are employed full time in this part of the service.

The hospice is free to all and receives state financing for pharmaceuticals and nutrition. The main part of the costs are covered by the private *Vale Fund*. Sometimes funerals are also paid by the *Vale Fund*. Private and corporate donations, contributions of government and non-governmental organizations, and church funding are sources of supplementary funding. As mentioned before, patients do not have to pay for services. Families and friends are allowed to donate money but no earlier than 40 days after the patients death to make clear the services are free of charge for everyone. Money donations have to be assigned to the clinic first, the hospice is only allowed to accept donations in kind: in the past relatives have donated for example a microwave, an aquarium and a refrigerator.

The patients are free to design their day according to their wishes and needs. They are allowed to smoke, drink alcohol, watch television, go for a walk. However this is sometimes difficult as the hospice is situated on the 7th floor. Due to that, many patients cannot leave the house. The relatives are allowed to visit the patients at any time of the day. Patients who are cared for at home, have the opportunity to call the inpatient unit for help at any given time.

According to the hospice's statistics, 80% of the patients have been members of the Orthodox Church. The hospice includes a small chapel. Each Sunday the Liturgy is performed. Every two weeks a general requiem is served for the rest of the departed. Those who, due to their condition, cannot be present at the services, have the opportunity of confession and to receive Holy Communion in their beds, if they wish.[37]

From Kalachov's point of view, *Vale Hospice* is the only hospice in the Ukraine that regards hospice care as more than pain treatment and symptom control. As stated by him, most services are most of all orientated medically. However the hospice care team should also support the patient psychologically and socially, adds Kalachov:

[34] cp. http://www.valehospice.org/kiev.html

[35] cp. *VALE Hospice International*: http://www.valehospice.org/rus/kiev.html

[36] cp. http://www.valehospice.org/kiev.html

[37] http://www.valehospice.org/kiev.html

"Our staff member never just sit in the office, they always talk with the patients." They speak about politics, everyday life and, if the patients wants to, about death as well. Death is not turned into a taboo, at the same time the patient should be encouraged not to lose hope. Some of the patients are able to talk about their fears: "They tell about their feelings and we listen to them. The sick are in fear when they leave us." [38]

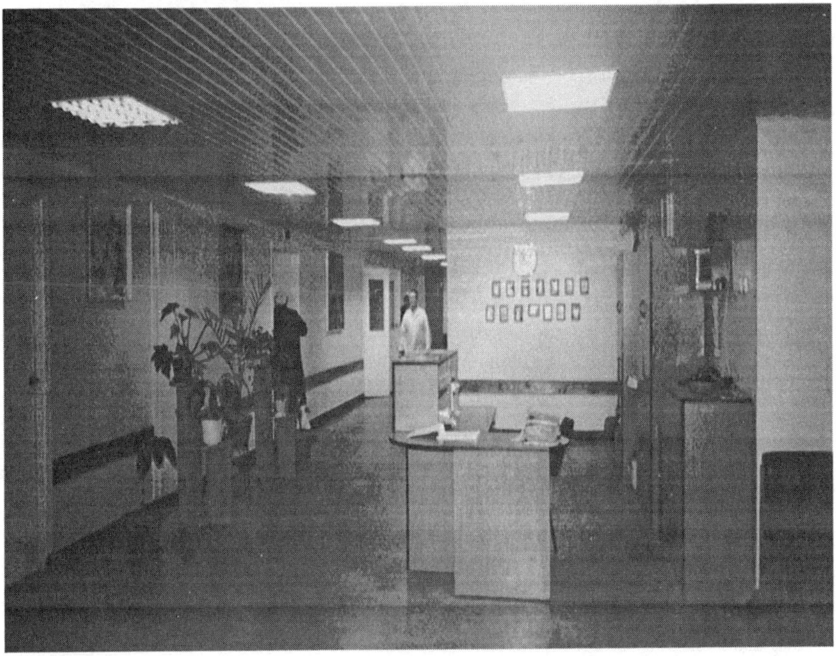

Vale Hospice, Kiev

3. Summary

The Ukraine faces enormous economical and social difficulties. The good care of the dying is one of the challenges for the future. Hospice and palliative care is still widely unknown in the population. There is no common sense among Ukrainian experts how to define hospice and palliative care. Only few experts are interested in the experiences made in other countries. However the situation is slowly changing, the media's interest for example is increasing, with reports on the subject being written more frequently. [39]

38 Personal communication with Elisabeth Glinka, 13 January 2004; Interview with Alexey Kalachov, 21 January 2004, in Kiev.

39 cp. Vladyslav Mykhalskyy: Palliative Care in Ukraine. EAPC East: http://www.eapceast.org

Many experts have identified the lack of state funding as one of the main problems for development of palliative care as it seems unrealisable that the government will cover all costs. The question of funding remains primary as palliative care is almost exclusively carried out by professionals as volunteers only play a minor role.

Sources and literature

Internet sources

Андріїшин, Л.І., Дацун, Н.Б.: Івано-Франківський хоспіс – досвід роботи, проблеми та перспективи. ONCOFORUM: http://oncoforum.iatp.org.ua/?r=newsmore_onco_t\&id=73\&razd=6

Дуб, Олена: Хоспіс: уміння лікувати собою."Львьвська газета" – Медична газета, No. 29 [Medical Journal Lvov]: http://www.gazeta.lviv.ua/2003/10/29.appendix/NewspaperArticle. 2003 - 10 - 29.2925

Звіт про діяльність Всеукраїнського лікарського товариства за 1999 - 2000 роки. Офіційна сторінка Світової Федерації Українських лікарських Товариств [World Federation of Ukrainian Medical Associations]: http://www.sfult.org.ua/news2.html

Eastern and Central Europe Palliative Care Taskforce: http://free.med.pl/ecept/en_index.html

Коник, Олег: Демографічна криза в Україні. "POSTUP", No. 34 (692), 1 - 7. March 2001. BRAMA – Gateway Ukraine: http://postup.brama.com/010301/34_4_4.html

Козирєва, Тетяна: Євген Москвяк: "Тільки Бог знає, як і коли людині піти з життя". Львівський портал. "Ратуша", 30.10.2003 [Lvov City Webportal] http://portal.lviv.ua/digest/2003/10/30/113806.html

Кузьмичов, Дмитро: Місія церкви. Газета "Хрещатик", № 45 (2056), 27.03.2002 [Magazine of Kiew local Government "Chreschtschatik"] http://kreschatic.kiev.ua/?id=2056\&page=6

Наказ від 28.10.2002 про затвердження переліків закладів охорони здоров'я, лікарських, провізорських посад та посад молодших спеціалістів з фармацевтичною освітою у закладах охорони здоров'.я Verkhovna Rada of Ukraine: http://zakon.rada.gov.ua/cgi-bin/laws/main.cgi

Отделение интенсивного сестринского ухода: Донецкий Областной Противоопухолевый Центр [Regional Centre for in Donetsk] http://www.oncohelp.dsmu.edu.ua/hospis.htm

Офіційний веб-портал київської міської влади -Новини [Portal of the local Government in Kiev – News]: http://kmv.gov.ua/news.asp?IdType=10\&Day=14\&Month=8\&Year=2003

Офіційний веб-сайт Волинської обласної державної адміністрації [Homepage of the Regional Governemnt of Volin – News]: http://www.voladm.gov.ua/?ukr/news/archive/june2002.htm

Проблеми фінансування сільської медицини. National Institute for Strategic Studies. Dnipropetrovsk Branch: http://www.db.niss.gov.ua/docs/region/monitor/nov_1-15_ukr.html

Програма діяльності Уряду: Підвищення якості життя населення. Міністерство праці та соціальної політики України [Ministry for Work and Social Politics] http://www.minpraci.gov.ua/pages.asp?id=525

Рай для приречених. The Day Weekly Digest "Äåíü", No. 105, 13.06.2002: http://www.day.kiev.ua/2002/105/den-ukr/du3.htm

Соціально-економічний розвиток Луцька за I півріччя 2002 року. OFFICIAL WEB-PORTAL OF LUTSK CITY COUNCIL: http://www.lutsk.ua/lutsk_ua/newz/showarticle.php?article=966\&articledate=20020725\&theme=2

Статистика – Стан репродуктивного здоров'я населення України: Caritas-Kyiv: http://www.caritas.iatp.org.ua/rod-dim/r-s-h-u.html

Только в столице Украины необходимо создать дополнительно 7-8 хосписов для безнадежно больных граждан. Новости медицины и фармации [News in Medicine and Pharmacy] http://www.mif-ua.com/arhiv/9a/35.php

Government portal. http://www.kmu.gov.ua

International Observatory on End of Life Care: Ukraine. http://www.eolc-observatory.net/global_analysis/ukraine_current_services.htm

Jones, Wendy: Palliative Care in Ukraine 2002. EAPC East. http://www.eapceast.org/

Mykhalskyy, Vladyslav: Palliative Care in Ukraine. EAPC East: http://www.eapceast.org/upload/Mikhalsky.pcProzent20inProzent20Ukraine,Prozent202002doc.doc

News "ElVisti": http://www.elvisti.com/2001/11/09/health.shtml

News Agency Unian: News from Ukraine: http://www.unian.net

Open Society Institute – Soros Foundations Network. Project on Death in America. International Directory of professional Palliative Care Associations: http://www.soros.org/initiatives/pdia/focus_areas/a_international_palliative/directory_associations

Pension Reform in Ukraine: http://www.pension.kiev.ua/Ukr/Law_Base/NonFormated/Goryuk_files/frame.htm

Public Radio: Stories: http://www.radio.org.ua/reports/?lid=331

The news of the 1+1 channel – news: http://1plus1.ua/news/?27-09-2002

Ukrainian Red Cross Website: http://www.redcross.org.ua/Ukrainian/tekst.htm

UNAIDS: Ukraine: http://www.unaids.org/en/geographical+area/by+country/ukraine.asp

VALE Hospice International: Kiev: http://www.valehospice.org/kiev.html

Population Division of the Department of Economic and Social Affairs of the United Nations Secretariat, *World Population Prospects: The 2002 Revision* and *World Urbanization Prospects: The 2001 Revision*. Official Homepage of the United Nations: http://esa.un.org/unpp

Population Division of the Department of Economic and Social Affairs of the United Nations Secretariat, *World Population Prospects: The 2004 Revision* and *World Urbanization Prospects: The 2003 Revision*. Official Homepage of the United Nations: http://esa.un.org/unpp

Zubov, A. and Mykhalskyy, V.: Palliative Care in Ukraine. International Association for Hospice and Palliative Care: http://www.hospicecare.com/regionalnews/reports.htm

List of Interviews (in chronological order)

- Nikolai Tkachjev (President) *NGO Palliative Care*
  Sevastopol, 14 July 2003
- Dr. Elizabeth Glinka (President) *VALE Hospice International* Cabot, VT, 13 January 2004
- Dr. Roman Krupnik (Physician) City Clinic Hospice Lvov, 19 January 2004
- Dr. Dzvenislava Chaykivska (Head) National programme “Home Care” Charity Ukraine Lvov, 19 January 2004
- Dr. Alexey Kalachov (Head) *VALE Hospice* Kiev, 21 January 2004

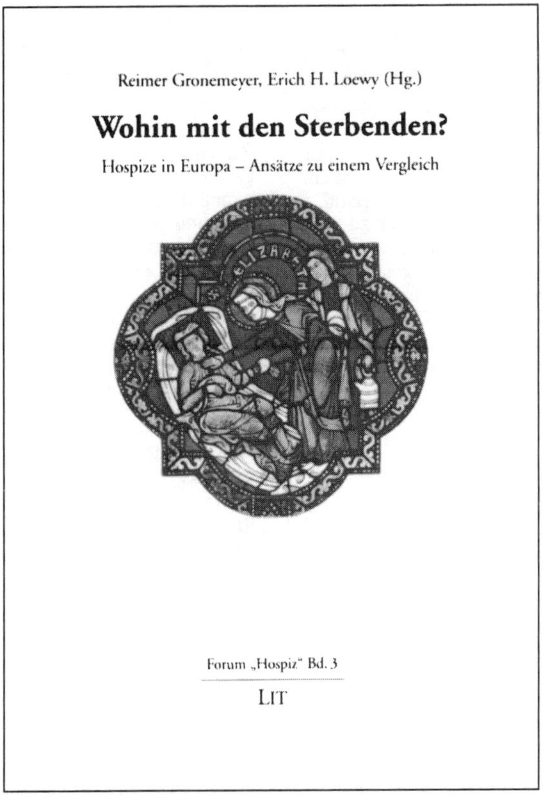

Reimer Gronemeyer; Erich H. Loewy (Hg.), in Zusammenarbeit mit Michaela Fink, Marcel Globisch und Felix Schumann

Wohin mit den Sterbenden?

Hospize in Europa – Ansätze zu einem Vergleich

In Deutschland wie in anderen europäischen Ländern treten die Konsequenzen eines noch nie dagewesenen demographischen Umbruchs zutage: Europas Gesellschaften sind alternde Gesellschaften. Davon wird auch der letzte Lebensabschnitt der Menschen tangiert: *Wohin mit den Sterbenden?* Die Familie sieht sich immer weniger zur Pflege imstande, das Krankenhaus ist eine problematische Ersatzlösung. In ganz Europa entstehen heute Hospize als Antwort auf die neue soziale Herausforderung. Dieser Band legt Berichte über Erfahrungen mit Hospizen aus verschiedenen europäischen Ländern vor.

2002, 240 S., 20,90 €, br., ISBN 3-8258-6011-6

LIT Verlag Münster – Berlin – Hamburg – London – Wien
Grevener Str./Fresnostr. 2 48159 Münster
Tel.: 0251 – 62 032 22 – Fax: 0251 – 23 19 72
e-Mail: vertrieb@lit-verlag.de – http://www.lit-verlag.de

Gertraud Aichmüller-Lietzmann
Palliativmedizin in der Praxis – dargestellt am Beispiel der Palliativstation des Johannes-Hospizes in München
"Grauenhafte Todeskämpfe" (Simone de Beauvoir) als Endpunkt einer schweren Erkrankung sind nicht nötig. Die Palliativmedizin hat ausreichend Möglichkeiten zur Hand, die Leiden schwerstkranker Menschen zu lindern – medizinisch, pflegerisch, psychosozial und spirituell. Sie kann dazu beitragen, den letzten Lebensabschnitt in Würde zu erleben. Die hier vorliegende empirische Untersuchung, durchgeführt an einer Münchener Palliativstation, macht deren Struktur und Arbeitsweise transparent.
1998, 216 S., 24,90 €, br.,
ISBN 3-8258-3975-3

Franco H. O. Rest
Leben und Sterben in Begleitung
Vier Hospize in Nordrhein-Westfalen – Konzepte und Praxis – Gutachten im Anschluß an eine wissenschaftliche Begleitung
Hospize sind Herbergen zur Lebensbegleitung sterbender Menschen. Vier stationäre Einrichtungen konnten während zweier Jahre für die Stiftung Wohlfahrtspflege des Landes Nordrhein-Westfalen wissenschaftlich begleitet werden. Die Arbeit der Hospize ist einerseits ein Beitrag zur veränderten Kultur im Umgang mit Sterben, Tod und Trauer, andererseits zur Euthanasie-Prophylaxe. Sterbebegleitung braucht gute Planungsdaten, eine Besinnung auf den historischen Ort, eine begründete Abwehr utilitaristischer Lösungen, sowie psychosoziale und spirituelle Kompetenzen der Begleitpersonen. Das vorliegende Buch zieht diesbezüglich Bilanz über Bemühungen der letzten zwanzig Jahre. Gleichzeitig werden Merkmale für die künftige Hospizentwicklung aufgezeigt. Es wird durch die Hospize auch ein Beitrag zur integrativen und toleranten Gesellschaft erwartet, in welcher Schwerkranke und Sterbende nicht länger ausgegrenzt werden.
1995, 200 S., 24,90 €, gb.,
ISBN 3-8258-2559-0

Doris Schubert
Hospizarbeit im Krankenhaus: ein Tätigkeitsfeld Sozialer Arbeit
Der psychosoziale Aspekt der ganzheitlichen Begleitung schwerkranker und sterbender Patienten im Krankenhaus hat an Bedeutung gewonnen. Welchen Beitrag könnte Soziale Arbeit in diesem Rahmen leisten, um auf die Situation der Sterbenden positiv einzuwirken? Die im vorliegenden Buch erarbeiteten Antworten auf diese Frage werden zudem anhand von Darstellungen bereits etablierter Konzeptionen der Hospizarbeit in sechs Krankenhäusern konkretisiert.
2003, 128 S., 14,90 €, br.,
ISBN 3-8258-6864-8

Andreas Stähli
"Ich will mitfliegen, aber ich habe noch keinen Platz"
Reflexion und Erfahrung über Kranksein, Sterben und Tod auf der Palliativstation "Johannes-Hospiz" in München
Die Hospizarbeit fordert in besonderer Weise das philosophische Denken zu einer Klärung und Vertiefung in ihr gemachter Erfahrungen. Fragen, die im Umgang mit Kranksein, Sterben und Tod aufbrechen, finden in der philosophischen Reflexion einen wichtigen Aspekt möglicher Beantwortung. Thematisiert wird im ersten Teil der vorliegenden Arbeit unter anderem die Frage nach der Theodizee, Fragen nach der Sprache, dem Willen und dem Bewusstsein des schwerkranken und sterbenden Menschen, aber auch die Frage nach der Zeit. In der Bemühung um eine Antwort ist stets die Nähe zur Praxis bedeutsam. Der zweite Teil stellt die Spiritualität in den Mittelpunkt seiner Ausführungen. Den Schwerpunkt bildet eine Betrachtung über das Gebet im Johannes-Hospiz.
2001, 192 S., 15,90 €, br.,
ISBN 3-8258-5107-9

LIT Verlag Münster – Berlin – Hamburg – London – Wien
Grevener Str./Fresnostr. 2 48159 Münster
Tel.: 0251 – 62 032 22 – Fax: 0251 – 23 19 72
e-Mail: vertrieb@lit-verlag.de – http://www.lit-verlag.de